CAMBRIDGE STUDIES IN LINGUISTICS
SUPPLEMENTARY VOLUME

General Editors: B. COMRIE, C. J. FILLMORE, R. LASS,
D. LIGHTFOOT, J. LYONS, P. H. MATTHEWS, R. POSNER,
S. ROMAINE, N. V. SMITH, N. VINCENT

---

*The acquisition of two languages
from birth: a case study*

In this series

20 JAMES FOLEY: *Foundations of theoretical phonology*
21 A. RADFORD: *Italian syntax: transformational and relational grammar*
22 DIETER WUNDERLICH: *Foundations of linguistics**
23 DAVID W. LIGHTFOOT: *Principles of diachronic syntax**
24 ANNETTE KARMILOFF-SMITH: *A functional approach to child language**
25 PER LINELL: *Psychological reality in phonology*
26 CHRISTINE TANZ: *Studies in the acquisition of deictic terms*
28 TORBEN THRANE: *Referential-semantic analysis*
29 TAMSIN DONALDSON: *Ngiyambaa*
30 KRISTJÁN ÁRNASON: *Quantity in historical phonology*
31 JOHN LAVER: *The phonetic description of voice quality*
32 PETER AUSTIN: *A grammar of Diyari, South Australia*
33 ALICE C. HARRIS: *Georgian syntax*
35 MARTIN ATKINSON: *Explanations in the study of child language development**
36 SUZANNE FLEISCHMAN: *The future in thought and language*
37 JENNY CHESHIRE: *Variation in an English dialect*
38 WILLIAM A. FOLEY and ROBERT D. VAN VALIN JR: *Functional syntax and universal grammar**
39 MICHAEL A. COVINGTON: *Syntactic theory in the High Middle Ages*
40 KENNETH J. SAFIR: *Syntactic chains*
41 J. MILLER: *Semantics and syntax*
42 H. C. BUNT: *Mass terms and model-theoretic semantics*
43 HEINZ J. GIEGERICH: *Metrical phonology and phonological structure*
44 JOHN HAIMAN: *Natural syntax*
45 BARBARA M. HORVATH: *Variation in Australian English: the sociolects of Sydney*
46 GRANT GOODALL: *Parallel structures in syntax: coordination, causatives, and restructuring*
47 JOHN M. ANDERSON and COLIN J. EWEN: *Principles of dependency phonology*
48 BARBARA A. FOX: *Discourse structure and anaphora*
49 LAUREL J. BRINTON: *The development of English aspectual systems*
50 DONNA JO NAPOLI: *Predication theory**
51 NOEL BURTON-ROBERTS: *The limits to debate: a revised theory of semantic presupposition*
52 MICHAEL S. ROCHEMONT and PETER W. CULICOVER: *English focus constructions and the theory of grammar*
53 PHILIP CARR: *Linguistic realities: an autonomist metatheory for the generative enterprise*
54 EVE SWEETSER: *From etymology to pragmatics: metaphorical and cultural aspects of semantic structure*

Supplementary Volumes

BRIAN D. JOSEPH: *The synchrony and diachrony of the Balkan infinitive*
ANNETTE SCHMIDT: *Young people's Dyirbal: an example of language death from Australia*
JOHN HARRIS: *Phonological variation and change: studies in Hiberno-English*
TERENCE MCKAY: *Infinitival complements in German*
STELLA MARIS BORTONI-RICARDO: *The urbanization of rural dialect speakers: a sociolinguistic study in Brazil*
RUDOLF P. BOTHA: *Form and meaning in word formation: a study of Afrikaans reduplication*
AYHAN AKSU-KOÇ: *The acquisition of aspect and modality: the case of past reference in Turkish*
MÍCHEÁL Ó SIADHAIL: *Modern Irish: grammatical structure and dialectal variation*
ANNICK DE HOUWER: *The acquisition of two languages from birth: a case study*

Earlier titles not listed are also available
*Issued in hard covers and as a paperback

THE ACQUISITION OF TWO LANGUAGES FROM BIRTH: A CASE STUDY

ANNICK DE HOUWER

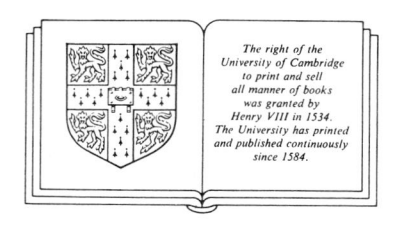

CAMBRIDGE UNIVERSITY PRESS
CAMBRIDGE
NEW YORK   PORT CHESTER
MELBOURNE   SYDNEY

Published by the Press Syndicate of the University of Cambridge
The Pitt Building, Trumpington Street, Cambridge CB2 1RP
40 West 20th Street, New York, NY 10011, USA
10 Stamford Road, Oakleigh, Melbourne 3166, Australia

© Cambridge University Press 1990

First published 1990

Printed in Great Britain at the University Press, Cambridge

British Library cataloguing in publication data

Houwer, Annick De
The acquisition of two languages from birth: A case
study. – (Cambridge studies in linguistics.
Supplementary volume.)
1. Bilingual children. Language skills. Acquisition
I. Title
401'.9

Library of Congress cataloguing in publication data

De Houwer, Annick.
The acquisition of two languages from birth: a case study
Annick De Houwer.
  p. cm.
Cambridge studies in linguistics. Supplementary volume – Ser. t.p.
Includes bibliographical references.
ISBN 0 521 36652 6
1. Language acquisition – Case studies. 2. Bilingualism in
children – Case studies. I. Title. II. Title: Cambridge studies in
linguistics. Supplement.
P118.D37   1990
401'.93 – dc20   89-22197   CIP

ISBN 0 521 36652 6

voor mama

Contents

List of tables		x
Symbols and abbreviations		xiv
Acknowledgements		xv
1 Introduction		1
2 Bilingual first language acquisition: methods and theories		9
2.1	Methodology in studies of BFLA	9
2.2	Theoretical issues in the field of BFLA	34
2.2.1	Introduction	34
2.2.2	Language separation: a useful concept?	36
2.2.3	The Independent Development Hypothesis	47
2.2.4	Bilingual and monolingual children compared	50
2.2.5	How does language presentation affect development?	54
2.2.6	Psycholinguistic explanations of the bilingual acquisition process	55
2.2.7	The state of the art in studies of bilingual first language acquisition	60
3 A new study of bilingual first language acquisition: aims and hypotheses		65
4 Case study of a bilingual child: introduction		71
4.1	Description of the study	71
4.1.1	The subject and her language background	71
4.1.2	Data collection	75
4.1.3	Transcription of the data	79
4.1.4	General procedure for analysis and coding systems	81
4.2	The data: an overview	85
4.2.1	Languages used by Kate per recording session	85
4.2.2	Mean Length of Utterance (MLU)	87
5 Language choice and Mixed utterances		90

	5.1	Language choice	90
	5.1.1	Introduction	90
	5.1.2	The language choice codes	90
	5.1.3	Analysis and results	92
	5.1.4	Comparisons with other bilingual children	100
	5.2	Linguistic characteristics of Kate's Mixed utterances	102
	5.2.1	Introduction	102
	5.2.2	Analysis and results	102
6	The noun phrase		115
	6.1	The marking of gender	116
	6.1.1	The adult systems	116
	6.1.2	Analysis and results	122
	6.1.3	Discussion	135
	6.1.4	Comparisons with monolingual children	142
	6.1.5	Concluding remarks	144
	6.2	Plural formation	145
	6.2.1	The adult systems	145
	6.2.2	Kate's plural NP's	146
	6.2.3	Comparisons with monolingual children	148
	6.2.4	Conclusion	149
	6.3	The use of diminutives	150
	6.4	NP's with an adjective as head	151
	6.5	Syntagmatic relations within NP's	153
	6.5.1	The adult systems	153
	6.5.2	Analysis and results	154
	6.5.3	Discussion	155
	6.5.4	Comparisons with monolingual children	155
	6.6	The noun phrase: concluding remarks	156
7	The verb phrase		158
	7.1	Introduction	158
	7.2	A catalogue of verb forms	159
	7.2.1	The adult verb systems	160
	7.2.2	The data	169
	7.2.3	Concluding remarks	189
	7.3	Kate's Dutch verb system	189
	7.3.1	Introduction	189
	7.3.2	Analysis and results	191

	7.3.3	Recapitulation	208
	7.4	Kate's English verb system	210
	7.4.1	Introduction	210
	7.4.2	Analysis and results	211
	7.4.3	Recapitulation	231
	7.5	The verb phrase: concluding remarks	233
8	Syntactic analysis		237
	8.1	Preliminaries	237
	8.1.1	Introductory remarks	237
	8.1.2	The syntactic codes	237
	8.2	Word order	241
	8.2.1	Dutch word order	242
	8.2.2	English word order	261
	8.2.3	A comparison between English and Dutch	274
	8.3	General syntactic development	281
	8.3.1	The Global codes	282
	8.3.2	Clauses	290
	8.3.3	Constituents	298
	8.3.4	Conclusion	304
9	The morphological and syntactic analyses: a recapitulation		306
10	Metalinguistic behaviour		310
	10.1	Introductory remarks	310
	10.2	Spontaneous repairs	310
	10.3	Elicited repairs	319
	10.4	Metalinguistic statements	325
	10.5	Hesitations and self-repetitions	331
	10.6	Other metalinguistic behaviour	332
	10.7	General discussion and conclusion	333
11	Findings and implications		338
References			345
Appendix			365
Index of names			385

List of tables

Tables as they appear in the main text

Table 2.1	Methodology in studies of BFLA
Table 4.1	List of countries visited by Kate
Table 4.2	Kate's daily language environment in Belgium
Table 4.3	Adults present at recording sessions
Table 4.4	Main activities engaged in by Kate and their associated interlocutors and languages
Table 4.5	Languages used by Kate
Table 4.6	Mean Length of Utterance calculations for Kate: results
Table 5.1	Language choice codes
Table 5.2	Kate's language selection in function of addressee
Table 5.3	Lexical insertions in Kate's Mixed utterances
Table 6.1	The basic English adult gender pronoun system
Table 6.2	The basic Dutch adult gender system
Table 6.3	Kate's use of syntactic gender marking in singular NP's
Table 6.4	English third person singular personal pronouns
Table 6.5	Dutch third person singular personal pronouns and independent demonstratives
Table 6.6	Animacy of neuter nouns and their use with Dutch gender determiners
Table 6.7	Proposed basic usage constellations of the personal pronouns IT, HE, HIM and SHE
Table 7.1	The basic English adult verb phrase formation system
Table 7.2	The basic Dutch adult verb phrase formation system
Table 7.3	Verbs with morphemes from both English and Dutch as used by Kate
Table 7.4	Kate's English verb forms
Table 7.5	Kate's Dutch verb forms
Table 7.6	Kate's Dutch past participles
Table 7.7	A cross-linguistic comparison of Kate's verb forms

Table 7.8	Kate's Dutch Subject--finite lexical verb combinations
Table 7.9	Kate's conjugation of HEBBEN
Table 7.10	Kate's conjugation of ZIJN
Table 7.11	Kate's Dutch verb system and how it compares with findings from monolingual acquisition
Table 7.12	Kate's English Subject--finite lexical verb combinations
Table 7.13	Full vs. abbreviated forms of BE
Table 7.14	The uses of DO
Table 7.15	Kate's English past forms: types
Table 7.16	Kate's English verb system and how it compares with findings from monolingual acquisition
Table 8.1	Kate's word order patterns in Dutch declarative MC's
Table 8.2	Y- and X -elements in Kate's Dutch declarative main clauses
Table 8.3	Barbara's word order patterns in some declarative MC's
Table 8.5	The elements occurring after non-finite verbs in Kate's Dutch MC's
Table 8.6	Kate's word order patterns in Dutch questions
Table 8.7	Syntactic functions of the question words occurring in Kate's full Dutch WH-questions
Table 8.8	Non-adult-like word order in the Dutch data
Table 8.9	Kate's word order patterns in English declarative main clauses
Table 8.10	Clause-initial elements in Kate's English declarative main clauses
Table 8.11	Kate's word order patterns in English multi-component VP's
Table 8.12	Kate's word order patterns in English questions
Table 8.13	Syntactic functions of the question words occurring in Kate's full English WH-questions
Table 8.14	Non-adult-like word order in the English data
Table 8.15	Kate's English and Dutch use of Subject--finite verb sequences
Table 8.16	Kate's English and Dutch inversion patterns
Table 8.17	The proportions of use of Kate's English and Dutch main clause WO patterns
Table 8.18	Fronting in Kate's English and Dutch declarative main clauses

Table 8.19   A comparison of Kate's English and Dutch main clauses with a multi-component verb phrase
Table 8.20   Kate's use of novel verb forms in English and Dutch interrogatives
Table 8.21   Kate's use of novel question words in WH-questions
Table 8.22   Kate's use of declaratives and interrogatives as compared to data from British children
Table 8.23   Kate's use of clause connectors
Table 8.24   Kate's English subclauses
Table 8.25   Structure types appearing at least 10 times
Table 9.1   Changes in Kate's language production after her third birthday
Table 10.1   Types of spontaneous repairs
Table 10.2   Improvement rating of Kate's spontaneous repairs
Table 10.3   Kate's responses to requests for clarification
Table 10.4   Kate's responses to requests for clarification as dependent on the formal adequacy of the original utterance

Tables as they appear in the appendix

Table 1   Kate's utterances: language preserving or not?
Table 2   Kate's utterances as a function of addressee and/or language addressed in
Table 3   Kate's mixed utterances as a function of addressee
Table 4   Types of insertions in Kate's Mixed utterances
Table 5   Occurrence of tokens of the parts of speech in the full corpus
Table 6   Overt syntactic gender marking in complex Dutch singular noun phrases
Table 7   Development in the appropriate use of overt syntactic gender marking in complex Dutch noun phrases?
Table 8   The marking of gender by means of pronouns
Table 9   Animate vs. inanimate reference as marked by means of pronouns
Table 10   Errors in the choice of gender pronouns and independent determiners
Table 11   Dutch corpus: independent vs. modifying use of DAT/DA/HET/'T/DIE/DEZE/DIT/DITTE

Table 12	Plural nouns
Table 13	NP's with an adjective as head
Table 14	Common nouns in combination
Table 15	Dutch subject--finite verb combinations
Table 16	The conjugation of Dutch HEBBEN
Table 17	Kate's independent vs. auxiliary use of Dutch modals
Table 18	Past reference in the Dutch corpus
Table 19	English subject--finite lexical verb combinations
Table 20	English subject--HAVE combinations
Table 21	English subject--BE combinations
Table 22	Use of WANT as auxiliary
Table 23	Use of DO as auxiliary
Table 24	Realizations of the English present continuous
Table 25	English past forms
Table 26	Kate's Dutch declarative main clauses
Table 27	Kate's Dutch interrogative main clauses
Table 28	Kate's English declarative main clauses
Table 29	Kate's English main clauses with a multi-component VP: word order patterns
Table 30	Kate's English interrogative main clauses
Table 31	The proportion of Kate's utterances with a Z vs. a U code
Table 32	Kate's utterances with a U code
Table 33	Kate's sentence types
Table 34	How many constituents per clause?
Table 35	Clause constituents
Table 36	Dutch and English spontaneous repairs

Symbols and abbreviations

A	the investigator
BFLA	Bilingual First Language Acquisition
D	Dutch
E	English
F	Kate's father
FCH	Formal Complexity Hypothesis
IC	interlocutor
IDH	Independent Development Hypothesis
M	Kate's mother
MC	main clause
MLU	Mean Length of Utterance
NP	Noun Phrase
SC	subclause
SDH	Separate Development Hypothesis
UB	Upper Bound
UVF	Unmarked Verb Form
VP	Verb Phrase
WO	word order

Phonetic realizations of sounds are indicated by [..]. All phonetic transcription is in broad IPA format.
Allomorphs and phonemes are indicated by /../.
Bound morphemes are indicated by {..}.
Items in <...> are translations of items preceding them.
Word for word glosses are indicated by dashes between all words.

Acknowledgements

The preparation of this book coincided with our daughter's first year. I hope that as she grows up I can give her as much freedom to learn as my parents have given me. If she ever goes on to higher education, I hope she will meet with encouragement and enthusiasm. These two things and much more I have received in abundance from my advisor, Prof. Dr. Hugo Baetens Beardsmore. I also wish my little girl, if she ever gets married, as helpful a husband as mine, Darius Clynes: without the computer programmes that he wrote for analysis, the data to be reported on in this book would have had to be analysed manually, adding many more months (and tedious computational work) to the research project. Thank you, Darius, not only for your computer help, but also for your general support and understanding.

In coming to grips with the practical and theoretical aspects of my work I have greatly benefited from conversations and/or correspondence with many individuals. Specifically, I would like to mention Léon Adriaens, Eve Clark, Sera de Vriendt, Paul Fletcher, Steven Gillis, Jürgen Meisel, Anne Mills, Rafaella Negro, George Saunders, Margreet van Ierland, Piet van de Craen, Jef Verschueren. Thank you.

I also thank my two anonymous reviewers for their encouragement and constructive criticism.

I am greatly indebted to the parents of Kate, the little bilingual girl who is the subject of the case study to be presented in this book.

Finally, I would like to thank Kate herself. She was a continuous source of wonder and without her joyous chatter this book could simply not have been written.

1 *Introduction*

In the field of child language acquisition studies, the emphasis has so far mainly been on monolingual children's language development. In their quest for explanations of this development researchers have increasingly turned to cross-linguistic studies, comparing with one another monolingual children acquiring different languages (see e.g. the recent collection of papers edited by Slobin 1985b). Such cross-linguistic research has, amongst others, been motivated by the question of the relative importance of language-universal vs. language-specific factors in acquisition (see e.g. Slobin 1985c, Berman 1986, Mills 1986c). It can be argued, however, that comparisons between monolingual children acquiring different languages are not the ideal empirical basis for addressing this issue. After all, in such comparisons most psycho-social variables cannot be held constant, and thus one can never be certain what the precise reasons are for any differences or similarities found in the acquisition patterns of children learning different languages: these may be due to purely linguistic factors, but also to other factors having to do, amongst others, with differences in cognitive development, cultural environment or socialization patterns.

A child growing up with two languages from birth, on the other hand, offers a unique opportunity for investigating general theoretical issues in the language acquisition field, since here the number of possibly influential variables is reduced to a minimum: the bilingual child comes the closest to being the 'perfect matched pair'. After all, the bilingual child is always at the same level of socio-cognitive development, and although he may be exposed to aspects of different cultures, and although the social interaction styles of the various speakers addressing the child may differ considerably if these speakers belong to distinct cultures [1], the main two variables are the bilingual child's two input languages. [2]

Obviously, however, studying bilingual children's language development is not only a worthwhile undertaking with reference to possible explanations of monolingual development, it is also a separate area of investigation with its own unique questions and hypotheses.

Throughout this century linguists, sociologists, psychologists and pedagogues have held a fascination with the phenomenon of children learning two languages from an early age on. In some of the empirical studies, authors have described their own development as a bilingual (see e.g. Elwert 1959), but most of the others (as is the case in studies of monolingual acquisition) concern reports on bilingual children who are either the author's own offspring or other people's (see e.g. Ronjat 1913).

There are various situations in which children can become bilingual: they may hear one language until they are two years old and only after this start to regularly hear a second language in addition to the first. Alternatively, this second language might entirely replace the first. A third possibility is that children may be regularly exposed to two languages from birth onwards, or at least from very soon after birth. Children may also hear more than two languages. These are just a few of the many possibilities.

McLaughlin (1978, 1984b) makes a distinction between <u>simultaneous</u> and <u>successive</u> acquisition of two languages: he speaks of 'simultaneous acquisition of two languages' when a child has been introduced to two languages before his or her third birthday and applies the term 'successive acquisition of two languages' to situations in which this criterion is not met. McLaughlin readily admits that the third birthday stipulation represents an arbitrary cut-off point. Taeschner (1983) accepts McLaughlin's stipulation, but Padilla and Lindholm (1984) do not. They speak of 'simultaneous acquisition of two languages' only when a child has been exposed to two languages from birth onwards. Anything else they regard as instances of 'consecutive' or 'successive' language acquisition.

It can be agreed with Padilla and Lindholm (1984) that McLaughlin's 'third birthday' criterion is to be rejected on the basis of its arbitrariness. Furthermore, it has yet to be empirically shown that children who grow up with two languages from birth exhibit similar acquisition patterns to children who have been exposed to a second language at, say, the age of one. There is no *a priori* reason to assume that indeed the acquisition patterns would be the same. In fact, the opposite would appear to be more realistic: after all, the child exposed to French after a year's exposure to only Russian might very well, due to his knowledge of Russian (however rudimentary this might still be at age one), start to use French in quite a different way from how a child exposed to both Russian and French from birth would use it at the same age. A possible underlying reason for such a difference might be the psychological principle that anything learnt has an effect on subsequent learning (see e.g. Kagan 1984). In addition, if any comparisons with monolingual children are to be valid, one must make sure that the basis for comparison is as solid as possible: comparing the acquisition of Cantonese in a monolingual child exposed to this language from birth and in a bilingual child exposed to it only from the age of six months onwards does not permit the disentangling of the two variables 'age of first exposure' and 'exposure to two languages'. It would thus seem that Padilla and Lindholm's (1984) suggestion to speak of 'simultaneous acquisition of two languages' only when a child has been exposed to two languages from birth onwards and to use the term 'consecutive' or 'successive' acquisition in all other cases is a reasonable one.

While I agree with the basic conceptual distinction that Padilla and Lindholm (1984) are making, I venture to suggest that the term 'simultaneous' acquisition of two languages not be used any more, since this term has been used with different meanings by different authors. This has had the unfortunate result that when researchers state they were studying a child 'simultaneously exposed to two languages' it is not at all clear whether the child was exposed to these languages very soon after birth, or came into contact with a second language some time between birth and age three.

Rather than use the term 'simultaneous' acquisition of two languages, then, I propose to use Meisel's (i.p.) term <u>Bilingual First Language Acquisition</u> (or, in short, BFLA). [3] Whereas Meisel uses this term to refer to situations in which a child is exposed to two languages from birth, the following definition is perhaps more workable: [4]

BFLA refers to those situations in which

(a) a child is first exposed to language B no later than a week after he or she was first exposed to language A, [5] and
(b) a child's exposure to languages A and B is fairly regular, i.e. the child is addressed in both languages almost every day. [6]

Obviously, within the BFLA situation there is a lot of variation possible. A child may start hearing two languages on a regular basis from birth onwards, but such regular exposure may cease at age one, with only one of the child's languages being used in the child's environment after this. However, most of the studies of BFLA to date have been concerned with children whose regular exposure to their two languages basically continued up to the time of observation, although regular exposure to either one of the languages may have briefly ceased due to holidays, stays in hospital, or other situations in which the person(s) providing the input in a particular language was/were absent. Except when indicated otherwise, the term BFLA in the following will be used to refer to the latter situation, i.e. to circumstances where children's regular exposure to two languages lasted at least up to the time of observation, but allowing for brief interludes in which such regular exposure was absent. For ease of reference, we shall continue to use the phrase 'a child exposed to two languages from birth' as shorthand for the new working definition of BFLA proposed above.

The most frequently asked questions in empirical studies of very young bilingual children have been whether, when and to what extent these children eventually come to speak two distinct languages. It will be argued that so far, this question remains fundamentally unresolved.

A first reason for this is that when asking the question (and certainly when attempting to find an answer), researchers have not usually taken into due account the potential importance of the nature of the child's exposure to his or her input systems. Although it is quite possible that differences in such exposure patterns are irrelevant to the acquisition process, this remains to be empirically investigated. Until such empirical investigations have unequivocally shown that indeed the nature of the child's exposure to his or her input systems has no impact whatsoever on the child's language development, we shall start from the common sense assumption that exposure patterns <u>might well be</u> important, and that it may matter a lot whether a child is exposed to two languages from birth or not, or whether the two input systems are presented separately or not (to name but a few possible variables). Not to recognize the possible relevance of different exposure patterns is unrealistic.

A second reason for why we consider as basically unresolved the question of whether, when and to what extent young children exposed to two languages eventually come to speak two distinct languages lies in the unfortunate fact that those few studies that do furnish sufficient background information on their subjects' linguistic environments often exhibit methodological flaws which make it logically impossible to accept as proven any conclusions reached concerning the issue under discussion.

Another issue that has been of major concern in studies of bilingual children is to what extent these children's language production resembles that of monolingual children in either language. This issue can be seen as fundamentally unresolved as well for the very same reasons as outlined above for the first question. Comparisons between bilingual and monolingual children must, after all, remain vacuous when the basic exposure patterns for the children to be compared are substantially different, or, indeed, are unknown: any differences found between children are then not necessarily relatable to the fact that the bilingual child is learning two languages and the monolingual only one, but may be directly relatable to factors such as the age of first regular exposure to a particular language and the extent to which the bilingual child's languages are presented in a separate fashion or not. Again, it is possible that such differences in exposure patterns are irrelevant, and that bilingual and monolingual children's language productions can be compared with one another regardless of how children came into contact with their languages, but until this has been proved beyond any reasonable doubt, researchers cannot start from the assumption that any differences in exposure patterns are irrelevant. Besides the fact that in drawing comparisons between monolingual and bilingual children researchers have often been comparing data that are not necessarily comparable, many of these comparisons have furthermore been methodologically weak.

In order to approach the issue mentioned at the very beginning of this chapter, namely what can bilingual children teach us about acquisition strategies in general (and thus also in monolingual children), we need detailed descriptive analyses of bilingual children's speech production. Unfortunately, as we shall attempt to show in Chapter 2, the body of proven empirical knowledge in the field of BFLA today is quite small, the result being that most of the available literature does not provide a solid enough basis for addressing this issue. In fact it will be argued that most of our present-day knowledge in the field of BFLA is even too limited to address the two main questions in the greater field of child bilingualism itself, i.e. the questions of the distinctness of the bilingual child's two languages and of the similarities or differences between bilingual and monolingual children's speech productions (see above).

The overall aim of this book, then, is twofold: first, to learn more about the process of bilingual first language acquisition in its own right, and second, on the basis of this newly acquired knowledge, to contribute to a better understanding of child language acquisition processes in general.

As pointed out in the preceding paragraphs, the total body of descriptively adequate knowledge about bilingual children's speech productions is very small. Hence it was imperative that new data be collected and analysed. The data to be presented here concern a single child's acquisition of English and Dutch. Since the subject of this study was exposed to her two input systems in a separate fashion from birth, we shall not be able to say anything about acquisition processes relevant to other exposure patterns identifiable in the field of child bilingualism. Any hypotheses set forth here, then, are to be interpreted solely as concerning the one basic exposure pattern where a child regularly hears two languages from birth and where each person when addressing the child basically uses one language only.

Our main concern in the analysis of the data will be to investigate the validity of what we shall term the separate development hypothesis. This hypothesis proposes that a bilingual child's morphosyntactic development proceeds along separate lines for each of the child's languages. Thus, the child's languages are seen as constituting largely self-contained systems. We shall approach the separate development hypothesis from two sides: first, from within the bilingual child's own speech productions, and second, on the basis of comparisons with monolingual English- and Dutch-speaking children.

It will further be argued that if the separate development hypothesis turns out to be an accurate characterization of the bilingual child's morphosyntactic development, this implies that development is very much guided by factors relating to the structural properties existing in the input and that hence language-specific elements play a major role in acquisition.

We regard the empirical investigation to be presented in this book as very much exploratory in nature, the main reason for this being that we see the body of 'solid' empirical knowledge in the field of bilingual first language acquisition to be quite limited indeed. In order to substantiate the latter claim we shall critically review most of the studies on BFLA available in the West today. In this review, which constitutes the first part of Chapter 2, we shall be focussing on methodological issues. The second part of Chapter 2 then considers the status of some major theoretical issues in the field of BFLA, only to find that these issues remain unresolved, partially because the empirical basis for them is lacking, or because the assumptions underlying some of the issues involved can be seriously questioned.

Chapter 3 introduces the separate development hypothesis and sets the scene for the empirical investigation following it.

Chapters 4 through 10 present a case study of a Dutch-English bilingual child for the age period between 2;7 and 3;4. In this case study, the main emphasis will be on morphosyntactic development, but attention will also be given to the subject's use of utterances containing morphemes from both languages and to signs of metalinguistic behaviour.

Chapter 11, finally, recapitulates the main findings and discusses their implications. Although Chapter 11 could be seen as the formal conclusion to this work, we chose not to call it that, since we regard the research project to be reported on as part of a continuing process of discovery that can only very gradually lend us any better insight in how children learn to speak (almost) like the people around them.

In the Appendix we present the bulk of the data in table format. There are a number of tables present in the main text as well, but these generally only give total figures for the entire period of observation, while the Appendix lists the data per recording session.

Notes
1 Such interaction styles, however, need not be determined by cultural differences: monolingual children growing up in the same culture may be exposed to greatly different interaction styles as well, depending on inter-individually defined variations between interacting speakers (see e.g. Wells 1986).
2 In referring to 'the child' in general, we will be using either one of the gender pronouns or both.
3 Meisel (i.p.) is a manuscript version of a chapter that at the time of the present book's going to press has been published in Hyltenstam and Obler (1989). Since during the preparation of the present book only this manuscript version was available we shall continue to refer to this version only.
4 Meisel's characterization is ambiguous: for instance, is it to be interpreted literally as meaning that in order to 'qualify' as a case of BFLA a baby would immediately after birth have to hear two languages spoken at once, or is a more liberal interpretation acceptable in which it is enough for a child to have heard two languages spoken alternately soon after birth?
5 The stipulation of a week was chosen because this would probably be the usual maximum period, even for children of mixed marriages, that initial contact with more than one language might be non-existent or difficult: at least in Western industrialized countries, a week would probably be the usual maximum period that a healthy newborn and its mother would spend in hospital after a hospital birth before going home, i.e. to an environment where a second language was used besides the language used by mother and/or nursing staff.

6 Although most of this book will be looking at the acquisition of two languages only, it is of course possible that children are exposed to more than two languages at an early age. No claims are made here about either differences or similarities between these two situations.

2 Bilingual first language acquisition: methods and theories

The study of children growing up with two languages from birth is comparatively new. As with any new area of investigation, there is an initial period for seeking a satisfactory method and paradigm in which to carry out valid work. This initial period is now perhaps starting to fade away: the clearest sign of this is that in general books on bilingualism, reference is made to findings from studies on young bilingual children in which these findings are presented as facts and generally accepted truths (see e.g. Grosjean 1982). Another sign is that scholars in first language acquisition are also starting to refer to findings from studies of young bilingual children (see e.g. E. Clark 1985). A third sign is the recent publication of various books on bilingual children aimed at answering parents' and other educators' questions on how to bring up children bilingually (see e.g. Kielhöfer and Jonekeit 1983, Arnberg 1987, Harding and Reilly 1987, Saunders 1988). In these books, findings from fundamental research are often quoted or taken as starting points for practical advice to parents and teachers.

The question now is: can indeed most of the findings from the available studies be taken as proven, unquestionable facts? Is there consensus in the field about these findings and how to interpret them? In other words, has a unified research paradigm developed that is methodologically sound enough to address theoretically pertinent issues?

It is the aim of the first part of the present chapter to examine the latter question. After this, we shall go on to discuss the theoretical repercussions of the answer to this question. We shall then also investigate whether what is often presented as factual information about bilingual children can indeed be seen as underpinned by methodologically solid fundamental research.

2.1 Methodology in studies of BFLA

In this section we present a method-oriented review of most of the empirical studies on bilingual first language acquisition readily availasble in the West today that present new data. Overviews such as the ones by McLaughlin (1978, 1984), Redlinger (1979), Lindholm (1980) and Padilla and Lindholm (1984), then, are excluded; Leopold's (1953) excellent article was not included either, since it primarily aims to test Jakobson's theories on language acquisition against data already reported on in Leopold's previous work; similarly, Leopold's (1978, c. 1954) article was excluded too, since it basically contains a summary of Leopold (1970, c. 1939-49).

In the review here, we shall only consider studies of young bilingual children, i.e. of children under the age of five, since most of the theoretical questions concerning BFLA pertain to the earliest stages of language acquisition. Excluded here because the subjects were older than five are - to name but a few - the studies by Kessler (1971), McClure and Wentz (1975), Tsushima and Hogan (1975), Chun (1978), Cummins (1978b), Hakuta (1978, c. 1974), Huang and Hatch (1978), Wong Fillmore (1979). Linnakylä (1980), Snow, Smith and Hoefnagel-Höhle (1980), Appel (1984) and Pfaff (1985).

A further limitation of the review here is that only naturalistic studies will be considered. We thus exclude from detailed review the non-naturalistic studies (i.e. experimental studies or formal test procedures) carried out by for instance Ianco-Worrall (1972), Bain (1976), Doyle, Champagne and Segalowitz (1978), Jarovinskij (1979), Lindholm, Padilla and Romero (1979), and Chesterfield and Pérez (1981). Experimental studies and formal test procedures are particularly useful for testing specific hypotheses about phenomena previously observed in natural settings. This in turn implies that one already has available data obtained in a naturalistic fashion, so that one has a 'base-line' to start from. For the study of bilingual children, the field at this point in time does not, I believe, have at its disposal an extensive body of generally accepted knowledge about these children's language development. At best, our knowledge is fragmentary (obviously, we have yet to demonstrate that this is indeed the case). In this situation, the time is not ripe for conducting tests or experiments with young bilingual children, and it is not clear how at the present moment any results from the few test procedures and experiments that have been carried out with young bilingual children as subjects should be interpreted. For any realistic interpretation to become possible, we first need many more studies of bilingual children's naturally occurring speech production.

The focus on naturalistic studies also means that studies using 'secondary data' gathered by means of questionnaires or caretaker interviews, such as the ones by Smith (1935), Métraux (1965), Ellul (1978), Arnberg (1979, 1981), and Harrison and Piette (1980), for instance, will not be reviewed here. These studies are very interesting for finding out more about parents' sociolinguistic attitudes towards a bilingual upbringing and about how parents see the rate of success of this upbringing, but tend to furnish little 'hard' data on children's language development. Third party reports are of course very useful, however, as a back-up source of information, and obviously, factual information about a child's private history (including his/her linguistic history) will have to be obtained through parental reports.

It should also be mentioned that we shall not be referring to papers presented at conferences insofar as they have not been published. As a consequence, the very promising studies by, amongst others, Lanza (1987) and Idiazabal (1988) were excluded, as was the one by Jisa (1987).

Finally, the review below concerns studies that clearly deal with the BFLA situation in the general sense, i.e., that report on children exposed to two (or more) languages from birth. Using the more precise definition of BFLA as introduced in Chapter 1 would have the awkward result that to date no studies of BFLA could be found - simply because authors have not used the newly proposed definition or have not described their subjects' linguistic history precisely enough to determine whether the new definition applies or not. Thus, the review below deals with studies in which authors specifically said that their subjects were exposed to two (or more) languages from birth and/or in which it was stated that a subject's parents had always used different languages when speaking to the child.

It must be emphasized that in considering a study on child bilingualism for review we did not interpret the phrase 'X was simultaneously exposed to languages A and B' as identical to 'X was exposed to languages A and B from birth' except when from additional exposure pattern information it was clear that indeed the study concerned dealt with a case of BFLA (cf. Chapter 1). Conversely, although authors may have stated that their subjects were raised with two languages "from the start" (Vihman 1981a: 2), the studies concerned were excluded from review if it was clear from additional information on exposure patterns that in fact these studies' subjects were not exposed to two languages from birth. Studies in which there was absolutely no information on exposure patterns were naturally excluded from review as well (see e.g. Bubenik 1978, Wagner-Gough 1978, c. 1975, and Vila and Zanón 1986).

There are quite a number of naturalistic studies that have as their subjects children under the age of five who were possibly exposed to two languages from birth. Unfortunately, though, authors do not always furnish enough exposure pattern information for the reader to decide whether these studies deal with cases of BFLA or not (just a few examples are Mikès 1967, Padilla and Liebman 1975, Vogel 1975, Redlinger and Park 1980, Nuckle and Lappin 1982 and Deuchar and Clark 1987).
(Often, authors simply stated that subjects were acquiring two languages 'simultaneously', without further explanation of this ambiguous term - see Chapter 1.) As a consequence, some of the results of these studies are uninterpretable and cannot be used to prove or disprove major theoretical issues in the field of BFLA such as the question whether children growing up with two languages from birth separate their language systems from the beginning or not (see the second part of this chapter). Furthermore, comparisons with other children, whether they be mono- or bilingual, cannot be made, since the basis for any meaningful comparison is lacking (one does not know whether one is comparing one type of apple with another, or whether one is comparing apples and pears). Until authors furnish sufficiently detailed information about exposure patterns we cannot assume that the studies concerned belong to the field of BFLA. Regrettably, they must be excluded from review.

Finally, then, we have come to naturalistic studies of pre-school children that unambiguously belong to the field of BFLA.

For the study of early child language development (whether bilingual or monolingual), the minimum aims of a scientifically sound empirical study as I see them at the present stage are (a) to gather data that most probably represent (a slice of) reality as it occurs when it is not being studied, (b) to describe these data in a comprehensive and knowledgeable manner so that other researchers may obtain a clear idea of what the data are, (c) to analyse the data using generally agreed upon methods of transcription and analysis, and (d) to interpret the results obtained by the analyses in as general a fashion as these logically permit in order to contribute towards a better understanding of the observed phenomena. Other criteria are: (e) truthfulness, i.e. the data should be what they are said to be, (f) objectivity, i.e. value judgements should be avoided unless it is made clear to the reader that indeed these are made as added comments to what otherwise are objective statements, (g) clarity of presentation of data and methods so that there is a chance for (h) comparison by other researchers. The investigation as a whole must in addition be (i) reproducible to as great an extent as possible (in studies of language acquisition it will not usually be practically possible to use the same subjects, but it should be possible to carry out a study with subjects who are very similar to the original subjects used). Obviously, all the criteria mentioned are related to one another (criterion (i) of reproducibility, for instance, will be violated if criterion (b) is not respected).

It is with the above criteria in mind that we present the following critical review of studies on BFLA.

A first question in our methodological investigation of studies on BFLA concerns the nature of the data, i.e. whether the data in a particular study are longitudinal or cross-sectional. As with experimental studies and test procedures, cross-sectional studies typically aim to probe specific issues that have emerged from longitudinal studies as being important, controversial, or simply unclear. In second language acquisition research, Rosansky (1976) has strongly advocated the use of longitudinal studies over that of cross-sectional ones. She argues that cross-sectional studies can be meaningful only once a 'base-line' of development has been established on the basis of longitudinal research. We shall have to investigate whether what Rosansky is claiming for second language acquisition research also holds for studies of BFLA or not, i.e., we shall have to see whether there are at present enough data from intensive longitudinal research that can act as a 'base-line' for cross-sectional studies.

Secondly, the data collection technique will be focused on: did the investigator(s) use a diary method, video- or audio-recordings, a mixed method, or perhaps only infrequent notes? Was the investigator the only data collector or was there a counterbalancing for both languages? It is clear that if one is interested in studying the course of development of both a child's languages one should make sure that environments for data collection are created in which there will be a reasonable chance that the child will in fact draw on her knowledge from two languages. (At the same time, of course, one must be careful to create an environment that is as natural as possible.) In addition, we shall indicate the investigator's relationship to the subject(s) as well as the quantitative extent of each study's corpus.

A third issue is the transcription method used (this applies only to media-recorded samples): was the transcription method clearly indicated? If researchers omit to describe their method of transcription, the exact nature of the data will not be clear and hence the study as a whole will be difficult to reproduce.

Fourthly, were the data (whether they were transcriptions or manual records) written down phonetically or orthographically? This question is particularly pertinent to studies that use subjects under the age of two: in writing down accurately what a very young child said on a particular occasion, use of phonetics is indispensable: if a one-and-a-half-year-old's vocalizations are written down orthographically at the transcription stage, the researcher might be over-interpreting what the child is actually saying. After all, children under the age of two do not yet have a fully established sound system (see e.g. Templin 1957, Olmsted 1971, Smith 1973, Ingram 1976; cf. also Leopold 1970, c. 1939-49, who points out the importance of phonetic training on the part of the researcher who wants to seriously study the language development of any child in the first two years). In order to avoid unwarranted over-interpretation of data on very young children, then, only phonetic transcriptions should be made (this does not imply, of course, that the use of phonetic transcripts automatically means that the quality of the transcripts is good).

A final question is whether authors used quantification. Quantification greatly expands the possibilities for empirical testing and often leads to new hypotheses and theories which, without the use of quantification, might not have arisen (van Ierland 1983). In the field of first language acquisition research, systematic frequency counts have often permitted the discovery of patterns in children's language behaviour that might not have been found without the use of quantification (van Ierland 1983). On the basis of these patterns, students of language acquisition have been able to formulate rule-models which reflect temporal changes in the frequency patterns observed. Frequency counts, then, are of great benefit to all research in the language acquisition field, and hence in the study of bilingual first language acquisition as well.

There is one aspect of quantitative information which has had a great impact in first language acquisition research, and that is the MLU or Mean Length of Utterance measure as developed by Brown (1973). On the basis of longitudinal studies of three American children, Brown (1973) found that age is not a good predictor of a child's level of language development.

Instead, he argued, an adequate measuring rod that allows children to be matched to each other as far as their stage of language development goes is the combined use of an MLU and upper bound (UB) measure. Roughly, MLU is the average number of morphemes per utterance within a transcript (for the exact rules for computing MLU, see Brown 1973: 54), and UB is the number of morphemes in the longest utterance in a transcript (again, length is expressed in number of morphemes).

There has been much debate on the general validity of MLU as an adequate tool of measuring children's language capabilities, but notwithstanding this, the measure continues to be used even today. Rather than repeat much of the criticism voiced by others (see e.g. Crystal 1974 and Wells 1985), I will briefly dwell on the main problem that I see with the use of MLU as a measuring rod in studies of BFLA, which is that it was developed for the analysis of standard English early child language only: one cannot, without extensive adaptation, apply MLU to other languages (see also Crystal 1974). This issue has been of some concern to researchers in the first language acquisition field wishing to compare children's monolingual acquisition of different languages, but has not, I feel, received sufficient attention in the field of BFLA research. Obviously, researchers in the latter field have recognized that a universally applicable measuring rod for determining children's language abilities is sorely needed if one wishes to compare the two sides of a bilingual child's speech production and if one is interested in comparing a bilingual child's use of language A with monolingual children's use of that language. Simply taking MLU as a basis for such comparisons, though, will not do, since at least one of the languages to be compared will not be standard English. The problem of finding an alternative instrument that could serve as an appropriate tool is both one of comparative and contrastive linguistics, and of child language research in general, and unfortunately we are far from developing such an appropriate alternative instrument (see also Wells 1985: 125).

Most of the studies that we shall be reviewing here did not make use of any formal coding system. In addition, more often than not the linguistic terminology used was not clearly defined, and only very rarely were the criteria set out that any stretch of speech production had to satisfy to count as an instance of a particular linguistic category. For instance, even in otherwise methodologically quite sound studies no working definitions are given of linguistic categories such as 'word' (Jekat 1985) or 'Subject'

(Meisel 1986). One might argue that most linguists will have a common understanding of these terms. Although this may be the case, the fact remains that such terms have been developed for the description of adult-like language. If, as in the case of Jekat (1985) and Meisel (1986), one uses these descriptive terms to refer to elements of a child's 'two-word sentences', however, an explicitation is needed of the criteria by which a particular form is assigned to a particular category. Since most of the studies reviewed below did not furnish sufficient information on any linguistic categorization decisions, the inclusion of an 'analysis rating' was rather pointless.

On the contents level, the languages that the subjects in each study were exposed to were listed, and a brief characterization was given of the type of exposure to each language. In addition, the number of subjects per study, their sibling status and sex were listed, as was the age range studied. We end with a succinct indication of each study's main analytical emphasis.

Answers to the methodological questions above were brought together in Table 2.1. This table also contains the factual information referred to in the previous paragraph. The note below explains some of the abbreviations and terms used in Table 2.1.

NOTE to Table 2.1

Nature of the data: LONG. stands for 'longitudinal', CRS. for 'cross-sectional'; OTHER will be explained in a footnote

Data collection technique: DIARY stands for 'diary method', VIDEO for frequent video-recordings, AUDIO for regular audio-recordings (if authors only spoke of 'recordings' or 'taped material', it was assumed that this referred to audio-recordings), VIDEO+A/N for regular video-recordings supplemented by occasional audio-recordings and manual notes, AUDIO+N for the use of regular audio-recordings supplemented by occasional manual notes, NOTES for the use of infrequent manual notes only. OTHER is always explained in an additional footnote

Ss stands for 'subjects'

Investigator's relationship to Ss: IND stands for 'independent, unrelated observer', i.e. a non-caretaker. Note that only information present in the publication under review is taken into account

Transcription method indicated: NO INFO stands for 'no information'; NA for 'not applicable' (these abbreviations will be used throughout Table 2.1); 'yes' means that there was some explanation of the transcription method present, however limited; 'no' means that no information whatsoever was given

Phonetic transcript: 'yes' here means that either the author stated that child utterances were written down phonetically (either in transcriptions or in manual notes), or that from examples given it was clear that most of the child data were written down phonetically; 'no' means that the author clearly indicated that child utterances were written down orthographically, or that there was no indication in the text that most of the child utterances were written down phonetically

Quantification used: MLU here means that the only quantitative information given concerns mean length of utterance; 'no' means that no quantification whatsoever was used, and 'yes' that some quantification beyond the indication of MLU was used

Nature of basic exposure: 1P/1L means that one parent addressed the child in one language only for most intents and purposes

Ss' sex and sibling status: G stands for girl and B for boy; a number between brackets after G or B indicates the number of girls and boys respectively (when no number is given, there was just one girl and/or boy subject)

Table 2.1 *Methodology in studies of BFLA*

	Aldenhoff 1979	Berkele 1983	Berman 1979
Methodology:			
Nature of the data	LONG.	LONG.	LONG.
Data collection technique	NOTES	VIDEO	OTHER [a]
One or two data collectors?	1	2	1
Investigator's relationship to Ss	father	IND	mother
Sampling frequency	NO INFO	38 tapes [b]	see fn a
Duration of each sample	NA	50 minutes	NO INFO [c]
Transcription method indicated	NA	yes	no
Phonetic transcript	no	no [d]	no
Quantification used	no	yes	no
Subject information:			
Ss' languages	French/German	French/German	Hebrew/English
Nature of basic exposure	1P/1L	1P/1L	complex [e]
Number of Ss	1	1	1
Ss' sex and sibling status	G: only child	G: firstborn	G: NO INFO
Age range reported on	1;0-2;6	1;9,16-3;6,16	3;11-4;6
Study's main emphasis:	morphosyntax	determiners	re-learning of Hebrew

[a] In the period from 3;11 to 4;2 a diary method was used; in the period from 4;2 to 4;6 sporadic notes were taken, supplemented by weekly tape-recordings (there is no information on the interlocutors present at these recordings; neither is there any other contextual information)

[b] The recordings were made every 2, 3, or 4 weeks

[c] I.e., for the weekly audio-recordings it was not stated how long each one lasted

[d] However, occasional use of phonetic symbols as shown in a few examples gives rise to the possibility that phonetic transcriptions were used in some cases after all

[e] While in Israel (periods birth-2;11; 3;11-4;6), the child's parents and grandmother were her source of English, while all other people, including adult siblings, spoke Hebrew; while in the U.S.A. (2;11-3;11), the child heard only English (from parents and environment at large)

Table 2.1 continued

	Clyne 1987	Hoffman 1985	Hoffmann & Ariza 1979
Methodology:			
Nature of the data	LONG.	LONG.	LONG.
Data collection technique	NO INFO	OTHER [f]	OTHER [g]
One or two data collectors?	NO INFO	2	2
Investigator's relationship to Ss	NO INFO	parents	mother
Sampling frequency	NO INFO	NO INFO	NO INFO
Duration of each sample	NO INFO	NO INFO	NO INFO
Transcription method indicated	no	no	no
Phonetic transcript	no	no	no
Quantification used	no	no	no
Subject information:			
Sts' languages	English/German	Spanish/German	Spanish/German/English
Nature of basic exposure	1P/1L	1P/1L	1P/1L
Number of Ss	1	1	2
Ss' sex and sibling status	G: NO INFO	G: NO INFO	G: NO INFO; B: not firstborn
Age range reported on	2;1-4;11	0;6-2;0	G: ca. 2;0-7;4; B: ca. 2;0-5;6
Study's main emphasis:	metalinguistic awareness	language choice	general development

[f] The authors state that they "have taken a large number of notes and many hours of recordings" (Hoffman and Ariza 1979: 3). Any further specification is lacking

[g] "My observations are based on notes, diary entries by both my husband and myself, recordings and test results (mainly of vocabulary recall tests)" (Hoffmann 1985: 481). Further information is lacking

Table 2.1 continued

	Huerta 1977	Jekat 1985	Kielhöfer & Jonekeit 1983
Methodology:			
Nature of the data	LONG.	LONG.	LONG.
Data collection technique	AUDIO+N	VIDEO	NO INFO
One or two data collectors	several	2	NO INFO
Investigator's relationship to Ss	IND	IND	NO INFO
Sampling frequency	8 tapes [h]	NO INFO [i]	NO INFO
Duration of each sample	ca. $1/2$ hr [j]	ca. 1 hour	NO INFO
Transcription method indicated	no	yes	NA
Phonetic transcript	no	no	no
Quantification used	no	yes	no
Subject information:			
Ss' languages	English Spanish	French/ German	French/ German
Nature of basic exposure	1 person, 2 languages	1P/1L	1P/1L
Number of Ss	1	2	2
Ss' sex and sibling status	B: NO INFO	G: NO INFO B: NO INFO	B1: firstborn B2: second [k]
Age range reported on	2;1-2;10	G: 1;2,19-3;5,5 B: 1;10,13-2;1,24	B1: 1;3-5;0 B2: 1;3-4;0
Study's main emphasis:	language separation	vocabulary	language choice

[h] I.e. spread out over 9 months of observation; the total material comprises "approximately four hours of discourse" (Huerta 1977: 2)

[i] Jekat (1985) does indicate how frequently data were recorded (every 2 weeks), but she does not indicate the number of recordings or transcriptions of recordings that she took as a basis for analysis

[j] This is my own calculation based on the information that 8 recordings furnished ca. 4 hours' worth of material

[k] B1 and B2 are brothers

Table 2.1 continued

	Leopold 1970, c. 1939-49	Meisel 1985
Methodology:		
Nature of data	LONG.	LONG.
Data collection technique	DIARY	VIDEO+A/N
One or two data collectors?	1	2 [k]
Investigator's relationship to Ss	father	IND
Sampling frequency	throughout	every 2 weeks [l]
Duration of each sample	NA	NO INFO [m]
Transcription method indicated	NA	yes
Phonetic transcript	yes	no
Quantification used	yes	MLU
Subject information:		
Ss' languages	German/English	French/German
Nature of basic exposure	1P/1L	1P/1L
Number of Ss	1 [n]	2
Ss' sex and sibling status	G: firstborn	G: only child/ B: second
Age range reported on	birth-12	1;0-3;6
Study's main emphasis:	general development	expression of time/aspect

[k] For each video-recording, two investigators speaking different languages collected the data; additional audio-recordings and manual notes were furnished by the subjects' parents. Since the bulk of the data concern the video-recordings, we only listed 2 principal data collectors (the same holds for Meisel 1986, i.p)

[l] The video-recordings were made every two weeks, the audio-recordings every two months, and there is no information about the frequency with which notes were made (see previous fn)

[m] There is no information about the length of the video-recordings; the audio-recordings lasted at least one hour each

[n] Although Leopold occasionally reported on some aspects of his second daughter's language development, he himself did not regard these reports as anything but anecdotal: he mainly concentrated on his first daughter's language development. This is why the number of subjects was indicated as one only

Table 2.1 continued

	Meisel 1986	Meisel i.p.
Methodology:		
Nature of data	LONG.	LONG.
Data collection technique	VIDEO+A/N	VIDEO
One or two data collectors?	2	2
Investigator's relationship to Ss	IND	IND
Sampling frequency	monthly [o]	monthly [p]
Duration of each sample	50/60 mins.	50/60 mins.
Transcription method indicated	no	no
Phonetic transcript	no	no
Quantification used	yes	yes
Subject information:		
Ss' languages	French/German	French/German
Nature of basic exposure	1P/1L	1P/1L
Number of Ss	2	2
Ss' sex and sibling status	G: only child/ B: second	G: only child/ B: second
Age range reported on	1;0-4;0	1;0-4;0
Study's main emphasis:	word order/ case marking	word order/subject-verb agreement

[o] Although video-recordings were made twice a month, not all tapes were transcribed, but a minimum of one tape per month of observation was. For additional material, see footnote k

[p] Although video-recordings were made bi-weekly, the corpus on which this study is based consists of a minimum of one transcription per month of observation

Methods and theories 23

Table 2.1 continued

	Porsché 1983	Ronjat 1913	Saunders 1980
Methodology:			
Nature of data	LONG.	LONG.	LONG.
Data collection technique	OTHER [q]	NO INFO [r]	AUDIO [s]
One or two data collectors?	NO INFO	NO INFO	NO INFO
Investigator's relationship to Ss	father	father	father
Sampling frequency	see fn q	see fn r	NO INFO
Duration of each sample	NO INFO	NA	NO INFO
Transcription method indicated	no	NA	no
Phonetic transcript	no	yes	no
Quantification used	yes	no	yes
Subject information:			
Ss' languages	English/ German	French/ German	English/ German
Nature of basic exposure	1P/1L	1P/1L	1P/1L
Number of Ss	1	1	2
Ss' sex and sibling status	B: firstborn	B: firstborn	B1/B2 [t]
Age range reported on	1;10-2;7	0;8-ca. 4;6	B1: 3;5-5;11 B2: 3;5-4;1 [u]
Study's main emphasis:	translation 'equivalents' + semantic relations	sound system/ language choice	language choice

[q] The data consist of 3 corpora: a word-list accumulated when the subject was aged 1;10, and transcriptions of two audio-recordings made at the ages of 2;3 and 2;7. This material is supplemented by sporadic manual notes

[r] Presumably, Ronjat used hand-written notes (there was no present-day recording equipment available at the time), but whether he kept a systematic diary as Leopold (1970, c. 1939-49) did for his study can only be guessed at

[s] For the elder subject, Thomas, "an analysis was made of taped material covering the two-year period from age 3;10 to 5;10" (Saunders 1980: 139). In addition, the Peabody Picture Vocabulary Test (PPVT) was administered once in both languages (at 3;7 for B2 and at 5;5 for B1). There was additional material gathered for Thomas, but since this was done after the age of 5 it falls outside the scope of the present review

[t] B1 and B2 are brothers (the same holds for Saunders 1982, 1988); B1 is the firstborn and B2 the second

[u] Saunders (1980) does not explicitly state what the period of observation was; the ages given here were arrived at by tracing the lowest and highest ages for any statements by Saunders about his sons' language use

Table 2.1 continued

	Saunders 1982	Saunders 1988 [v]
Methodology:		
Nature of data	LONG.	LONG.
Data collection technique	AUDIO [w]	AUDIO [x]
One or two data collectors?	NO INFO	NO INFO
Investigator's relationship to Ss	father	father
Sampling frequency	NO INFO	NO INFO
Duration of each sample	NO INFO	NO INFO
Transcription method indicated	no	no
Phonetic transcript	no [y]	no
Quantification used	yes	yes
Subject information:		
Ss' languages	English/German	English/German
Nature of basic exposure	1P/1L	1P/1L
Number of Ss	2	1
Ss' sex and sibling status	B1/B2 [z]	G: third
Age range reported on	B1: 2;2-8;0	G: 2;4-6 [aa]
	B2: 1;4-6;0	
Study's main emphasis:	sociolinguistic aspects; general proficiency	sociolinguistic aspects; general proficiency

[v] This study is a sequel to Saunders (1982): it offers new data on Saunders' two sons for the later child years and early teens, and also presents mostly new data on the author's daughter Katrina for her first six years of life (Saunders 1983 had already briefly reported on Katrina's very early language development). The general methodology in Saunders (1988) is essentially the same as for Saunders (1982), and the new data for Katrina are presented in a fashion virtually identical to the data presentation for B1 and B2 (Thomas and Frank) in Saunders (1982). In order to avoid repetition, the Methodology and Subject information sections for Saunders (1988) above refer only to the new data for Katrina - the information in Table 2.1 for Saunders (1982) is still valid for the parts of the 1988 book that concern Thomas and Frank's development until the age of 5

[w] Saunders (1982) simply speaks of 'taped material'; in addition, data collection before the age of 5 included the administration of the PPVT when B2 was 3 years and 7 months old

[x] The author simply speaks of 'taped material'; he also gives results of the administration of the PPVT at the ages of 2;4 and 4;3

[y] When Saunders (1982) quotes some utterances by B2 under the age of 2;8, he does so using phonetics occasionally; the bulk of the examples given, however, are printed orthographically

[z] See footnote t above

[aa] The lower age indication is approximate only: it may be that throughout the text, examples occur that are situated earlier (Saunders 1988 does not explicitly state when data collection for Katrina began or from what age on he is reporting on her development)

Table 2.1 continued

	Swain 1972	Swain & Wesche 1975
Methodology:		
Nature of data	CRS.	LONG.
Data collection technique	AUDIO	AUDIO
One or two data collectors?	2	2
Investigator's relationship to Ss	IND	IND
Sampling frequency	every 2 weeks	every 2 weeks
Duration of each sample	60/90 minutes	60/90 minutes
Transcription method indicated	yes	yes
Phonetic transcript	no [bb]	no
Quantification used	yes	yes
Subject information:		
Ss' languages	English/French	English/French
Nature of basic exposure	1P/1L	1P/1L
Number of Ss	2	1
Ss' sex and sibling status	B1: second B2: first	B: second
Age range reported on	B1: 3;2-3;9 B2: 4;0-4;5 [cc]	3;1-3;10
Study's main emphasis:	question formation	'lexical mixing' [dd]

[bb] I.e., except when morphemes could not be unambiguously determined

[cc] These ages include the age ranges reported on, not the age ranges for which data were gathered. For B1, the total amount of data reported on consists of the child's questions produced in 6 recording sessions, with 2 each covering the periods 3;2-3;3, 3;6-3;7 and 3;8-3;9. For B2, the total amount of data reported on consists of the child's questions produced in 4 recording sessions, with 2 each covering the periods 4;0-4;1 and 4;4-4;5

[dd] I.e. the use of 'Mixed' utterances (see Chapter 4)

Table 2.1 continued

	Taeschner 1983	Volterra & Taeschner 1978
Methodology:		
Nature of data	LONG.	LONG.
Data collection technique	AUDIO+N.	AUDIO+N
One or two data collectors?	2	2 [ee]
Investigator's relationship to Ss	mother	IND+mother
Sampling frequency	"bimonthly" [ff]	twice a month [gg]
Duration of each sample	45 minutes	30 minutes
Transcription method indicated	yes	yes
Phonetic transcript	no [hh]	no
Quantification used	yes	yes
Subject information:		
Ss' languages	Italian/German	Italian/German
Nature of basic exposure	1P/1L	1P/1L
Number of Ss	2	2
Ss' sex and sibling status	G1: firstborn	G1: firstborn
	G2: second [ii]	G2: second
Age range reported on	G1: 1;6-5;0	G1: 1;5-3;6
	G2: 0;11-4;0	G2: 1;2-2;6
Study's main emphasis:	general development	lexical development

[ee] "The data collected by the authors [..]" (Volterra and Taeschner 1978: 312)

[ff] This refers to the audio-recordings only; unfortunately, the term "bimonthly" is ambiguous and can mean 'twice a month' or 'once every two months', the difference between these two being rather significant

[gg] This refers to the audio-recordings only

[hh] "The transcripts were not phonetic; rather, they reflected the way in which the children spoke" (Taeschner 1983: 20)

[ii] G1 and G2 are sisters; the same holds for Volterra and Taeschner (1978)

In the ensuing critical review of the studies mentioned in Table 2.1, we draw a distinction between studies primarily aimed at a lay audience (parents, educators) and those primarily aimed at an academic, scholarly audience.

Table 2.1 makes reference to three publications whose main goals it is to inform parents and educators about young bilingual children's language development and to help parents and educators in making various decisions concerning a bilingual upbringing. These publications are Kielhöfer and Jonekeit (1983) and Saunders (1982, 1988).

The thoughtful book by Kielhöfer and Jonekeit (1983) is full of valuable insights about young bilingual children and their upbringing. Furthermore, what many more scholarly publications on bilingual children lack but what Kielhöfer and Jonekeit's book abounds with is extensive background information about the authors' subjects. However, the observations that Kielhöfer and Jonekeit make about their two subjects' language production are mainly meant as a structure around which issues of interest to educators can be discussed. The authors' primary aim is not to investigate basic theoretical questions in the field of BFLA. As a result (and quite appropriately), an explanation of their methodology is lacking. In addition (and just as appropriately), their presentation of various characteristics of their subjects' language use is quite informal, and does not follow the format expected of purely academic publications. All this does mean however that, in spite of all its merits, Kielhöfer and Jonekeit's book does not contain sufficient information on the basis of which inferences could be made about the bilingual acquisition process.

The much appreciated and highly recommended books by Saunders (1982, 1988) offer very detailed information about the author's children's linguistic environments, and present a detailed, sensitive analysis of sociolinguistic aspects of the subjects' language use. There is some quantification present as well. Unfortunately, however, there is very little information on data collection procedures. The reader is given no information on the extent of the audio-recordings made, in what contexts they were made, how it was made sure that both languages would be represented on tape, and what the transcription method was. Again, the most probable reason for this is that it was Saunders' (1982, 1988) main aim, like Kielhöfer and Jonekeit's (1983), to present an informal picture of communication in a bilingual family and to offer advice about various aspects of immediate concern to educators confronted with a bilingual child, rather than to present and analyse data in order to address various theoretical issues about the bilingual acquisition process. Although the observations on Thomas, Frank and Katrina (Saunders' sons and daughter) are more central perhaps to Saunders' work than, *mutatis mutandis*, is the case for Kielhöfer and Jonekeit's, they are primarily to be seen as a - quite solid - background against which issues of general parental concern are discussed. This manner of presentation, whereas fully appropriate in the context of a book aimed at a more general public, does mean, however, that the data presented in Saunders (1982, 1988) cannot easily be used to probe the theoretical issues to be discussed later in this chapter.

Among the more 'scholarly' studies mentioned in Table 2.1 above there is a group of studies in which the data collection procedures were not explained or were inadequate, and in which the treatment of the data was very cursory and anecdotal. These studies typically did not use any quantification, and their data analysis sections mainly consisted of the listing of a few child utterances followed by often far-reaching claims about general developments. In the methodological information sections of Table 2.1, these studies have more 'NO INFO' and 'no' ratings than anything else. The studies concerned are Huerta (1977), Aldenhoff (1979), Berman (1979), Hoffman and Ariza (1979), Porsché (1983), Hoffmann (1985) and Clyne (1987). Since any findings and conclusions cannot be taken for granted if a study's methodology is largely unsatisfactory (or, indeed, unknown), these studies' findings cannot be taken at face value or properly evaluated. Thus, even though the studies listed above might and do in many cases contain quite valuable insights on various aspects of bilingual children's language use, as they stand they are not rigorous enough to act as solid sources of knowledge about how children acquire two language from birth. This unfortunately implies that they cannot be referred to in order to evaluate the theoretical issues in the field of BFLA to be discussed in the second part of this chapter.

Each of the remaining studies in Table 2.1 will be looked at separately in chronological order below.

The first study is the one by Ronjat (1913). Although a major pluspoint of Ronjat's study is that Ronjat wrote down his son Louis' utterances phonetically and was apparently able to note down quite subtle articulatory variations, the lack of information about data collection procedures is very unfortunate. How, for instance, did Ronjat make sure that he could obtain data for German? After all, he always addressed his son in French. A second question is on what basis Ronjat could decide what a particular child vocalization stood for or meant. Related to this is the issue on what basis it could be determined in the early stages of language production whether a particular vocalization was modelled on a French or German word. These drawbacks are balanced by Ronjat's quite thorough analysis of his son's language productions: they are not by any means anecdotal. On the contrary, Ronjat supplies the reader with a wealth of data which are carefully analysed and compared to the few data from monolingual children available at the time. Furthermore, Ronjat explains his son's linguistic environment in great detail and carefully notes any modifications in his son's language use as possibly dependent on changes in this linguistic environment. Notwithstanding these obviously commendable features, the lack of information about data collection and analysis procedures means that Ronjat's study cannot be seen as a methodologically strong one.

Leopold's (1970, c. 1939-49) monumental study of his daughter Hildegard is unique in that it presents the only existing detailed, thorough, and systematic account of a bilingual child's phonetic, phonological, lexical and syntactic development before the age of two. In analysing his data, Leopold is very careful, opting for minimal, rather than maximal, interpretations. Nevertheless, Leopold's diary study has the regrettable disadvantage that data collection was carried out by one person only (viz. Leopold himself, who always addressed Hildegard in German), and that any data obtained when Leopold's subject was interacting with her English-speaking mother were recorded in his presence, which might have had a considerable effect on the type of language produced by the child. There is no way of knowing whether the language that she produced in Leopold's absence was substantially different. This possibly confounding sociolinguistic variable, then, was not controlled for, although it might be an important variable to consider in any data interpretation. On the whole, though, Leopold's (1970, c. 1939-49) study is by far the best to date, certainly as far as developments before the age of two are concerned. One may regret the lack of any quantification beyond occasional vocabulary counts, but in Leopold's case any such lack is completely redeemed by the careful, sensitive, crystal-clear and insightful analyses and discussions.

The next study is the one by Swain (1972). Although in this study quite acceptable data collection techniques were used and the transcription method was indicated, there are two fundamental methodological problems. The first one has to do with the choice of subjects, and the second with the data collectors.

It was Swain's (1972) aim to carry out a cross-sectional study in which the data could be taken together and considered as reflecting a developmental picture for any one child's learning of English and French from birth. However, two of Swain's subjects (viz. Monica and Douglas) might not have been regularly exposed to both English and French from birth. On the other hand, the other two subjects most probably were, since their parents had always addressed them in a different language each. Even if one were to argue that Monica and Douglas were in fact regularly exposed to two languages from birth, there is still the problem that the exposure patterns differed quite extensively for all the four subjects involved. It is obvious that one cannot, in this case, simply assume that the combined data from these four children with widely different linguistic backgrounds give an accurate picture of any one child's learning of English and French from birth. In a cross-sectional study, the subjects must be fully matched for everything except age and/or level of language development. If not, one is again comparing apples and pears.

In Swain's (1972) study two data collectors were used, but these were interacting with the subjects at the same time. It was not the case that one data collector receded into the background while the other one fully engaged in interaction, or that data collectors each made separate recordings. Furthermore, the children were told that each data collector spoke only one language. Apart from the fact that this recording setting was not very natural, in that it probably was very different from any other social situation the children had found themselves in before, the recording setting was very restricted, and any data gathered might be highly dependent on the recording setting used. Even from a lay-man's point of view, it would seem only natural that, when a child is 'forced' to interact with two speakers of different languages at the same time, a lot of alternate language use, both within utterances and at utterance boundaries, would occur. In any later analyses and interpretations, this point would have to be taken into account. It is unfortunate that instead, far-reaching conclusions are drawn which could only have been made on the basis of a more diversified data-collection approach in which a variety of sociolinguistic settings were represented.

Swain and Wesche's (1975) study, however - although it comprises only five two-columned pages - contains all the features that make it a methodologically sound study: the data collection procedure is clearly indicated and adequate for the subject's age, sufficient data were gathered relative to the period observed, the transcription method was indicated and two transcribers were involved in the transcription (which obviously greatly enhances reliability), analytical categories were clearly defined, quantification was used and the results were clearly presented. As a result, the data presented form a solid basis for any later theoretical interpretation.

Then comes the frequently quoted article by Volterra and Taeschner (1978). This study can be partially seen as a preliminary to Taeschner's

(1983) monograph: both Volterra and Taeschner (1978) and Taeschner (1983) deal with basically the same research project, although Taeschner's study is much more extensive and detailed than the Volterra and Taeschner article. It is not clear, however, why Volterra and Taeschner (1978) state that recordings lasted 30 minutes each, and why Taeschner (1983) writes that they lasted 45 minutes each: presumably, both studies are reporting on essentially the same set of materials. Because Volterra and Taeschner (1978) say that recordings were made twice a month (one for each language), we can assume that in Taeschner (1983) the ambiguous term 'bimonthly' means 'twice a month'. Since Taeschner (1983) is in fact a sequel to Volterra and Taeschner (1978), we shall focus on the former only: all comments made in the following essentially apply to the Volterra and Taeschner (1978) article as well.

For evaluating Taeschner's (1983) study a distinction must be made between the data collection procedures used before and after the subjects' second birthday. Throughout the period of observation, data were gathered using mainly audio-recordings. Whereas this method is probably adequate for when subjects are older than two, it is not well-suited to the time before a child's second birthday. After all, very young children's language production tends to be strongly linked to the particular context in which it is uttered (see e.g. Nelson, Rescorla, Gruendel and Benedict 1978; Barrett 1983), and audio-recordings, even if they are supplemented by careful contextual notes, cannot furnish the level of detail required for later accurate interpretation of various aspects of recorded interactions. Particularly in the case of Taeschner (1983) it would seem that the method for data collection chosen at the early stages was perhaps not the best: the author is primarily concerned with the demonstration of the existence of a stage in which the young bilingual child's languages form a single system, a system which later "splits up" in two, so to speak (see the second part of this chapter). I maintain that the kind of data that Taeschner (1983) relies on to address the separation issue are inadequate: audio-tapes do not provide access to the kind of detailed situational and contextual information that would be needed to start to investigate this issue.

Another methodological problem has to do with the transcription. Taeschner writes that in the transcriptions, "particular attention was given to the context in which the statements [sic] were made. The speakers' actions and gestures were described, as were the objects to which they referred" (Taeschner 1983: 19). There are two questions here that spring to mind: first of all, if the material consisted of audio-tapes only, then how was it possible for the transcriber to transcribe "speakers' actions and gestures"? There is no word, unfortunately, on how transcribers were able to have access to the kind of detailed information that reportedly was included in the transcripts. A second comment springs from an inherent ambiguity in "as were the objects to which they referred" (see above). What does "they" refer to in this clause? It could refer to "The speakers' actions and gestures" or, indeed, to "The speakers". In the case that 'they' refers to the former, our previous comment applies. In the case that 'they' refers to 'the speakers', the question arises what the decision procedures were to decide what a particular child was referring to by using a vocalization before the age of 2. The question of reference in very young children's speech is a highly complex one that has eluded many scholars (see e.g. Gillis 1984). Hence at least some operational definitions would have been useful to explain what were seen as 'object-referring' vocalizations (that is, if the second meaning of 'they' applies).

For transcriptions of Taeschner's material for the age periods between 1;6 and 2;0 (for G1) and 0;9 and 2;0 (for G2) there is the additional problem that they were not phonetic. As mentioned in our introduction to Table 2.1 above, phonetic transcription can be considered a *conditio sine qua non* in the case of subjects younger than two years of age.

Keeping in mind the problems with the choice of data collection procedure and transcription methods for the period when G1 and G2 were younger than two it is clear, then, that any analysis based on Taeschner's corpus collected before the subjects were two years old must be approached with great care.

Then we have the study by Saunders (1980). This study, which is later expanded upon in Saunders (1982), can best be seen as a progress report. There is some quantification present, and the analysis of the subjects' language choice is interesting and informative. Unfortunately, just like Ronjat (1913), Saunders (1980) offers very little information on data collection procedures, although there is ample information about the subjects' linguistic environments.

On the whole, the data collection procedures used in the studies by Berkele (1983), Jekat (1985) and Meisel (1985, 1986, i.p.) are clearly explained and generally quite adequate. In these five studies data were collected using mainly video-recordings (even for subjects older than two) and by employing two data collectors it was made sure that data could be gathered for both languages. It is regrettable, though, that video-recordings were made only twice a month, even when the subjects were considerable younger than age two. This means that possibly important developments might not have been 'caught'. Furthermore, the apparent lack of phonetic transcriptions for recordings involving subjects under the age of two is very unfortunate, and there is little or no information on transcription methods used.

This brings us to the end of our methodological review of studies in BFLA. The results may seem disappointing: after all, we have been able to find but a very small number of studies of young children growing up with two or more languages from birth that can be seen as forming a sufficiently solid basis for hypotheses-testing purposes.

While it is unfortunate that so few studies of BFLA can be seen as offering methodologically sound, substantial contributions to the field, it is perhaps not surprising that this is the case. In monolingual first language acquisition research, which as a discipline is more evolved than BFLA research, scientists have had to search for appropriate methodologies for quite some time, and have developed generally acceptable, but time and effort consuming data collection and analysis procedures. On the whole, the present section has taken the methodologies developed in monolingual first language acquisition research as a guideline, but unfortunately, the complexity of the phenomena to be observed in the field of BFLA means that these methodologies have to be expanded, so that the work and effort involved in conducting methodologically sound studies on young bilingual children becomes, so to speak, double that of studies on monolingual children. If one adds to this the obvious requirement that either one investigator must have a thorough knowledge of both of her subjects' languages, not only as a language user, but also as a linguist, or that two investigators whose knowledge of the languages involved is complementary must be engaged, then it is quite understandable that few researchers have so far attempted to carry out studies on bilingual children, and that those studies that have been carried out have not always been quite successful on the methodological level.

Since the number of scientifically acceptable empirical studies on BFLA is so small, the field of BFLA research as a whole is still very much in its infancy. This begs the question whether certain claims about how young children acquire two languages from birth are actually supported by the data available. The second part to this chapter will examine this question in detail against the background of some major theoretical issues concerning young bilingual children's language development and the 'better' studies in the field of BFLA as reviewed above.

2.2 Theoretical issues in the field of BFLA
2.2.1 *Introduction*

Grosjean (1982) writes that the following are found "repeatedly" in bilingual children:

> the initial mixed language stage; the slow separation of the two language systems and increasing awareness of bilingualism; the influence of one language on the other when the linguistic environment favors one language; the avoidance of difficult words and constructions in the weaker language; [...] the final separation of the sound and grammatical systems but the enduring influence of the dominant language on the other in the domain of vocabulary and idioms (Grosjean 1982: 181).

Saunders (1982) adopts a similar view: he states that "generally, [...] [bilingual children] will pass through a three-stage developmental sequence" (Saunders 1982: 43), in which the first stage is characterized by the fact that "children really possess only one lexical system containing words from both languages" (ibid.). In a second stage, the bilingual child has acquired "an active vocabulary comprising words which designate the same item, action or function in both languages and [...] will increasingly use the appropriate language when addressing different people" (Saunders 1982: 44). In the third (and final) stage, "the child [...] speaks the two languages differentiated in both vocabulary and syntax" (Saunders 1982: 48). Arnberg (1987) writes that "initially, the bilingual child does not appear to differentiate between the vocabularies of the two languages but has one system composed of words from each language" (Arnberg 1987: 69), and that as the child grows older, "the two vocabularies and grammatical systems become increasingly differentiated" (Arnberg 1987: 70).

In all these views, the bilingual child who has come into contact with two languages from an early age is seen as starting out with an undifferentiated, hybrid system which incorporates elements from both of the languages the child is exposed to. Language separation or differentiation becomes a point of primary concern: the child must, eventually, come to produce two separate language systems, and this process is seen as taking a lot of time, depending on the individual child.

An entirely different view is taken by Bergman (1976), who has proposed the Independent Development Hypothesis (IDH), which in its strongest form runs as follows:

> In cases of simultaneous language acquisition, each language will develop independently of the other, reflecting the acquisition of that language by monolingual children, unless it is the case that the lines between the two languages are not clearly drawn in the linguistic environment of the child. In such a case, which may be caused by code-switching patterns in the bilingual community or by deviations [sic] in the adult language of the child's environment from the norm in the monolingual community, the child will sort out the two systems according to the input that he receives (Bergman 1976: 94).

Padilla and Lindholm (1984) also believe that from a very early age onwards, bilingual children are able to differentiate their two linguistic systems. They further write that the view that a bilingual child will grow up to speak "a hybrid mixture of the two languages [...] must be rejected" (Padilla and Lindholm 1984: 34). Similarly, Padilla and Liebman (1975) strongly oppose the view that in the earliest stages of acquisition bilingual children do not differentiate their languages into two linguistic systems.

Then there is the issue of the degree to which a young bilingual child's language development resembles that of monolingual children. Taeschner believes that "the development of speech is very similar in bilingual children and in monolingual children" (Taeschner 1983: 227). Grosjean writes: "whether a child acquires only one language and becomes monolingual or acquires two languages and becomes bilingual, the rate and pattern of language development are the same" (Grosjean 1982: 181). Lindholm states that "bilingual children acquire their linguistic structures in a fashion similar to monolinguals [...] at about the same time" (Lindholm 1980: 257). Padilla and Lindholm (1984) claim that simultaneous bilinguals show no differences with monolingual children. Swain suggests that the child, "whether in a bilingual or a monolingual environment, employs what is basically one and the same set of strategies in learning the linguistic skills of his particular linguistic milieu" (Swain 1972: 19). Vihman and McLaughlin (1982), however, prefer to stress the point that children exposed to more than one language (either simultaneously or not) go through a different experience than the monolingual child.

Another issue has been the importance of the type of exposure to the two languages that the child receives. Authors have argued that in order for children to most easily grow up speaking two distinct languages, children should be exposed to their languages in a separate fashion, i.e., basically, each person should address the child in mainly one language only (see e.g. Arnberg 1987, Kielhöfer and Jonekeit 1983, Ronjat 1913). (Authors do generally warn, however, that whichever exposure type is used, it should be as 'natural' as possible.) On the other hand, it has been suggested that in a child's bilingual development it does not substantially matter whether the child hears both languages in a 'separated' fashion or not (Huerta 1977).

Although the above issues are not the only ones involved, they are the ones most frequently mentioned in connection with young bilingual children in general. We shall take these issues as a starting point for critical discussion and examine what the empirical basis is for the various claims made.

First we shall address the language separation issue: is there indeed such a process as language separation, or is Bergman's (1976) IDH a more adequate characterization of how a bilingual child acquires his/her languages? These questions will be explored in sections 2.2.2.and 2.2.3. Secondly, what is the evidence to date that bilingual children's language development resembles that of monolingual children's for each of the languages involved? Section 2.2.4 will try to answer this question. In section 2.2.5, we briefly look at the type of exposure issue.

Section 2.2.6 departs from the issues mentioned above and considers the assumptions underlying some theoretical psycholinguistic explanations of bilingual children's language development. In section 2.2.7, a short 'state-of-the-art' summary will be presented centring around the question: what is the extent of our current knowledge in the field of BFLA?

2.2.2 *Language separation: a useful concept?*

The term separation obviously only makes sense if previous to any separation there was a state of unity or togetherness. Similarly, the concept of language separation in young bilingual children implies that prior to any such separation there is something to be separated or differentiated, namely a so-called 'mixed' or 'hybrid' stage in which two languages are interwoven with each other.

The first researcher in the West to mention such a 'mixed' or 'hybrid' stage was Werner Leopold. The two sets of data that Leopold takes as a basis for stating that at the age of two "there was no attempt yet to split the one medium of communication into two parallel ones" (Leopold 1970, c.1939-49, Vol. III: 186) consist of the child's sound system and the occurrence of early two- and three-word utterances containing lexical items from both languages.

As far as the phonological level goes Leopold claims that at the end of the second year, his subject Hildegard "was still trying to weld two linguistic systems into one unit" (Leopold 1970, c.1939-49, Vol. II: 206). The evidence for this statement is quite puzzling. Preceding it we find the following text:

> The sounds of English and German are too similar to produce differentiations in the child's early rough imitation. Those in which they differ [...] belong to the latest sounds learned by monolingual children, and had not yet entered into Hildegard's store of sounds. (Leopold 1970, c. 1939-49, Vol. II: 206)

In fact, then, Leopold is basing his 'one unit' interpretation on empirical data that reflect adult input systems which have a great deal in common, and, as he himself admits, whose differences are too complex or too subtle to be incorporated in any child's speech sound production before the age of two (see also Leopold 1978, c. 1954: 25). It is clear, though, that evidence for a 'one unit' or 'single system' interpretation can only be based on an examination of children's acquisition of areas reflecting structural differences between the two languages they are exposed to (cf. Meisel i.p.; see also later in this section). In the present case, it is logically impossible to determine whether Hildegard operated with two separate phonological systems before the age of two or not, and Leopold's claim about her using 'one linguistic system' as far as phonology goes must be rejected as not founded on sufficient empirical evidence. Furthermore, Leopold does not claim that Hildegard used a single syntactic system before the age of two, even though the situation for syntax is highly similar to that of the sound system: as Leopold himself states (Leopold 1970, c. 1939-49, Vol. III: 186), any structures that one would expect the very young child to be able to manipulate would be highly similar across languages (at least, for the pair English-German), and thus there is no real possibility for investigating whether the child operares with two distinct

There is a certain inconsistency, then, when on the basis of an equivalent situation for phonology, Leopold posits 'one linguistic system', but refrains from doing so for the area of syntax.

In the last paragraph we challenged Leopold's claim with reference to the child's sound system. Remains for discussion, then, Leopold's reference to 'mixed utterances' as evidence for the existence of one 'hybrid system'.

Leopold found that before the age of two, Hildegard freely mixed English and German vocabulary within two- or three-word utterances (Leopold 1970, c. 1939-49). This Leopold interpreted as a sign that she did not yet use "two separate systems of speech" (Leopold 1970, c. 1939-49, Vol. I: 179), but that instead she used "one medium of communication" (Leopold 1970, c. 1939-49, Vol. III: 186).

First there is an empirical question: did Hildegard ever use two- or three-word utterances containing only lexical items from one language? The answer to this question is positive: throughout his third volume, Leopold (1970, c.1939-49) gives many examples of fully English two- and three-word utterances. It is not clear why Leopold chose to focus on his daughter's 'mixed' rather than her 'non-mixed' two- and three-word utterances. After all, when the occurrence of 'mixed utterances' is seen as evidence for a 'one unit' system, by the same token the simultaneous appearance of 'non-mixed' utterances can be seen as evidence against such an interpretation.

There is also the distinct possibility that Leopold's data collection procedure had an effect on Hildegard's language choice (this point was first raised by Bergman 1977: 54-56). As we mentioned in section 2.1, Leopold was the only data collector. He was a fluent bilingual, and spoke both English and German in the home. He usually addressed Hildegard in German, except when monolingual English-speaking visitors were present. Whenever data were gathered, Leopold was always present, with or without Hildegard's mother being there as well. Although the latter spoke very little German, apparently she was proficient enough to spend three months in Germany with Hildegard (and without Leopold). Hildegard must have heard her mother speak German in that time. Data collection, then, always took place with at least one bilingual speaker present (i.e., Leopold). The third person present was not strictly speaking a monolingual English speaker either. Since there were no data collected when Hildegard was only in the company of monolingual speakers of either language, we do not know what her speech production was like in these sociolinguistic situations. It is possible that Hildegard did not use many 'mixed utterances' when she was addressing monolingual speakers. Even though empirically the issue here can obviously not be solved, the very possibility that the lack of sociolinguistic variation in the data collection situation had an effect on the child's speech production casts doubt on Leopold's 'one unit' interpretation as being the only one.

More fundamentally, even if most of the bilingual child's early two- and three-word utterances contain lexical items from both languages and even if the child produces these 'mixed utterances' in a variety of sociolinguistic situations, there is little reason to speak of a 'hybrid system' or 'one medium of communication'. What this hypothetical child is doing is drawing on all her vocabulary knowledge and not addressing one person entirely in one language (cf. "at this time Hildegard did not associate the languages with definite persons" - Leopold 1970, c.1939-49, Vol. III: 175). In other words, the child has yet to acquire a particular type of sociolinguistic knowledge. Whether on the psycholinguistic level (i.e., on the process level) the child in using 'mixed utterances' operates with two different sets of knowledge or only one is an unresolved question (and perhaps even an unresolvable one - see below).

Leopold does not specifically speak of language separation or differentiation, but it is clear that in any discussion of this concept his claims about a 'hybrid stage' must be approached with caution.

The notion of language separation or language differentiation in bilingual children was actually first developed by Volterra and Taeschner (1978), who proposed a three-stage model of bilingual children's early language development (it should be noted that this model is considered to apply to children who become bilingual "from early infancy" (Volterra and Taeschner 1978: 312), and not necessarily only to children who have come into regular contact with two languages from birth). In Stage I, "the child has one lexical system which includes words from both languages. A word in one language almost always does not have a corresponding word with the same meaning in the other language" (Volterra and Taeschner 1978: 312); in Stage II, "the child distinguishes two different lexicons, but applies the same syntactic rules to both languages. For almost any word in one language, the child has a corresponding word in the other language. Moreover, words drawn from the two lexicons no longer occur together in constructions" (Volterra and Taeschner 1978: 312); finally, in Stage III, "the child speaks two languages differentiated both in lexicon and syntax, but each language is associated with the person using that language: 'une personne - une langue' (Ronjat 1913)" (Volterra and Taeschner 1978: 312). In Taeschner (1983) this three-stage model is further developed and it is emphasized that the bilingual child "learns first to differentiate between the two vocabularies and only later to distinguish between one syntax and the other" (Taeschner 1983: 16).

In discussing the three-stage model here, we shall be referring to the Volterra and Taeschner (1978) article and Taeschner's (1983) book as if they were one study, since the data reported on in Volterra and Taeschner (1978) and the ideas presented in this article are recapitulated and expanded upon without substantial changes in Taeschner (1983). V&T in the following, then, refers to both Volterra and Taeschner (1978) and Taeschner (1983).

First we turn to the proposed Stage I. The evidence that V&T use to support the notion of their Stage I comes from the early speech production of Taeschner's two daughters Lisa and Giulia and of Leopold's daughter Hildegard (Hildegard's development is only taken as a data base in Volterra and Taeschner 1978) - in the present critique we shall only refer to V&T's discussion of the data for Lisa and Giulia (a critique of Volterra and Taeschner's 1978 analysis of Leopold's data can be found in De Houwer 1987).

Stage I "lasts for an average of 6 months" (Taeschner 1983: 29), which period starts when the child "begins speaking" (ibid.). For Lisa, Stage I reportedly lasted from 1;7 to ca. 2;2, whereas for Giulia, it lasted from 1;2 to 1;10. Stage I, then, is situated mainly in the second year of life. In Stage I, according to V&T, terms are used in one language that have "no equivalent meaning corresponding to the terms in the other" (Taeschner 1983: 24). As evidence, V&T list German and Italian words used by Lisa and Giulia, and 'neutral' words, "which are the same in sound and meaning in both languages" (Taeschner 1983: 25). The few 'equivalents' (V&T never clearly define this term, although Taeschner 1983: 23 uses the term 'equivalent' to mean 'interlingual synonym' - this being yet another term that needs a stringent operational definition) that Lisa and Giulia use at this stage are, V&T say, not considered as equivalent by the children, i.e., they are used in different contexts. Thus, V&T conclude that "all the words of the child's speech appear to form one lexical system" and that the bilingual child at this stage "speaks only one language which is a language system of his own" (Volterra and Taeschner 1978: 317).

There are several problems with V&T's approach. As pointed out above, the crucial term 'equivalent' is not satisfactorily explained, leaving independent researchers wishing to investigate V&T's hypothesized Stage I 'in the cold', so to speak (cf. also Jekat 1985). A second problem also having to do with a lack of clarity concerns the question of how many 'equivalent pairs' are actually allowable in Stage I: Volterra and Taeschner (1978) state that in Stage I, "A word in one language <u>almost always</u> does not have a corresponding word with the same meaning in the other language" (Volterra and Taeschner 1978: 312; emphasis mine). Unfortunately, it is not explained how "almost always" should be interpreted in quantitative terms. Taeschner (1983), on the other hand, speaks of "terms used in one language having <u>no</u> equivalent meaning corresponding to the terms in the other" (Taeschner 1983: 24; emphasis mine). Apparently, then, there are two different criteria about the allowability of 'equivalent pairs' in Stage I. Yet the lists of 'words' used by Lisa and Giulia in the first stage in both Volterra and Taeschner (1978) and Taeschner (1983) are virtually identical (for Lisa they are completely identical; for Giulia 'si' is listed in Taeschner 1983 but not in Volterra and Taeschner 1978, and 'ò!ò!' and 'tò!tò!' are listed in Volterra and Taeschner 1978 but not in Taeschner 1983).

In addition, not only did V&T not use phonetic transcriptions, which makes it unclear what the precise bases were on which they decided which language a particular vocalization belonged to, they also did not use video-recordings or other methods that can furnish extensive contextual information (cf. the methodological review in section 2.1). Thus, their material does not allow for any careful analysis of meaning or reference that could even start to address the issue of whether bilingual children use 'equivalents'.

A much more basic problem is that the definition of V&T's Stage I depends on a form's <u>absence</u>. However, a form's absence is difficult if not impossible to prove in acquisition studies: unless one has a complete list of all of a child's vocalizations, one can never be sure that she did not produce a particular form. To take a form's absence as the only criterion for a theoretical construct, then, is treading on dangerous ground, and for this reason alone V&T's Stage I is empirically virtually unprovable.

It would be possible, however, to empirically dis̲prove the hypothesized Stage I: acceptable counterevidence would consist of the quasi-simultaneous appearance in a bilingual child's second year of life of a number of 'equivalent'-pairs (or even of just one of these if Taeschner's 1983 characterization is followed - see above). Thus, if a child used form A with interlocutor X in situation H1 and used form B with interlocutor Y in situation H2, with form A unequivocally belonging to language A and form B to language B, and situation H1 being the same as situation H2, except for the time at which each takes place, then the child could be credited with an 'equivalent' pair.

So far, I am not aware of any counterevidence that would disprove V&T's hypothesized Stage I. Jekat (1985) has attempted to interpret her data from a German-French bilingual girl, Caroline (see Table 2.1), according to V&T's Stage I (Jekat 1985 only refers to Taeschner's 1983 monograph). Even though Jekat had the use of protocols of video-recordings (but not, apparently, of phonetic transcriptions), she found it very difficult to decide whether the members of a possible 'equivalent' pair as produced by Caroline were actually used with the same meaning or not. Perhaps a more detailed analysis than the one Jekat used would have offered a better basis on which to decide the issue. It is telling, however, that with a better data base than V&T's, and with a much more in-depth analysis than V&T's, an independent researcher has been unable to find sufficient grounds for either accepting or rejecting the possibility that the bilingual child she was studying did not have any 'equivalents' available for production.

We can now turn to V&T's Stage II proposal. Obviously, the existence of their proposed Stage II strongly depends on the existence of a Stage I, at least as far as the 'lexical' part of Stage II is concerned. We repeat that for Stage II it is hypothesized that "For almost any word in one language, the child has a corresponding word in the other language" (Volterra and Taeschner 1978: 312). A first problem here is the vagueness of the phrase 'almost any word': how many words are allowable for which the child does not have a corresponding word in the other language? Secondly, what does it mean to say that a child 'has' a word in a language? Does 'has' refer to productive, adult-like use, or is passive knowledge relevant? Thirdly, what is 'a corresponding word in the other language'? Is it a translation equivalent from the adult point of view?

On the whole, it is unclear what the independent criteria would be for deciding whether a child is in 'Stage I' or 'Stage II'. After all, in both stages the child is seen as producing words from both languages, some of which may at more or less the same time in development appear to be used as 'equivalents': even in Stage II, an 'equivalent' may not appear until 3 months after one word has been acquired in one language only: "in creating a bilingual lexical system, the child tends not to produce two words for one object or event at the same time. First he acquires one word in one of the two languages, and only when he has mastered it well and used it for a while does he begin to use its equivalent" (Taeschner 1983: 33). If one just had available the Volterra and Taeschner (1978) article, one might conclude that the empirical difference between 'Stage I' and 'Stage II' is primarily a matter of degree, with 'Stage I' containing hardly any 'equivalent' pairs, and 'Stage II' containing a very high proportion of them. However, Taeschner (1983) lends no support to such a conclusion. She writes: "Even when the child is well into the second stage and uses a considerable number of equivalents, he continues to acquire more new words than equivalents" (Taeschner 1983: 30). Thus there seem to be no clear empirical grounds on the basis of which one could decide whether a child is in 'Stage I' or 'Stage II'. And since any information about analytical procedures used is lacking, the distinction between 'Stage I' and 'Stage II' (at least as far as lexical development is concerned) is impossible to make.

This brings us to the second part of Volterra and Taeschner's proposed Stage II, which addresses syntactic rather than lexical development. It should be emphasized here that whereas Volterra and Taeschner (1978) propose one model which combines lexical and syntactic development (the three-stage model), Taeschner (1983) does not do so explicitly, but speaks of two stages in lexical development (which are the same as Volterra and Taeschner's Stage I and Stage II), and of two 'periods' in morphosyntactic development, which appear to be fairly equivalent to Volterra and Taeschner's two proposed stages for syntactic development, except that Taeschner (1983) addresses morphosyntax while Volterra and Taeschner (1978) addressed syntactic elements only (more precisely, they looked only at the expression of possession, and the relative placement of adjectives and nouns on the one hand and negatives and verbs on the other).

In Taeschner's proposed first period, "the [morphosyntactic] rule systems are not yet bound to their respective languages, and some of the rules are superextended to both" (Taeschner 1983: 167) - the term 'superextended' here appears to have the meaning of the more current term 'overgeneralized'; in the second, "the child very gradually realizes that the rules involved in linguistic processing must be separated" (ibid.). Taeschner proposes these periods in a summary of her fourth chapter on the acquisition of morphology and syntax. As Mills (1986b) has pointed out, many of the analyses and discussions in this chapter are all too brief, vague, and sometimes inaccurate. It can be added that the definition of the proposed second period is based on an empirically untestable concept, i.e. the child's 'realization' of a particular notion. Without further objective criteria it remains unclear what Taeschner (1983) used as a basis for deciding whether her subjects had entered the hypothesized second period.

In the literature so far, however, it is the original Volterra and Taeschner (1978) model that is most frequently referred to. Meisel (i.p.) has written a well-taken critique of the syntactic aspect of Volterra and Taeschner's (1978) alleged Stage II. Since we share most of Meisel's views here, we shall suffice by summarizing his main points of criticism.

A first point of criticism raised by Meisel (i.p.) is the vagueness of Volterra and Taeschner's definition of the syntactic part of their hypothesized Stage II. All the reader gets as information is that in Stage II, the child "applies the same syntactic rules to both languages" (Volterra and Taeschner 1978: 312), i.e. the child is seen as using 'syntactic mixing' (note that the latter is Meisel's own 'translation' of 'applying the same syntactic rules to two languages' - Volterra and Taeschner do not use the term 'syntactic mixing'). No independent criteria are given on the basis of which the definition of Stage II was arrived at. Meisel (i.p.) further notes that although Volterra and Taeschner define the second part of their Stage II proposal in terms of the occurrence of syntactic mixing, such mixing itself, according to the same authors, is not limited to Stage II, but may already occur in Stage I and continue to exist in Stage III (although Meisel i.p. does not point this out, in Stage III the alleged application of the same syntactic rules to both languages is suddenly called 'interference', without there being any clear reason given for this - see Volterra and Taeschner 1978: 325). One then wonders, Meisel writes, how the alleged occurrence of syntactic mixing can be seen as a sufficient definition for Stage II. Furthermore, in attempting to provide evidence for their Stage II, Volterra and Taeschner give examples of their subjects' utterances produced when apparently Stage III had already set in. Meisel concludes: "I do not believe that the empirical evidence and/or the theoretical justification given is sufficient to support the hypothesized phase II of the three-stage model" (Meisel i.p.: page 5 in manuscript).

Meisel (i.p.) then goes one to consider "what kinds of empirical evidence could be accepted as instances of syntactic mixing or of differentiation between syntactic systems" (Meisel i.p.: page 6 in manuscript). He proposes that one can only examine those aspects of grammar "where the two adult target systems differ" (ibid.). Even when one does this, however, Meisel writes, the interpretation of the data might not be straightforward: one may find that young bilingual children produce forms which appear to reflect structural regularities existing in only one of the target languages. In this case there are two possibilities for interpretation: first, if the bilingual children's forms are identical to those produced by monolingual children for either language at a similar point in development one might be dealing with quite universal acquisition processes, and it will be logically impossible to decide whether the bilingual children are processing both languages as one system or whether they are using two underlying systems which just happen to overlap for a particular structural domain at a given point in linguistic development (Meisel i.p.: page 7 in manuscript). Secondly, any "commonalities in the use of the two languages may be the result of transfer from the dominant language" (ibid.), this theoretical possibility being, of course, the clearest counterargument to the positing of a 'single grammar', since in the transfer argument, two systems are seen as interfering with each other (Meisel i.p.).

In sum, it is very difficult, if not impossible, to find positive evidence for the one syntactic system-hypothesis.

Finally we have come to Stage III of Volterra and Taeschner's (1978) model, which partially corresponds to the second period of morphosyntactic development as proposed by Taeschner (1983).

We already pointed out some difficulties with Taeschner's (1983) proposed second period of morphosyntactic development (see above). As far as Volterra and Taeschner's (1978) hypothesized Stage III goes, there is contradictory information: on the one hand "the child speaks two languages differentiated both in lexicon and syntax" (Volterra and Taeschner 1978: 312) , but at the same time "there still are, in the same period, many examples of interference" (ibid.: 325). Unfortunately, the latter term is not explained, and it is not indicated what the acceptable percentage of "examples of interference" would be at Stage III. For the same reason that it was unclear whether the child was still in Stage II (see above), it is impossible from the information given to decide what exactly would constitute sufficient empirical evidence to show that the child is in Stage III.

We can conclude, then, that the three-stage model of bilingual children's early language development as it was first developed by Volterra and Taeschner (1978) and later confirmed with slight modifications by Taeschner (1983) is at the moment not founded on positive evidence. Furthermore, because of certain theoretical assumptions and lack of precision and clarity, doubts exist as to whether the model in its present form could ever be used as an adequate explanation of bilingual children's early language development. This means that it is premature for reviewers of the literature on young bilingual children to present the stages as proposed by Volterra and Taeschner as established, unshakable fact.

Finally, another author who strongly supports the initial 'mixed language' stage hypothesis is Vihman (1985). However, since Vihman founds her hypothesis on the basis of data from a child regularly exposed to a second language only 7 months after birth, the hypothesis falls outside the scope of the field of BFLA.

In summary, then, it appears clear that there is at present no conclusive empirical evidence supporting the hypothesized existence of an initial 'mixed' or 'hybrid' stage in early bilingual development. Furthermore, it is not clear what exactly authors mean when they speak of a non-differentiated system: is this term meant to be descriptive only, or does it refer to a certain type of language processing? When Leopold (1970, c. 1939-49) considers the use of lexical items from both languages within one utterance as evidence for a non-differentiated system, for instance, he does not further define the latter term: is he making a descriptive summarizing statement, or does he intend to say that psycholinguistically, the child operates with a single rule system with lexical items from both languages?

In Volterra and Taeschner's (1978) case a child's never using a lexical item from language A in situations where the child already uses a lexical item from language B is seen as evidence for a non-differentiated lexical system. It would appear here, then, that the notion of a 'mixed' system refers to a sociolinguistic feature, viz. the child's choice of a particular language. That Volterra and Taeschner's (1978) article leaves open the possibility that indeed the authors' conception of a 'mixed' system has to do with the sociolinguistic inappropriateness (from the adult's point of view) of a particular lexical item is clear from Saunders (1982), who in his summary of Volterra and Taeschner's (1978) work wrote that in the supposed second stage of early bilingual development, the bilingual child "will increasingly use the appropriate language when addressing different people" (Saunders 1982: 44), although Volterra and Taeschner (1978) themselves do not mention this (they situate the beginnings of addressee-differentiation in their Stage III). It remains unclear exactly how Volterra and Taeschner would precisely define the concept of a 'mixed' stage, and thus of language separation., although their use of phrases such as "the child <u>has</u> one lexical <u>system</u>" and "the child <u>distinguishes</u> two different lexicons" (Volterra and Taeschner 1978: 312; emphasis mine) gives rise to the interpretation that these concepts are meant to be psycholinguistic terms.

In our critical discussions in this section, we have in fact usually interpreted the terms 'hybrid' or 'mixed' system and 'language separation' as psycholinguistically relevant ones. If these terms are indeed meant to have psycholinguistic significance, it is not clear to this author how they would have to be defined and what would constitute clear empirical evidence for them. On the other hand, if 'language separation' is meant to indicate the process by which a bilingual child learns to address interlocutors in a sociolinguistically appropriate fashion (implying that before such a separation children typically do not use the 'right' language with the people they talk to), matters would appear to be much more straightforward. In order to show that indeed there is a 'mixed' stage in which a bilingual child's language choice does not discriminate between interlocutors, a careful analysis of such a child's utterances in a variety of sociolinguistic contexts at various times in development would in principle be sufficient to settle the issue. That such a process of addressee-differentiation or 'sociolinguistic language separation' (admittedly an awkward term) probably does take place in most cases is confirmed by almost all reports on very young bilingual children.

The concept of 'language separation', then, is probably a useful one if it refers to a sociolinguistic rather than a psycholinguistic process.

2.2.3 *The Independent Development Hypothesis*
Some researchers have claimed that as long as children have been regularly exposed to two languages from birth and have received a fairly balanced

input in both languages, whether in a separate or non-separate fashion, they will develop two differentiated language systems from very early on in the acquisition process. The most vocal proponents of this view have been Lindholm and Padilla (see e.g. Lindholm and Padilla 1978a, 1978b and Lindholm 1980). Since none of the studies quoted here - insofar as they are not reviews - can be unambiguously accepted as studies of children regularly exposed to two languages from birth, the data provided in these studies cannot be considered as a sufficient basis for investigating the proposed hypothesis.

As mentioned in section 2.2.1, Bergman (1976, 1977) is also a strong proponent of the view that bilingual children develop their languages independently from one another from early on. However, she emphasizes that such independent development can only be predicted in cases where the child is exposed to both languages in a separate fashion (cf. the Independent Development Hypothesis (IDH) as quoted in section 2.2.1 above). Bergman (1976, 1977) primarily bases her IDH on the data from her daughter Mary, who was regularly exposed to a second language (Spanish) from the age of 7 months onwards. Hence, according to our definition (see Chapter 1), Mary's is not a case of bilingual first language acquisition. Whether the IDH can really account for the language development of a child exposed to two languages from birth, then, cannot be ascertained from the data that Bergman presents.

Much earlier than Padilla, Lindholm and Bergman, Ronjat (1913) had already concluded that his bilingual son, Louis, acquired his two languages in a largely separate fashion: Ronjat (1913) strongly insists that from the very beginning his son used both languages as separate tools of expression. He writes:

> dès les débuts la prononciation de Louis est dans des deux langues celle d'un enfant indigène; on ne peut relever aucun fait authentique et durable [...] d'influence d'une langue sur l'autre (Ronjat 1913: 103);

and in addition,

> le développement de la syntaxe se fait parallèlement dans les deux langues [...], et il en est de même pour la morphologie [...]. Dès le début commencent à se constituer deux vocabulaires à usage distinct (Ronjat 1913: 105).

Ronjat (1913) does mention, though, that Louis produced utterances containing lexical items from both languages, or, more accurately, that words from one language were inserted into sentences in the other language. Although Ronjat does not explain how frequent such 'mixed utterances' (see Chapters 4 and 5) were, there are many examples throughout his monograph of utterances containing lexical items from one language only, and Ronjat also reports that at the same time that Louis inserted French words into German sentences, he produced entirely French monologues.

Unlike the studies by Padilla, Lindholm and Bergman, Ronjat's is clearly one of a child exposed to two languages from birth. Furthermore, this child's development was followed from very early onwards, i.e. from when the child's first 'words' appeared. Ronjat's (1913) study, then, seems to offer the minimal basis for finding evidence that from very early on, the bilingual child develops two separate linguistic systems. Unfortunately however, as pointed out in section 2.1, Ronjat's study is not free from some major methodological drawbacks, which, ultimately, means that his interpretations and conclusions cannot be taken at face value. At best, his study indicates that there is possibly a basis for the suggestion that bilingual children do indeed develop their two languages separately from a very early age on. Positive proof for this, however, Ronjat's study does not supply.

It appears, then, that there is as little positive evidence for the position that bilingual children develop two separate linguistic systems from the earliest stages of acquisition on as there is for the claim that bilingual children start out with a single linguistic system which is later differentiated or separated into two linguistic systems. Furthermore, as was the case for authors arguing for the existence of an initial 'mixed' stage, proponents of the IDH do not indicate what exactly is meant by claims that a bilingual child's languages develop independently from one another from the start. Most importantly, one would like to know what kind of evidence would be acceptable for an IDH interpretation in the early stages of bilingual language development. Is it sufficient, perhaps, that a young bilingual child's vocalizations include some that can be traced to one input language and others that can be traced to the other input language, regardless of interlocutor or context, either linguistic or extra-linguistic? Or are there other criteria? Until questions such as these are answered, the IDH, just like the 'mixed' stage hypothesis, must remain a vague and basically meaningless construct that contributes little to our actual understanding of the bilingual acquisition process.

2.2.4 *Bilingual and monolingual children compared*

What is the empirical evidence to date for the claim made by Swain (1972), Lindholm (1980), Grosjean (1982) and others (cf. section 2.2.1) that bilingual children's language development resembles that of monolingual children for each of the languages involved?

In the most general of terms, bilingual children seem to follow the patterns of language development observed in monolingual children: there are no reports of bilingual children whose first productive vocalizations consist of fully adult-like complex sentences, for instance. Neither have major delays been reported concerning the ages at which bilingual children start using two-word utterances (to list but one possibility) as compared to monolingual children. Rather, it appears that like monolingual children, bilingual children go through an initial babbling stage, followed by the one-word stage, the two-word stage, and the multi-word stage (we leave out of consideration here the stage between the babbling and the one-word stages during which monolingual children are reported to produce 'phonetically consistent forms' - cf. for instance Dore, Franklin, Miller and Ramer 1976. In the literature on bilingual children, there is no mention of such a stage. This is not necessarily because such a stage does not exist, but perhaps because researchers have simply failed to notice it).

More detailed comparisons of bilingual and monolingual children's language development are few and far between. When we restrict ourselves to the few methodologically more acceptable studies of BFLA that were reviewed in section 2.1, there are only five (!) that specifically compare their data to reports on monolingual acquisition. These are the studies by Meisel (1986, i.p.), Ronjat (1913), Swain (1972) and Taeschner (1983). We shall briefly look at each of these. (In Leopold's work I have been able to find only one passing remark on monolingual acquisition, namely when Leopold writes that Hildegard's 'mistakes' in English at age 4 "are characteristic of monolingual children as well", Leopold 1970, c. 1939-49, Vol. IV: 59.)

In Meisel (1986, i.p.), MLU values are given for French and German, even though the author in each case emphasizes that he is aware of the shortcomings of the MLU measure. Nevertheless, he says, MLU values can furnish at least some basis for comparison with other children. Meisel

(1986, i.p.) explains that in the calculation of MLU values Brown's (1973) and Bloom and Lahey's (1978) recommendations were followed. It can thus be assumed that Meisel adopted Brown's more or less child-centred approach rather than an 'adultomorphic' one. However, if this assumption is correct, it would have been useful had Meisel explained how he solved certain ambiguities that must have arisen. Unfortunately, Meisel (1986, i.p.) only states that plurifunctional morphemes were counted as consisting of just one morpheme.

On the basis of the available evidence for French and German monolingual acquisition Meisel (1986, i.p.) found that the use of word order by his bilingual subjects was "markedly less variable than in the speech of monolingual French and German children" (Meisel i.p.: p. 12 in manuscript - a similar conclusion is reached in Meisel 1986). Case-markings appeared earlier in the German speech production of Meisel's (1986) bilingual subjects than in German monolingual children. No comparisons between the French speech production of his bilingual subjects with that of French monolingual children could be made due to the lack of comparison material. As regards the acquisition of Subject--finite verb agreement, Meisel states that bilingual children "acquire each of the two languages very much like monolingual children" (Meisel i.p.: p. 16 in manuscript). Unfortunately, the validity of the latter statement can be doubted, since, as Meisel himself notes on the same page, Subject--finite verb agreement has apparently not been reported on in studies of monolingual French children. If there are no data available, then no comparisons can be made. Meisel's conclusion here is obviously too far-reaching, and must be toned down to include only the data for German.

In sum, Meisel (1986, i.p.) has found both differences and similarities between his bilingual subjects' speech productions in each language and those of French- and German-speaking monolingual children.

Ronjat's main purpose in conducting his study, as he himself states, was "de comparer les faits observés chez [my bilingual subject] Louis avec ceux qui ont été observés chez des enfants monoglottes" (Ronjat 1913: 43). He complains, however, that he does not have the disposal of sufficiently detailed information on monolingual children's language development. Ronjat also makes the point that in order for substantial comparisons to be drawn, he would need to know a great deal more of the exact circumstances in which the monolingual children reported on learned to talk, and what type of language they were exposed to (Ronjat finds it very important that he and his wife spoke 'franc' to their son, i.e., that they used no baby talk, and he laments the fact that observers of monolingual children do not usually comment on whether their subjects heard baby talk or not). Nevertheless, he states that his son's pronunciation in French and German was not any different from that of comparable monolingual children, although he admits that perhaps Louis was a bit late (i.e. ca. 5 months) in using the 'correct' pronunciation in comparison with some monolingual children. If there is indeed a delay, Ronjat writes, it is certainly not due to his son's bilingualism (unfortunately the author does not explain what he would attribute the 'delay' to instead). Any further explicit comparisons (besides passing remarks) are lacking (Ronjat does draw some comparisons with another bilingual child exposed to French and German and concludes: "Les faits concordent en général avec ceux qui ont été observés chez Louis"

Swain (1972) has compared her data for the acquisition of interrogative structures by bilingual children with the data available at that time for monolingual children (actually, detailed data for the latter were only available for one of the languages to be compared, i.e. English). On the whole, Swain claims, the order of acquisition of the structures examined runs parallel in bilingual and monolingual children, although bilingual children appear to be slightly delayed in comparison with monolingual children as far as their first use of inversion in Yes/No questions is concerned. Since, however, Swain's study is a cross-sectional one in which the subjects were not matched as far as their language input is concerned (see section 2.1), the data obtained for all the subjects together cannot be seen as adequately representing a sequence of development that any one child would exhibit if observed longitudinally. Hence any comparisons with other data that do represent longitudinal development are vacuous.

Then we come to Taeschner's (1983) monograph. In Taeschner's second chapter we find a first explicit comparison of the data for Taeschner's two bilingual subjects with those of two monolingual Italian-speaking children at times when apparently all four children were in the one-word stage or in the beginning of the two-word stage. Apart from the fact that there is very little information on the monolingual children and on data gathering procedures (Taeschner simply states that monthly recordings were made using the same techniques as she employed in her own data collection on her bilingual subjects - cf. Taeschner 1983: 20), it is difficult to see how a comparison of the number of verbs produced by the four children involved could furnish logical and conclusive evidence for the far-reaching conclusion that "the bilingual child easily manages to acquire two lexicons without exhibiting a lexical development greatly differing from that of the monolingual child" (Taeschner 1983: 56).

In the third chapter Taeschner compares her bilingual daughters' acquisition of sentence structure with that of German and Italian monolingual children. As a framework, Taeschner takes that of Parisi and Antinucci (1973). A first problem is the unclear analysis and presentation of results. There is also the problem that "The exact criteria for classification are in general not clearly presented, so that the reader who is not familiar with all the details of Parisi and Antinucci is left puzzling about the categorization of particular utterances" (Mills 1986b: 827). This setback is relevant to the analysis of both the bilingual and the monolingual data. Thirdly, again there is hardly any information on the data from the monolingual children. Taeschner's conclusion, then, that "bilinguals acquire typical sentence structure in the same sequence as the monolinguals of each language" (Taeschner 1983: 111), can only be accepted on faith: its empirical validity cannot be ascertained from the scanty information provided (it is furthermore not explained what is meant by 'typical sentence structure').

The same problems as mentioned in the preceding paragraph crop up in Taeschner's fourth chapter, in which various morphosyntactic aspects are discussed. Additional problems are that comparisons are made with monolingual children regardless of their ages or some other criterion that could be used as a basis for comparison. Furthermore, occasionally reference is made to quantitative analyses, but no results are presented. In some sections, no real comparisons are drawn but only concluding statements of similarity or difference are made. When in her summary of her fourth chapter Taeschner writes that on the whole, bilingual children's morphosyntactic development proceeds along the same lines as monolingual children's in each language, we again have to see this as only a very tentative conclusion.

It appears, then, that it is certainly premature to state that "the process of monolingual and bilingual language acquisition is similar" (Lindholm 1980: 224). At the moment, the available literature simply does not provide sufficient evidence to support this statement (cf. also McLaughlin 1984b): very few comparisons have been carried out, and the ones that have done so in a more or less systematic fashion involve a maximum of only three languages (i.e., German, French and Italian). It is clear that much more methodologically sound research is needed before any general conclusions in this area can be formulated.

2.2.5 *How does language presentation affect development?*
Meisel (i.p.) has suggested that some of the findings by Volterra and Taeschner (1978) and Taeschner (1983) which they seem to interpret in terms of 'psycholinguistic stages of bilingual development' (my terminology) might in fact be the result of social-psychological factors: he proposes that certain factors such as the use of 'mixing' in the child's linguistic environment, dominance of one language, or social-psychological biases in favour of one language (the list is incomplete) may lead to the appearance of 'language mixing' or code-switching, and Meisel implicitly criticizes Volterra and Taeschner (1978) and Taeschner (1983) for not paying any attention to such sociolinguistic factors when they present their three-stage and two-stage/two-periods models respectively.

Whereas Meisel's points here are well-taken, there is at the moment no empirical basis whatsoever available for systematically approaching the issues he raises. Although intuitively it does seem quite acceptable that there is a rather direct link between the way in which children are exposed to their two languages and the way children learn to use them, there have been no studies, as far as I know, that have carefully compared bilingual children who were exposed to their two languages in a separate manner (i.e. one person always used mainly one and the same language when addressing the child) with children who heard their two languages spoken by the same people in their environment.

Thus, when 'guide-books' for parents advise educators to follow the 'one person/one language' principle, they are probably making a reasonable suggestion that does not go against common sense. However, so far there is no evidence that other 'methods' should fail, be more 'difficult' for the child, lead to language delay, or otherwise have disadvantageous results. We shall have to wait for methodologically sound research before these issues can be meaningfully addressed, and before the question in the title can be answered.

2.2.6 *Psycholinguistic explanations of the bilingual acquisition process*

So far we have mainly been concerned with descriptive, empirical questions. Proponents of the 'mixed stage' hypothesis, for instance, do not usually try to explain why there should be a 'mixed stage', or through which psycholinguistic processes (if any - see section 2.2.2) the alleged 'language separation' can take place. In addition, when it is claimed that bilingual children go through essentially the same developmental phases as monolingual children, it is again not normally indicated what the reasons for this might be.

Oddly enough, suggestions for explaining the sequence of development of particular forms in bilingual children have not originally come from researchers primarily studying bilingual children, but have been made by Dan Slobin, a specialist on monolingual acquisition.

In his search for possible explanations of the order of development of grammatical devices in the course of children's language acquisition in general, Slobin (1973) took as his empirical starting point reports on bilingual children by Imedadze (1960), Mikès and Vlahovic (1966), and Mikès (1967) (Imedadze's work is only mentioned in passing). [1] It is primarily the data by Mikès and her colleague that are at the focus of attention. More in particular, Slobin concentrates on the data for the grammatical expression of locatives. It appears that Mikès' two bilingual subjects learning Serbo-Croatian and Hungarian first produced the grammatical expression of locatives in Hungarian, while they produced the Serbo-Croatian locative expressions only much later (in Hungarian case endings are used for expressing locatives, and in Serbo-Croatian locatives are expressed using a preposition placed before a noun with occasionally an additional suffix as well - see Slobin 1973).

Thus, there are two observations to be taken into account: (i) in language A, form X is acquired at age {N} to express a semantic notion F; (ii) in language B, form Y is acquired at age {N + some time} to express a semantic notion F (this formulation briefly summarizes Slobin's 1973 points). The logical consequence of the combined action of (i) and (ii) is that form Y is acquired later than form X. On the basis of observations (i) and (ii) and their logical consequence, Slobin concludes that form Y is formally more complex than form X. Slobin (1973) then goes on to try and explain what it is that apparently makes one form psycholinguistically more complex for a child than another one, and proposes his theory of 'operating principles', recently updated in Slobin (1985a).

I shall not discuss Slobin's 'operating principles' here, but will only be concerned with the crucial link between the observations of bilingual children on the one hand and the theory of 'operating principles' on the other: this crucial link is what could be called the Formal Complexity Hypothesis (or FCH), i.e. the claim that the differential order of acquisition across languages of formal elements expressing similar semantic notions is due to a difference in formal complexity between those formal elements.

A first question that can be raised is whether differences in formal complexity are the only possible explanation for why one form should be acquired earlier than another one. At least one other viable explanation - which is not necessarily mutually exclusive with the FCH - may be that certain forms are acquired earlier than others because they are more productive or more frequent in the input that the child receives (cf. e.g. Clark and Hecht's 1982 "principle of productivity"; see also Bowerman 1985).

A second question concerns the basic assumption underlying the FCH that it is unproblematic to cross language boundaries and draw comparisons between forms in language A with forms in language B. I would argue that such an assumption is not necessarily appropriate, and that one might equally well start from the assumptions that languages form closed systems and that it yet needs to be empirically determined whether formal elements can in fact be meaningfully compared across languages. Connected with the 'universalist' assumption made by the FCH is the implicit belief that formal linguistic elements are primarily linked to semantic functions rather than to other formal elements within the same language system. For anyone not sharing this belief, the FCH has little to offer.

Even if theoretically one accepts that formal elements from different languages can be compared to one another, there still remains the third question of what the basis for comparison should be and how 'formal complexity' should be operationally defined. In the literature, the example of English vs. Egyptian Arabic plural noun formation is often quoted as a prime instance of a case where the English system is much simpler than the Arabic one, since the Arabic system morphologically marks semantic distinctions between various types of plurality which are not morphologically marked in the English system, although English may mark these distinctions by means of separate lexical items (cf. Clark and Clark 1977: 338-339). Hence, from an English-centred point of view, the system will indeed appear to be more complex. On the other hand, one may wonder whether an Egyptian Arabic linguist would say the same thing: Arabic is a highly inflectional language (see e.g. Breston 1970) in which the modulation of meaning by means of bound morphemes is extremely productive. With this system as a background, the Egyptian linguist studying English might find the forms of nouns expressing plurality in English to be more complex than in Arabic, since English relies on different types of lexical items as well as on inflectional morphology to express plurality.

The above example shows two things: first, in comparing levels of formal complexity between languages, one must take care to start from identical semantic functions in both languages (this being an integral part of the FCH), which is not always easy, and may even be impossible. The English-Arabic plural system comparison above limits itself to the 'one vs. more than one' distinction in English (as commonly expressed by singular vs. plural nouns), but goes on to compare the expression of this distinction with the expression in Arabic of many more finely-tuned distinctions between various types of 'more than one'. No wonder, then, that one concludes that the Arabic system is more complex! Secondly, the example shows how much the initial choice of a semantic distinction to be taken as a basis for comparison is determined by the formal system that the psycholinguist is best acquainted with: since the 'one vs. more than one' distinction is morphologically marked in English, it presents itself as a 'logical' separate semantic function to the English-speaking linguist. The Egyptian-Arabic linguist, on the other hand, might choose as a 'logical' separate semantic function the distinction between pairs of things and collections of things, since, as Clark and Clark (1977: 338) note, this is a distinction which is morphologically marked in Egyptian Arabic.

Supposing, now, that the above problems have been solved and that both the English and the Egyptian linguist are satisfied with the delimitation of the semantic function to be taken as a basis for comparison: then remains the problem of comparing the formal means of expressing this semantic function. Here we are faced with the difficulty that there are no generally accepted independent criteria for defining formal complexity (cf. Clark and Clark 1977) and that one's linguistic description of any language system will strongly determine one's evaluation. In the absence of independent criteria of what constitutes formal complexity, then, the FCH becomes quite difficult to investigate. Nevertheless, interim solutions can be suggested, one of which is to consider formal complexity in terms of the number of exceptions to a given rule (cf. Clark and Clark 1977). [2] Meisel (1986) has further suggested that "Homonymous, plurifunctional and phonetically nonsalient forms contribute to the complexity of certain forms" (Meisel 1986: 177).

The FCH is repeatedly referred to in reviews of bilingual children's language development, but rarely in its original form. Arnberg (1987) for instance writes:

> if certain forms are equally difficult in the two languages, they will appear at approximately the same time in the two languages; if a form is easier or more difficult in one of the languages, it will appear early or late (Arnberg 1987: 68).

In this characterization any reference to equal levels of semantic or cognitive complexity, which are so central in Slobin's (1973) original proposal, has been simply abandoned. The same problem crops up when Lindholm (1980) writes that in the bilingual child's acquisition of two languages, "The rate of structural development will vary depending on the complexity of the structure" (Lindholm 1980: 226).

The two quotations above are misleading for two reasons: first of all, they misrepresent Slobin's (1973) original proposal, and secondly, they present the FCH as if it had been empirically proven. This, however, is not the case: as shown above, the FCH stands on shaky ground, and until the three main questions that were brought up as problems have been satisfactorily addressed, the FCH remains very much a hypothesis.

Until very recently, the FCH was the only psycholinguistically oriented hypothesis attempting to explain the acquisition of formal elements in a bilingual child's language development. After an investigation of his bilingual subjects' acquisition of word order, case-markings and Subject--finite verb agreement, Meisel (1986, i.p.) found that they differentiated between the grammars of their two languages from the moment they began to use multi-word utterances. On the basis of this finding, Meisel has suggested that

> the grammatical mode of language processing plays an important role even during early phases of language development, and that formal aspects of coding semantic and pragmatic functions have to be viewed as being of crucial importance. This aspect of the mental processing of language, performative complexity of the coding devices, determines

the underlying logic of language development <u>in a more decisive manner than semantic-pragmatic factors or input frequency</u> (Meisel 1986: 179; emphasis mine).

Whereas it is clear that indeed children must be closely attending to the formal peculiarities of their two languages from a very early age in order to produce language-specific morphosyntactic elements from that early age, it is not at all clear that this automatically means that young (bilingual) children are operating with <u>primarily</u> a 'grammatical mode of language processing' at the expense of semantic-pragmatic aspects or input frequency. Since Meisel did not look at the input frequencies of various morphosyntactic devices in the languages addressed to his subjects, he cannot logically discount the possibility that input frequencies may be of major importance in the language acquisition process. Furthermore, although one of Meisel's (1986) main concerns is to criticize functionalist explanations of early child language development, which claim that the acquisition of formal properties of languages can be explained as a direct result of functional needs in communication (see e.g. Bates and MacWhinney 1982), proponents of such functionalist explanations would have a point if they were to claim that Meisel has not unambiguously shown that the 'grammatical mode of language processing' is <u>more important</u> than the semantic-pragmatic mode. Proponents of functionalist explanations would have to admit, though, that their explanations alone cannot account for the data that Meisel presents. Indeed, since from a very early age the bilingual children studied by Meisel used certain structures in one language but not in the other, and this "without any recognizable functional motivation" (Meisel 1986: 139), it is clear that semantic-pragmatic functions are not the sole determinants of children's early language development.

Meisel's work, then, has clearly offered counterevidence against purely functionalist models of language development. However, it has not, I believe, offered clear evidence for the existence of an autonomous area of grammatical language processing. Although it can be accepted on the basis of Meisel's analyses that "new means of expression are acquired simply because they are part of the target system" (Meisel 1986: 177), this finding cannot at the moment be interpreted as constituting unambiguous evidence for the need to capture the child's developing grammatical and pragmatic competence by means of language-specific abstract categories (cf. Meisel

1986: 139). Until other possible interpretations have been investigated and found irrelevant or inapplicable, Meisel's explanation must remain hypothetical. It is quite possible, for instance, that the mechanism underlying the child's early capability to initially acquire the formal devices present in his or her input systems is the result primarily of the child's attention to the most frequently heard patterns in the input which are stored in memory as unanalysed 'chunks' (Peters 1983) and accessed as such in the production of speech - this being but one rival possibility that needs to be empirically investigated before it can be discounted.

The two psycholinguistic hypotheses so far offered as explanations for bilingual children's language development, then, are not entirely satisfactory. Whether it is at all possible at the present time to formulate satisfactory explanations is doubtful: since researchers in monolingual first language acquisition have yet to agree on a unified theory to explain monolingual acquisition (see e.g. the various theoretical points of view reflected in the papers in Wanner and Gleitman 1982 and Fletcher and Garman 1986), it is unlikely that in the near future researchers will be able to come up with generally acceptable hypotheses concerning the even more complex phenomenon of bilingual first language acquisition.

In the mean time, though, searches for possible explanations must continue, and with each new proposal the hope is that we gain more knowledge of how children (whether they be mono- or bilingual) acquire language. The less ambitious a new proposal is, the more chance it probably has of being a step in the right direction. The modest proposal to be mapped out in this book (see Chapter 11) is, I hope, such a step. Before we present the basis for it in Chapter 3, however, a brief summary is in order of what our current knowledge of children acquiring two languages from birth consists of.

2.2.7 *The state of the art in studies of bilingual first language acquisition*
Although it is quite clear that many children exposed to two languages from birth have grown up to be sociolinguistically highly sensitive and fluent bilingual speakers (see Saunders 1982, 1988 for particularly insightful reports on two such children), the extent of our knowledge about how these children acquired their two languages is very limited: there are many more questions than there are answers. The 'big' questions remain basically unanswered: we do not know whether bilingual children in general develop their languages separately from one another or not. We are

also fundamentally ignorant about how bilingual children's language development compares with that of monolingual children. And we know nothing about the degree of influence of a bilingual child's type of language exposure on his or her linguistic development.

However, primarily because of the work undertaken by Jürgen Meisel and his collaborators in the framework of the DUFDE project (i.e. Deutsch und Französisch - Doppelter Erstspracherwerb), some promising pointers and beginning answers do exist. So far, data have been analysed and reported on from a total of either 4 or 5 children who have been exposed to German and French from birth onwards (see the publications by Berkele 1983, Jekat 1985 and Meisel 1986, 1985, i.p. - cf. Table 2.1 in section 2.1). [3]

In Berkele's (1983) work, the acquisition of articles is the focus of interest. However, questions about bilingual acquisition *per se* are not specifically addressed in Berkele's dissertation. Rather, Berkele's main concern is to describe and explain the acquisition of her subject's French and German article systems in terms of functional categories suggested in the literature. In her admirable attempt to do so, she finds that the acquisition of the article system cannot be approached as an independent area of investigation, but convincingly argues that this issue must be linked up with the more general problem of object reference and the acquisition of the pronominal system.

For her functional analyses, Berkele approaches the data as if they consisted of two fairly closed sets (one German, the other French). This assumption, however, is an implicit one, the validity of which Berkele did not investigate. She does state, though, that "Mit einer geringen zeitlichen Verschiebung von ca. 2 Wochen macht [...] jede Sprache eine ähnliche Entwicklung durch" (Berkele 1983: 70), but a detailed and clear presentation of the data in a fashion that would unambiguously show this is unfortunately lacking. While Berkele's (1983) work is a substantial contribution to our knowledge of language acquisition processes in general, entirely different analyses are required to address issues specific to the language development of bilingual children in particular.

Jekat's (1985) Master's thesis has two main goals: first, to give an overview of various theories concerning the development of word meaning, and, more pertinent to our concerns here, to document the vocabulary development of bilingual children and test existing hypotheses. As mentioned previously, Jekat specifically tried to test Taeschner's (1983) hypotheses concerning the development of the bilingual lexicon. Jekat was unable to find confirming evidence for Taeschner's (1983) two-stage model of lexical development, but on the positive side she did find evidence for Taeschner's (1983) claim that up to a certain age, bilingual children acquire more lexical items expressing new meanings than cross-linguistic synonyms for already acquired meanings.

Finally, there is Meisel's work. First we consider his 1985 publication. Meisel's main question here is: how does the very young child linguistically learn to disengage himself from the *hic und nunc* ? As with Berkele's (1983) dissertation, Meisel does not specifically address issues pertaining to bilingual development *per se* , but focuses on the development of his subjects' temporal-modal-aspectual system (or TMA system) as a whole, starting from semantic notions such as [± irrealis] to see how these might be expressed in his subjects' speech productions from the age of 12 months to 3;6. As Meisel notes, "Puisque les moyens morphologiques et syntaxiques sont assez limités à cet âge-là, il ne faut pas encore s'attendre à des différences très significatives dans le développement de deux systèmes grammaticaux" (Meisel 1985: 323). Nevertheless, I think that Meisel presents some indication that already from an early age, there is a language-specific development of certain morphosyntactic features used to express elements of the TMA system: "les enfants bilingues utilisent en allemand des 'adjectifs' ou des 'adverbes' dans des contextes où, en français, ils se servent de 'verbes au participe passé'" (Meisel 1985: 347).

In Meisel (1986, i.p.), the analyses are much more focussed on issues relating to bilingual development. In both publications, it is emphasized that from the two-word stage onwards, young bilingual children already use a variety of language-specific morphosyntactic devices in both their languages. For word order phenomena, for instance, Meisel found that from the moment that his subjects start using multi-word utterances,

> the children follow the requirements of the grammatical systems of both target languages quite closely, even when these merely express grammatical necessities without any apparent semantic-pragmatic motivation. In other cases, certain constructions may well be motivated pragmatically such as the topicalization of complements, yet their formal properties are merely determined by the respective grammatical system (Meisel i.p.: p. 14 in manuscript).

Meisel (1986, i.p.) also adduces convincing evidence from analyses of the acquisition of case-markings and Subject--finite verb agreement.

Obviously, Leopold's (1970, c. 1939-49) work offers a wealth of data as well. However, as explained before, his claims about the nature of his daughter's bilingual development before the age of two must be approached with caution. Much of his diary for Hildegard after the age of two focuses primarily on her development of English, since it seems that Hildegard only started productively and regularly to use fully German utterances towards her fifth year (before this time she did insert German nouns in otherwise entirely English utterances, however). Whether in her total speech production Hildegard distinguished between the morphosyntactic rules of each language before this time, then, is a question that cannot be addressed. There is no indication, though, that Hildegard's morphosyntactic development of English was in any way influenced by her passive knowledge of German.

There is not only the issue of whether bilingual children apply the morphosyntactic rules of the languages they are exposed to in a language-specific manner, but there is also the related issue of the use and nature of utterances containing lexical, morphological or syntactic elements from both languages. Swain and Wesche's (1975) study has clearly shown that in the bilingual three-year-old, such utterances account for only a small proportion of the total recorded output, and that most of these 'Mixed utterances' consist of the insertion of a noun from language A into an utterance that is otherwise entirely in language B (see also Chapter 5). This finding again suggests that influence from one language on the other is minimal, and cannot be seen as a driving force behind the acquisition process.

Since the preceding findings are based on quite disparate data from only 7 or 8 children and since they concern just a few areas of language development and a handful of languages, we have as yet but a very sketchy and fragmentary picture of how bilingual children go about acquiring their languages. The 'base-line' of bilingual development (if such a thing exists) still needs to be established. What is direly needed in the field of BFLA, then, is many more in-depth, methodologically sound case studies of bilingual children covering a wide range of linguistic phenomena and, obviously, a wide range of languages. It is hoped that the empirical investigation to be presented in this book can serve as a first attempt towards the fulfilment of this need.

Notes

1 Due to my lack of knowledge of Serbo-Croatian and Russian, I have not been able to personally consult the work by Mikès and Vlahovic (1966) and Imedadze (1960). The only publications by Mikès and Imedadze that were accessible to me are their 1967 and 1978, c. 1967 articles respectively. In these short articles unfortunately no indication is given of the exact nature of exposure to the two languages, so it is not clear whether we are dealing with cases of BFLA or not.
2 This suggestion, though, is not ideal either, since the delineation of a 'rule' will greatly depend on the particular linguist describing it.
3 Meisel (1985, 1986, i.p.) reports on the girl C and the boy P; Jekat (1985) reports on the boy François and the girl Caroline; Berkele (1983) reports on the girl Claudine. Whether there are 4 or 5 children in total reported on depends on whether the girl C was Caroline or Claudine, or yet a third girl.

3 A new study of bilingual first language acquisition: aims and hypotheses

The conclusion of section 2.2 in Chapter 2 made the point that at the moment we lack sufficiently detailed knowledge about the 'base-line' of bilingual development. The empirical investigation to be presented in the remainder of this book hopes to rectify this situation somewhat.

The new data to be investigated comprise a detailed case study of a child exposed to English and Dutch from birth onwards. The fact that one of the child's languages is Dutch contributes to the diversification needed in this field, since Dutch is a language hitherto not studied in the field of BFLA. Although we have not been as ambitious as Taeschner (1983), who reports on her daughters' language development over several years, and have limited ourselves to a relatively short age period as a basis for investigation (viz. the 8 months between the ages of 2;7 and 3;4), it is hoped that the level of detail and the thoroughness of the analyses can make up for this lack of temporal scope.

It should be stressed that the English-Dutch bilingual child who is the subject of the case study to be presented was exposed to her two languages in a separate fashion: she heard Dutch from one set of interlocutors, and English from another. Any hypotheses or other theoretical points made in the following are intended to apply to such a separate input situation only.

In the analyses, the emphasis will be on morphosyntactic development. We shall also look at the possible determinants of language choice, the use and nature of what we shall call 'Mixed utterances', and signs of metalinguistic behaviour. Conspicuously lacking are phonetic, phonological, semantic and pragmatic analyses, and there is no investigation of language comprehension, even in the morphosyntactic domain. We cannot claim, therefore, that our analyses present anywhere near a complete picture of the child's linguistic capabilities. Nevertheless, the incomplete picture that will be drawn will be solid enough, it is hoped, to address some major theoretical issues.

The first and most important theoretical issue to be addressed is the question of whether and to what extent the bilingual child's morphosyntactic development proceeds in a language-specific manner. I see fundamentally two ways in which this question can be answered.

A first possibility is that from the beginning of morphosyntactic development onwards the bilingual child uses morphosyntactic elements in language A that properly belong to language B and vice versa. Within such a 'transfer theory', it is predicted that any morphosyntactic device belonging to input system A will be used in the child's speech production in utterances containing only lexical items from language B and vice versa. In other words, the child's total speech production will consist of utterances containing a total mixture of structural properties of both input systems. Utterances with lexical items from input system B and morphosyntactic devices belonging to the same input system may occasionally occur, but will in this view be accidental. Evidence against a transfer theory would be the more frequent occurrence of utterances with lexical items from one input system and morphosyntactic devices belonging to the same input system as compared to other types of utterances.

This brings us to the second possible answer to the question of whether and to what extent the child's morphosyntactic development proceeds in a language-specific manner. In this second answer, the bilingual child is seen as developing two distinct morphosyntactic systems. It is further proposed that there is hardly any relationship between the child's two languages, i.e. the morphosyntactic development of the one language does not have any fundamental effect on the morphosyntactic development of the other. Thus, the bilingual child's two languages are seen as forming structurally fairly closed sets which are undergoing a separate

What would constitute evidence for this separate development hypothesis? In order to answer this question, a distinction must be made between morphosyntactic devices that are highly similar in the child's two input systems, and between those that are clearly different (clearly, we are here starting from the assumption that forms can actually be compared across languages). We shall first consider the latter.

Suppose form X of input system A is substantially different from a comparable form Y of input system B. With 'comparable' here we are referring to generally recognizable areas of language that play a role in both languages. What is comparable across languages will greatly depend on the languages concerned. 'Word order in Yes/No-questions', for instance, is a meaningful concept in the description of both English and Dutch, and thus any type of Yes/No-question word order in English (form X, say) can be seen as comparable to a type of Yes/No-question word order in Dutch (form Y, say). If the bilingual child only uses said form X in utterances with lexical items belonging to input system A and at the same age only uses said form Y in utterances with lexical items belonging to input system B, this is the ideal type of supporting evidence for the separate development hypothesis. Another type of supporting evidence would be the occurrence of form X only in utterances with lexical items belonging to input system A even in the complete absence (at the same age) of form Y (this is again if form X of input system A is substantially different from the comparable form Y of input system B). In other words, any language-specific morphosyntactic devices that occur in one language as used by the bilingual child but not in the other are evidence for the separate development hypothesis.

Evidence against the separate development hypothesis <u>might</u> consist of language-specific morphosyntactic devices that occur in both the child's languages, but we are here confronted with eternally ambiguous data: even if one finds that at the same age a bilingual child is using form X in language A and an apparently 'translated' form X in language B, this does not automatically mean that the child is not acquiring both input systems in a separate fashion. After all, the use of the apparently 'translated' form X in language B may be developmentally determined. How can one choose between the one possibility that indeed there is inter-linguistic interaction and the other that what may look like such inter-linguistic interaction is actually the result of the child going through developmentally determined stages of acquisition <u>within one linguistic system</u>? The alternative here is to go and look at monolingual children's language development: if it is found that at a comparable age or overall stage of development the apparently 'translated' form X in language B produced by the bilingual child is also part of the speech production of the monolingual child exposed to only input system B, there is a high chance that the 'translated' form X in language B is the result of the bilingual child learning language B rather than language A, although of course the latter possibility can never be entirely dismissed. On the other hand, if it appears that the 'translated' form X in language B does not occur in monolingual children's speech production, there may be problems for the tenability of the separate development hypothesis (but see later in this chapter).

Then there are areas where both input systems use highly similar or identical morphosyntactic devices. Here of course, if the bilingual child uses form W in language A as well as in language B, there is no positive proof for the separate development hypothesis (nor, it should be noted, against it). However, if at a certain age form W appears only in language A and does not get used in language B until much later, this again constitutes positive evidence for the separate development hypothesis. In this case, the hypothesis would get even more support if monolingual A-speaking children use form W at roughly the same time as the bilingual child when she is speaking language A and if monolingual B-speaking children use form W at roughly the same time as the bilingual child when she is speaking language B.

Thus, if there is such a thing as the separate morphosyntactic development of a bilingual child's two languages, a number of fairly straightforward situations providing positive evidence for such a development could be found. Although the absence of such positive evidence does not necessarily mean that the separate development hypothesis must be rejected, there are in addition cases that would constitute fairly reasonable counterevidence against it. The separate development hypothesis, then, is testable.

As noted above, the transfer theory is testable as well. In effect, if the separate development hypothesis is found to be applicable, this very fact constitutes the strongest evidence against the transfer theory. Similarly, positive evidence for the transfer theory is immediate counterevidence against the separate development hypothesis. The results of investigating the one, then, have direct implications for the other.

In the preceding discussion we have repeatedly referred to 'utterances containing only lexical items from input system A (or B)'. Indeed, in order to investigate whether there is any structural influence from one linguistic system on another, one needs a basis for comparison. The most clear-cut basis (and, of course, the only one possible for comparisons with monolingual children) consists of a corpus of utterances containing lexical items from one input system only, and this for both of the child's languages. Obviously, if there are no such utterances to be found in the corpus, neither the transfer theory nor the separate development hypothesis can be investigated as they stand, and alternatives would have to be formulated. Since it is fairly clear from the literature, though, that from an early age on bilingual children do produce quite a few utterances containing lexical items from one input system only, delving into such alternatives is not a fruitful exercise.

There remains for discussion the issue of the relative quantitative importance of the number of utterances containing lexical items from both input systems (or 'Mixed' utterances - see Chapters 4 and 5) and those containing lexical items from just one input system. What if a young bilingual child produces many more 'Mixed' than 'single lexicon' utterances? Would this finding have major consequences for either the transfer theory or the separate development hypothesis? Not necessarily so: the very occurrence of 'Mixed' utterances could be sociolinguistically determined, and does not automatically have psycholinguistic repercussions. If one feels that one does not have the disposal of enough 'single lexicon' utterances and if it is impossible to collect more data, it might still be feasible to use some of the 'Mixed' utterances as a basis for investigating the transfer theory or the separate development hypothesis: one could focus on those 'Mixed' utterances which contain a clear majority of lexical items from one input system. However, any conclusions about separate or non-separate morphosyntactic development based on an analysis of these 'Mixed' utterances could only be tentative: after all, one would never with certainty be able to say that rules from one language were transferred to the other, since it would not be clear which language exactly was doing the 'influencing' and which one was being 'influenced'.

In the study to be presented in the remainder of this book, we shall try to find evidence for the separate development hypothesis. The reason for this is twofold: first, from a theoretical point of view, I could not see any compelling reason why a child exposed to two languages from birth in a separate fashion should not try to speak like the people around him. In fact, that indeed a bilingual child does not initially try to speak like the people around him is an implicit assumption of the transfer theory. The separate development hypothesis, on the other hand, does not start from any such assumption. Furthermore, before formal data collection began, I had known the bilingual child who is the subject of the present empirical investigation for approximately 6 months. During this time, informal observations had already given a strong indication that she was producing utterances that were morphosyntactically (in addition to lexically and phonetically) fully relatable to one language only. Whether this impression is supported by detailed analyses of the data will have to be decided by the results.

Earlier on we me ntioned the possibility of using data from monolingual children as an additional basis for interpreting data from bilingual children. It should be stressed, though, that the answer to the question of whether and to what extent a bilingual child's morphosyntactic development proceeds in a language-specific manner does not ultimately depend on whether a similarity or dissimilarity with monolingual children's linguistic development can be found. That would be buttressing one hypothesis with another, rather than with 'hard' evidence. The issue of separate development or not can strictly speaking only be addressed on the basis of a corpus of data on bilingual children's development. Similarities or dissimilarities with comparable monolingual children's linguistic development can only be used as secondary evidence for hypotheses that were arrived at on independent grounds. It is, for instance, quite possible that a bilingual child develops his or her two languages in a separate fashion without there being any fundamental similarity with monolingual children's language development for either language.

On the other hand, though, if there are strong and consistent similarities between monolingual and bilingual children's language development, this should automatically mean that bilingual children develop their languages in a separate manner, and in this case it should be quite impossible to find substantial evidence against the separate development hypothesis.

In the present case study, we shall be comparing the bilingual data with reports on monolingual children wherever possible. By referring to findings available in the literature, we follow common practice in studies of monolingual acquisition in which monolingual children acquiring the same language are compared with each other. Such comparisons are not ideal, but in the present case they are the only practical possibility. Perhaps at a future time it will be feasible to carry out a carefully controlled comparative study in which both the mono- and bilingual data are part of the same research project and handled in the same way. Since we will for the moment only be able to draw comparisons on the basis of other researchers' findings which were arrived at using often widely different methods of analysis, any conclusions can be suggestive only. In order to draw comparisons that are as solid as possible, though, care will be taken to compare children in similar age ranges who were exposed to similar varieties of language.

4 *Case study of a bilingual child: introduction*

4.1 Description of the study
4.1.1 *The subject and her language background*

The subject of this study is an only child, Kate, who has been exposed to English and Dutch virtually from birth onwards. The age period studied covers the 8 months from 2;7 to 3;4.

Kate's case is one of bilingual first language acquisition in the more narrow sense of the term as we defined it in Chapter 1: as will be explained below, first exposure to two languages occurred within the period of a week, and exposure to two languages was regular up to and including the period of investigation to be reported on here.

Kate was born of an American mother and a Flemish father in a hospital near Antwerp, Belgium, where the language used by the nursing staff in conversations with patients is a standard-like variety of Dutch as spoken in Flanders. Kate roomed in with her English-speaking mother, who stayed in hospital for a week. Kate's Dutch-speaking father was present at the birth and afterwards visited daily. In her first days of life, Kate heard English spoken to her by her mother, and Dutch by her father and various members of the nursing staff. Thus, first exposure to two languages occurred within the period of a week.

Kate lived with both her parents up to and including the period of investigation and was usually addressed in a different language by each parent. Apart from short intervals when one of the parents was away on a trip, or when both Kate and her mother were in the United States without Kate's father, exposure to two languages took place virtually every day.

Kate's mother, who is also her most regular care-giver, almost always addresses the child in mainstream American English with a slight Midwestern accent. The term 'mainstream American English' here is meant to refer to the variety of English that on the morphosyntactic level is not substantially different from the type of language used on national United States television.

Kate's father almost always addresses Kate in standard Dutch with a slight Ghent accent. The term 'standard Dutch' here refers to the "supraregional variant" (Willemyns 1981: 23) of the language spoken in the Belgian region of Flanders and in most of the Netherlands.[1] It is obvious that neither mainstream American English nor standard Dutch are monolithic entities, and that there may be a great deal of intra-variant variety. This will be taken into account in the ensuing analyses wherever relevant.

Both parents are university graduates and hold prestigious jobs: Kate's mother is a part-time free-lance journalist for a variety of international publications, and Kate's father is a university professor. Kate's social background thus could be described as upper middle class. Kate's parents speak English with each other, since Kate's mother speaks a heavily accented, ungrammatical Dutch (she understands a lot more than she can produce herself), whereas Kate's father speaks English with a close to native competence.

At the beginning of the study, Kate's mother was asked to fill out a form with questions about the child's language background up to the time of the study. The information obtained is represented in Tables 4.1 and 4.2.

Table 4.1 *List of countries visited by Kate*

Age	Country	Approximate duration
birth-0;4	Belgium (Antwerp)	3 months
0;4-0;9	Australia (Canberra)	6 months
0;10-0;10	USA and Great Britain	3 weeks
0;10-1;6	Belgium (Antwerp)	8 months
1;7-1;8	USA	5 weeks
1;8-2;5	Belgium (Antwerp)	9 months
2;5-2;5	USA	2 weeks
2;6-3;4	Belgium (Antwerp)	11 months

As Table 4.1 shows, the family's home base has mostly been Antwerp, a fairly large city in Belgium with much international activity mainly due to the presence of a major sea-port and a large diamond industry. Many languages are spoken in the streets but the language of the local inhabitants is a distinct Antwerp dialect which is significantly different from standard Dutch on the phonological, lexical and morphosyntactic levels (see e.g.

Smout 1980, Stoops 1980, Van de Craen 1982: 610-634). Kate, however, has had little contact with speakers of this Antwerp dialect, and it can be said to be of little importance in a discussion of her language background. Before the age of 3;4, Kate spent 8 and a half months in English-speaking countries compared to about 2 years and 7 months in a Dutch-speaking region. The local environment has thus been mainly Dutch-speaking. The type of Dutch that non-relatives (including peers) would tend to use with Kate is fairly standard, with regionally coloured accents. The media use standard Dutch. In the English-speaking environments, Kate has been exposed to a variety of regional dialects from Australian to British to American.

Table 4.2 *Kate's daily language environment in Belgium (age 2;5-3;4)*

	Language	Estimated frequency
Care-givers		
mother	English	average 6 hrs. a day
father	Dutch	average 4.5 hrs. a day
paternal grandparents	Dutch	average 5 days a month
neighbour babysitter	Dutch	irregularly
Visitors/visits		
most visitors	English	average 5 hrs. a week
some visitors	Dutch	irregularly
most people visited	English	average 5 hrs. a week
some people visited	Dutch	irregularly
peers outside school	Dutch	irregularly
Group situations		
pre-school	English	average 20 hrs. a week
playgroup	English	3 hrs. a week
Media		
television	Dutch & English	average 1 hour a day
Other		
shops and services	Dutch	short periods daily

On week-days, English is heard by the child much more often than Dutch, with an average of about 10 hours of English versus about 4 hours of Dutch a day (of course part of the day will include an overlapping of both languages, e.g. when both parents are interacting with the child in the same room). This is mainly due to the fact that Kate goes to an English-speaking pre-school, a small private school with a low pupil to teacher ratio. (Before Kate started going to school at age 2;6, the input for both languages on week-days was about equal: for three mornings a week she was cared for by a Dutch-speaking neighbour.)

On week-ends, Dutch tends to be heard more often than English (Kate's father spends more time with her then, and this is mostly the time when the grandparents are present; also visits to Dutch-speaking acquaintances and friends tend to take place at the week-ends). Kate occasionally spends a week alone with her monolingual Dutch-speaking grandparents in the holidays or during the school-term when her parents are away on business trips.

On the whole, it might be said that for the period from 2;5 to 3;4, Kate has slightly more contact with English than with Dutch. For both languages, she is exposed to a wide variety of accents. Most of the people that Kate meets address her in only one language, and certainly her caregivers use mainly one language with her. Kate has thus grown up in a one person/one language situation.

On the information form filled out by her mother, Kate was described as a talkative child "in both languages". From my own observation of the child I can confirm this. In addition, Kate is a healthy child with no history of hospitalization or illnesses. She has never had to stay away from school because of a cold or other ailment. Kate is used to meeting a lot of different people from various ethnic backgrounds and is not shy in communicating with them. There is no reason to assume that she is exceptionally intelligent or has lower than normal intelligence.

Finally, a word should be said about the attitudes in the child's environment towards her developing bilingualism. Although no formal investigation of this issue was carried out, informal observation during the study, as well as before and after it, have shown there to be no negative or outspokenly positive attitudes present. Rather, the child's bilingualism at the age period studied seemed to be accepted by the environment at large as a matter of course, which was not commented on in either positive or negative terms. Kate's parents themselves only mentioned their daughter's bilingualism to outsiders when they were proudly recounting her 'bilingual jokes'. Bilingual individuals who were in regular contact with the child, however, were made aware by Kate's parents that they preferred that person to use mainly one language with her.

4.1.2 *Data collection*

The investigator (A) first met Kate when she was about 2 years and 2 months old (6 months before data collection began) and was in regular contact with her after the initial meeting. The child saw A as a close friend of the family's and felt perfectly at ease with her. The investigator used Dutch with Kate most of the time throughout this initial acquaintanceship and the recording period. When data collection started, the child was not aware that her language was A's field of interest. There was no difference noticeable between Kate's behaviour towards A before data collection began and afterwards. In total, 19 one hour recordings were made. Although the aim was to make a recording a week, the sessions ended up being irregularly spaced due to the family's unexpected absences or visitors which made data collection impossible. Data collection was carried out in the child's home using a good quality portable cassette-recorder with a built-in multi-directional microphone. This recorder was placed on the floor or on a table close to where interaction was taking place and received little interest from the child, except on some infrequent occasions when A was asked to "turn the music on". There is no reason to believe that the interaction and the linguistic choices made were influenced by the presence of the recorder.

Frequently, interactions were recorded while Kate was playing with A in the kitchen while M (Kate's mother) was cooking. Thus, at most of the recording sessions both languages were present, but since M was busy cooking and A was usually Kate's focus of attention (after all, A was there "to play with her", as M frequently told Kate), interactions between M and Kate were rather less frequent than interactions between A and Kate. This is reflected in the rather big differences between the total amount of Dutch vs. English material on the tapes (see also later). On many of the tapes, then, there are three speakers present, and each of these may interact with either one of the others. This situation, by the way, was quite usual in Kate's life: her parents had visitors almost daily, and the very hospitable atmosphere in Kate's house meant that more often than not, a visitor stayed for lunch or dinner.

Favourite games played during the recording sessions included 'flying', in which Kate would repeatedly ask A to lift her high up in the air, playing with an animal farm, pretending to be a lion or some other animal, making pretend 'dinner' and 'tea' and naming colours. In M's interactions with Kate during the recording sessions, discussions of past and future featured prominently (again nothing unusual in Kate's life: each day before going to bed Kate had a conversation with M about the events of that day or the next). Other interaction between Kate and her mother frequently concerned the eating or preparing of food. There are not many examples of playing between Kate and her mother. As M has reported to the investigator, she does not usually play with Kate, except when Kate needs someone to give pretend 'tea' or 'dinner' to.

Table 4.3 *Adults present at recording sessions*

Tape	Adult(s) present		Duration of presence
1	M (English) + A (Dutch)		entire session
2	M (English) + A (Dutch)		entire session
3	M and A's friend	English	entire session
	A and F	Dutch	entire session
4	A	Dutch	entire session
	F	Dutch	on and off
5	M	English	entire session
	A and F	Dutch	entire session
6	A	Dutch	entire session
7	M and Kate's aunt E	English	entire session
	A	Dutch	entire session
	F	Dutch	end of session
8	F	Dutch	first half of session
	M	English	second half of session
	A	Dutch	entire session
9	M	English	second half of session
	A and grand-parents	Dutch	entire session
10	M	English	second half of session
	A	Dutch	entire session
11	M (English) + A (Dutch)		entire session
12	M (English) + A (Dutch)		entire session
13	M	English	entire session
	A	Dutch	entire session
	F's colleague R	Dutch	first half of session
	F	Dutch	second half of session
14	M	English	entire session
	F	Dutch	second half of session
15	M (English) + A (Dutch)		entire session
16	M (English) + A (Dutch)		entire session
17	M (English) + A (Dutch)		entire session
18	A	Dutch	entire session
	F	Dutch	second half of session
19	A and F	Dutch	entire session

There are a few recording sessions where Kate's father (F) is present as well. In addition, Kate's aunt, her grandparents and a colleague of F's are briefly present at some sessions. Overall, though, the data consist of mainly Dutch interactions between Kate and A, and mainly English interactions between Kate and M. The language used between A and M is English. For a detailed representation of the adults present at each recording session, see Table 4.3.

As is clear from Table 4.3, at most recording sessions at least one Dutch-speaking and one English-speaking adult were present. This method had as its most obvious disadvantage the fact that there was no strict control over how much each of the adults present would interact with the child, and consequently, to what extent one language would be used rather than the other, both by the adults and the child. Obviously, more of a balanced output could have been expected if all recording sessions had taken place in the presence of only one interlocutor, with the one week a Dutch speaker and the other week an English speaker for instance. The latter possibility, however, would have been slightly contrived, since in Kate's home environment both languages tend to be present at the same time (see above). In deciding on the data collection method, then, a choice was made in favour of naturalness and the risk was taken that the data might be abundant for one language and rather scarce for the other.

Table 4.4 lists the main activities that Kate engaged in during the recording sessions, together with an indication of who the major interacting adult was for each activity and which language they would tend to use in addressing the child.

It is clear from this table that the method of data collection produced the kind of imbalance pointed out above: in general, A tended to interact much more with the child than M, the result being than the child was addressed in Dutch much more frequently than in English. As will be shown later, the child's choice of language reflects this situation. Yet there are sufficient English-interlocutor interactions to allow comparisons between Kate's use of both languages. However, a more balanced combination of the single- and double-interlocutor methods would have been preferable. At present, there is only one recording session (Tape 14) where most of the interaction takes place between M and Kate. Yet even at this session F is present for some time, if mostly on the background, i.e. as a non-participant.

Table 4.4 *Main activities engaged in by Kate and their associated interlocuors and languages*

Tape	Activity	Main interaction with:	Main language used by adult
1	Naming colours/	A	Dutch
	general conversation	A	Dutch
2	Recounting a visit/	A	Dutch
	arranging cushions/	A	Dutch
	naming colours/	A	Dutch
	discussing past and imaginary future events	M	English
3	Acting out boating scene	A	Dutch
4	Pretending to be cooking/	A	Dutch
	pretending to be sleeping/	A	Dutch
	pretending to be a sick lion/	A	Dutch
	pretending to shoot a bird	A	Dutch
5	Requesting and insisting on having candy/	M	English
	being thrown up in the air/	F/A	Dutch
	hiding game/	F/A	Dutch
	pretending to be a fish, a rooster and a chicken	A	Dutch
6	Playing with animal farm/	A	Dutch
	singing/	A	Dutch
	general conversation/	A	Dutch
	pretending to be a fish, a rooster and a chicken	A	Dutch
7	Discussing school events/	A/M/E	English/Dutch
	discussing a visit to a museum/	A/M/E	English/Dutch
	singing/	A	Dutch
	requesting and insisting on having candy/	M	English
	pretending to be a rooster and a chicken	A	Dutch
8	Drawing/	F/A	Dutch
	making and serving pretend dinner/	M/A	English/Dutch
	requesting and insisting on having a banana/	M	English
	playing with animal farm	A	Dutch
9	Naming colours/	A	Dutch
	playing with a doll/	A	Dutch
	requesting food stuffs	M	English
10	Playing in the bath tub/	A	Dutch
	getting dressed	M	English
11	Discussing past	M/A	English/Dutch

Case study of a bilingual child: introduction

	and imaginary events/		
	joking around/	M/A	English/Dutch
	making and serving	M/A	English/Dutch
	pretend dinner		
12	Playing in the bath tub/	M/A	English/Dutch
	getting dressed/	M	English
	discussing the food	M	English
	M is preparing		
13	Discussing an upcoming trip/	M/A	English/Dutch
	discussing the past week-end/	M/A	English/Dutch
	'helping' M prepare food/	M	English
	discussing food	F	Dutch
14	Making matches 'dance'/	M	English
	learning about food stuffs/	M	English
	learning about cooking/	M	English
	singing/	M	English
	general conversation/	M	English
	chattering nonsense	F	Dutch
15	Discussing school events/	M	English
	general conversation/	M	English
	requesting food stuffs/	M	English
	riding tricycle/	M	English
	discussing upcoming trip/	M	English
	discussing past trip to the seaside/	A	Dutch
	bed-time monologue	self	-
16	Being thrown up in the air/	A	Dutch
	hiding game/	A	Dutch
	naming colours/	A	Dutch
	requesting food stuffs/	M	English
	general conversation	M	English
17	General conversation/	M	English
	cutting up strawberries/	A	Dutch
	requesting food to cut up	M	English
18	Making and serving pretend dinner/	F/A	Dutch
	discussing school event/	A	Dutch
	general conversation/	F/A	Dutch
	joking around	F/A	Dutch
19	Hiding games/	F/A	Dutch
	playing with a ball/	F/A	Dutch
	general conversation/	F/A	Dutch
	making and serving pretend dinner/	F/A	Dutch
	discussing upcoming trip	F/A	Dutch

4.1.3 *Transcription of the data*

The tapes were transcribed orthographically by the investigator as soon as possible after their recording. Contextual information was added where necessary for later disambiguation (some of this information was occasionally spoken in on tape in the course of a recording session when Kate was briefly in another room and thus outside hearing range).

In transcription, a simple one-column format was used in which each speaker's turns were listed sequentially, preceded by the speaker's initial. Any contextual or other additional information was noted between brackets after the utterances to which it was relevant. Partially overlapping utterances by different speakers were indicated by using slashes (/) at the start and end points of overlap. For sound sequences that could not be unambiguously interpreted, phonetic transcriptions were used (in IPA format), and when even phonetic transcriptions were impossible, gaps were indicated by '??' or, for sequences probably longer than one syllable, '?...?'. Bits of transcriptions which were doubtful were indicated by a single question mark at the beginning and the end of the relevant sequence. Short pauses within utterances of less than a second were indicated by commas, longer pauses were indicated by dots (..).

All interactions were transcribed in full (including hesitations, false starts, repetitions, self-made songs, and nonsense utterances). Extended conversations between the adults that did not include the child in any way were not transcribed (this was indicated by a comment between brackets), but all other adult utterances were included in the transcription.

The boundaries of both child and adult utterances were determined intuitively on the basis of intonation contours (this procedure is unfortunately far from ideal). Utterances were separated from one another using full stops unless there was clear question intonation (in which case a question mark was used), or unless the utterance was uttered in a fairly loud and/or excited voice (in which case an exclamation mark was used).

The following text is an example of a bit of transcription taken from Tape 5 at 2;10,5 when Kate and the investigator were playing in the kitchen (English glosses of Dutch utterances are given in <> brackets; these glosses, however, are not part of the original transcript):

K: Waar's de vis? <Where's the fish?>
   (K is pretending to be a fish)
A: Ik weet het nie, de vis is verdwenen! De vis is weg! Helemaal weg!
   <I don't know, the fish has disappeared! The fish is gone! All gone!>
   (K laughs and hides)
A: Waar is de vis nu? Zou de vis gaan zwemmen zijn?
   <Where can the fish be? Do you think the fish has gone for a swim?>
K: De vis gaat nu zwemmen. <The fish is going for a swim now.>
A: Ah!

K: ?..? de vis nu? De vis gaat in het water!
 <?..? the fish now? The fish is going in the water!>
A: Ah, de vis gaat in het water zwemmen, ja! .. En wat ziet hij in het water? Andere visjes?
 <I see, the fish is going in the water for a swim, right! .. And what does he see in the water? Other little fish?>
K: De visjes! <The little fish!>
A: Andere? <Other ones?>
K: Nu gaat de kleine visjes. <Now the little fishes goes.>
A: Kleine visjes? <Little fishes?>
 (short pause in interaction)
K: Ja ben jij een vis? Klein visje?   <Yes are you a fish? Little fish?>
 (K is speaking to an imaginary little fish that supposedly she has caught in her hand)
K: ?..? een klein visje! <?..? a little fish!>
A: O zeg da's een klein visje! Mag ik et ook 's ebbe?
 <O hey that's a tiny little fish? Could I hold it for a second?>
K: Ja! <Yes!>
 (K gives the imaginary little fish to A)

Although every effort was made to carry out the transcriptions as meticulously as possible, with an average of 15 hours' transcription time per hour of recorded interaction, the lack of verification by a second transcriber is regrettable. The main reason for why no second transcriber could be engaged for even a portion of the recordings is that it was impossible to find a person not only capable of carrying out the transcriptions (someone was needed who was trained in linguistics and preferably also in phonetics and who was sufficiently proficient in both the varieties that Kate was exposed to) but also willing to do so.

4.1.4 *General procedure for analysis and coding systems*
After transcription, all child utterances were entered on computer disks, coded along various dimensions, and analysed using specially designed programmes written by Darius Clynes. The hardware consisted of an Apple Macintosh Plus computer.

Although the corpus on disk was limited to only the child utterances, coding took place on the basis of the full transcription. The coding system includes a language choice code, a morpheme count, utterance characterization codes, morphological codes per individual word and syntactic codes.

The language choice codes will be briefly referred to in section 4.2 below and are presented in more detail in section 5.1 of Chapter 5. This chapter deals with aspects of Kate's language production which by their very nature are linked to her bilingualism and cannot be investigated in monolingual children, viz. the possible determinants of language choice and the linguistic characteristics of Mixed utterances (for a definition, see section 4.2).

For further information on the morpheme counts the reader is referred to subsection 4.2.2.

Each utterance in the corpus could in principle be given an optional utterance characterization code referring to general characteristics of the utterance and/or pertaining to the more 'performance' oriented aspects of an utterance. Rather than list the utterance characterization codes utilized, we shall refer to them and define them where relevant in the ensuing analyses.

As a general guideline in the design of both the morphological and syntactic coding systems it was decided that the level of detail present in the codes should follow the limitations and complexities present in the material. For instance, in order to construct a coding system to be used for analysing the speech productions of a child still in the 'two-word' stage, it will hardly be necessary to include a morphological code 'auxiliary, non-modal, finite verb', since there might not be even one of these present in the corpus. At the 'two-word' stage, one would probably need only two or three different verb codes to adequately capture the range of variation in the material (cf. e.g. de Haan 1986b). Since several preliminary readings of the transcripts for Kate had shown her to be well into the multi-word stage, and since she used a wide variety of verb forms, it was deemed necessary to include a large range of quite detailed verb codes in the coding system. For other word classes, other decisions were made on the same principle.

The decision to use a data-driven approach in the setting up of the coding systems meant that it should be possible during the coding process to adapt and expand them. The flexible format of the coding and analysis programmes allowing the addition of new word-level codes at any time during coding ensured that this requirement could be met.

A second major determinant in deciding on the codes to be included in the coding system was the existence of specific research questions. One of these questions, for instance, was whether the absence of a syntactic gender system in English as marked by the use of articles had any influence on the child's learning of the Dutch syntactic gender system. With only the first guideline, it might have been sufficient to distinguish between definite and indefinite articles, and to treat all singular nouns identically. Since a specific research question in this area existed, however, more detail was added and a distinction was made between neuter and non-neuter nouns, and the neuter and non-neuter definite article.

The example above shows that for the one language detail needed to be added that was quite meaningless in the other (Dutch has syntactic gender whereas English does not), which might be seen as an argument for the setting up of separate coding systems for each language. In addition, if the view is taken that languages form formally closed systems, their description should be entirely language specific. While these arguments are perfectly acceptable, it was decided that only one morphological and one syntactic coding system should be used to describe the whole corpus. This was much more efficient in terms of computer handling and in terms of the learning of the two coding systems. It also circumvented the problem of the Mixed utterances: should we have opted for a coding-system-per-language-solution, then perhaps there ought to have been separate coding systems for these as well, resulting in a minimum total of three times two coding systems. This would have been very cumbersome, and besides, it would not have been clear at all what separate coding systems for Mixed utterances should look like. The theoretical problem of the need for a language specific description was partially solved by the admission of codes that could only be applied to elements from one language and not the other.

The morphological and syntactic coding systems as a whole, then, are the result of many compromises, a situation which probably cannot be avoided, even if an approach is chosen that is pre-determined by a theoretical model rather than a data-driven approach as is the case for the present study (see also Wells 1985). However, the two less-than-ideal coding systems do seem to be capable of capturing most of the variation and complexity of the data, while at the same time they are efficient in terms of computer handling. The main argument against the coding systems as they stands is that the description of both languages is not sufficiently language-specific. This argument is a valid one, but it is believed that the present coding procedures have allowed highly language-specific elements to be included where necessary, thus limiting the danger of non-language-specific description to an acceptable minimum. This danger has further been reduced by the versatility of the coding and analysis programmes, which have always allowed 'on-the-spot' decisions to be made where they were felt to be necessary.

Finally, for both the morphological and syntactic coding systems we have used adult terminology. It should be emphasized, though, that this does not imply that the child is attributed knowledge or awareness of the categories used: the terminology employed is meant to be purely descriptive (see also Crystal, Fletcher and Garman 1976: 62).

Each interpretable word in the corpus was assigned at least one morphological code.[2] As with the language choice codes, we shall refer to the specific morphological codes used where relevant in the ensuing analyses, which are presented in the morphologically oriented Chapters 6 and 7. The focus of these chapters will be on Kate's use of noun and verb phrases respectively, and the main research question will be to what extent the use of bound morphemes and other closed class items (Quirk and Greenbaum 1973) is language specific, rather than relatable to the child's knowledge of the other language.

We shall further clarify the syntactic coding system at the beginning of Chapter 8, which deals with word order and general syntactic development. It will be investigated again to which extent these aspects are language specific, rather than relatable to the child's knowledge of the other language.

The general working procedure in Chapters 6, 7 and 8 will consist of a form-oriented analysis comparing the relevant forms used in either language (short summaries of the main characteristics of the adult input systems act as a framework for this analysis), followed by an investigation of any developments over time in the frequency patterns and the nature of the forms under investigation. Finally, comparisons will be made with reports on the language productions of both monolingual children within approximately the same age range as Kate.

It should be noted that in all comparisons with other English- and Dutch-speaking children, preferably only data from children exposed to mainstream colloquial American English and standard colloquial Dutch will be used. The same holds for any reference made to input data. The reason is that Kate was mainly exposed to the two varieties mentioned here.

In cases where data from mainstream American English are lacking, only data from speakers of standard British English will be used as a basis for comparison. This is admissible, it is believed, since, although there a number of morphosyntactic differences between the two varieties, these are generally few, and quite well-known from contrastive descriptions, so that areas of difference can easily be recognized and dealt with accordingly. In cases where data from standard Dutch are lacking, other data will only be used as a basis for comparison if it is certain that they are not examples of clearly definable regional dialects.

Before we go on to Chapter 5, we present a general overview of the data in section 4.2.

4.2 The data: an overview
4.2.1 *Languages used by Kate per recording session*

The language codes used to characterize each child utterance contain three elements: the first one refers to the language used by Kate, the second to the language that Kate's utterance was a response to (if Kate's utterance was not a clear response to any utterance by an interlocutor the second element was coded as 'I' for initiation), and the third element defines the interlocutor. For now we will only be concerned with the first element, viz. the language used by Kate.

A child utterance was coded as being English if all the lexical items and bound morphemes in it were unambiguously and fully English (a lexical item is here defined as "a word as it occurs in a dictionary" (Quirk, Greenbaum, Leech and Svartvik1985: 68)). One phonetic feature from Dutch was allowed to occur (e.g. a Dutch quality [r]). An example of an English utterance by Kate is:

'Mommy I want a waffle.' (Age: 2,10,28)

An utterance was coded as being Dutch if all the lexical items and bound morphemes in it were unambiguously and fully Dutch. One phonetic feature from English was allowed to occur (e.g. an aspirated stop). An example of a Dutch utterance by Kate is:

'Waar is de haan?' (Age: 2,10,28)

It should be noted that the few linguistic forms which in principle could belong to either Dutch or English were not taken into account in deciding which language an utterance was. A case in point is the fairly frequently occurring allophone [s] functioning as an abbreviation of the third person singular present tense of the copula or auxiliary BE in English and ZIJN in Dutch: this allophone exists both in English and in Dutch, and thus can be said to be 'neutral' in any decision procedure concerning the language Kate was using.

An utterance was coded as Mixed if there was a lexical item consisting of one English and one Dutch morpheme, if there was a Dutch lexical item next to an English-one, or if it contained a 'blend', i.e. a free morpheme which without any doubt combines phonological elements from both languages (only two of these occur in the entire corpus). An example of a Mixed utterance by Kate is:

'On jij kop!' (Age: 2,10,28) <On you head!>
{three-morpheme utterance consisting of the English preposition ON followed by a Dutch personal pronoun in the subject form and a Dutch noun}

In a few cases Kate produced non-adult-like lexical items in which the bound morpheme(s) could belong to either language. In these instances it was decided to consider the bound morpheme(s) as belonging to the same language as the free morphemes they were attached to. Further analysis will have to show for each individual case whether this was the right decision.

A final subgrouping is that of the 'Non-language specific' utterances. A 'Non-language specific' (NLS) utterance contains no elements referable to either English or Dutch, but consists only of gibberish or onomatopoeic sounds. Apart from a short mention later on, these utterances will not be analysed any further, which is not to say that they are unimportant in an account of language acquisition: they may fulfil important pragmatic roles, and may reveal much about a child's general interest in sound play and imitation for the sheer fun of it. In Kate's language production, NLS utterances account for only 1.7% of her entire recorded output. Presumably, this is within normal bounds although no data exist in the literature that could be used as a basis for comparison. An example of an NLS utterance by Kate is:

'[pip pip pi:k]' (Age: 2,10,28)

It must be pointed out that the division into language groups here is purely descriptive: at this stage, no claims are made of any separate development of the languages involved.

Table 4.5 lists the total number of utterances per recording session and the extent to which the child makes use of any of the four 'language' subgroups. As was mentioned in section 4.1, the data collection method used carried as a risk the possibility that there might be abundant data for one language and rather scarce data for another. And indeed, there is quite an imbalance in the material as far as the quantity of English vs. Dutch child utterances is concerned: there are about three times as many Dutch utterances than there are English. It is believed, though, that the total number of English utterances (1099) is still quite sufficient for a detailed analysis to take place.

Table 4.5 Languages used by Kate [a]

Tape	Age	Dutch	English	Mixed	NLS	Totals
1	2;7,12	68.8	23.4	7.8	0.0	77
2	2;7,17	42.7	38.2	18.8	0.3	335
3	2;8,8	45.9	27.0	21.6	5.4	37
4	2;9,0	94.7	0.5	3.2	1.6	374
5	2;10,5	60.8	36.6	0.9	1.7	232
6	2;10,13	95.8	0.4	3.6	0.2	527
7	2;10,28	69.3	26.1	4.1	0.4	241
8	2;11,14	72.5	20.8	6.7	0.0	284
9	3;0,6	52.3	38.6	9.1	0.0	88
10	3;0,11	52.3	36.2	11.5	0.0	130
11	3;0,17	16.2	68.4	15.4	0.0	117
12	3;1,6	45.2	48.8	6.0	0.0	84
13	3;1,12	52.7	45.1	2.2	0.0	91
14	3;1,13	5.2	85.8	6.7	2.2	134
15	3;1,18	10.7	77.2	5.4	6.7	224
16	3;1,26	53.5	36.0	3.5	7.0	258
17	3;2,7	55.9	38.8	3.3	2.0	245
18	3;3,9	88.3	1.1	5.5	5.1	274
19	3;3,16	89.3	2.6	7.9	0.3	392
Entire corpus		65.2	26.5	6.5	1.7	4144

[a] the decimal figures are percentages based on the totals for each tape

4.2.2 Mean Length of Utterance (MLU)

Although the usefulness of MLU counts can be debated, especially when languages other than English are involved (see Chapter 2), MLU counts for Kate are presented in the following in order to obtain at least a rudimentary basis for comparisons with other children in either language.

In determining the number of morphemes in each of Kate's utterances Brown's (1973) criteria were not followed, since it was felt that these criteria carry with them already too much data interpretation. Instead, for the data from Kate an adult-oriented morphemic analysis was adopted for

The acquisition of two languages from birth: a case study 88

both languages, but of course no claim is made that a form used by the child has the same analytical value that it might have for an adult.

Brown (1973) and Miller (1981) both suggest basing the MLU count on 100 consecutive and fully transcribed utterances, starting with the 51st utterance in the transcript. For the material at hand, this procedure could easily be followed were it not that in each recording session more than one language is used. As a solution one could apply Brown and Miller's suggestion within each language, but use the first 50 utterances in each tape, regardless of language, as the portion to be disregarded. In the data at hand, there are 10 tapes for which a Dutch MLU could be computed following this procedure. For English, though, there are only two tapes for which a MLU value could be computed this way. In order to obtain a larger basis for comparison with English-speaking children, it was decided to do away with the '50-for-nought'-rule (Kate knew the investigator quite well, and there is no reason to assume that the first 50 utterances in each recording session are significantly different from the others) and to lower the number of utterances used to base the MLU count on to 80. The results of the computations can be found in Table 4.6. This table includes upper bound (UB) counts as well (from now on, 'D' in tables will be an abbreviation for 'Dutch', and 'E' in tables will be an abbreviation for 'English').

Table 4.6   *Mean Length of Utterance calculations for Kate: results*

Tape	Age	D MLU	D UB	E MLU	E UB
2	2;7,17	3.15	11	4.90	22
4	2;9,0	4.00	15	-	-
5	2;10,5	2.18	9	4.04	10
6	2;10,13	2.41	11	-	-
7	2;10,28	2.16	15	-	-
8	2;11,14	3.32	12	-	-
11	3;0,17	-	-	5.11	14
14	3;1,13	-	-	4.86	23
15	3;1,18	-	-	3.85	32
16	3;1,26	2.04	10	3.33	17
17	3;2,7	4.73	26	5.58	21
18	3;3,9	5.30	21	-	-
19	3;3,16	3.32	21	-	-

We now turn to the analyses and results.

Notes
1 We are using the term 'standard Dutch' to refer to that variant that Willemyns (1981) calls "Netherlandic".
2 It was possible with the computer programmes used to have more than one morphological code associated with any word - this was useful in cases of doubt (operator OR) or in cases where indeed two or more codes applied (operator AND).

5 *Language choice and Mixed utterances*

5.1 Language choice
5.1.1 *Introduction*

In section 4.2 of Chapter 4 an overview was given of the quantitative use of English, Dutch, Mixed and 'Non-language specific' utterances by Kate. The question now is: what determines Kate's choice of language? In the small range of literature on the subject, the main determinant of language selection by bilingual children is seen to be the interlocutor (see e.g., Bergman 1976, McClure 1977, Fantini 1978a, Saunders 1982). It seems that in general, bilingual children address their interlocutors in a language they know they will understand and will be able to respond in. McClure (1977: 101), for instance, writes: "Inappropriate choice of language when addressing a monolingual is rare". To see to what extent Kate is similar to other bilingual children, we decided to categorize each of her utterances in terms of interlocutor and in terms of which language the interlocutor used to address the child. In the following subsection the categorization system will be explained in more detail. After this, the data are analysed and discussed.

5.1.2 *The language choice codes*

As was mentioned before, the language choice codes consist of three elements. The criteria for deciding on the first element have already been outlined in section 4.2.1.

The second element in the code refers to the language that Kate's utterance was a reaction to. There are two main categories here: initiations and responses. An utterance was coded as an 'initiation' if (1) it occurred after a lull in the conversation and could not be considered a delayed response to an adult's query, or (2) Kate had inserted an utterance in the middle of a conversation by adults and the utterance had both meaningwise and structurally no connection with what any adult was saying, or (3) the utterance was a response to a non-verbal action by an adult. An utterance was considered to be a 'response' in all other cases, and was given the code English, Dutch, or Mixed as second element. These codes refer to the

Language choice and Mixed utterances

language used by the interlocutor in the utterance preceding the child's utterance. The criteria for deciding between the three 'language' groups are the same as the ones for the first element in the language choice code (cf. section 4.2.1). It should be pointed out here that a non-initiating code is contingency-oriented and descriptive only: no claim is made of conscious addressee-directedness on the child's part at this stage. The code EEE, for instance, only means that after an English utterance by an English speaker Kate produced an English utterance. This brings us to the third element, the interlocutor code.

There are three possibilities for the interlocutor code: the interlocutor (IC) is a Dutch or an English speaker (codes D and E), or the interlocutor code is X, which means that the interlocutor could be either a Dutch or English speaker - and it is not clear which - or both an English and a Dutch speaker, or Kate is speaking to herself. By definition, an IC code X can only follow an initiation code, except when Kate is talking to herself. The IC codes D and E were only used when through the context or elements in the child's utterance (such as Vocatives) it was quite clear what type of speaker the utterance was directed at. In this study the child's mother (M) and aunt (E) were categorized as being English speakers, while all others were categorized as being Dutch speakers.

In Table 5.1 the reader will find the total catalogue of language choice codes as used in the present study.

The group of Mixed utterances by Kate was subcategorized into (1) mainly Dutch, (2) mainly English, and (3) 'Dutlish' utterances. The criteria for subcategorization depend on the number of morphemes (both bound and free) clearly referable to one language: a Mixed mainly Dutch (or MMD) utterance has more than 50% Dutch morphemes (example 1), a Mixed mainly English (or MME) utterance has more than 50% English morphemes (example 2), and a 'Dutlish' utterance contains as many English as Dutch morphemes (example 3). This subcategorization was utilized because it allows a more detailed approach to the problem under consideration and smooths out the rather sharp, and possibly too arbitrary, division between Dutch and English utterances on the one hand, and Mixed utterances on the other.

(1) 'Nog één, nog een song.' (Age: 2;10,28)
    <Another one, another song.'>
        {five-morpheme utterance in which four morphemes are Dutch
        and the fifth and last one is English - MMD}
(2) 'You don't bring me off the zetel!' (Age: 2;7,17)
        {eight-morpheme utterance in which all morphemes except the
        last one are English; the last one is a Dutch morpheme
        consisting of a noun meaning CHAIR - MME}
(3) 'Yellow bos.' (Age: 2;7,17)
    <Yellow wood.>
        {two-morpheme utterance consisting of an English and a
        Dutch morpheme - Dutlish}

Table 5.1   *Language choice codes*

First term of three-term code: one code to be chosen among the following
D = Dutch
E = English
M = Mixed
X = Non-language specific

Second and third terms of three-term code: one code to be chosen among the following
<u>Initiations</u> (no clear response to an interlocutor's preceding utterance)
ID = directed at a Dutch speaker
IE = directed at an English speaker
IX = addressee not clear: could be either an English or a Dutch speaker

<u>Responses</u> to an interlocutor's preceding utterance
DD = in response to a Dutch utterance by a Dutch speaker
DE = in response to a Dutch utterance by an English speaker
MD = in response to a Mixed utterance by a Dutch speaker
ME = in response to a Mixed utterance by an English speaker
ED = in response to an English utterance by a Dutch speaker
EE = in response to an English utterance by an English speaker

---

5.1.3 *Analysis and results*

Table 5.2 gives an overview of the 'languages' used by Kate in function of addressee. Utterances addressed to 'X' are not included, and this explains why the totals do not add up to 4144 as in Table 4.5 in Chapter 4.

Although the absolute number of child utterances addressed to a Dutch speaker is more than three times that of utterances addressed to an English speaker (78.1% versus 21.9% on a total of 3897 utterances), it is striking how the distributions of the 6 'language' subdivisions are equally dissimilar for both types of addressee. No statistical tests are required to see that the language selection patterns for a Dutch addressee would be a mirror image of those for an English addressee if the actual 'pictures' were not each other's inverse. This finding strongly confirms the hypothesis that addressee is a major determinant of language selection. In addition, Table 5.2 clearly shows that there is a very strong tendency for Kate to use English with an English speaker, and Dutch with a Dutch speaker. Spearman rank correlation tests examining the relationship between the total number of utterances directed at a Dutch speaker and the number of Dutch utterances directed at a Dutch speaker show there to be a highly positive correlation ($p < .01$). The same holds, *mutatis mutandis*, for English utterances. This suggests that there is no developmental trend showing a significant change over time in Kate's tendency to use English with an English speaker and Dutch with a Dutch speaker. There is a slight change in Kate's use of non-language specific utterances over time: these start to be used only from Tape 11 onwards with an English speaker, but are used much more consistently with a Dutch speaker throughout. However, since for both types of addressee these NLS utterances account for only 1.3 and 1.2% of all utterances, any differences here are quite insignificant. From now on, NLS utterances will be excluded from any calculations and will not be discussed any further.

Table 5.2 *Kate's language selection in function of addressee* [a]

Addressing a Dutch speaker		Addressing an English speaker	
Dutch	85.7	English	89.3
English	6.3	Dutch	4.7
Mixed mainly Dutch	3.7	Mixed mainly English	3.2
Dutlish	2.5	NLS	1.2
NLS	1.3	Dutlish	0.9
Mixed mainly English	0.6	Mixed mainly Dutch	0.7
TOTALS	3044		853

[a] The decimal figures are percentages based on the totals at the bottom

The question arising from the previous finding is: how can the 'deviations' from the 'norm' in the data be explained? After all, there are still four language selection patterns that are not relatable to type of addressee.

It is possible that the language that the child was addressed in is a second major determinant of language selection. To investigate this possibility, the data were arranged in function of the language that Kate was addressed in (obviously, initiating utterances were excluded from this analysis). On a total of 2987 utterances, 89.2% were in the same language as Kate was addressed in, 7.5% were in a different language than she was addressed in, and 3.3% were very similar to the language she was addressed in (this final group includes MMD utterances in response to Dutch utterances, and MME utterances in response to English utterances). Again no developmentally determined pattern can be discerned.

It is clear that the language the child was addressed in indeed plays a major role in her language selection. Obviously, however, type of addressee and language addressed to the child are very interconnected: after all, type of addressee is defined by the language an individual usually addresses Kate in. The adults interacting with Kate during the study only very rarely address Kate in a different language than they are used to. On the few occasions that this happens, Kate tends to respond in the language addressed to her, but the data are too scant here for statistical treatment. It does seem, then, that if type of addressee and language addressed to the child are collapsed, the remaining child utterances are the 'marked' ones that need closer scrutiny.

Table 1 in the Appendix represents the data in this 'collapsed' manner. Dutlish utterances were not included: they will be analysed separately further on. English utterances in Table 1 include MME utterances as well; the same goes for Dutch and MMD utterances. If either the second or the third code in the language choice code was the same, then Kate's utterance was classified as 'language preserving' (E/MME-E or D/MMD-D). In all other cases, the utterance was classified as 'not language preserving' (E/MME-not E or D/MMD-not D).

In Table 1 the total figures for Kate's English and Dutch utterances are quite different: her English utterances are 'preserving' in only 81% of the cases, while her Dutch utterances are so in 99.2%. To see whether this difference reflects a consistent pattern throughout the study, a Wilcoxon matched pairs signed-ranks test was run on the 'preserving' data (rows E/MME-E and D/MMD-D) where there are figures available for both languages and where the number of utterances is greater than 20 per language (the numbers used for the Wilcoxon test are underlined in Table 1). The results of this test are highly revealing (N=11; T=0; one-tailed: p < .005): Kate shows a very high tendency to use Dutch only with a Dutch speaker or when addressed in Dutch, whereas the tendency to use English only with an English speaker or when addressed in English is significantly lower. A further quantitative comparison of Kate's use of Dutch with a Dutch speaker and English with an English speaker, regardless of which language the interlocutor used, suggests that the variable 'addressee' is sufficient to expose the differentiated behaviour (again, a Wilcoxon test was used with the same ground rules as for the data in Table 1 in the Appendix. Results: N=10, T=4, p [one-tailed] < .01. The data for this computation are not shown). A qualitative comparison shows that Kate's 18 Dutch utterances directed at her mother (M) are very limited in nature: more than half of them are single words, some of the remainder are repetitions of the Dutch part of a previous Mixed utterance by M, and the one or two that remain could have been classified as addressed to a Dutch as well as to an English speaker. When the English utterances directed at a Dutch speaker are considered, the picture is quite different: a whole range of utterances with varying degrees of syntactic and conceptual complexity is used here.

In order to start and approach the question as to why this differentiated behaviour *vis-à-vis* M on the one hand and A and F on the other exists, a short discussion of Kate's use of colour terms might be relevant. Dutch colour terms start to be used in larger numbers only from Tape 16 onwards. Before that, use of Dutch colour terms is only sporadic, and nearly half of them are imitations of the interlocutor's previous mention of a colour term. This is in contrast with English colour terms, which appear quite regularly from the beginning of the study. In addition, the absolute number of English colour terms is much higher than that of Dutch colour terms, despite the fact that Dutch utterances as a whole occur three times as often as English utterances. More than 30% of English colour terms appear in English utterances directed at a Dutch speaker. Most of the colour terms used in Mixed utterances are English. Thus, except for the end of the study, Kate tends to refer to colours in English rather than in Dutch. This suggests that Kate is not as familiar with Dutch as with English colour terms. Some characteristics of the child's language input may explain this: colour terms are learned mainly at Kate's English school, and at home M frequently discusses colours with Kate whereas F does not.

The preceding paragraph has shown that one possible determinant of language selection when it is not determined by addressee is reference to the colour domain. There are no other topics, however, that can be said to fulfil the same function. This is in accordance with Fantini (1978b), who reports that his bilingual children did not switch languages as a result of a change in topic.

If topic does not exert any major influence on language selection in young bilinguals, then perhaps language dominance plays an important role. Language dominance is usually defined in terms of fluency, but the problems connected with measuring fluency in one language vs. the other are quite daunting (see e.g. Baetens Beardsmore 1982, Grosjean 1982). In the present study, no experiments or association tasks could be administered, and thus it was decided to analyse the naturally occurring disfluencies in the transcript by means of a 'hesitation' code, which was applied whenever an utterance contained a disfluency in the form of a brief silence or an 'er'. In order to find out whether Kate is more fluent in one language than the other, the number of hesitations in each language per recording session was expressed as a percentage of the total number of utterances for the corresponding language. Then a Wilcoxon matched pairs signed-ranks test was run on the data where there are figures available for both languages and where the number of utterances is greater than 20 per language. The results of this test are negative: there is no statistically significant difference between the number of hesitations in Dutch vs. that in English (N=10; T=17). This means that no dominant language as measured by the number of hesitations exists. Baetens Beardsmore has suggested that the direction of 'interference' - which is defined as the occurrence of "observable features of one code used within the context of the other" (Baetens Beardsmore 1982: 40) - may show which of a bilingual's languages is the dominant one. In order to investigate this possibility, Kate's MMD and MME utterances were compared to each other (Baetens Beardsmore1982 does not define what precisely a code's 'context' is; for the purposes of this study 'context' was interpreted as meaning 'utterance'). In absolute numbers, there are many more Mixed utterances that have English words inserted into an otherwise largely Dutch utterance than the other way round. However, this finding masks the fact that there is no significant difference between MMD and MME utterances when response patterns are analysed: MMD utterances are mainly directed at a Dutch speaker, while MME utterances are mainly directed at an English speaker. This strongly suggests that the differences in the absolute numbers for MMD and MME utterances should be seen in terms of addressee-relatedness rather than language dominance.

It is clear, then, that using the measures available, no language dominance configuration for Kate can be specified. Baetens Beardsmore (1982: 30) suggests that in this case it might be better to speak of language preference, a concept introduced by Dodson (1981) to refer to the fact that bilinguals feel more at ease using one of their languages for a particular activity rather than the other. It is of course hard to measure whether a person 'feels at ease' in anything, but if frequency of occurrence patterns can be used as an indicator, then Kate's preferred language for discussing colour terms probably is English (see the discussion above). As was pointed out before, no other domain or topic can be isolated that is discussed primarily in one language rather than the other. At this point in her life, there are no strong indications that Kate has a dominant or preferred language. Hence we must look further for an explanation of Kate's language selection patterns that are not determined by the type of addressee.

It is possible that the presence of both an English and a Dutch speaker fosters the use of English in response to Dutch and vice versa. If this is true, then recording sessions where only speakers of one language are present should show a substantial reduction in the number of non-language preserving utterances. To investigate this possibility, the data were arranged according to whether they were in response to English (or an English speaker) or Dutch (or a Dutch speaker), the data base for this analysis being the same as the one used for Table 1 (see above). Within each group the percentage of preserving vs. non-preserving utterances was calculated; the results are shown in Table 2 in the Appendix.

From Table 4.3 in Chapter 4 it is clear that at recording sessions 4, 6, 18 and 19 only Dutch interlocutors were present. There is no recording session at which only an English interlocutor was present. The figures in Table 2 show that four of the five lowest percentages in the row E/MME-not E are to be found in tapes 4, 6, 18 and 19 (see the underlined numbers). This supports the hypothesis that 'type of speaker present at a recording session' is a relevant variable that helps explain the language selection patterns. However, the finding here still does not account for the significant difference in the language selection patterns for a Dutch vs. an English interlocutor: yet another explanation must be found. [1]

In the preceding we have always referred to A and F as Dutch speakers, and to M as an English speaker. This classification was arrived at on the basis of which language the adults use when addressing Kate, and is a valid classification, since F and A address Kate in Dutch as much as M addresses her in English. However, another classification is possible as well, namely one that is based on which languages the adults use within the child's hearing range. Whereas M nearly always uses one language (viz. English), this cannot be said of A and F: A and F frequently use both Dutch and English when Kate is within hearing range. They use English with M, and in addition Kate hears her father speak English with the many English-speaking guests that visit the house regularly. A and F use Dutch with each other, with Kate's grandparents and Kate herself, as well as with bilingual or Dutch-speaking visitors. When A and F use English, they do so easily and fluently. In contrast, Kate hears her mother use Dutch only in isolated sentences and in rare, brief interactions with delivery-men or the occasional plumber. M's Dutch is, as was pointed out in section 4.1, heavily accented and full of grammatical errors. It is certainly not fluent. Rather than classify A and F as Dutch speakers, then, they may as well be categorized as <u>bilingual</u> speakers. If it is accepted that Kate categorizes her main interlocutors in terms of which language(s) they use in general, then the fact that she regularly uses English with A and F but not Dutch with M is accounted for. In deciding on which languages to use with whom, the child thus relies on knowledge which she has gained through attending to the language <u>not</u> addressed to her.

The last paragraph has offered a viable solution for the 'problem' of the 'deviating' language selection patterns: the 'problem' is not a problem at all if the child is attributed a solid knowledge of her interlocutors' language abilities. The outcome of this knowledge is that she will only use the language that she is confident her IC will be able to respond in. However, if Kate knows that A and F are able to respond equally well in English as in Dutch, why does she not use more English with them? After all, the majority of her utterances addressed to them are still in Dutch, whereas if knowledge of the IC's language abilities were the only determining factor, then a 50/50 distribution would be expected. Here the role of the language actually used in the interaction takes on its importance, as well as the language habits built up over the years (and in A's case, months): Kate has of course heard her father and A use mostly Dutch with her, and this apparently prompts her in turn to use mainly Dutch with them. It is clear that while knowledge of the IC's language abilities is important in language selection, for Kate the language normally used in interaction with a particular interlocutor is a much more influential factor.

So far little attention has been given to Mixed utterances as a separate group. Does Kate use more or fewer of these as she gets older, or are there any major changes in the types of Mixed utterances over time? Table 4.5 in Chapter 4 lists the percentage of Mixed utterances in terms of the total number of utterances per recording session. When Tapes 2 and 3 (which are a-typical in many ways) are not taken into account, the distribution of these percentages is fairly normal, and the proportion of Mixed utterances over time remains more or less constant (i.e. close to 6.5%), but with a slight increase for Tapes 10 and 11. There is no major decrease or increase in the proportions of Mixed utterances in terms of their total number. Thus no developmental trend can be discerned. For MMD and MME utterances it was shown earlier that their occurrence is strongly influenced by the type of interlocutor, so a further analysis of distribution patterns is pointless. Although they are used more with a bilingual Dutch than a monolingual English speaker (see the next paragraph), the distribution of the total number of 'Dutlish' utterances per tape remains fairly constant over time, both when expressed in terms of proportion of all Mixed utterances and in absolute numbers.

Swain and Wesche (1975) found that their three-year-old English-French bilingual subject Michael used considerably more Mixed utterances when he was interacting with monolingual speakers of his two languages than when only speakers of one language were present. For Kate no such distinct behaviour can be observed: the percentages of Mixed utterances for tapes 4, 6, 18 and 19 where only bilingual Dutch speakers were present are not significantly lower than for other tapes. Of course, the difference between Kate and Michael might be linked to the fact that the latter was led to believe that his interlocutors each understood only one language, whereas Kate was quite used to hearing her Dutch interlocutors use English as well.

To see whether there are any major changes in the kinds of Mixed utterances used over time, the three types of Mixed utterances were arranged according to type of addressee. The results may be found in Table 3 in the Appendix. This table shows in more detail that indeed the occurrence of MMD and MME utterances is strongly influenced by the type of interlocutor. In addition, 'Dutlish' utterances are used significantly more frequently with a bilingual Dutch speaker than with a monolingual English speaker, and the percentage of MME utterances to a monolingual English speaker is quite a bit higher than that of MMD utterances to a bilingual Dutch speaker. This again suggests a different 'treatment' of the first versus the latter, which finding in turn constitutes the clearest evidence for the appropriateness of the initial coding distinction between MME, MMD and Dutlish utterances. In the literature, this distinction is not usually made, which is unfortunate, since thus significant regularities might go completely unnoticed. There are changes over time in the distribution of MME, MMD and Dutlish utterances per type of interlocutor, but these occur in a fairly random fashion. There is no developmental trend to be discovered, but in general the patterns found in the Totals for each addressee are present throughout (obviously, though, not much can be concluded in this respect for the Mixed utterances addressed to a monolingual English speaker, since their total amounts to just 41).

Quantitatively, then, Mixed utterances are a constant feature of Kate's language production: no major changes occur as she gets older, either in frequency patterns as a whole or in terms of the three types. The question of whether any qualitative or structural changes occur will be addressed in section 5.2. In that section it will also be discussed why Mixed utterances should occur at all.

5.1.4 *Comparisons with other bilingual children*

There are few quantitatively similar data presented in the literature that could be used as a basis for comparing the above findings. However, the few findings that are reported on support much of the preceding. Some of the relevant literature on children growing up bilingually from birth is discussed below.

Kielhöfer and Jonekeit (1983) discuss their subjects' language selection patterns in great detail although they present no quantitative data (see Chapter 2). They report that the two French-German boys in their study used mainly one language with speakers who they knew to be monolingual, but that they were much more inclined to use either language with an individual whom they knew to be bilingual. They also suggest that Mixed utterances may be a determinant of language choice, in that they may act as a 'bridge' between two languages (Kielhöfer and Jonekeit 1983: 42).

In Taeschner's (1983) work it is pointed out that the two bilingual girls reported on used Italian with their Italian monolingual father and friends, but frequently used both Italian and German with their mother, who addressed the girls mainly in German but who spoke Italian to most other people, including the girls' father. Taeschner further notes that bilingual children are more prone to using Mixed utterances with bilingual interlocutors than with monolingual addressees.

Saunders (1982) also reports that his bilingual sons initially tended to use significantly more Mixed mainly German (in the terminology used here) utterances with their father, clearly a 'bilingual German' speaker, than Mixed mainly English utterances with their mother, who used primarily English. These findings confirm the language selection patterns found for Kate.

Thus, our interpretation that Kate's language selection patterns are to a large extent determined by her knowledge of her interlocutors' linguistic abilities is corroborated by similar interpretations in at least three other studies of young bilingual children.

How does Kate's quantitative use of Mixed utterances compare with that of other young bilingual children? Unfortunately, there is little information in the literature on BFLA as far as the quantitative use of Mixed utterances is concerned: we have only been able to find two publications that deal with this aspect in any detail, viz. Swain and Wesche (1975) and Taeschner (1983).

In their much quoted article, Swain and Wesche (1975) write that their bilingual subject Michael showed "remarkably little mixing": less than 4% of his recorded multi-word utterances contained words from both languages. This low figure is not far removed from the one found for Kate's corpus.

A comparison with Taeschner's (1983) material is less straightforward. All recorded Mixed utterances (in our sense) are represented on a graph in percentages (Taeschner 1983: 170). Unfortunately, it is not indicated what these percentages are based on, and the graph only shows figures up to age 3;1. If the percentages are based on the total number of recorded utterances, then the values for the third quarter of the third year are quite high (an approximate average of 15%). The values do decrease dramatically, however, to a low average of 5%, which is more consistent with the findings for Kate. Taeschner says that most of the Mixed utterances as shown on the graph were of the type that we have called

'Dutlish', and that as her children grew older, the Mixed utterances were almost exclusively 'lexical interferences'. Whereas Taeschner's findings seem to be fairly consistent with the data in the present study for the time after her daughters' third birthdays, the data before this time are not. However, Taeschner's findings do show great differences between the two girls' behaviour, which suggests that the relative use of Mixed utterances may be strongly defined by individual preferences. Certainly much more research is needed in this area.

Although the basis available for comparisons is quite meagre, it does seem to be the case that on the whole, Kate's language selection patterns are very similar to those of other bilingual children acquiring different sets of languages. This suggests that language selection patterns are perhaps not so dependent on the individual languages being acquired, but are subject to more general constraints. Further systematic study is needed, however, to investigate what these constraints might be and to what extent they are determined by characteristics of the child's immediate environment or by more universal psycho-social factors.

5.2 Linguistic characteristics of Kate's Mixed utterances
5.2.1 *Introduction*

Mixed utterances were defined in terms of the co-occurrence within one utterance of morphemes from both languages (see section 4.2 in Chapter 4). The question now is whether there are any formal characteristics of Mixed utterances that might account for these intra-utterance language switches. In order to find a possible answer to this question we present the ensuing analysis, which will have as its focus a classification of the types of words and morphemes that occur at the switching points between language A and language B.

5.2.2 *Analysis and results*

In analysing the linguistic characteristics of Kate's Mixed utterances a primary distinction was made between MME and MMD utterances on the one hand, and 'Dutlish' utterances on the other (for a definition of the terms MME, MMD and Dutlish, see section 5.1). For MME and MMD utterances it was tabulated what part of speech the 'inserted' Dutch (for MME) and English (for MMD) elements belonged to. These 'elements' are in the most cases single, free morphemes. Occasionally, they consist of a free morpheme and a bound morpheme. There are no insertions of just a bound morpheme from the other language. This last finding is highly significant, and its importance will be discussed in the morphological analyses later on (see Chapters 6 and 7). For Dutlish utterances the point(s) was(were) defined at which an item from language B was found after one of language A (a 'switching point'), and the part of speech of the item from language B was determined. Since most Dutlish utterances consist of only two or three words, only one such switching point could be found.

In tabulating the preceding, the distinction between addressees (as in Table 3 in the Appendix) was retained (utterances addressed to an unspecified speaker were tabulated as a third category). After all, the patterns for a bilingual Dutch addressee might well be quite different from those for a monolingual English addressee. This, however, was not found to be the case: the distributions of the various types of insertions and items found at switching points in Dutlish utterances were quite similar for both types of addressee. This finding is quite significant: it suggests that although the occurrence of Mixed utterances is sociolinguistically determined, their linguistic forms are not. Since there was no need to uphold the distinctions made (i.e. for the different types of addressees), the data were collapsed according to their linguistic categories. In addition, the distinction between insertions and items found at switching points in Dutlish utterances was collapsed as well. A 'NOUN insert' thus is shorthand for 'an insertion of just a noun of language B into an utterance otherwise wholly in language A' or 'the occurrence of a noun immediately after a switching point in a Dutlish utterance'. The results can be seen in Table 4 in the Appendix.

It is clear from Table 4 that most frequently (viz. in 89.4% of all Mixed utterances), insertions (in the larger sense) consist of only one word. Insertions consisting of more than one word (row 'MORE THAN 1 insert') involve a variety of combinations. More often than not, these insertions consist of two words following each other that belong to the same syntactic constituent (e.g. a noun phrase consisting of an article and a noun, or a noun phrase consisting of an adjective and a noun). The class of 'Remaining inserts' consists of a variety of cases not covered by any of the other six groups. For these cases other major groupings would have made little sense, since the relevant utterances would consist of only one or two per grouping. One of the groups in Table 4 concerns the insertion of a preposition. Whereas this type of insertion might seem strange from the adult point of view (Baetens Beardsmore, personal communication),

Swain and Wesche (1975) have found there to be a small number of these in their material as well. It is well possible, then, that the insertion of just prepositions into otherwise unilingual sentences is a feature occurring only in young bilingual children's speech productions

Whereas it has been found that adult bilingual subjects use not only single word insertions in what we have termed Mixed utterances, but quite a few insertions of complex constituents and entire subclauses as well (see e.g. Lipski 1978, Poplack 1980, Sridhar and Sridhar 1980), it comes as no surprise that the latter are infrequent in Kate's production. After all, her knowledge of the possible structures in her two languages is only in an incipient stage at age three: Kate is just starting to use complex constituents and subclauses and she does not yet use all sentence constituents with equal ease (see the syntactic analyses in Chapter 8 below). Kate's use of mainly single-word insertions in Mixed utterances, then, can be seen as reflecting the greater limitations of her language production in general. Other bilingual children of pre-school age have also been found to use mainly single-word insertions in Mixed utterances (see Swain and Wesche 1975, Taeschner 1983).

Since most of Kate's Mixed utterances involve single-word insertions, there is not much opportunity for checking whether the constraints on the structure of Mixed utterances as put forward by Lipski (1978), Poplack (1980) and Sridhar and Sridhar (1980) apply to the Kate corpus as well. However, if one reads Kate's MMD and MME utterances as if they were fully Dutch and English respectively, then there are no structural anomalies noticeable. It is, in fact, as if insertions act as virtual synonyms (see also Sridhar and Sridhar 1980). The fact that Kate's Mixed utterances are 'well-formed' (Huerta 1977) means that the child has "internalized sufficient knowledge of either language to be able to manipulate and combine items from both of these languages into a grammatical whole" (Huerta 1977: 17). Poplack (1980) takes a similar view: in order to produce Mixed utterances ('intra-sentential switches' in Poplack's terminology), "the speaker must [...] know enough about the grammar of each language, and the way they interact, to avoid ungrammatical forms" (Poplack 1980: 605). Structurally adult-like Mixed utterances, then, show quite a sophisticated knowledge of the separate rule systems of the two languages involved, and hence cannot be invoked as evidence that a speaker has no control over these separate rule systems.

Another major finding is that noun insertions account for nearly half of all the Mixed utterances, and that while other types of insertions may be absent at some recording sessions, noun insertions are present whenever Mixed utterances are. In addition, no other type of insertion comes close to noun insertions as far as frequency goes: the difference with the next most frequent type (adjective insertions) is a full 34%. In one out of two cases, then, the very existence of Mixed utterances is determined by the usage of a single noun from the other language.

In order to investigate whether the distribution patterns as shown in Table 4 are at all correlated to the occurrence of the various parts of speech in the corpus as a whole, all the tokens of the parts of speech listed as 'inserts' in Table 4 as well as all occurrences of pronouns were counted. The results of these calculations are represented in Table 5 as percentages of the total number of lexical items per recording session.

When Tables 4 and 5 are compared with one another it is obvious that no similarity between them exists: in the full corpus, verbs form the most frequently occurring word class, with pronouns as a close second and nouns as a distant third (the OTHER category, which strictly speaking comes in third place, consists of a large variety of smaller subgroupings. It can thus be compared to the 'Remaining inserts' in Table 1, and is of equally small importance numerically). The distribution of the various word classes occurring as insertions in Mixed utterances thus does not reflect the distribution of these word classes in the corpus as a whole.

The finding here that single-word insertions in Mixed utterances most frequently are nouns strikingly resembles that of other studies of both adult and child bilinguals. Sridhar and Sridhar (1980), for instance, found that adult subjects produce quite a number of nouns when using single words in 'code-mixed' utterances.(Sridhar and Sridhar 1980 use the term 'code-mixed utterances' for what is called 'Mixed utterances' in the present study, but whereas the latter is used purely descriptively, 'code-mixing' is used as both a descriptive and a theoretically significant term.) Second in frequency were adjectives, third adverbs and fourth verbs. Nouns and adjectives are the two most frequent insertions in Kate's Mixed utterances as well, and adverbs and verbs come fourth and third. Poplack (1980) also found for adult subjects that nouns and noun phrases are amongst the most frequent items to be used as insertions in the host language. The frequency patterns of insertions found for Kate are remarkably similar to those reported by McClure (1977) in a study of Mexican-American children:

single nouns were inserted in about half of all Mixed utterances (these findings relate to the 'Junior' group), second in frequency were adjectives (most of these were colour terms), third in frequency were verbs, and fourth adverbs. This order of frequency is nearly identical to what was found for Kate, although McClure's study was methodologically very different from the present one, and although the languages investigated were Spanish and English. Lindholm and Padilla (1978b) found that their bilingual Spanish-English child subjects mostly inserted nouns in their 'lexically mixed' utterances (this term coincides with what are called 'Mixed utterances' in the present study). Swain and Wesche (1975) report that their three-year-old bilingual French-English subject most frequently substituted nouns in 'lexically mixed' utterances.

Since the findings in the latter three studies of bilingual children were based on quite different populations, and since distinct methodologies were used, the confirmation of the main finding by the present study based on naturally occurring child speech suggests that we are dealing with a psycholinguistically highly significant phenomenon: more than any other word class, it is single nouns that account for the very occurrence of Mixed utterances. This implies that there is a saliency about nouns which makes them more moveable than any other linguistic element. More studies, of course, are needed in both monolingual and bilingual research to explore this hypothesis further. [2] The evidence so far, however, does support the notion that the distribution patterns for word class insertions found for Kate are not idiosyncratic but are a consequence of more general psycholinguistic processes.

The question that arises from the preceding is: why does Kate use lexical insertions at all? Huerta (1977) and Lindholm and Padilla (1978b), for instance, have put forward the suggestion that such insertions may be the result of the child's not knowing a particular lexical item's translation equivalent (in the lay sense of the term) in the other language. [3] From the adult's point of view, the child has a 'lexical gap' as it were, which can only be filled by the word from the 'wrong' language. It must be pointed out, though, that from the child's point of view there may be no such 'lexical gap': a word may be tagged in memory as belonging to both languages, without the child realizing in any way that it in fact belongs to only one. The term 'borrowing' (see e.g. Baetens Beardsmore 1982), which implies that a word tagged for a particular language is used instead of a word tagged for the speaker's other language, would thus not appear to be generally applicable to the use of lexical insertions by young bilingual children. In addition, one should not assume that 'translation equivalents' carry the same meanings for the child.

With the above *caveats* in mind, a list was drawn up of all the single-word insertions in Kate's Mixed utterances. Colour terms were not included, since, as it was shown in the previous section, these most probably are mainly known to Kate in English only (certainly at the beginning and middle of the study). For colour terms, then, a lexical gap (from the adult's point of view) may be said to exist. The remaining single-word insertions are presented in Table 5.3.

For English and Dutch insertions we examined whether the respective translation equivalents had been produced by Kate in either a previous or the same recording session (column 1). Based on the investigator's familiarity with the situation and using the adults' utterances in the transcript, an estimate was then made of whether the respective translation equivalents were ever used in the child's home or school environment (column 2). In some cases, their most definite absence could be established, since both parents and grandparents would label an object with a word from one language only. These special 'family words' are of course known by the child in only one language. For other words, there was often no way of determining whether they were heard by the child in the other language as well. These are marked by a question mark in the relevant column. In a third column, a judgement was made as to whether Kate could be said to know both the English word and its translation equivalent. A definite 'yes' was used only when Kate had actually used a word's translation equivalent earlier or in the same tape (however, no claims are made that the elements of a pair of 'translation equivalents' are synonymous or at all related from the child's point of view). 'No' was used only when this was not the case and in addition when Kate had most probably not heard the translation equivalent used at home. A question mark was used when there were not enough data to make a decision.

First we turn to part 3 of Table 5.2, which lists Kate's use of 'blends' and lexical items containing morphemes from both languages. This list comprises only two blends. Hence, further discussion is not fruitful. It is interesting to note, however, that in monolingual child language production certain forms appear which greatly resemble the blends referred to above. De Vooys (1916) in his perceptive account of the Dutch language acquisition of his children, for instance, gives a detailed account of their use of words consisting of elements of two semantically related words. An example is *MIEG, a melting together of MUG <mosquito> and VLIEG <fly>. In young children, De Vooys writes, such words may 'stick', i.e., they may continue to be used for a long time if they are not expressly corrected (see also Vihman 1981b).

Table 5.3   *Lexical insertions in Kate's Mixed utterances* [a]

PART 1: English insertions into otherwise Dutch utterances

	Translation	1	2	3
Nouns				
boating	<varen>	no	no	no
counter	<keukenwerkblad>	no	no	no
fireplace	<open haard>	no	no	no
ice show	[no translation]	no	no	no
jelly	[no translation]	no	no	no
seaside	<kust, zee>	no	no	no
study	<studeerkamer>	no	no	no
corn	<maïs>	yes (rep. only)	probably not	probably not
lamp post	<lantaarnpaal>	no	probably not	probably not
tights	<kousen>	no	probably not	probably not
apple juice	<appelsap>	yes (rep. only)	?	probably
dinner	<eten>	no	yes	?
dress	<kleed, jurk>	no	?	?
duck	<eend>	no	?	?
face	<gezicht>	no	yes	?
fist	<vuist>	no	?	?
kitchen	<keuken>	no	yes	?
sauce	<saus>	no	?	?
shirt	<hemd>	yes (rep. only)	?	?
strawberry	<aardbei>	yes (rep. only)	?	?
suit	<pak>	no	?	?
toys	<speelgoed>	no	?	?
song	<liedje>	yes	?	yes
ball	<voetbal>	yes	yes	yes
beaker	<beker>	yes	yes	yes
present	<kado, geschenk>	yes	yes	yes
spoon	<lepel>	yes	yes	yes
tea	<thee>	yes	yes	yes
train	<trein>	yes	yes	yes
tree	<boom>	yes	yes	yes
Verbs				
broke	<is gebroken>	no	?	?
look	<kijk>	no	yes	?

paste	<plakken>	no	?	?
cook	<koken>	yes	yes	yes
throw	<gooi>	yes	yes	yes

Miscellaneous

just	<zomaar, alleen>	no	probably not	probably not
back	<terug>	no	yes	?
full of	<vol (met)>	no	yes	?
I think	<ik denk>	no	yes	?
off	<uit> [b]	no	yes	?
when	<als>	no	yes	?
also	<ook>	yes	yes	yes
this	<dit>	yes	yes	yes
on	<op> [c]	yes	yes	yes
then	<dan>	yes	yes	yes
with	<met> [d]	yes	yes	yes

PART 2: Dutch insertions into otherwise English utterances

	Translation	1	2	3

Nouns

boebel	<bump>	no	no	no
kermis	<fair>	no	probably not	probably not
bos	<woods>	no	?	?
schop	<shovel>	no	?	?
emmer	<bucket>	no	yes	?
frigo	<fridge>	no	yes	?
kin	<chin>	no	yes	?
koek	<cake>	no	yes	?
melk	<milk>	no	yes	?
mond	<mouth>	no	yes	?
slaapkamer	<bedroom>	no	yes	?
spiegel	<mirror>	no	yes	?
streep	<stripe>	no	yes	?
telloor	<plate>	no	yes	?
vliegtuig	<airplane>	no	yes	?
water	<water>	no	yes	?
banaan	<banana>	yes	yes	yes
fietsje	<bike>	yes	yes	yes
kussen	<cushion>	yes	yes	yes
schoenen	<shoes>	yes	yes	yes
vuilbak	<garbage>	yes	yes	yes
zetel	<chair>	yes	yes	yes

Miscellaneous

alleen	<only>	no	yes	?
[kaput]	<broken>	no	yes	?
op	<finished: all gone>	no	yes	?
klaar	<finished: all done>	yes	yes	yes

| ook | <also> | yes | yes | yes |

PART 3: *Blends and lexical items consisting of morphemes from both English and Dutch*

	Consists of:	Fully E or D word used earlier or in the same tape?	Single-language term known in D and E?
Nouns			
[o:lə]	E ALL + D plural morph.	E ALL and D AL DE	yes
['mu:zik]	E ['mjuzik] + D [my'zi.k]	E MUSIC and D MUZIEK	yes
[i:ren]	E EAR + D plural morph.	no: E EARS/EAR, D OOR/OREN never occur	?
karpijt	E CARPET + D TAPIJT	no: E CARPET or D TAPIJT never occur	?
Verbs			
boaten	E BOAT + D infinitive morph.	no: E verb BOAT or D VAREN never occur, but E BOATING does occur once	probably not
[laikt]	E LIKE + D 3rd person sg. present tense morph.	E LIKE, not D HOUDEN VAN	probably not
[mu:ft]	E MOVE + D 3rd person sg. present tense morph.	E MOVED, never D BEWEEGT	probably not
touchen	E TOUCH + D infinitive morph.	no: E TOUCH or D AANRAKEN never occur	probably not
cooken	E COOK + D infinitive morph.	E COOK and D KOKEN	yes
eaten	E EAT + D infinitive morph.	E EAT and D ETEN	yes
looken	E LOOK + D infinitive morph.	E LOOK and D KIJKEN	yes
tellen	E TELL + D infinitive morph.	E TELL and D ZEGGEN	yes
throwt	E THROW + D 3rd person sg present tense morph.	E THROW and D GOOI	yes

a   'rep.' stands for 'repetition'; 'morph.' stands for 'morpheme'.
b   I.e. used as Subject Complement.
c   I.e. used as preposition.

d   It should be noted that before the occurrence of WITH in MMD utterances, Kate uses Dutch MET always in its instrumental meaning; in MMD utterances, however, WITH never has this instrumental meaning, but is used in the meaning of 'together with'.

Although it is still quite short, the list of lexical items in part 3 of Table 5.3 containing morphemes from both languages is somewhat longer. In the literature, similar forms have been reported on (see e.g. Saunders 1982, Kielhöfer and Jonekeit 1983, Taeschner 1983), and on the whole they seem to occur as infrequently as is the case in the Kate corpus. While these forms are non-existent in Kate's language environment and thus are highly marked in her speech production (this is one reason why they were listed separately in Table 5.3), they are qualitatively no different from lexical insertions.

As part 3 of Table 5.3 shows, all the items listed happen to be English free morphemes with Dutch suffixes added to them. There is no way of telling whether this is a coincidence or not. The occurrence of these forms in otherwise wholly Dutch utterances is highly significant, however, since the functional markers (the bound morphemes in this case) fit in with the main language of the utterance. In the morphological analyses later on this point will be dealt with further, especially in relation to our proposed principle of morphological language stability (see Chapters 6 and 7). Another important point here is that, since these 'bilingual' items have never been heard by the child, her production of them is the result of creative analysis: these forms would not have been possible without some sort of 'knowledge' about Dutch infinitive and third person singular present tense endings.

It is clear from parts 1 and 2 of Table 5.3 that most frequently there is not enough material available to decide whether an item fills a lexical gap or not. It can, after all, not be assumed that a word's translation equivalent is not known simply because it is not present in the transcripts. Swain and Wesche (1975) were more fortunate in this respect: about half of the insertions in their subject's Mixed utterances were used in "the equivalent word in the other language" (Swain and Wesche 1975: 18) while the investigators were present to observe them. Table 5.3 does show, however, that in a number of cases a word from language A is inserted into language B although the equivalent in language B was used before. In these cases, then, the lexical gap hypothesis is no satisfactory explanation for the use of other-language insertions, and so other explanations must be found.

Swain and Wesche (1975) found that an item's insertion could be attributed to its occurrence previously in the conversation. They speculate that "increased availability of an alternative item in another language in the form of a memory trace may shortcut normal lexical retrieval" (Swain and Wesche 1975: 19), resulting in a Mixed utterance. While occasionally the inserted element in a Mixed utterance by Kate had occurred earlier in the interaction, no main effect of this on the choice of insertions could be discerned.

Kielhöfer and Jonekeit (1983) argue that the occurrence of Mixed utterances is determined by the language that a concept was first learned in, or by the frequency of a particular item in one language rather than the other in the child's environment. It is a pity that no quantitative data are presented to support these interesting hypotheses. [4] Saunders (1982) suggests that a lexical insertion from language A in language B (a 'lexical transfer' as Saunders calls it) may be used by the child "to make a [semantic] distinction in one language which is normally not made in the other" (Saunders 1982: 198). The data from Kate, unfortunately, do not allow the above valuable suggestions to be investigated. Finally, Huerta (1977) proposes 'language preference' as an explanation for insertion in Mixed utterances in cases where lexical equivalents exist.

In conclusion, then, other-language insertions in Mixed utterances addressed to a bilingual Dutch speaker may be the result of one or a combination of the following: the existence of a 'lexical gap', easier retrievability from memory because of previous mention, earlier learning or higher frequency in input, or even perceptual saliency ('perceptual saliency' is particularly mentioned by Lindholm and Padilla (1978b). Unfortunately they do not offer an operational definition of this term, which makes it difficult to see how exactly perceptual saliency accounts for their data). Other factors may be important as well.

As was seen in section 5.1, however, while Mixed utterances addressed to a bilingual Dutch speaker follow Kate's general tendency not to exclusively use Dutch with such a bilingual speaker, the occurrence of Mixed utterances addressed to a monolingual English speaker is fairly anomalous, since Kate exhibits a very strong preference for addressing a monolingual English speaker only in English. It is argued, therefore, that Kate's Mixed utterances addressed to an English speaker are for the most part slips of the tongue. Although this explanation is hardly ever mentioned in the literature, a few other researchers on child bilingualism have made this suggestion as well (see Bergman 1977, Kielhöfer and Jonekeit 1983). In adult bilinguals, Mixed utterances directed at a strictly monolingual speaker will be very rare or even non-existent (see e.g. Grosjean 1982). If they do occur, they will be repaired promptly, since the adult has available the use of a sophisticated repair mechanism. The young child, however, does not possess quite this level of sophistication yet, and so insertions from another language that are sociolinguistically inappropriate remain unrepaired. As later analysis will show (see Chapter 10), there is a dramatic increase in Kate's use of spontaneous repairs and other signs of language awareness around the age of 3;3. Before this time, spontaneous repairs occur very infrequently. This can be seen to indicate that Kate's repair mechanism is not quite as sophisticated as after the age of 3;3, and that consequently repairs to 'inappropriate' Mixed utterances - i.e, Mixed utterances that are inappropriate within the child's system, since they do not follow her preferred pattern of using just English with a monolingual English speaker - are simply not yet in the realm of what Kate is capable of doing.

We briefly return to our suggestion above that in Kate's Mixed utterances addressed to a primarily monolingual speaker we are dealing with speech errors or slips of the tongue. What could be the reason for their occurrence? Slips of the tongue might be seen as the result of insufficient pre-production editing (or 'covert monitoring' - see Laver 1973). In the language production process, 'competing plans' (Fromkin 1980b) may be present at the same time, i.e. two possible forms, only one of which is really appropriate, may have been activated simultaneously from memory storage and are both ready to be produced. Since only one of the forms can actually be produced (it is impossible to produce two words at the same time - except perhaps in blends), the monitor (see Chapter 10) must make a decision between the two forms in 'competition' (see also Bowerman 1985). Occasionally, the monitor makes an inappropriate decision, resulting in an utterance that must be edited. In a bilingual, two competing forms may be cross-language (near-) synonyms. The production of a form from language A in an utterance largely in language B can then be seen as not very different from the monolingual's choice of the 'wrong' word. As Lattey writes: "speech errors, slips of the tongue, and bilingual code-switches are related" (Lattey 1981: 49). When 'code-switches' occur "in the context of monolinguals" (Lattey 1981: 50), we are dealing with 'slips of the bilingual tongue' (Lattey's term). Although Kate's Mixed utterances addressed to a bilingual Dutch speaker are structurally identical to those addressed to a monolingual speaker, the former are not 'slips of the bilingual tongue': they are simply realizations of one of two competing forms from different languages where the choice for the one vs. the other is not necessarily clear, i.e. the status of the two forms, as long as they express the speaker's communicative intentions, is identical. It is the sociolinguistic situation which determines whether it is meaningful to speak of 'slips of the tongue' or not.

In conclusion, then, the main linguistic characteristic of Kate's Mixed utterances is that they are Mixed due to the insertion of single-word items from language A in an utterance that is otherwise completely in language B. More often than not, the single-word insertions are nouns. Mixed utterances are not necessarily sociolinguistically inappropriate: whether they are so or not highly depends on who they are addressed to. Structurally, however, Mixed utterances with more than two or three words follow the regularities existing in the main language of the utterance. As such, these Mixed utterances cannot be seen as evidence that the bilingual child does not make use of two separate language systems. Instead, they show her creative manipulation of the tools for fluent speech production: a bilingual lexicon, and two closed linguistic rule systems. It is those linguistic rule systems that we turn to next.

Notes
1 It should be noted that this difference again appears in Table 2 (results of a Wilcoxon matched-pairs test run on the rows D/MMD-D and E/MME-E: N=11, T=5, p [one-tailed] <.005).
2 There is at least one study of monolingual speakers that indicates that single nouns have a special status in speech processing: in his study of speech errors made by Dutch adult speakers, Nooteboom found that "substantives in particular seem to have more chance of attracting slips of the tongue than any other word class" (Nooteboom 1969: 123-124).
3 From a theoretical point of view, however, it is valid (and necessary) to question whether 'true' translation equivalents can actually exist, and if so, what the theoretical repercussions of this are.
4 Kielhöfer and Jonekeit (1983) also maintain that insertions in Mixed utterances may be used quite consciously because the inserted item is felt to express a particular meaning more adequately than its equivalent in the other language. While this may be relevant to more mature bilinguals, it is not clear that the subject matters that three-year-olds usually talk about already pose these problems of subtlety.

6 *The noun phrase*

English and Dutch noun phrases are quite similar on the functional level. They express similar meanings and pragmatic functions, and can be used in similar syntactic positions. However, whereas the internal structure of singular noun phrases and the types of items that can feature within them are fairly similar for both adult English and Dutch, there are major differences in the paradigmatic choices that need to be made: in English, a natural gender rule is used which operates on personal and possessive pronouns, but not on articles, adjectives, or demonstrative pronouns. In Dutch, on the other hand, a syntactic gender system largely determines the form of all these five types of elements, in combination with a natural gender rule which applies to some pronominal elements only. In order to approximately speak like most of the people around her, then, one of Kate's main tasks in learning to produce formally acceptable singular noun phrases lies in the marking of syntactic-cum-natural gender in Dutch and the marking of just natural gender in English. Furthermore, Kate will also have to learn that Dutch plurals are more variable in form than English ones, and that Dutch uses a productive diminutive suffix whereas English does not. Just applying the rules from one language to the other, then, will not work: this would result in non-adult-like overgeneralizations, or non-adult-like underextensions.

In the following, we shall examine to what extent Kate produces overgeneralized or underextended patterns within any one language that can be seen as the result of the application of a rule or mechanism from the other language.

The areas that we shall be focussing on are Kate's handling of the respective gender systems, plural formation, the use of diminutives, noun phrases with an adjective as head and noun phrase-internal syntagmatic structure.

6.1 The marking of gender
6.1.1 *The adult systems*
As was said above, Dutch and English differ quite markedly as far as the marking of gender goes. English has no syntactic gender, whereas Dutch does. Both English and Dutch formally express natural gender, but the extent to and manner in which this is done in each differ markedly. Rather than offer a contrastive presentation of the English and Dutch gender systems, though, we shall indicate the main characteristics of each language's gender system separately, and only occasionally make some comparative/contrastive comments.

Note that in all of the following, we shall be concerned with the gender marking system insofar as it is used to refer to singular, specific, definite referents. Hence, we shall not discuss the use of gender marked forms to refer to any class of beings in general (such as 'man' in its sense of 'any member of the human race', or 'the ordinary tabby' in its sense of 'any member of the class of ordinary tabbies').

In English, only some personal and possessive pronouns can be used to express gender distinctions. These gender distinctions are mainly based on a natural gender rule, interacting with an animacy rule.

The pronouns IT and ITS are most generally used to refer to inanimate referents and to animate, non-human referents which are not specified for sex. Whereas an inanimate singular referent will virtually always be referred to by IT or ITS, except in case of personification (Mills 1986c: 23), animate, non-human referents can easily be referred to by either the feminine or masculine pronouns. Whether a speaker will actually do so, highly depends on a speaker's knowledge of the referent's sex, on a speaker's desire to mark a referent's sex or other variables (again, personification may be such a variable) (see Mills 1986c: 21 and 23).

Any one of the trio HE/HIM/HIS is primarily used to refer to male human beings. Similarly, any one of the trio SHE/HER/HERS is primarily used to refer to female human beings. Since there is usually a one-to-one relationship between the two trios HE/HIM/HIS and SHE/HER/HERS on the one hand and biological gender on the other, these pronouns are called the natural gender pronouns. The natural gender pronouns, however, are not exclusively used to refer to human beings of either sex: their second main use is to refer to non-human animates when the sex of these referents is accessible. Thirdly, the natural gender pronouns may be used to indicate a personification of a non-human, animate referent or of an inanimate referent. This use, however, can be seen as peripheral. The main features of the English gender system have been summarized in Table 6.1. 'Personification' use of the natural gender pronouns was not included. For a more detailed and complete description of the English gender system, see Mills (1986c).

Table 6.1 *The basic English adult gender pronoun system*

From form to referent					
IT/ITS		HE/HIM/HIS		SHE/HER/HERS	
inanimate	animate	+ human	animate	+ human	animate
	- human	male	- human	female	- human
	gender		male		female
	indeterminate				

From referent to form	
inanimate	IT/ITS
animate, - human, gender indeterminate	IT/ITS
animate, - human, male	IT/ITS/HE/HIM/HIS
animate, - human, female	IT/ITS/SHE/HER/HERS
animate, + human, male	HE/HIM/HIS
animate, + human, female	SHE/HER/HERS

In the Dutch adult gender system a combination of elements plays a role in determining the exact shape that noun phrases (NP's) will actually take. In many cases, a syntactic gender system regulates the choice of personal and demonstrative pronouns, definite articles, and the forms of some adjectives. In addition, there exists a natural gender-cum-animacy rule which applies to pronominalized elements only, and which operates either on the basis of the syntactic gender system, or independently of this. The interplay between the syntactic and the semantic rules here is not always obvious, and in some cases there may be a conflict between them, in which case discourse elements may determine the choice of pronoun.

It should be noted that pronominal reference to non-human entities (both animate and inanimate) is not a straightforward matter. Indeed, there exist a number of preferential differences between speakers of standard Dutch. These differences are greatest between Belgian speakers of Dutch and Dutch speakers of Dutch (see e.g. Geerts, Haeseryn, de Rooij and van den Toorn 1982, de Vriendt to appear).

Broadly speaking, in pronominal reference to non-human entities by means of personal pronouns, Dutch speakers of Dutch mainly draw a distinction between neuter and non-neuter singular nouns, and they will refer to these by HET <it> and HIJ/HEM <he/him> respectively, even when the referent is a female animate being such as KOE <cow>. This practice, however, is a tendency, and since not all Dutch speakers of Dutch use a pronominal binary system (see e.g. de Vriendt to appear) we cannot really speak of a 'rule'. In fact, the standard Dutch personal pronoun system (both in the Netherlands and in Belgium) is very much in a state of flux (De Jonghe and De Geest 1985: 59; de Vriendt to appear).

Belgian speakers of Dutch do not, by and large, employ a pronominal binary system. Rather, in their choice of personal pronoun they are still primarily led by a three-way syntactic gender system distinguishing between neuter, feminine and masculine gender (de Vriendt to appear). Historically, this three-way syntactic gender system used to be expressed in the article and demonstrative pronoun systems as well (see e.g. Rijpma and Schuringa 1971), but in the standard variety of Dutch spoken in Belgium and the Netherlands this appears not to be the case any more: instead, there is a two-way syntactic gender system which distinguishes between neuter and non-neuter singular common nouns (Rijpma and Schuringa 1971).

Since there are such important differences between the standard Dutch as spoken in the Netherlands and as spoken in Belgium, it is crucial to decide what kind of system Kate was exposed to. de Vriendt (to appear) points out that, with some exceptions, Belgian speakers find the Dutch 'pronominal habits' to be quite odd indeed. I would venture to say that Kate's father, who is her Dutch language model on a daily basis, is not a typical Belgian speaker of standard Dutch, and that consequently, he produces some of these 'odd' pronouns: due to his many contacts with Dutch speakers of Dutch and his profession, his knowledge of standard Dutch as spoken in the Netherlands is quite profound, and his sociolinguistic allegiance is perhaps more oriented towards the Netherlands than to Belgium. It seems fair to say that in his personal pronoun usage, he represents some middle ground between the 'Northern' habits (with the system based on two syntactic genders only) and the 'Southern' habits (with the system based on three syntactic genders): for inanimate referents, he tends to follow the neuter/non-neuter distinction, i.e. he does not usually distinguish between masculine and feminine

The noun phrase 119

gender within the class of non-neuter nouns. In referring to non-human animates, he would use ZE/HAAR <she/her> only in the very most obvious cases of female sex (for instance, in the case of KOE <cow> and KIP <chicken>). Otherwise, he would use HIJ/HEM <he/him>. Of course, Kate is not exclusively exposed to the Dutch that her father uses, but interacts with both Flemish and Dutch speakers from various dialect backgrounds. It is obvious, then, that pronoun usage in her entire Dutch input will be quite variable, with the entire range of possibilities present. However, since her closest and most regular contact with Dutch is mainly embodied by her father, it was his system that was taken as a basis for Table 6.2, which summarizes the basic elements of the Dutch adult gender system.

Table 6.2 *The basic Dutch adult gender system* [a]

Articles and demonstrative determiners in complex NP's	Syntactic gender	Natural gender	Animacy
DE/DIE/DEZE <the/that/this>	non-neuter	0	0
HET/DAT/DIT <the/that/this>	neuter	0	0

Independent demonstrative pronouns	Syntactic gender	Natural gender	Animacy
DIE/DEZE <that-one/this-one>	non-neuter	0	0
DIE/DEZE <that-one/this-one>	neuter	0	animate
DAT/DIT <that-one/this-one>	neuter	0	0

Third person singular personal pronouns (Subject and object forms)	Syntactic gender	Natural gender	Animacy
HET <it>	neuter	0	0
HIJ/HEM <he, him>	non-neuter	{irrelevant}	inanimate
HIJ/HEM <he, him>	0	indeterminate/male	animate
ZE/HAAR <she, her>	0	female	animate

[a] a zero (0) mark means that any of the possibilities within the corresponding category may be used

As can be seen from Table 6.2, singular definite articles and demonstrative determiners exclusively mark the neuter/non-neuter syntactic gender distinction: they never mark natural gender or animacy.

Natural gender is obviously restricted to animate referents, and there is a three-term distinction between male, female, and indeterminate gender. Only the pronouns HIJ/HEM and ZE/HAAR can be used to distinguish natural gender (cf. the situation in English), but note that, unlike with the English pair HE/HIM, the use of HIJ/HEM is not restricted to male beings: when an animate being's gender is indeterminate, the Dutch speaker has the choice between HIJ/HEM (focusing on the referent's animacy, not natural gender) or HET (which can only be used if the referent's syntactic gender is neuter). In English, an animate being with indeterminate gender would normally (except in cases of personification) be referred to by IT/ITS.

Note that English SHE and Dutch ZE come close to being translation equivalents (their use is equivalent for animate reference); English HE and Dutch HIJ, on the other hand, are not functionally equivalent in the adult system (the use of HIJ includes that of HE and many other uses - compare Tables 6.1 and 6.2).

'Animacy' in Table 6.2 refers to the animate-inanimate distinction. For the independent demonstrative pronouns DIE/DEZE and DAT/DIT, animacy plays a role insofar that it can override syntactic gender. Natural gender never acts as a basis for a choice between DIE/DEZE on the one hand and DAT/DIT on the other. In the choice of third person singular personal pronouns, the syntactic gender of animate nouns can play a role only if these nouns have been previously mentioned in discourse; the syntactic gender of inanimate nouns, on the other hand, plays a major (but not exclusive) role in all cases.

The three categories (syntactic gender, natural gender and animacy) do not interact with each other in any predictable manner, i.e. no rules of the type "an animate noun will mostly have non-neuter gender" can be formulated (although there are certain tendencies of co-occurrence). The following examples reveal some of the complexities involved in pronominal reference by means of TPSP's (for a more in-depth description of the Dutch system, see Geerts, Haeseryn, de Rooij and van den Toorn 1982):

(1) 'Het meisje' <the girl> : 'meisje' refers to an animate female referent and is a neuter noun (hence the use of the article HET). Later pronominal reference to 'meisje' can, in some restricted stylistic contexts, occur through HET (focussing on syntactic gender) or, more usually, through ZE (focussing on natural gender and animacy).
(2) 'De koe' <the cow> : 'koe' refers to an animate female referent and is a non-neuter noun (hence the use of the article DE). Later pronominal reference to 'koe' may occur through HIJ (focussing on non-neuter syntactic gender) or ZE (focussing on natural gender, or, alternatively, on feminine syntactic gender).
(3) 'Die vork' <that fork> : 'vork' refers to an inanimate referent and is a non-neuter noun (hence the use of the demonstrative DIE). Later pronominal reference to 'vork' can occur through HIJ or ZE, depending on whether the speaker makes a masculine-feminine distinction within the class of non-neuter inanimate nouns (see previous discussion).
(4) 'Deze vis' <this fish> : 'vis' refers to an animate referent with indeterminate gender and is a non-neuter noun (hence the use of the demonstrative DEZE). Later pronominal reference to 'vis' can occur only through HIJ (it so happens that 'vis' historically has masculine syntactic gender - here, then, applying the 'non-neuter'- rule or the 'historical gender'-rule have the same effect).
(5) 'De soep' <the soup> : 'soep' refers to an inanimate referent and is a non-neuter noun. Later pronominal reference to 'soep' can occur through HIJ, ZE, or, in some cases, HET. [1]
(6) 'Het mes' <the knife> : 'mes' refers to an inanimate referent and is a neuter noun. Later pronominal reference to 'mes' can occur through HET.

Besides determiners and pronouns, there is another type of word-class that may be used to mark syntactic gender, viz. changeable adjectives (not shown in Table 6.2). These adjectives can occur in their root form or in a form in which an {–e}-suffix is added to this root (Extra 1978 provides a clear succinct overview of which adjectives are changeable and which are not). The root + {–e} form in standard Dutch is mostly used in front of singular non-neuter nouns and all plural nouns, as e.g., in DIE LAGE PRIJS <that low price>, where LAGE is the root + {–e} form of LAAG. The root form is mostly used in front of neuter nouns preceded by an indefinite determiner, although when the adjective is preceded by HET/DAT/DIT, a possessive pronoun or a genitive, the root + {–e} form may be used as well. Here again there are differences between Belgian speakers of Dutch and Dutch speakers of Dutch (de Vriendt to appear), with Dutch speakers predominantly using the root + {–e} form and Belgian speakers the root form only. Some examples are:

(7) 'groen water' <green water> : zero article + adjective in root form + neuter noun

(8) (a) 'het groene water' <the green water> : definite article + adjective in root + {–e} form + neuter noun (this is typical of 'Northern' use) [2]
(8) (b) 'het groen water' <the green water> : definite article + adjective in root form + neuter noun (this is typical of 'Southern' use).

6.1.2 *Analysis and results*

The data base for the present investigation consists of two major sets of material: first, the use of definite articles and modifying demonstratives in complex noun phrases (complex NP's contain a singular head and at least one determiner), and second, the use of TPSP's and independent demonstratives (although in the adult systems modifying possessives take part in the gender system as well, third person possessives did not occur frequently enough in the data to be included in any detailed discussion here).

As far as complex NP's are concerned, the material under investigation quite clearly shows unique patterns for each language: in Dutch, Kate uses various kinds of morphological markers that are relevant to the syntactic gender system, whereas in English all forms reflect the input language, that is to say, no syntactic gender marking is apparent. In the following subsection, then, only the Dutch data will be discussed.

6.1.2.1 The marking of syntactic gender: Dutch

In order to construct fully appropriate complex NP's in standard Dutch, the speaker must have discovered three related features: first, that there are basically two types of singular nouns, and that their difference is determined by the kinds of determiners and modifiers they can be combined with. Since there exists a complementary distribution of the relevant markers (cf. e.g. Rijpma and Schuringa 1971), a decision for one type or the other determiner or adjective must be made. There are few morphological, phonological or semantic aspects which indicate whether a noun is neuter or non-neuter. As Deutsch and Wijnen note, there seems to be "no correlation between the article form and the phonetic structure of a simple noun" (Deutsch and Wijnen 1985: 749), but "there are some correlations involving noun affixes" (ibid.). The most relevant of these for child language is the class of diminutive nouns, which are all neuter (although their non-diminutive form may be non-neuter). A second major point is that the speaker must know which are the actual forms of the various determiners and adjectives that express the distinction between

The noun phrase 123

nouns and which are not. Finally, the speaker must have discovered what nouns can be combined with what gender marking forms.

The acquisition data show that Kate has learned the first feature. Secondly, she has isolated most of the forms that are used to mark syntactic gender distinctions in Dutch. Thirdly, she is still fully in the process of learning the third feature, i.e. what nouns can be combined with what gender marking forms. The relevant data for these claims are summarized in Table 6.3 (a detailed breakdown of all the relevant data may be found in Table 6 in the Appendix).

Table 6.3   *Kate's use of syntactic gender marking in singular NP's* [a]

	Non-neuter	Neuter	Total
The use of zero article and the indefinite article			
zero article	68 %	32 %	164
indefinite article	61 %	39 %	94
The use of determiners			
	Non-neuter	Neuter	Total
DE/DIE	85 % (234)	<u>15 % (42)</u>	276
HET/DAT	<u>12 ± 4 % (4)</u>	88 ± 4% (29)	33
Appropriate vs. inappropriate use of all determiners and changeable modifying adjectives			
	Non-neuter	Neuter	Total
appropriate	246	45	291 (83%)
inappropriate	12	46	58 (17%)
TOTAL	258 (74%)	91 (26%)	**349**

[a]   non-adult-like usage is underlined

The fact that Kate has learnt that there are different kinds of singular nouns and that this difference is marked by the types of determiners and modifiers they are combined with, is clearly shown by the very fact that she uses formally different determiners and modifiers that are functionally equivalent, viz. HET, DE, DAT, DIE, modifying adjectives in the root form and modifying adjectives in the form with {-e} (DIT and DEZE do not occur as demonstrative determiners in the corpus). In addition, a number of neuter nouns are treated differently from non-neuter nouns, although 50% of all neuter nouns following a determiner or changeable adjective are treated as if they were non-neuter (see the third part of Table 6.3). Some examples are:

(9) 'Ik stap uit op de garage' (Age: 2;7,17)
    <I'm getting out at the garage.>
        {appropriate use of DE with a non-neuter noun}
(10) 'Ga bij bij bij de andere leeuw.' (Age: 2;9)
    <Go to to to the other lion.>
        {appropriate use of DE and an adjective in root + {–e} form with a non-neuter noun}
(11) 'De vis gaat in het water!' (Age: 2;10,5)
    <The fish is going into the water!>
        {appropriate use of DE with a non-neuter noun and of HET with a neuter noun}

It was claimed above that Kate has isolated most of the forms that are used to mark syntactic gender distinctions in Dutch. This implies that she has also learned which determiners are irrelevant to the gender marking system (e.g. zero article and the indefinite article EEN). That this is indeed the case is shown by the absence of any tendency to use only neuter nouns with zero article and non-neuter nouns with the indefinite article or vice versa (see the first part of Table 6.3). The proportions of use of both these articles with both types of nouns are virtually the same, and closely follow the distribution of neuter vs. non-neuter singular nouns in the whole of the corpus (for every 10 singular nouns, 7 are non-neuter). Furthermore, whenever a definite article is inappropriately omitted (there are only 15 such cases in the entire corpus), there are as many errors on neuter as on non-neuter nouns (7 cases where DE is missing vs. 8 where HET is missing). Errors involving the use of EEN instead of a definite article occur only twice, so no conclusions can be drawn here.

The claim that Kate only marks syntactic gender through forms which in the adult system can do so as well is further substantiated by the distribution patterns for the two types of nouns when preceded by a definite article: the middle section of Table 6.2 show a marked differential treatment of both types of nouns when they are preceded by DE/DIE vs. HET/DAT (the picture is the reverse for these), and the extent of this differential treatment in each case is larger than one would expect on the basis of the overall distribution of neuter vs. non-neuter nouns in the corpus. This is quite different from the usage patterns for zero article and the indefinite article (cf. the top part of Table 6.2 and the preceding paragraph).

While Kate can be seen to have isolated most of the forms that are used to mark syntactic gender distinctions in Dutch, there is evidence that she has not fully learned that HET can function as an article. In the following, we shall try to substantiate this claim.

In the corpus, HET occurs in quite different ways from DE. The frequency of occurrence of DE is significantly related to the number of Dutch utterances per recording session, whereas occurrence of HET appears to be quite random: there is no link with the total number of Dutch utterances per recording session, and there is no obvious relationship between age and occurrence of HET either (for detailed figures, see Table 6 in the Appendix) [3]. The types of combinations that both definite articles enter into are quite different as well: DE is clearly overgeneralized, in the sense that it is often used in circumstances where it is non-adult-like to do so, viz. in combination with neuter nouns (see example 12). This is in contrast with HET, which is nearly always used in an adult-like fashion, i.e. in combination with a neuter noun (on 21 occasions, HET is used with a neuter noun, vs. three instances where it is used with a non-neuter noun). Furthermore, inappropriate use of DE - with 34 instances - far exceeds appropriate use of HET - with 21 instances - (for more detail, compare parts C.a and C.b in Table 6 in the Appendix).

(12) 'Ze gaan naar de park!' (Age: 2;10,13)
<They're going to the park.>
{inappropriate use of DE with a neuter noun}

In the corpus under investigation, diminutives are never used with HET (contrary to adult usage), although they do occur with the non-adult-like DE (see examples 13 and 14). On the basis of cases like the one in example 14, one might argue that the use of DE with diminutives is linked to the non-neuter syntactic gender of the base forms. However, while DE does occur in front of diminutives which have a non-neuter base form, there are quite a number of diminutives which have a neuter base form and are still preceded by DE: for every ten diminutives, seven have a non-neuter base form and three a neuter one. This pattern follows the overall distribution of non-neuter vs. neuter nouns in the corpus.

If Kate fully knew that HET is an article, and that it is functionally equivalent to the other definite article DE, it would be very easy for her to combine HET with a diminutive, even long before she has learnt which non-diminutives are neuter and which are not. After all, in the input language there are no exceptions for diminutives: they form a class of neuter nouns that are morphologically clearly marked as distinct from any other noun, namely by the addition of the suffix {–je} (which can have various allomorphs) to the singular form of the noun (see section 6.3 below). They are never used with the non-neuter article DE or the non-neuter demonstratives DIE or DEZE in the adult system, and since Dutch-speaking adults often use diminutives when talking to young children (Snow, Arlman-Rupp, Hassing, Jobse, Joosten and Vorster 1976), and frequently use only the diminutive form of a particular lexical item rather than its non-diminutive variant, it is particularly peculiar that Kate should never use diminutives with their appropriate definite article.

One could object to the reasoning in the preceding paragraph that incomplete knowledge of HET's article-status accounts for the non-adult-like use of DE with diminutives by pointing out that perhaps Kate might not yet see diminutives as a separate form class, and that it is lack of this piece of knowledge that is the stumbling block as far as non-usage of HET is concerned. This hypothesis can be rejected, though, since there is ample evidence that Kate treats diminutives as a separate form class (see section 6.3 below).

(13) 'Wa doe de aapje nu?' (Age: 2;10,13)
    <Wha's the monkey doing now?>
    {inappropriate use of DE with a diminutive}
(14) Investigator: 'Waar ben je geweest?' <Where did you go?>
    Kate: 'Op - op de wieleke?' [with rising intonation] (Age: 3;2,7)
      <On - on the little wheel?>
      {inappropriate use of DE with a diminutive}
    Investigator: 'Mm?' [request for clarification]
    Kate: 'De - de grote wiel'. (Age: 3;2,7)
      <The - the big wheel.> [i.e. at the fairground]
      {inappropriate use of DE with a neuter noun but appropriate use of the root
      + {–e} form of the adjective}

The as yet not fully established status of HET as an article is further evidenced by its patterns of occurrence: the article HET is used in only 9% of all NP's with a definite article and a noun, whereas DE is used in 91%. One might argue that this difference can be explained by the higher frequency in the corpus of non-neuter nouns. While this element may indeed play a role, one would still expect this difference to be less pronounced, since neuter nouns in the corpus occur in a 3 to 7 proportion as compared to non-neuter nouns. A final point is that when the article HET appears at all, it is never followed by an adjective and noun combination, whereas such a combination frequently follows DE.

If Kate had fully learned that HET is in fact an article, and if the problem was only to discover which nouns go with HET and which with DE, one would not expect to see the many restrictions on the usage of HET, and most certainly, the very clear overgeneralization strategy that is apparent now would not occur. That at least a beginning has been made towards the realization that HET is an article is shown by the occasional appropriate use of HET and certainly by its occasional inappropriate use with a non-neuter noun.

The fact that Kate is not fully aware that HET is a definite article does not prohibit her from learning which nouns are neuter and which are not. After all, there are other elements besides the definite articles which mark the syntactic gender distinction and which may be employed to predict later appropriate uses of HET once its article-status has become more established.

In the corpus, the demonstrative determiners DAT and DIE occur much less frequently than the definite articles. A quarter of the time, DIE is used inappropriately (see example 15), and the other three quarters it is used as an adult would (see example 16). For DAT (with only 9 occurrences preceding a noun), use is nearly always appropriate (in one instance, DIE would have been the adult-like choice). The usage pattern of DAT, then, closely resembles that of HET. Although DIE is clearly the overgeneralized form, its 3 to 1 appropriate use is half the 6 to 1 appropriate use proportion of the corresponding non-neuter DE. DIE, one might suggest, appears to be better 'known' than DE, but due to the small number of occurrences (DIE is used in front of a noun on only 24 occasions) this conclusion can be very tentative only.

(15) 'Ik speelt met die stuk'. (Age: 3;3,9)
<I'm playing with that piece.>
{inappropriate use of DIE with a neuter noun}
(16) 'Die kangeroe valt altijd hee?' (Age: 2;10,13)
<That kangaroo is always falling down, isn't it?>
{appropriate use of DIE with a non-neuter noun}

Two thirds of the changeable modifying adjectives in the corpus are used appropriately, and one third is not (see example 17). Although the absolute number of changeable modifying adjectives is greater than that of demonstrative determiners (51 vs. 31), again the number is too low for any major conclusions to be drawn.

(17) 'Wij gaan naar Engeland met een groot boot!' (Age: 3;1,12)
    <We're going to England in a big boat!>
    {inappropriate use of the root form of the adjective with a non-neuter noun}

When the data for changeable adjectives and modifying demonstratives are combined, however, thus forming about a quarter of all complex NP's showing syntactic gender, 79% of all cases are used in an adult-like fashion and 21% are not. This suggests that a firm beginning has been made towards learning which nouns are neuter and which are not.

The notion of the existence of syntactic gender, then, seems to be definitely present at the end of the study, although full familiarity with all the gender marking forms is still absent, as well as complete knowledge of which nouns are what gender. For a discussion of the possibility that a semantically based rule may play a role in the errors on syntactic gender, see the discussion later on.

The period studied shows no clear developmental pattern or trend as far as the relation between adult-like and non-adult-like usage goes (see Table 7 in the Appendix). There are bursts of overgeneralization strategies throughout, which level off towards Tape 19, but there is no marked increase in appropriate or inappropriate combinations as time goes on. In any one recording session, all neuter nouns may be appropriately marked as such, whereas in the following session they may all occur with inappropriate determiners. Errors on neuter nouns occur mainly in two big bursts at Tapes 6 and 8, but as indicated before, these tapes contained many instances of neuter nouns, and the number of diminutives in these tapes is also much higher than usual. This means that there is a lot more opportunity for errors to be made here in comparison with other recording sessions. Thus there is no compelling ground for attaching any major developmental significance to the data in Tapes 6 and 8.

6.1.2.2 Natural gender and animacy: Dutch and English

We now come to the analysis of the marking of natural gender and/or animacy by means of third person singular personal pronouns and independent demonstrative pronouns. This analysis only includes forms of which the referent could be determined beyond any doubt. Forms referring to actions and 'dummy' forms without a referring function were excluded from analysis, as well as 'identification' markers in sentences such as '<u>Da</u>'s gordijn' <That's curtain> or 'What's <u>that</u>?'. It should be emphasized that also excluded were instances of HET in Dutch where it was not precisely clear whether HET referred to a specific entity, or to a 'situation', as for instance in 'Hier is je rijst. Pas op, <u>het</u> is nog warm!' <Here is your rice. Watch it, it's still hot!', where HET may be seen as referring to the non-neuter noun RIJST, but also to 'the food on your plate'. Alternatively, HET here may be seen as an empty filler pronoun. When Kate referred to food or drink by means of a pronoun, this pronoun often was HET, where HET fulfilled the ambiguous function of either pointing to the item of food or drink in particular, or to 'thing to be consumed' in general, or where HET could be seen as a filler (or a combination of these). Use of HET (or any other pronoun) in this ambiguous function was not taken up in the data analysis.

Kate's use of third person singular personal pronouns and independent demonstrative pronouns is quite distinct for both languages. The first point is that the English natural gender pronouns HE or SHE occur later than their Dutch pseudo-translation equivalents: there is no pronominal reference to either male or female entities present in the English corpus before the age of three, while such reference is already widely present in the Dutch corpus two months earlier. This piece of evidence, though, may not be as significant as it appears: since there are fewer data for English than for Dutch before Kate's third birthday, the result here may be due to sampling. More important, however, is that the use of the natural gender pronouns is fully language-specific: e.g., first use (at age 2;7,17) of HIJ <he> in the corpus is restricted to animate referents with indeterminate gender. Such usage (of the corresponding HE) is unusual in adult English and restricted to personification (see earlier), and it is doubtful that the Dutch data follow this unusual English usage. Rather, the source of the Dutch data can be traced directly to consistent patterns existing in the Dutch input system (see later for a detailed discussion).

When the English masculine and feminine pronouns appear, they are always used according to the appropriate English natural gender rules. Their use is restricted to human beings: while in Dutch Kate frequently refers to gender-neutral animate beings by means of a personal pronoun (viz. HIJ), such reference does not occur in the English corpus. In other words, Kate does not treat HIJ and HE as translation equivalents. A third point is that when errors occur, they are not necessarily relatable to the child's knowledge of the other language. In the English data, the 7 errors are due to the choice of the singular IT or THAT rather than a more appropriate plural form. In the Dutch data, the 25 errors are quite varied in nature, and while some could be attributed to influence from the English system, others cannot (for a more detailed analysis, see below). Finally, there is no sign of the Dutch system being imposed on English as far as the use of English demonstrative pronouns goes: usage here completely follows the adult English system (except for the errors pointed out above). In Dutch, a distinction is made between the neuter and non-neuter demonstratives and so no influence from English is apparent: after all, if the English system were used in Dutch, one might expect to find an underextended use of only one type of demonstrative.

The above preliminary findings suggest that the development of gender marking through the use of pronouns proceeds in a largely independent fashion in both languages. In the following separate analyses for English and Dutch more evidence will be given to support this claim.

As said before, no pronominal reference to male or female individuals is made in the English data until just after Kate's third birthday. From the age of 3;0,11 onwards, the feminine and masculine pronouns start to appear, usually in reference to human beings only (see example 18). These human beings are all persons familiar to Kate (a friend of the family's, Kate's teacher, a little boy at school, ...), and although Kate always uses the natural gender pronouns appropriately, there is no basis on which to argue that Kate has yet any productive knowledge of the distinction between HE and SHE: it is well possible that she uses these pronouns in a pseudo-associative way (see section 6.1.4 lbelow).

There is no reference to any animate beings through the use of English pronouns before the age of 3;0,11, and the personal pronoun IT is always used to refer to inanimate entities (see example 19), even after the masculine and feminine pronouns have started to occur with some regularity. IT is thus underextended, since in the adult system it can be used to refer to animate, non-human beings (viz. animals) as well. However, it is possible that due to sampling there was very little opportunity for Kate to refer to animals in the English corpus (but see the discussion later on in this section for an alternative interpretation): a review of the types of words that Kate uses in English reveals that she hardly ever talks about animals.

Reference to dolls is made through masculine and feminine pronouns rather than IT. This might be seen as support for the underextension of IT, but since children often view dolls as animate, or even 'humanized' objects, and since their environment encourages them in this, the non-use of IT here is of little significance (the four instances of SHE or HE being used to refer to dolls have been counted as human reference). HIM occurs only twice in the data, and HIS only once. HER occurs both as personal and as possessive pronoun. Use of HIM/HIS/HER is always gender appropriate. Third person singular reference also takes place through the use of THAT or THIS (or occasionally, THAT-ONE or THIS-ONE). When all the independent demonstratives and personal pronouns are added together, natural gender pronouns account for only 33% of the total.

The order of first appearance for the English pronouns under consideration is the following: IT/ THAT (age: 2;7,12), THIS (age: 2;7,17), HER (age 3;0,11), SHE (age: 3;0,17), HE (age: 3;1,6), HIS (age: 3;1,13), HIM (age: 3;1,18).

(18) Mother: 'Does David like soup?'
 (addressed to investigator; 'David' is not present, and is a favourite adult friend of Kate's)
 Kate: 'Ma, is he coming?' (Age: 3;1,18)
 {use of HE by Kate to refer to an animate, male, human referent}
(19) Mother: 'You wanna say goodnight to the sun?'
 Kate: 'Look it's orange!' (Age: 3;1,6)
 Mother: 'Yeah, he's going down, he's going dodo too.'
 {use of IT by Kate to refer to an inanimate referent even where she could have used HE and thus personified the referent as her mother did in the next conversational turn}

The main findings for the English data, then, concern the rather late appearance of the full range of natural gender pronouns and the underextended use of all the personal pronouns: Kate is still far from having acquired the English third person singular personal pronoun system at the age of 3;4, although the increased diversification of the pronoun system after the age of three is a clear sign that she is well underway to working out the complexities involved.

Table 6.4 *English third person singular personal pronouns* [a]

	IT	SHE	HER	HE
absolute frequency	58	28	7	8
referent	inanimate	+ human female	+ human female	+ human male

[a] Only pronouns that occurred 5 times or more have been included

Kate's use of the English personal pronouns has been summarized in Table 6.4 (this table also lists the total number of occurrences per type of pronoun for the whole of the corpus). Detailed overviews listing the data per recording session can be found in the Appendix: Table 8, part B, lists the distributions of all English third person singular personal pronouns and independent demonstratives per tape and for the whole of the corpus. Table 9, part B, shows the extent to which inanimate vs. animate referents are referred to by means of pronouns. Finally, Table 10, part B, gives a breakdown of the errors made in the choice of English pronouns.

In Dutch, the masculine and feminine personal pronouns already appear from the age of 2;7,17 onwards. HIJ <he> is the most frequent of all the pronouns considered in this section (for a summary of the Dutch data, see Table 6.5). ZE <she> occurs much less frequently, and is restricted to clearly female referents which may or may not have been previously mentioned by name and which refer to persons familiar to Kate. Use of Dutch ZE, then, is virtually the same as that of English SHE, although English SHE starts to appear much later than Dutch ZE. HIJ is used most frequently in reference to animate, non-human entities (see example 20), although reference to clearly male referents is present as well. The syntactic gender of the noun that HIJ refers to is mostly non-neuter, but neuter gender also occurs, in which case the choice of HIJ is appropriate, since the referent is animate and has indeterminate gender (the fact that non-neuter nouns are pronominalized much more frequently than neuter nouns is probably a direct result of the distribution of non-neuter vs. neuter nouns in the corpus). HEM <him> and HAAR <her> occur only sporadically.

The personal pronoun HET <it> is mainly used to refer to inanimate referents, whatever their syntactic gender (see example 21). Indeed, most

The noun phrase 133

of the 25 pronoun errors occur because HET is used to refer to non-neuter nouns. Additional evidence for this failure to take into account the syntactic gender of the referent comes from 6 errors made in the use of the independent demonstrative pronoun DAT <that>, which is inappropriately used to refer to non-neuter nouns (3 remaining errors are also due to the not taking into account of syntactic gender, and the last 4 errors occur because a singular demonstrative was used instead of a plural one). Thus the main reason for (the relatively few) errors in pronoun usage are due to the ignoring or non-marking of syntactic gender (Table 10, part A, in the Appendix provides a detailed breakdown of the above pronominal errors per recording session).

Since HIJ and ZE are mainly used to refer to animate referents and HET mainly to inanimate ones, Kate can be seen as largely using a semantic animate-inanimate distinction as a guideline in her choice of Dutch third person singular personal pronouns. While this strategy usually works quite well for animate referents, since in the adult system the speaker may choose to ignore the syntactic gender of animates, the strategy fails when used to refer to inanimate referents with non-neuter syntactic gender.

(20) Investigator: 'Slaapt de leeuw?' <Is the lion asleep?>
    (Kate is pretending to be a lion)
    Kate: 'Nee.' <No.> (Age: 2;9,0)
    Investigator: 'Nee?' <No?>
    Kate: 'Hij slaapt nie meer'. <He's not asleep anymore.>
    {use of HIJ to refer to an animate being with indeterminate gender}
(21) Kate: 'Jij mag aan de stoel zitten'. <You can sit at the chair.> (Age: 2;7,17)
    {appropriate use of DE with a non-neuter noun}
    Investigator: 'Ah, ik mag op de stoel zitten. Maar de stoel is ook hard. En de stoel is klein.'
    <Oh, I can sit on the chair. But the chair's also hard. And the chair is little.>
    Kate: 'Het is klein.' <It is little.>
    {inappropriate use of HET to refer a non-neuter noun}

Kate's usage of independent demonstratives, however, does not follow any animate-inanimate strategy (see Table 6.5): the proportion of animate nouns referred to by independent DIE vs. DAT is approximately the same, and both DIE and DAT are mainly used to refer to their appropriate syntactic genders, although some errors occur with DAT (see previous main paragraph). As in the adult system, Kate basically uses a syntactic gender rule to distinguish between both types of demonstratives.

Developmentally, unlike in the English corpus, there is no major increase or decrease in the number of pronominalized animate or inanimate referents (cf. Table 9, part A, in the Appendix). Non-neuter referents are constantly strongly represented, while neuter referents appear rather sporadically and in a seemingly random fashion. There does seem to be some development as far as erroneous pronoun usage goes: half of all the 25 inappropriate uses of HET, DAT, HIJ and DIE occur in the last two tapes (see Table 10). At the age of 3;4, Kate is thus producing relatively more inappropriate pronouns than before. Finally, the order of first appearance for the pronouns under consideration is the following: HET (age: 2;7,12), HIJ/ ZE/ ZIJ/ ZIJN/DIE (age: 2;7,17), DAT/DIT (age: 2;9,0), HEM (age: 2;10,13), HAAR (age: 3;0,11).

On the whole, then, acquisition of the Dutch adult third person singular personal pronoun system is by no means established by the age of 3;4. Not all the third person singular personal pronouns existing in the adult system are used, and the general frequency of occurrence of certain forms is quite low. More importantly, a semantic rule is used throughout (except for the independent demonstratives), and unless Kate learns to apply a syntactic rule to pronouns as well, she will not be able to produce fully adult-like forms.

The noun phrase 135

Table 6.5 *Dutch third person singular personal pronouns and independent demonstratives* [a]

Third person singular personal pronouns

	Animacy	Natural gender	Syntactic gender	N
HIJ \<he\>	animate	indeterminate	non-neuter	64
		male	non-neuter	11
		male	neuter	2
	inanimate	{irrelevant}	non-neuter	5
			neuter	<u>2</u>
HET \<it\>	inanimate	{irrelevant}	neuter	9
			<u>non-neuter</u>	<u>11</u>
	animate	indeterminate	neuter	1
			<u>non-neuter</u>	<u>1</u>
ZE \<she\>	animate	female	{irrelevant: proper noun}	13

Independent demonstrative pronouns

	Syntactic gender	Animacy	N
DIE \<that\>	non-neuter	animate	8
	non-neuter	inanimate	17
	<u>neuter</u>	<u>inanimate</u>	<u>1</u>
DAT \<that\>	neuter	animate	4
	neuter	inanimate	11
	<u>non-neuter</u>	<u>animate</u>	<u>1</u>
	<u>non-neuter</u>	<u>inanimate</u>	<u>6</u>

[a] Only pronouns that occurred 5 times or more have been included; in the column headed by N the total number of tokens for the whole corpus is indicated; the non-adult-like cases have been underlined

6.1.3 *Discussion*

The previous analyses have shown that Kate's production of the third person singular pronominal gender systems in both English and Dutch is not subject to any discernible influence from the Dutch syntactic gender system. Furthermore, the regularities observed within Kate's third person singular personal pronoun system are quite different for both languages, suggesting that development of the two gender systems proceeds in an independent manner for both languages. However, while the errors in Kate's use of HET in Dutch were interpreted as a result of the child's not taking into account syntactic gender, an alternative explanation is that Kate is actually transferring her usage pattern for English IT to Dutch. If we just had the disposal of the data for HET and IT, a choice between the competing explanations would be impossible. However, since no other pronoun usage patterns occur where influence from one language on the other could be used as an explanation, the first interpretation for the errors in HET still seems the most acceptable one.

It is not surprising that by the age of 3;4 all the formal complexities of the Dutch syntactic gender system have not been established yet. After all, the adult system is quite complex, and shows very little mutual predictability. In addition, there are but few clear phonological or semantic regularities which may be used to predict which nouns are what gender (see earlier in section 6.1.2). This implies that in many cases, rote-memorization is the only way of acquiring the correct forms and of discovering what the entire paradigm look like. In order to learn which nouns are neuter and which are not, then, one must have had extensive experience with a large variety of nouns. This experience only comes with growing up, and it may take a very long time for any learner of Dutch to confidently manipulate the syntactic gender distinction. The question in the mean time, however, is why we are seeing the overgeneralizations from DE to HET in Kate's handling of the syntactic gender system, and why Kate has apparently not really discovered that HET can be used as an article.

One might suggest that an animacy-based rule is the governing factor in Kate's production of Dutch determiners (after all, such a rule was found to be paramount in her production of third person singular personal pronouns). This, however, is not generally the case: in the corpus, the article DE is not restricted to combinations with only animate or inanimate nouns, but is used with either throughout in approximately the same proportions. The article HET <u>does</u> exhibit a strong tendency of occurring only with inanimate nouns. At first sight, this might be interpreted as showing a semantically based distinction in an area where only a syntactic rule is applied in the adult system. However, most of the neuter nouns in the corpus (including diminutives) happen to be inanimate, and singular neuter inanimate nouns occur more frequently with DE than with HET (see Table 6.6). Both these additional findings are counterevidence to a semantic interpretation: it appears that the combination of HET with inanimate nouns is a purely distributional consequence of the generally high proportion of neuter inanimate nouns. And if there was indeed a semantic distinction to be discovered, one would hardly expect to see the frequent combinations of DE with neuter inanimate nouns: rather, one

The noun phrase 137

might expect neuter animate nouns to be used exclusively with DE, and neuter inanimates with HET.

Table 6.6 *Animacy of neuter nouns and their use with Dutch gender determiners*

	Animate	Inanimate	Total
neuter nouns following HET/DAT	1	18	19
neuter nouns following DE/DIE	4	32	36
ALL NEUTER NOUNS	17.2%	82.8%	**134**

The determiner DAT occurs only sporadically and shows no preference pattern linked to animacy. The determiner DIE occurs more regularly, and is used in front of both inanimate and animate referents, although there is a strong tendency for Kate to use DIE in combination with inanimate nouns, especially towards the end of the study. Often, the resulting NP is non-adult-like, since syntactic gender is not respected, i.e. also neuter nouns are combined with DIE (rather than DAT). DIE, in fact, behaves very much like DE (see also section 6.1.2.1).

In general, then, no trend to impose an animate-inanimate distinction on the determiner system can be discerned.

Alternatively, one might propose that there is an input frequency factor at work here. In a recent study of the language input to a monolingual Dutch-speaking child between the ages of 1;6 and 1;11, it was found that adults use the article DE (whether in front of singular or plural nouns) about 4 times as frequently as the article HET (Verlinden 1987). This proportion is virtually the same as the one found by de Jong (1979), who carried out frequency counts based on adult-to-adult colloquial Dutch. In de Jong's data, HET as an article occurs much less frequently than DE (de Jong 1979: 117), with HET occurring in only 25% of the cases and DE in 75% (presumably, the use of DE here again includes its usage in front of plurals). Although the present study has not permitted any analysis of frequency counts of the input to Kate, the above findings strongly suggest that Kate will have heard DE followed by a noun much more frequently than HET followed by a noun. Furthermore, within Kate's own system, the lexical item HET occurs very frequently as an independent impersonal, personal or indefinite pronoun. This usage is fully adult-like as well, and in fact, adult use of the pronoun HET is much more common than use of the article HET, with HET occurring as article in 38% of the cases, and as independent pronoun in 62% of the cases (de Jong 1979: 117). Kate's frequent use of HET as an independent pronoun may be a rather direct result of the frequency of this use in the adult system.

The underrepresentation of HET as an article, then, may be seen as the result of a strong one form/one function strategy: the lexical item HET is so to speak already reserved for pronoun usage, and temporarily blinds the child's view to consider other uses (for a similar suggestion, see Wijnen 1984; a similar interpretation to ours of comparable findings for the bilingual first language acquisition of French and German has been put forward by Berkele 1983). The same might be true of the neuter demonstrative pronoun DAT, which is frequently used as an independent demonstrative in the corpus, and only very rarely as a determiner (the quantitative data supporting the differences between independent vs. dependent use of the various forms are tabulated in Table 11 in the Appendix): it is DIE, the non-neuter demonstrative pronoun, which occurs far more frequently as a determiner than DAT (again, these data strongly resemble data from frequency counts of spoken adult usage - see de Jong 1979). Obviously, however, when here the existence of a strong one form/one function strategy is hypothesized, the notion 'function' must be interpreted in the grammatical rather than the semantic sense: HET and DAT are both used in a multitude of semantic functions. They may both indicate an action or a specific referent in the context or discourse; both may equally be used as 'dummies', i.e. without any specific referring function. Their use at Kate's present stage of development, however, is not identical: HET does not have the clear 'pointing' meaning that DAT does, and in addition HET does not occur as an introduction to the naming of objects or people (thus, for instance, utterances such as 'Het is een boek' do not occur - although they would be perfectly adult-like; conversely, there are many instances of utterances of the form 'DA'S EEN {noun}'). When it is claimed that HET and DAT share two functions, then, it is their <u>grammatical</u> functions (viz. pronominal vs. modifying use) rather than any semantic functions that are the focus of attention.

In adult Dutch, some elements of the third person singular personal pronoun system are loosely connected with the syntactic gender system, but there is, again, little predictability. Syntactic gender of the referent is of great importance, however, when the referent is inanimate (see Table 6.2). However, the data in this study show that Kate does not usually mark syntactic gender through the use of third person singular personal pronouns. Rather, third person singular personal pronouns are mainly used to mark animacy and natural gender distinctions.

What might be the reason for the latter finding? A possible answer may be found in the purely distributional differences between the various third person singular personal pronouns in the adult system.

When reference to animate beings is made, the pair HIJ/HEM will have the best chance of being used, and the pair ZE/HAAR will have the second best chance of being used. Although these generalizations are perhaps too strong (after all, use of HIJ/HEM vs. ZE/HAAR will highly depend on the topic of conversation), there are some arguments suggesting that in fact they do reflect major trends: there is some indication from frequency counts of spoken adult Dutch (de Vriendt-de Man 1971) that the pair HIJ/HEM occurs more frequently than the pair ZE/HAAR: when all the occurrences of HIJ/HEM, ZE as subject pronoun and HAAR as object pronoun are added up together, HIJ/HEM accounts for 63% of the cases and ZE/HAAR for 37% (calculations based on de Vriendt-de Man 1971: 216). Furthermore, the pair ZE/HAAR is mostly only used when the referent's biological sex is clearly female, and its usage potential is thus more restricted than that of the pair HIJ/HEM, which is used both when the referent's biological sex is male and when it is undetermined. HET will stand the least chance of being used when reference is made to animate beings (use of HET for neuter, animate nouns is the stylistically marked case).

For inanimate beings, both HET (for neuter nouns) and HIJ/HEM/ZE/ HAAR (for non-neuter nouns) may be used, with no clearly distinct distribution patterns.

Kate's early abundant use of HIJ to indicate animate referents (cf. Table 6.5) may be seen as following the main usage pattern for this pronoun in the adult system: relative to the other third person singular personal pronouns that can be used to refer to animates, HIJ is simply the most frequently used (in distributional terms). [4] The quasi-exclusive use of the personal pronoun HET to refer to inanimates, on the other hand, may be considered to be the result of two combined features: first, when HET is used in the adult system, chances are that it will refer to an inanimate rather than an animate entity. Secondly, a strong one form/one function strategy operating within the child's own system can be posited: HIJ is already 'reserved' for animate beings, and thus, when inanimate reference is made, HIJ will initially not be used (although there is no *a priori* distributional frequency pattern in the input that lends more weight to HET than HIJ or ZE for inanimate reference). It is the particular state of the child's system, then, which makes it difficult for the child to mark syntactic gender, since she would have to start using a form that is already linked to a well-specified function (viz. HIJ). In addition, the syntactic gender system *per se* is still far from completely developed, and even if Kate were fully ready to use HIJ in a second function, i.e. to refer to inanimates, she would not necessarily be able to apply HET and HIJ appropriately, due to incomplete knowledge of which nouns are what gender, or indeed, to an absence of knowledge that syntactic gender needs to be taken into account at all (that Kate's system is already changing towards a more syntactically based one is evidenced by the occasional use of HIJ to refer to inanimates as shown in Table 6.5).

I am not aware of any data on input frequencies and usage patterns of the various pronouns in speech addressed to Dutch-speaking children. If we had such data, we would at least have a starting basis allowing us to empirically test the hypothesis that the acquisition of many morpho-syntactical elements is highly dependent on the interaction between absolute and distributional frequencies of certain forms in the input and the state of the child's own developing system at any particular time.

For English, we do have relevant frequency information available. There is clear evidence from adult input to English-speaking children that in absolute terms IT occurs much more frequently than the other third person singular personal pronouns: Wells (1985: 361) has found that the personal pronoun IT accounts for 170 tokens per 1000 adult-to-child utterances, while HE, HIM and SHE account for only 86 such tokens (Wells gives no figures for HER, from which it may perhaps be concluded that HER hardly ever occurred in his corpus). When specific third person singular pronominal reference is made by adults addressing young children, then, IT appears in 66% of the cases, while HE, HIM and SHE taken together appear much less frequently, i.e. in only 34% of the cases.

As far as the distributional frequencies of the various pronouns of interest here are concerned, there is a high predictability for two major cases: inanimates are (nearly) always referred to by IT, while humans are (nearly) always referred to by HE, HIM, HER or SHE (see Table 6.1).

The English data from Kate (cf. Table 6.4) may be seen as largely reflecting the characteristics of the English input system as outlined in the preceding two paragraphs: after all, Kate has isolated the most 'consistent' input patterns (cf. Karmiloff-Smith 1979) for the various pronouns: she uses a [+human/-animate] distinction, with natural gender marked in function of the [+human] feature. In addition, Kate uses IT more frequently than the feminine and masculine forms. One may also look upon the earlier occurrence of IT vs. the natural gender pronouns as being determined by the higher absolute frequency of IT in the presumed input system (obviously, however, we need data from Kate's own environment to truly substantiate any claims about possible influence on her language development from the frequencies of certain forms in the specific input she received). In addition, the fact that the child has to work out the male/female distinction may have a slowing-down effect on the later occurrence of the HE/SHE pair relative to the occurrence of IT.

Table 6.7 *Proposed basic usage constellations of the personal pronouns IT, HE, HIM and SHE*

Adult English spoken to children (source: Wells 1985)			
Referent	*Pronoun*	*Usage*	*Absolute frequency*
inanimate	IT	ALWAYS	HIGH
+ human	HE/SHE/HIM	ALWAYS	±LOW
- human, animate	IT	unmarked	± high
- human, animate	HE/SHE/HIM	marked	± low
Kate corpus			
Referent	*Pronoun*	*Usage*	*Absolute frequency*
inanimate	IT	ALWAYS	HIGH: 58
+ human	HE/SHE/HER	ALWAYS	±LOW: 43
- human, animate	/	absent	/

The absence of errors on the use of IT and the HE/SHE pair, with IT never applied to humans and HE/SHE never to inanimates, may be related to the absence, both within the adult model and the child's own developing system, of other forms to express the same functions. The absence of IT to refer to non-human animates may be the result of a strong one form/one function strategy yet again (cf. the interpretation offered for Kate's much more frequent use of Dutch HET as a pronoun rather than as an article). The main points made in the preceding three paragraphs have been summarized in Table 6.7.

6.1.4 *Comparisons with monolingual children*

Regrettably, there have as yet been no published naturalistic studies of young standard Dutch-speaking children which analyse their use of HET versus DE, or DAT vs. DIE. Schaerlaekens (1977: 146) only mentions that DE is used 'adequately' in the last quarter of children's third year, and that HET appears later than DE, and is in fact often not present until the child's third birthday (it is not clear whether the term 'adequately' refers to pragmatic adequacy or syntactic gender adequacy). Schaerlaekens and Gillis (1987) note that the article HET is not necessarily used by children aged three. Children that do use the article HET around this age do not use it appropriately (i.e. 'correctly' as far as syntactic gender goes), and Schaerlaekens and Gillis (1987: 124) further claim that even the article DE is not used appropriately as far as syntactic gender goes. This latter statement, however, contradicts many of the examples that Schaerlaekens and Gillis (1987) give in which children around and even before the age of three are quoted as using DE appropriately in front of non-neuter nouns.

The data from Kate show that use of DE is already well-established at the beginning of the study, and that HET is used occasionally before her third birthday. Thus, Kate seems to be slightly ahead of the monolingual children reported on as far as her usage of the actual forms of the definite article goes. Because of the ambiguity in Schaerlaekens and Gillis (1987) concerning the gender appropriate use of DE around age three no comparisons with the data from Kate are possible here. Kate's problems with HET do seem to reflect Dutch-speaking monolingual children's usage as reported by Schaerlaekens and Gillis (1987).

Evidence from two experimental studies suggests that complete knowledge of the Dutch syntactic gender system may take a long time to acquire: Extra (1978) and Wijnen (1984) have shown that four-year-olds still make quite a few errors in their choice of HET versus DE (Extra (1978) found a similar situation for DAT vs. DIE). In addition, their analyses of these errors shows the existence of a clear overgeneralization strategy resulting in the use of non-neuter determiners where the neuter forms would have been appropriate (Extra 1978: 124-126; Wijnen 1984: 38). Examples from the spontaneous speech of monolingual Dutch children also show the overgeneralization of the non-neuter determiners with neuter nouns, including diminutives (see e.g. examples given in Extra 1977 and Verhulst-Schlichting 1985).

Dutch children use HIJ from quite an early age onwards (Bol and Kuiken 1986): first recorded usage appears at the age of 1;8. Regular use of HIJ seems well-established by the age of 2;6. The use of ZE (as the feminine pronoun) and HET in Subject position lags far behind, and were used only occasionally by Bol and Kuiken's (1986) subjects in the age range of one to four. The respective object and possessive pronouns occur very infrequently as well (including HEM). The possessive HAAR was not used by any of Bol and Kuiken's (1986) subjects until the age of 3;10. Unfortunately, although Bol and Kuiken mention that in the learning of the pronoun system their subjects did not make many mistakes, they do not present any error analysis. Neither do they indicate in which functions the pronouns under consideration were used. A comparison with the Dutch data from Kate clearly shows that as far as production of the forms *per se* goes, Kate behaves very much like the children studied by the above authors (cf. the frequent use of HIJ, the less frequent use of HET, the occasional use of ZE, HEM, ZIJN).

Schaerlaekens (1977) briefly mentions that in the period from 2;6 to 5 years of age, Dutch-speaking children make quite a few errors in the choice of the personal and possessive gender pronouns (this is in contrast with the findings of Bol and Kuiken above), and that it takes a long time for both natural and syntactic gender to be established (this point is repeated in Schaerlaekens and Gillis 1987: 130). She gives a few examples of utterances by children around the age of three in which the male pronouns are used to refer to clearly female entities (Schaerlaekens 1977: 145). Unfortunately, further data and quantification or error analyses are lacking, so no real comparisons with the data from Kate can be made.

The English data from Kate for the acquisition of natural gender pronouns are similar to those reported on in studies of children acquiring English as far as the relatively late occurrence of the masculine and feminine pronouns goes. In a longitudinal study of a monolingual English-speaking child by French (1987), for instance, no natural gender pronoun had been produced by the age of 2;9. In fact, it seems that in monolingual English acquisition, masculine and feminine pronouns generally start to appear regularly only well after the child's third birthday (Wells 1985). Often, however, usage is inappropriate, with HE being overgeneralized to cases where SHE would be the adult choice (Chiat 1978; for an experimental study, see Mills 1986a and 1986c). Such inappropriate usage is not found in the data from Kate, but on the other hand there is evidence from a case study by Fletcher (1985) that not necessarily all monolingual English children start out by using inappropriate gender assignments: the little English girl that Fletcher reported on never made any errors in her choice of natural gender pronouns. These apparently contrasting findings in the monolingual literature here may largely be due to the different data collection methods used in the various studies: the data that Chiat (1978) refers to in her longitudinal study were not gathered in the child's home environment but in a school setting, and the topics of conversation revolved around dolls and pictures. Significantly, when Sophie in Fletcher's (1985) study appropriately uses gender pronouns, she is mostly referring to people very familiar to her. The same is true of Kate. It may be, then, that in their initial use of gender pronouns, Sophie and Kate used them as alternatives to proper names, and, given the restricted number of people familiar to them, appropriate choice of a gender pronoun is the result of a strong, memory-based association, rather than a productive rule of the form 'female person>>SHE' or 'male person>>HE'. Since in the data reported by Chiat (1978) most inappropriate use of gender pronouns occurred when her subjects were presumably referring to pictures or dolls, not to familiar individuals, these data do not necessarily contradict either the data for Fletcher's (1985) Sophie or for Kate. In her use of gender pronouns, then, Kate behaves very much like at least one monolingual child.

Kate's very early and abundant use of IT coincides with the usage patterns found in monolingual English speaking children (see e.g. Chiat 1986). At the age of five, English children's use of IT is strongly associated with inanimacy (Mills 1986c). Kate is showing this strong association already at age three. Finally, English-speaking children do not attempt to use any syntactic gender marking. Neither does Kate when she is speaking English.

On the whole, then, Kate uses similar gender marking forms to monolingual children from within the same age range, and while some of Kate's usage patterns resemble those found in at least some monolingual children, other usage patterns cannot be compared due to lack of data.

6.1.5 Concluding remarks
At the age of three years and four months, Kate is still very much in the middle of learning the intricacies of the Dutch and English gender

systems, although there are great differences between Kate's use of her two languages: from the beginning of the study, her use of both gender systems is fully language specific, and most non-adult-like usage is relatable to formal and semantic characteristics of the separate input languages. The child's other language cannot be taken as a guide for predicting patterns of use.

The preceding analysis has further shown that the child marks syntactic and natural gender within their appropriate spheres of application. Errors occur due to an as yet incomplete knowledge of the bases for the various distinctions within each gender type, and for the Dutch third person singular personal pronoun system, errors occur due to the non-application of a syntactic rule. These errors can be explained in terms of restrictions imposed by the child's own developing system: a strong one form/one function strategy seems to play a major role in determining which forms are (not) used. Then there are also 'errors of omission' (Bowerman 1985): in both languages, some pronoun forms are clearly used in an underextended fashion. It can be argued that this underextended use is due to the ignoring of finer distinctions made in the adult systems: only the most general cases find expression in the child's system.

6.2 Plural formation

In this section the focus will be on plural noun phrases (NP's) with a noun as head.

6.2.1 *The adult systems*

In the adult systems, there are no syntagmatic differences between English and Dutch as far as plural NP's are concerned. Gender distinctions are of no importance either, but in Dutch a distinction needs to be made between changeable and non-changeable adjectives (most changeable adjectives get a suffix {–e} when used in combination with a plural noun).

In producing a regular Dutch plural noun, a choice must be made between the plural allomorphs /–ə/ and /–s/. The 'choice' here often depends on the final phoneme of the singular form and on whether this phoneme was preceded by a schwa or not. In the most general of terms it can be said that singular words ending in a consonant preceded by a schwa or ending in a vowel form their plural with the allomorph /–s/, and that singular words ending in a consonant not preceded by a schwa form their plural with the allomorph /–ə/. Most of the time, the plural allomorphs are in complementary distribution, i.e. a decision for either one or the other must be made.

In English, the speaker has to choose between the three plural allomorphs /-s/, /-z/ and /-iz/. Again, the choice is phonologically determined, with /-s/ being used after plosives, /-iz/ after sibilants, and /-z/ after any other type of sound.

Both in English and Dutch there exists a small group of nouns which have an irregular, non-productive plural form.

6.2.2 Kate's plural NP's

The acquisition data from Kate show very little difference between English and Dutch as far as 'correctness' of the forms is concerned: in both languages, most plural nouns are formed in an adult-like fashion. The two exceptions are English POTSES instead of POTS, which is a case of overmarking, and Dutch NAGELLAKKEN <nail polishes>, where the actual plural allomorph is well-chosen, but where the plural does not exist, since NAGELLAK is an uncountable substance, and, as is the case in English, adult Dutch does not pluralize these nouns.

More interesting perhaps is the overall usage pattern of all the plural allomorphs. Should Kate be mainly using the /–s/ allomorph in Dutch, then we might be seeing an underextension of the Dutch system due to influence from English. A mirror-argument could be made if the /–s/ allomorph were the main one being used in English. As it is, however, neither of these possibilities materializes.

Kate uses all three English plural allomorphs, but /–iz/ appears only twice (in *POTSES and NOISES). More than two thirds of the remaining plural types are formed with /–z/, and slightly less than a third with /–s/. Already it is clear that /–s/ is not the main allomorph used in Kate's English plurals, contrary to what a 'transfer' theory of early bilingual acquisition might predict. Furthermore, five of the plural types ending in [s] are 'disguised' plurals, i.e. there is no real singular alternative for them (e.g. PANTS). On the other hand, there is but one plural type ending in [z] that is not a 'real' plural (i.e. CLOTHES). In addition, only two plural types that end in [s] also occur in the singular elsewhere in the corpus, whereas for plural types ending in [z], the number occurring in the singular as well is 12. It appears, then, that /–z/ is the most productive plural allomorphs in Kate's system, and that perhaps /–s/ is not yet productive. There is no sign of any transfer from the Dutch system to English.

In Dutch, transfer from English is not clearly detectable either. Whereas the allomorph /–s/ is the most frequently occurring plural allomorph, the allomorph /–ə/ appears quite frequently as well (the two allomorphs are used in a 3:2 proportion). There is thus no clear preference for just plurals ending in [s]. We do not, however, find that the /–s/ allomorph is used in a possibly non-productive fashion as evidenced by a relatively large proportion of 'disguised' plurals or plural types that did not occur in the singular, as was the case for English. In fact, it seems as if the Dutch /–s/ and /–ə/ allomorphs are equally productive: the proportion of plural types ending in [ə] that do not appear in the singular is about the same as that for plural types ending in [s]. Striking, however, is that three quarters of the plural types ending in [s] are plural forms of diminutives. This, then, could perhaps be seen as a slight underextension of the usage possibilities of the /–s/ allomorph, which, again, takes us away from a transfer interpretation.

Irregular plurals occur only three times in the entire corpus and are all adult-like in form (Dutch: BLADEREN <leaves>; English: TEETH and FEET).

In the actual plural forms produced by Kate, then, there is no evidence that the other language had any effect on the allomorphs used. Rather, in each language Kate follows the possibilities of the respective input system.

Plurals occur fairly infrequently throughout (on the average, they occur once in every 20 utterances), but in both languages there is a clear increase in the number of plural nouns from the middle of the study onwards. For each language this increase is evident in both the absolute number of plurals, as well as in the percentage of the total number of utterances per tape containing a plural noun (see Table 12 in the Appendix).

In both languages, plural nouns occur mostly without a determiner or with just the definite article, although there are some other combinations as well. There is a wide variety of lexical entries that are used in the plural: i.e., no clear stereotypical usage is apparent, even not at the beginning of the study.

Since on a total of 225 plural nouns only two occur that are inappropriate, and since there is a great variety of pluralized nouns, it is likely that Kate has already passed the pre-analysis, rote-memorization stage which is characteristic of children at an earlier age (Schaerlaekens 1977). Neither in the Dutch or the English data is there any trace of an overgeneralization strategy, and although "systematic errors and overgeneralizations provide convincing evidence that the child has a productive rule" (Cazden 1973: 228), the absence of such errors does not imply that the child does not have a productive rule. Appropriate, frequent and varied use (i.e. across a large number of different lexical items) can also indicate a productive rule. Given these criteria, Kate can be said to have already acquired productive knowledge of the English /–iz/ allomorph and the Dutch /–∂/ allomorph. Although the Dutch /–s/ allomorph occurs with a variety of different lexical items, it is largely linked to a class of nouns, viz. the diminutives. Whether the Dutch /–s/ allomorph is actually productive, then, is uncertain. Firm beginnings towards the appropriate marking of plural nouns have been made, but until irregular forms start being produced and until the as yet only weakly represented allomorphs start to be used in greater numbers the acquisition of plural formation will be far from complete.

6.2.3 *Comparisons with monolingual children*

Bol and Kuiken (1987) write that already in the first half of the third year plurals have become productive in the speech productions of their Dutch-speaking subjects (unfortunately Bol and Kuiken (1987) do not indicate how often plural forms occur, and in what proportions they continue to be used after their first occurrence). Although it is not defined what the authors mean by "productive", the term does suggest that plurals are present regularly from quite an early age onwards.

This latter finding is in contrast with data reported on by Schaerlaekens (1977): she writes that although plural forms consisting of a singular noun and a plural suffix start to appear in the first half of the third year, regular use of plural forms contrasting with singular ones appears only towards the child's third birthday. Schaerlaekens (1977) further emphasizes that the development of plural formation is a long drawn-out process. The reasons for the discrepancies between Schaerlaekens' analysis, on the one hand, and the early 'productive' use of plurals as noted by Bol and Kuiken (1987) have yet to be explained (it is not impossible, for instance, that Bol and Kuiken found a large token number of plural forms which were mainly restricted to just a few vocabulary items).

Schaerlaekens (1977) further notes that even by the age of six children may still be making errors on the formation of irregular forms (experimental studies have also found that Dutch plural formation takes a long time to acquire - see Snow, Smith and Hoefnagel-Höhle 1980 and Vogel, Harder, Jogman, Nagtegaal, den Os, van Reydt and Slockers 1980). The regular forms are usually acquired by the age of four. Before this time, Schaerlaekens (1977) writes, overgeneralizations of the /–s/ allomorph occur quite regularly, while overgeneralizations of the /–ə/ allomorph are much less frequent. Schaerlaekens and Gillis (1987), however, state that overgeneralizations occur in both directions.

The Dutch data from Kate show the regular use of plurals from her third birthday onwards, which is in accordance with Schaerlaekens' (1977) findings, but the overgeneralizations mentioned by Schaerlaekens (1977) and Schaerlaekens and Gillis (1987) do not occur. There are two possibilities: either Kate is still in the pre-analysis, rote-memorization stage (despite the large variety of forms produced), or Kate is ahead of Dutch-speaking monolingual children in that she has already learnt the regular rule. At the moment, no choice between these two possibilities can be made.

The data for English-speaking children reported on by Wells (1985) show that plural nouns occur quite consistently from the age of 1;6 onwards, but that their relative frequency compared to that of singular nouns is quite low. This was also found to be the case in the present study. Wells does not discuss what types of plurals are produced: there is no breakdown of the number of regular and irregular forms, and thus the findings for Kate cannot be compared.

6.2.4 *Conclusion*

It should be stressed again that plural morphemes do not travel between languages, but are language-specific. This is but a first instance of the general <u>principle of morphological language stability</u>, which proposes that in the acquisition of two languages from birth where exposure to either language is separated by person or situation, bound morphemes belong to the main language of the utterance from the very beginning of their occurrence. More evidence for this principle will be presented throughout the rest of this and the following chapter.

6.3 The use of diminutives

A striking difference between adult English and Dutch is the existence in Dutch of a very productive diminutive marker, which can be added not only to most nouns (but not all, contrary to what Snow, Arlman-Rupp, Hassing, Jobse, Joosten and Vorster 1976 claim), but also to adjectives when they are nominalized and even to some adverbs. In English, such a marker exists only in a few stereotyped forms (e.g. COOKIE, MOMMY, DUMMY, and in first names such as TIMMY).

The acquisition data from Kate reflect the difference existing in the adult systems. There is no tendency whatsoever to apply diminutive markers to English words where this would be inappropriate (even in a 'translated' fashion: for instance, words like *CHAIRIE do not occur, whereas Dutch STOELTJE <chair-ie> is fully adult-like). Conversely, there is no striking absence of diminutives in Dutch as might be expected within a 'transfer' theory of early bilingual language acquisition.

In Dutch, Kate uses the various diminutive allomorphs quite appropriately (but so far mainly on nouns). There is one case of overmarking in which a noun is produced with two diminutive suffixes instead of just one (viz. *BEDJETJE <little bed> instead of BEDJE). In another isolated case, Kate has used the allomorph /–kə/ instead of /–əkə/ or, alternatively, /–jə/ (viz. in *POTKE <little pot> instead of POTTEKE or POTJE). In all the other cases, Kate uses a range of appropriate allomorphs attached to a large variety of nouns. The actual allomorphs that she produces are /–jə/, /–tjə/, /–kə/, /–əkə/ and /–ətjə/.

Kate uses 52 types of diminutive nouns in the whole corpus (a singular and a plural rendition of the same root using the same diminutive allomorph was counted as one type only). Of those 52 types, at least 6 cannot be used in their non-diminutive form: they are diminutives in disguise (e.g. SNOEPJE <piece of candy>: the root SNOEP does not exist in the same meaning, although it means 'candy' in general, as a type of food. SNOEPJE, however, is not the diminutive form of SNOEP - although formally speaking, it certainly looks as though it is!). We are thus left with 46 'real' diminutives. 21 of those also appear in their non-diminutive form. This last finding, combined with the fact that a great variety of diminutive allomorphs occurs, suggests that knowledge of the diminutive marker is quite productive.

One may argue that this productive knowledge of the diminutive marker is the result of a combination of factors: diminutives are quite salient perceptually, since they are always one syllable longer than the root of the noun (or adjective, or adverb). In addition, they are a very frequent and constant feature of language input to young children (see Snow, Arlman-Rupp, Hassing, Jobse, Joosten and Vorster 1976; most native speakers of Dutch will accept this statement as a matter of course). Furthermore, apart from plural morphemes, they are the only type of suffix that is ever attached to a noun without resulting in a change of word class. Since the plural suffix is so different in function, there is no competition whatsoever from other morphemes, either in the adult or in the child system.

Finally, when diminutives are pluralized, the resulting form preserves adult order relationships, with the plural morpheme as the final suffix. The theoretically possible form *(noun + plural + diminutive suffix) never occurs.

Developmentally, there is no major increase or decrease in the number of diminutive forms in the singular, although clear peaks occur in sessions 6 and 8 (44% of all the 54 singular diminutives (tokens) occur in these sessions). The number of pluralized diminutive forms, on the other hand, increases drastically towards the end of the study, just as the number of Dutch non-diminutive plurals does (see section 6.1.2), which implies that rather than a learning of diminutive formation we are here seeing a learning of plural formation.

All the above evidence combined strongly suggests that by the age of three, Kate has learned most that there is to learn about Dutch diminutives. This finding is not surprising if one considers that the diminutive suffix is one of the first bound morphemes to be used by Dutch-speaking monolingual children (Schaerlaekens 1977, Bol and Kuiken 1987), and this in an abundant and usually appropriate fashion. Kate, then, resembles monolingual children in her similarly abundant and usually appropriate use of diminutives.

6.4 NP's with an adjective as head

The next topic is the use of NP's with an adjective as head. These forms are particularly interesting because we are here dealing with functionally identical but both morphologically and syntagmatically different forms that are not inherently more or less complex in one or the other language: in English, an NP with an adjective as head contains at least a determiner, followed by an adjective and the pro-form ONE. In Dutch, an NP with an adjective as head contains at least a determiner, followed by an adjective in the root + {–e} form (that is, if the adjective is changeable). The prediction traditionally for the acquisition of different languages in monolingual children here would probably be that both forms would be used at about the same time and with similar error rates (see e.g. Slobin 1973). A logical implication of this view is that the hypothesis should also apply to children who happen to acquire two languages simultaneously. In the case of NP's with an adjective as head, one would predict the simultaneous occurrence of both the English and the Dutch forms.

The data from Kate, however, do not support this prediction, since usage of the determiner+adjective+pro-form ONE syntagm in English is much more established than the Dutch counterpart determiner+adjective in {–e}. Briefly, the findings for this conclusion are that in absolute terms the English forms greatly outnumber the Dutch ones, even though the number of Dutch utterances in the corpus more than doubles the number of English utterances. In addition, the English forms are used much more consistently and much more frequently throughout than the Dutch forms. Usage in Dutch of NP's with an adjective as head, then, is very marginal, whereas this is not so in English. No clear developmental pattern appears for either language. The relevant data have been tabulated in Table 13 in the Appendix.

The reasons for the differences between Kate's Dutch and English may be due to many factors. A first one lies in the great perceptual difference between the clear pronominalizer ONE and the unclear, unstressed {–e} suffix with the same function in Dutch: it is possible that because of this perceptual difference, the child has been able to pay attention to the English form first. Another reason may be the 'explicitness-factor': the English syntagm is fully explicit, while the Dutch one is in a sense elliptical. Children in their development of language often show a preference for explicit markers, as was noted by Slobin (1985a). We may here be seeing an instance of this. These explanations, however, are again expressed in terms of a comparison between both languages. There are also intra-linguistic reasons that might explain the differences. For instance, the English pattern follows exactly the same syntagmatic pattern as a full NP with a noun as head: the noun is simply replaced by ONE as a fairly free variation (but see Wells 1985: 264 who suggests that in development, it is the noun which replaces ONE rather than the other way round). In Dutch, an element is 'left out' as it were. As was seen in the analysis of overt syntactic gender marking, Kate is in the midst of learning what nouns go with what determiners and modifiers. To recognize that these determiners and modifiers can be used by themselves may be a step situated on a different level that the child has not yet reached.

A final point concerning the use of adjectives as heads of NP's is that bound morphemes do not travel between languages. In addition, language specific syntagms are not readily transferred to the other language. More precisely, in English there is no transfer of the Dutch {–e} morpheme, except in one instance (ALLE, with English ALL as root - see also Table 5.2 in Chapter 5). In Dutch, translated forms of the English syntagm that are theoretically possible do not appear. This is again evidence for the principle of morphological language stability.

For completeness' sake, however, it should be mentioned that in English there are nine instances of errors due to the omission of ONE. We may here be dealing with transfer of the Dutch pattern (although no {–e} is added to any English adjective). This possibility is highly unlikely though, given the very rare use of an adjective as head of an NP in Kate's Dutch. Conversely, the error may be developmentally determined, in which case monolingual English children should produce similar forms. Unfortunately, the relevant literature gives no clues in this respect, and thus a well-founded explanation cannot be given.

6.5 Syntagmatic relations within NP's
6.5.1 *The adult systems*
We now turn to an analysis of the syntagmatic relations existing within Kate's NP's with a common noun as head. This analysis was added in order to present a more complete picture of Kate's use of NP's, but cannot address the separate development hypothesis, since in adult Dutch and English the ordering relationships within NP's with a common noun as head are virtually identical. Abstracting from various sematically based restrictions (there are combinatory restrictions based on semantic characteristics of nouns; in addition, there are ordering restrictions for multiple modifying adjectives), the basic adult ordering relationships can be summarized as follows: there are three elements in any noun phrase with a common noun as head, viz. a first, middle and final element. First and middle elements may be empty, but the final element always is a common noun (i.e. the head of the NP). If the first element is not empty, it may be filled with one of the following, and only one: an article, a

pronoun, or an adverb. If the middle element is not empty, it may be filled with one or more adjectives (note that an empty first element may be followed by a 'filled' middle element - thus an adjective can be a first element in disguise). After this brief characterization of the adult systems we turn to the data.

6.5.2 *Analysis and results*

All the NP's in the material with a common noun as head were categorized into nine major subgroupings. The results of this grouping can be found in Table 14 in the Appendix.

As is clear from Table 14, the first seven subgroupings occur in the same global order of frequency of occurrence for both languages. These seven subgroupings are the following combinations (listed from most to least frequent): definite article+noun, zero article+ noun, pronoun+noun, indefinite article+noun, adjective+noun, indefinite article+adjective+noun, and definite article+adjective+ noun.

In order to find out whether in the course of the study there were any major differences or similarities between English and Dutch in the proportional use of the most frequently occurring NP syntagms, Wilcoxon T-tests were run on the four most frequent types of NP's with either a singular or plural noun as head, comparing Dutch and English per type of combination. Only those data were taken into account where there existed more than 10 noun combinations in each language for any one session. This resulted in four series of 10 x 2 numbers (underlined in Table 14). The results are: significant relation between English and Dutch definite article+noun combinations ($p < .05$; one-tailed); significant relation between English and Dutch zero article+noun combinations ($p < .005$; one-tailed); significant relation between English and Dutch indefinite article+noun combinations ($p < .025$; one-tailed); non-significant relation between English and Dutch pronoun+noun combinations. These results suggest that on the whole, the development of the four most frequent noun combinations runs parallel in both languages.

In both languages, there is a diversification of the subgroups which gains momentum at around the middle of the study, i.e. when Kate is ca. three years old. Before this, nouns mainly get combined with zero article, an indefinite or a definite article.

In both languages, use of just the indefinite article with a noun decreases drastically after the middle of the study. This finding can to some extent be related to a slight overall decrease in identifying expressions (of the sort THAT'S A NP), but the main reason for it seems to be the fact that other determiners and modifiers simply take over.

A final but highly significant finding is that adult order of determiners, modifiers and nouns is preserved at all times, even in those few cases where more than one adjective occurs within an NP. This complete lack of syntagmatically inappropriate forms in either language suggests that syntagmatic relations may be easier to detect than paradigmatic ones (cf. Kate's very incomplete knowledge of the Dutch syntactic gender marking system but her fully appropriate use of intra-noun phrase word order).

6.5.3 *Discussion*

The fact that for both English and Dutch the relative usage of various types of noun combinations is very similar probably reflects the similarity of the syntagmatic relationships in adult usage in both languages. The finding that no errors in the combinations occur (e.g. no two articles or pronouns are used within the same NP) may be due to the clarity and lack of exceptions in the input languages. In addition, the child never hears, for instance, two articles used in front of a noun, so why should she produce these sequences herself? One might object to this 'you-don't-produce-what-you-don't-hear' interpretation that in the marking of gender in Dutch NP's, Kate does produce sequences she never hears. This of course cannot be denied, but the significant difference between the syntagmatic combinations and the paradigmatically oriented forms is that neither in the child's developing system nor in the input language is there competition of other possibilities for the syntagmatic combinations, whereas for the morphological choices to be made, there is competition from other forms in the child's system, which possibly blinds the child to even perceiving certain features in the input language.

6.5.4 *Comparisons with monolingual children*

There is very little information on Dutch-speaking monolingual children's syntagmatic use of NP's. The only study that furnishes some information in this regard is the one by Bol and Kuiken (1987). They) write that adjective+noun combinations (without another determiner) are used productively in the first half of the third year. Only after their third birthday do children start to use determiner+adjective+noun combinations (Bol and Kuiken 1987). Although in the Kate corpus adjective+noun combinations are only the fifth most frequently occurring ones, these combinations do appear quite steadily and regularly from Tape 2 onwards, and use hence seems to be productive. Kate also uses determiner+ adjective+ noun combinations (even before her third birthday). Thus, Kate appears to be maybe slightly ahead of Dutch-speaking monolingual children as far as her use of NP's containing a modifying adjective is concerned. Unfortunately, comparative data from Dutch-speaking monolingual children about NP's without a modifying adjective are lacking.

Fortunately, there is more information available for English-speaking monolingual children. Wells (1985) gives a highly detailed account of the types of noun phrase structures found in the speech production of English-speaking children. For the age of 36 months, we see that of all the NP's with a noun as head, the four most frequent combinations are the same as the ones found for Kate (cf. Table 14 in our Appendix and Table A16 in Wells' Appendix A2). Comparisons for the adjective+noun and adverb or adjective+ adjective+noun combinations cannot be made, since Wells' table does not list these. The remaining infrequently occurring combinations in our Table 14 also occur quite infrequently in Wells' table. Thus, as far as the structure of NP's with a noun as head goes, Kate behaves quite similarly to English monolingual children.

6.6 The noun phrase: concluding remarks

At the age of three years and four months, Kate is still very much in the middle of learning the intricacies of the noun phrase in both English and Dutch. Development in either language is largely separate for each language. Although no sufficiently detailed comparisons can be made due to lack of comparable data in the literature, there exists a general similarity for most aspects analysed in the above between the bilingual data and data reporting on the acquisition of English and Dutch in monolingual children.

Notes
1   This use of HET occurs fairly frequently, but operates with ill-understood restrictions (see Geerts, Haeseryn, de Rooij and van den Toorn 1982: 170). It is not even certain whether HET in this usage refers to just the preceding non-neuter noun, and hence this usage was not included in Table 6.2 or in the data analysis.
2   'Northern' use refers to standard Dutch as used in the Netherlands; 'Southern' use refers to standard Dutch as used in Flanders (cf. also Willemyns1981).

3 In part C of this table, recording sessions 6 and 8 show a surge in the number of neuter nouns preceded by a determiner. This may be attributed to the fact that during these recording sessions, Kate was intensely practising new names of various animals, and repeatedly referring to neuter nouns such as PAARD <horse> and VARKEN <pig>; furthermore, recording sessions 6 and 8 contain the highest numbers of diminutives over the whole recording period.
4 Unfortunately, I have not been able to find any frequency counts of use of the various pronouns in connection with animacy or natural gender. De Jong (1979) does present figures for the use of the lexical items involved, but there is no breakdown according to type of referent.

7 The verb phrase

7.1 Introduction

English and Dutch verb phrases (or VP's) exhibit a number of similarities and differences. Both languages express time and aspect distinctions through the morphological marking of lexical items referring to actions, states and events (i.e., verbs). [1] In addition to the affixing of bound morphemes to these verbs (cf. Dutch 'speel' <play> vs. 'speel**de**' <play**ed**>), separate free morphemes which themselves are renditions of verbs are relied upon heavily in order to further encode time, aspect and mood distinctions (cf. English 'The child washed his doll' vs. 'The child **had** washed his doll'). Another similarity between English and Dutch is that there exists a system of person and number agreement between the grammatical subject (typically not a verb) of the sentence and one part of the verb phrase. This part has traditionally been labelled the 'finite' verb (see e.g. Palmer 1974, Quirk, Greenbaum, Leech and Svartvik 1985) and we shall follow this tradition here. All other components of the verb phrase are by definition non-finite. Both languages make use of the copula, time, mood and aspect auxiliaries, modal auxiliaries and 'full' or lexical verbs (the functions of the auxiliaries are not always equivalent in both languages, though).

English and Dutch differ widely, however, in the way and extent to which they map time and aspect distinctions onto specific verb phrases. For instance, where one language would use a one-unit verb phrase for a time or aspect indication the other language might use a periphrastic form (for example, upon seeing the rain fall down in the street, a Dutch speaker might suddenly yell out 'Kijk! Het **regent**!' <Look! It rains!>, whereas an English speaker would disappointedly say 'Look! It**'s raining**!'); furthermore, where one language would use one kind of verb phrase (VP) to mainly situate the time that an action or event takes place, no straightforward morpheme-by-morpheme translation would necessarily express such a time indication in the other language (for instance, the Dutch 'Ik heb de vaat gedaan' <I-have-the-dishes-done> may refer to some time

time in the near or distant past without any further implications; an English speaker using the formally equivalent 'I've done the dishes' expects his housemate to be appreciative of the just accomplished task: the same utterance cannot normally be used to refer to an action taking place at a well-defined point in the past, and in fact it has been argued (Lyons 1977) that the perfect's main role is that of indicating aspect rather than tense. An additional difference is that the English agreement system mainly distinguishes between third person singular and all other persons, whereas in the Dutch system a distinction usually has to be made between first, second and third person singular and the plural persons.

The above characterization of the main similarities and differences between Dutch and English as far as use of the verb phrase goes has of course been very succinct, but it will be clear that Kate will not be able to latch on to either adult system simply by transferring knowledge that she may have from the one language to the other. This is true not only for the marking of Subject--finite verb agreement and other paradigmatic choices to be made (e.g. the formation of past participles), but also for the choice of 'tense' (i.e. the particular morphological configuration used to encode any one time and/or aspect distinction).

If it is found that Kate uses English and Dutch verb forms mainly within their respective linguistic contexts, and if her functional use of the tenses is mostly language specific, then we shall have gained more evidence for the hypothesis that the morphosyntactic development of a bilingual child's two languages involves two fairly separate processes that are by logical implication strongly guided by the linguistic input that the child is exposed to, rather than primarily by the existence of universal cognitive or linguistic categories.

7.2 A catalogue of verb forms

In this section we shall address the question to what extent Kate stays within the formal boundaries of each of her languages in attaching bound morphemes to verb roots and in combining auxiliaries with non-finite elements. Before we go on to analyse the data, however, a more detailed overview of the adult systems that the child is exposed to is presented below.

7.2.1 The adult verb systems

In Tables 7.1 and 7.2 below a short overview of some of the formal characteristics of the adult English and Dutch VP systems is presented. As in Chapter 6, only those features have been included which are pertinent to the acquisition data under discussion. Thus, for instance, the table presenting relevant elements of the adult English system does not include the present perfect for the simple reason that in the corpus there was no English present perfect to be found.

Before we go on to the analysis of the corpus, a few clarifications of elements in the tables may be necessary.

Both Tables 7.1 and 7.2 are mainly organized around the various types of verbs: in the adult systems, lexical verbs clearly behave differently from auxiliaries or the copula, both as far as inflectional morphology and combinatorial possibilities with other verb elements go. One of the basic prerequisites for the child to produce adult-like verb phrases is distinguishing between the various types of verbs: only on the basis of the distinction between these can further details be learned (that is, if any 'rule system' is accepted to lie at the basis of VP production).[2] Our later data analysis will closely follow the format of Tables 7.1 and 7.2.

One section of Tables 7.1 and 7.2 that does not have anything to do with a presentation based on distinctions between the various types of verbs is the section that lists the various verb forms that can be used to express future time reference. This deviation from the general structure of the tables was thought to be necessary because in English, and to a lesser extent in Dutch as well, there is no single 'future' verb form which could be listed under e.g. 'lexical verbs' and which would apply to lexical verbs only, as for instance the regular past inflection. Instead, both languages utilize a number of different verb forms to express future time reference which overlap with other verb forms that may be used in entirely different contexts (thus, for instance, the Dutch 'present tense' form may be used to refer to general situations, or actions going on at the time of speaking, or to actions that have yet to take place, to list but a few possibilities. The actual 'time' reference expressed by the verb form will strongly depend on any adverbs used in combination with it, or by elements in the extralinguistic context).

A final general remark concerning both tables has to do with the amount of abstraction present in them. In both tables, only written verb forms have been included, with, for the English system, an emphasis on contracted verb forms, which are typical of informal conversation (see e.g. Crystal and Davy 1969). Obviously, however, the young language-learning child is not exposed to written forms, but to spoken verbs, which show a much greater phonetic diversity than is apparent from a catalogue of the written forms alone. In the more detailed clarification for each adult system below, the main discrepancies between the written and spoken forms will be indicated where necessary.

In adult English, lexical verbs in affirmative clauses take the bound morpheme {-s} in the third person singular of the simple present tense. This morpheme has three major phonetic realizations, viz. [iz], [s] and [z]. The choice between them is determined by the form of the preceding phone (see e.g. Palmer 1974: 245-246). The same holds for the past {-ed} morpheme, which is realized as [id], [t] or [d] (see e.g. Palmer 1974: 246-247).

For the simple past forms only regular past formation was tabulated; irregular past formation is fairly idiosyncratic for each lexical item, although certain 'rules' or 'schemas' may apply to 'subclasses' of irregular verbs (Bybee and Slobin 1982). At any rate, in the adult system irregular verb formation is not a productive principle any more, and the number of irregular verbs is quite limited. Past participles are formed in the same fashion as simple past forms, except for irregular verbs and BE, HAVE and DO: here past participle forms may differ from the simple past ones. Past participles were not tabulated, though, since, as was said before, Kate did not make use of the present perfect, which in English is made up of a form of HAVE followed by a past participle.

English lexical verbs in the interrogative and negative are formed by the addition of an auxiliary than can also function as a lexical verb, viz. DO. This auxiliary follows the conjugation paradigm of lexical verbs in the present, with the finite forms being DO and DOES (DON'T and DOESN'T in the negative). When DO is used as an auxiliary, it is followed by a non-finite verb in the Unmarked Verb Form (UVF). An Unmarked Verb Form is that form of a verb that is minimally present in any regular inflectional paradigm, actually participates in such a paradigm and that can be used without a bound morpheme. The UVF's of the irregular verbs BE and HAVE thus are /bi:/ and /hæv/, rather than for instance /iz/ or /hæz/, since, although these forms can be used by themselves, they cannot be combined with any of the three bound verb morphemes {-s}, {-ed} or {-ing}. The modal verbs, then, have no UVF. DO as auxiliary can also be used for emphasis (in affirmative clauses) and in tag questions.

Note that for lexical verbs, English interrogatives are not always formed by means of the DO-periphrasis: when addressing another person, a speaker might ask a Yes/No-question using YOU + UVF or simply a UVF alone. This use is mainly restricted to informal styles, and to 'experiential' verbs such as WANT, REMEMBER and THINK.

Not included in the class of lexical verbs is HAVE: although HAVE can function as a full lexical verb in the basic meanings of 'to possess' or 'to take, eat, drink', it was separated out from the large class of lexical verbs since in the present tense form HAVE behaves slightly differently from these verbs on the morphological level, and secondly, since the lexical item HAVE can be used as an auxiliary or as a modal verb (in HAVE TO) as well - uses which are impossible for most other lexical verbs. Note that all the full finite forms of HAVE listed in the table have abbreviated alternatives as well, which are quite common in informal conversation (cf. Crystal and Davy 1969). For the negative and interrogative forms, HAVE (in American English) when used as a lexical verb needs DO-periphrasis, whereas it does not utilize this periphrasis when it is used as an auxiliary (except when it appears in HAVE TO: then DO-periphrasis is used in American English).

Since BE does not usually function as a lexical verb but is used as a copula or auxiliary it was treated separately as well. Furthermore, its morphology is quite distinct from that of other English verbs. Note that again, abbreviated forms are quite common. The abbreviated third person singular, simple present form 'S is homophonous with the corresponding 'S form of HAVE. No distinction was made in Table 7.1 between VP's in affirmative, negative and interrogative clauses, since basically the same forms are used in each of these modes. However, all the interrogative and negative forms use only the non-abbreviated forms, except in the first person singular negative, where there is a choice between AM NOT and 'M NOT. This first person singular negative is also the only one where the abbreviated negative particle N'T cannot be used. In the negative interrogative form, the first person singular is again an exception, since, unlike all the other persons, which simply take the negative form, there is choice for the first person singular between AM I NOT? and AREN'T I?.

The verb phrase   163

Table 7.1   *The basic English adult verb phrase formation system*

	Person	Affirm	Interrog [a]	Negative
Lexical verbs [b]				
SIMPLE PRESENT	all but 3psg	UVF	do UVF?	don't UVF
	3psg	UVF + {-s}	does UVF?	doesn't UVF
SIMPLE PAST	all	UVF + {-ed}	did UVF?	didn't UVF
IMPERATIVE [c]	-	(you) UVF	-	don't UVF
PRES. CONT. [d]	all: simple present form of BE and UVF + {-ing} [e]			
HAVE				
SIMPLE PRESENT	all but 3psg	have/'ve	do have? have?	don't have haven't
	3psg	has/'s	does have? has?	doesn't have hasn't
SIMPLE PAST	all	had/'d	did have? had?	didn't have hadn't
IMPERATIVE	-	have	-	don't have
PRES. CONT.	all	simple present form of BE and HAVING		
BE				
SIMPLE PRESENT	1psg	am/'m		
	2psg/plural	are/'re		
	3psg	is/'s		
SIMPLE PAST	1psg/3psg	was		
	2psg/plural	were		
IMPERATIVE	-	be (positive)/don't be (prohibition)		
PRES. CONT.	all persons	simple present form of BE and BEING		
VP's with a modal as finite verb				
SIMPLE PRESENT	all persons	modal (NOT) UVF		
Future time reference				

* the simple present form of BE + going to/gonna [f] and UVF + {-ing}
* the present continuous form of all lexical verbs (including HAVE and DO)
* the simple present form of the modals WILL and SHALL

---

[a] Affirm = affirmative; interrog = interrogative

[b] Used as heads of VP's (and used without a modal verb in the same VP)

[c] There is no interrogative form here (this is true of all the imperatives); positive commands may be issued using a strongly emphasized YOU followed by a UVF or by a UVF alone

[d] PRES. CONT. stands for PRESENT CONTINUOUS

[e] The simple present form of BE here must be in a person-appropriate form of course; the interrogative present continuous has the same morphological form as the affirmative although there may be differences in word order; negatives are made by adding the negative particle to the form of BE. The comments made here are applicable to all cases of the present continuous as presented in Table 7.1

[f] GONNA is relevant here because it is a form typical of informal American English, which is the variety of English that Kate is exposed to

In Table 7.1, the group of 'modals' includes only the verbs CAN, MAY, WOULD, WILL, SHALL, SHOULD and the contracted forms 'LL and 'D. The adult system uses other modals as well, but these do not occur in the data. HAVE TO will be treated separately.

Modals cannot be used by themselves, but must be followed by at least one non-finite verb in the UVF. This UVF can yet be followed by other (non-modal) non-finite verb forms. The minimal unit, however, consists of FINITE MODAL + NON-FINITE UVF. English modals furthermore are morphologically defective, in that they cannot take the {-s}, {-ing} and {−ed} morphemes that many lexical verbs can be combined with. In the table, only the simple present form was listed: imperatives of modals are non-existent, and past forms are quite a complicated matter. In fact, some of the modals (e.g. COULD, WOULD and SHOULD) may already contain an element of past reference (although not necessarily so); in other cases, a periphrastic form with HAVE is used (as in 'I **may have called** him, I don't remember'). Since in the corpus the modals do not refer to past time, this use was not tabulated. Modals can also occur in the continuous form (e.g. 'He **may be fishing**') but since this use did not occur in the corpus either it was not listed.

Only Subject--finite verb inversion distinguishes interrogative and affirmative clauses with a modal as finite verb, i.e. there is no DO-periphrasis. Modals form their negatives with the simple aid of NOT or with the contracted form N'T (again there is no DO-periphrasis). The contracted negative modals may be phonetically quite distinct from the non-contracted ones: compare for instance WILL NOT [wil not] and WON'T [wount]. The difference between CANNOT [kænot] and CAN'T [kænt], on the other hand, is not very great (at least not in American English, which is the main focus of interest here, since this is the variety that Kate was exposed to).

It can be argued that there is no specific future tense in English (Palmer 1974): rather, a number of different verb forms can be used to express future time reference. The most common ones have been listed at the end of Table 7.1 (the list is by no means complete). Among these, the 'BE GOING TO + UVF' construction is the most relevant to the data and typically denotes "future fulfilment of the present" in the adult system (cf. Quirk and Greenbaum 1973: 50).

For a more detailed and more complete description of the basic elements of the adult English VP system, see Palmer 1974.

In adult Dutch, lexical verbs take the bound morpheme {-t} in the third and second persons singular of the simple present tense, but this morpheme is not present when there is Subject--finite verb inversion with a second person singular subject (the second person pronoun U, however, which is the formal equivalent of JIJ and JE in standard Dutch, is grammatically treated as a third person singular form and is always combined with a finite lexical verb carrying the bound morpheme {-t}). The bound morpheme {-t} is virtually always pronounced as [t]. For plural persons, Dutch lexical verbs in the present take the bound morpheme {-en}, which is realized as [∂] when the final phone of the preceding stem is a consonant, and as [n] when the final phone of the preceding stem is a vowel. There are two important points to be noted here, however: the first one is that the bound morpheme {-t} is not realized when the stem of the verb already ends in [t]. The second major point is that, unlike in English, the phonetic realizations of stems of a number of lexical verbs are not necessarily the same across the whole conjugation paradigm. The reason for this is that in Dutch there is a devoicing rule which says that all free morpheme-final, voiced, non-nasal consonants must be pronounced voiceless if they are word-final or followed by a bound morpheme consisting of or starting with a consonant (the devoicing rule may become void when there is assimilation with the first phone of the word following the form that would undergo the devoicing rule if pronounced in relative isolation).

Consider for instance the verb BEVRIEZEN (/b∂vri:z∂/) <to freeze>: the stem of this verb is the free morpheme {bevriez} (/b∂vri:z/). The isolated pronunciation of this free morpheme is [b∂vri:s] (the orthographic form BEVRIES reflects this change of voice). The word BEVRIEZEN would be pronounced [b∂vri:z∂], since here the devoicing rule does not apply (the free morpheme-final phoneme /z/ is not in word-final position, and it is not followed by a consonant but by a vowel). The word BEVRIEST <freezes>, on the other hand, is pronounced [b∂vri:st]: after all, the free morpheme-final phoneme /z/ is followed by a bound morpheme {-t} consisting of a consonant. BEVRIEZEN, then, has two phonetic realizations of the stem, viz. [b∂vri:s] and [b∂vri:z].

Note that the singular forms of the present tense cannot be used to predict what the plural forms will sound like: if a child encounters IK EET [ik e:t] <I eat>, there is no information as to whether the plural form is going to be pronounced [e:də] or [e:tə]. It is only on the basis of hearing the infinitive or plural forms that their exact shape can be determined. However, once the infinitive or plural forms are known the exact shape of the singular forms can be determined, given of course that the speaker is able to apply the devoicing rule. It is clear, then, that the morphological rules as presented in Table 7.2 are a strongly simplified presentation of the actual learning task that the child is faced with.

In view of the preceding, the term 'stem' in Table 7.2 refers to that part of the infinitive that can be obtained by taking away the {-en} infinitive morpheme. The plural forms of lexical verbs in the present are identical to the infinitive form.

Dutch imperatives may be of two kinds: first there is a 'true' imperative form, which is always in clause-initial position, and secondly there is the infinitive form, which occurs in clause-final position. There is a distinct difference between both 'imperatives': the 'true' imperative form (e.g. SLAAP! <sleep!>) can be said to be more direct and 'authoritarian' than the infinitive form (e.g. SLAPEN! <try and go to sleep now!>). Both forms can be combined with a negative particle to express a prohibition.

Note that unlike in English, Dutch does not make use of any kind of periphrasis for forming negatives or interrogatives: affirmative, negative and interrogative VP's are identical, except that negative VP's contain a negative particle.

Whereas the English corpus contains no instances of a present perfect tense, the Dutch corpus contains hardly any instances of simple past tenses, whereas there are quite some instances of the Dutch present perfect. This is why for lexical verbs the simple past is not mentioned in Table 7.2, while the present perfect is.

The Dutch present perfect is made up of an auxiliary (the present tense form of ZIJN <be> or HEBBEN <have>) and a past participle. This past participle may be formed according to a regular paradigm, or may have an irregular form. Only regular past participle has been tabulated; irregular past formation is again (as for English) fairly particular to each lexical item. In regular past participle formation, a discontinuous morpheme consisting of a prefix {ge-} and a suffix {-t} is added to the verb stem. Stems that end in a voiced, non-nasal consonant are devoiced before they receive the suffix {-t} (the same procedure is applied as for the simple present tense); note that the suffix {-t} may be spelled either as -D or -T. The prefix {ge-}

The verb phrase 167

is not actually realized when the stem already appears to begin with a prefix-like element such as VER–, BE–, ONT–, GE– etc. (such elements are quite common in Dutch).

Besides regular past participle formation, there is irregular past participle formation as well. Irregular past participles usually contain the prefix {ge–} (except when the root already appears to begin with a suffix - cf. above). However, instead of the {–t} suffix they may use an {–en} suffix. In addition, irregular past participles often use a vowel-changed form as root rather than the stem.

In Table 7.2 the verb HEBBEN <have> has been separated out from the large class of lexical verbs, since, as in English, the present tense form of HEBBEN behaves differently from these verbs, and since the lexical item HEBBEN can be used as an auxiliary as well - uses which are impossible for most other lexical verbs. The simple past and past participle forms of HEBBEN are irregular.

The copula and auxiliary ZIJN <be> was tabulated separately since its morphology is quite distinct from other Dutch verbs. There is one abbreviated form: the third person singular present tense form may be rendered as [s] rather than [is]. The simple past and past participle forms of ZIJN are irregular, as is the 'true' imperative WEES.

Following De Schutter and van Hauwermeiren (1983), the class of 'modals' in Table 7.2 refers to the verbs KUNNEN, MOGEN, MOETEN, WILLEN, and ZULLEN (again, only modals are listed that actually occur in the data). Unlike in English, Dutch modals do not always have to be followed by a non-finite verb: in fact, four out of the five listed can be used as transitive verbs without an overt non-finite verb (the exception is ZULLEN). (One could argue that in cases where a Dutch modal is only followed by an (obligatory) object, the non-finite verb is 'understood' or 'ellipted' in some sense: 'ik kan het' = 'I can it' <I can do it>, for instance, is often equivalent to 'ik kan het doen' = 'I can it do' <I know how to do it, or: it's possible for me to do it>.) When modals are followed by a non-finite verb, this verb is in the infinitive form. The actual forms that modals take in the singular present tense are irregular, in the sense that they do not follow the paradigm of lexical verbs. This is why the singular forms were listed separately. The plural forms in the present are 'regular' in the sense that they are the same as the infinitive form and thus seem to follow the general rule applicable to lexical verbs (the fact that no stem + {-en} rule was tabulated is because it is hard to say what exactly the 'stem' of each modal verb would be). Dutch modals have past tense inflection and also occur in past participle forms. In addition, they can be used in the infinitive in combination with non-modal finite forms. However, none of these uses (i.e. Dutch modals in the simple past, past participle or infinitive form) occurred in the corpus, and hence were excluded from Table 7.2. Dutch modal auxiliaries show many more syntactic characteristics of lexical verbs than their English counterparts do, and the term 'modal auxiliary' may not be the best description in the case of the Dutch forms (Hofmans 1980).

Finally, Table 7.2 includes a separate section for the expression of future time reference (again, the list is by no means complete). One of the possibilities listed is the inchoative GAAN <go> + infinitive periphrasis, which may be used to indicate an action in the immediate future that may already have started or that is about to take place (as with some of the other verb constructions dealt with so far (e.g. the English present continuous) there are severe restrictions on the types of verbs that can be used in the non-finite part of this construction. A discussion of these restrictions here would lead us too far, however, and more detailed reference to them will only be made when this is of immediate concern to the acquisition data). The use of this construction is very similar to that of the BE GOING TO + UVF construction of English.

In Table 7.1 above the English 'present continuous' was tabulated. A periphrastic form used in Dutch more or less expresses some of the functions that this English present continuous encodes: the form in Dutch consists of a combination of a simple present form of the auxiliary ZIJN followed by AAN HET + infinitive (e.g. 'Hij is aan het eten' <he is eating>). Instead of ZIJN another (semi-)auxiliary indicating a durative meaning such as LIGGEN <lay>, ZITTEN <sit> or STAAN <stand> may be used. Any of these, however, are followed by TE + infinitive. This periphrastic 'durative present' was not included in Table 7.2, since it was not present in the corpus (at least not in its fully adult form - see below).

For a more detailed description of the Dutch VP system, see e.g. Geerts, Haeseryn, de Rooij and van den Toorn 1982.

Table 7.2 *The basic Dutch adult verb phrase formation system*

Lexical verbs [a]
SIMPLE PRESENT   1psg + 2psg (inversion)   stem
                        2psg (no inversion) + 3psg   stem OR stem + {-t}
                        plural persons   stem + {-en}
PRESENT PERFECT   all persons: present form of ZIJN or HEBBEN
                        + past participle
IMPERATIVE   -   stem OR stem + {-en}
HEBBEN
SIMPLE PRESENT   1psg + 2psg (inversion)   heb (/hep/)
                        2psg (no inversion)   hebt (/hept/)
                        3psg   heeft (/he:ft/)
                        plural persons   hebben (/hebə/)
SIMPLE PAST   singular persons   had (/hat/)
                        plural persons   hadden (/hadə/)
PRESENT PERFECT   all persons: pres. form of HEBBEN + gehad
IMPERATIVE   -   heb OR hebben
ZIJN
SIMPLE PRESENT   1psg + 2psg (inversion)   ben (/ben/)
                        2psg (no inversion)   bent (/bent/)
                        3psg   is OR 's (/is/ or /s/)
                        plural persons   zijn (/z in/)
SIMPLE PAST   singular persons   was (/was/)
                        plural persons   waren (/wa:rə/)
PRESENT PERFECT   all persons: pres. form of ZIJN + geweest
IMPERATIVE   -   wees OR zijn
The modals
SIMPLE PRESENT   1psg + 3psg   kan/mag/moet/wil/zal
                        2psg   kan OR kunt/mag OR moogt/moet/
                                                          wil OR wilt/zal OR zult [b]
                        plural persons   kunnen/mogen/moeten/willen/zullen
Future time reference
* the simple present form of GAAN or ZULLEN and the infinitive

[a] Used as heads of VP's (and used without a modal verb in the same VP)

[b] MOOGT and WILT are forms that can be used with the pronoun GIJ. This pronoun tends to be used more frequently in Flanders than in the Netherlands, and consequently, the modals MOOGT and WILT, while perfectly standard, are also somewhat regionally defined. These modals were listed because Kate used each of them once

7.2.2 The data

We now go on to see to what extent Kate's verb forms reflect the different Dutch and English systems. The analyses and discussions here will focus only on the actual forms that Kate uses, rather than on any developments within any one system: after all, it is only when it has been determined that Kate in fact produces fully Dutch and fully English VP's, rather than some 'Mixed' or 'Dutlish' VP's, that those Dutch and English VP's can be considered as pertaining to separate, closed systems that can be treated independently from the other language.

The data base for the following analyses consists of all Dutch, English and Mixed utterances containing at least a finite verb or an imperative. The terms 'finite verb' and 'imperative' were defined in a purely descriptive manner: a verb form was coded as being a finite verb when it had a grammatical Subject, whether this subject was actually present or not (if it was not, though, it had to be unambiguously clear from the on-going discourse), and a verb form was coded as being an imperative when its function was to issue a command to another person solely through the use of this verb form. At this level of categorization, no claims are made about the status or relevance of these and other descriptive categories in the child's acquisition process.

For clauses containing just a finite verb, the present analysis will only consider the verb forms themselves rather than how they are combined with particular subjects (the question of Subject--finite verb agreement will be taken up in sections 7.3.2.1 and 7.4.2.1). The present analysis will, however, look at the combinations of elements in complex VP's (i.e., VP's containing a finite verb and at least one non-finite element) in order to see to what extent they reflect both input languages.

7.2.2.1 Ambiguous finite verb forms

In the classification of Kate's utterances according to language used, guidelines were followed which were based on the morphological make-up of lexical items (cf. Chapter 4, section 4.2). However, in some cases where Kate produced non-adult-like forms, it was not unambiguously clear to which language specific lexical items belonged. It is these cases that will be discussed in this subsection.

As far as single-morpheme verb forms are concerned, there were three types where any decision about what language they should be classified as was bound to raise questions later: Kate occasionally used the forms HEEF, EM and KEN in otherwise completely Dutch utterances. HEEF was mostly used to mean 'have', and EM was mostly used as one would use AM (of the verb BE) in English, or BEN (of the verb ZIJN) in Dutch.

KEN was very much used like the English modal CAN. In the following paragraph, we shall look at each of these three items in closer detail.

First we turn to Kate's use of HEEF. This non-adult-like form might derive from the third person singular, present form of Dutch HEBBEN, viz. HEEFT, with the /t/ analyzed as a bound morpheme (by analogy with the regular pattern existing for lexical verbs - see Table 7.2 above) and omitted in HEEF to form a new 'stem' that happens to be non-existent in adult usage. Alternatively, HEEF [he:f] might be seen as a phonological or phonetic adaptation of the English HAVE [hæv]. It will be argued here that HEEF derives from the Dutch HEEFT, since in the literature on monolingual Dutch children forms of HEBBEN have been reported on that could only be produced on the basis of an analysis of Dutch HEEFT as consisting of a 'stem' HEEF and a separable {–t} morpheme : the non-adult-like infinitive HEVEN [he:və] is mentioned by Schaerlaekens (1977: 163), and Tinbergen (1919) and Van Ginneken (1917) give many examples in which their respective subjects Luuk and Keesje use HEEF around the age of three. Obviously, however, the fact that some Dutch-speaking children misanalyzed HEEFT does not prove that Kate did the same (she might accidentally have arrived at a form that Dutch-speaking children produce but Kate might have followed an entirely different route). Even though our interpretation of HEEF as being a form of Dutch HEBBEN can remain only hypothetical at this stage, we saw enough reason to categorize the utterances containing HEEF as being part of the Dutch rather than the Mixed corpus (that is, of course, if HEEF was the only possibly non-Dutch portion of the utterance as a whole). In the following, then, any discussion of Kate's use of Dutch HEBBEN <have> will include her use of HEEF.

The second non-adult-like form to be discussed, viz. EM [em], is always used in combination with the first person singular subject pronoun IK <I> and occurs a total of nine times in the whole corpus. Phonologically, this form is much closer to the English AM [æm] than to the Dutch BEN [ben], so it seems more reasonable to see EM as a 'translation' from English into Dutch accompanied by a phonetic adaptation than was perhaps the case for HEEF. On the other hand, in the English corpus the item AM occurs only once or twice, whereas the abbreviated form M is used abundantly, and so one may argue that since the English full form AM seems to be hardly present it cannot really exert a big influence on the Dutch system. Quite a different possibility is that here we are seeing an influence from the form EM from the Antwerp dialect meaning <have> and used in combination with the first person singular subject pronoun. There are two main arguments against this interpretation: first of all, Kate does not hear the Antwerp dialect on a daily basis (although one of her regular baby-sitters may have used IK EM instead of the standard IK HEB); secondly, how could a form of HEBBEN have an influence on the use of the copula ZIJN? That in fact Kate herself is not always clear on the boundaries between forms of HEBBEN and ZIJN is shown in the following examples where there appears to be a clear influence from HEBBEN on ZIJN (see examples 1 and 2):

(1) 'Nee ik [em] - ik [ep] Kate!' (Age: 3;3,16)
    <No I ?am? - I have Kate!>
    {EM repaired into HEB}
(2) 'Ik [ep] - ik [em] ook een kip.' (Age: 2;10,13)
    <I have - I ?am? also a chicken.>
      (Kate is pretending to be a chicken)
      {HEB repaired into EM}

While influence from the Antwerp dialect is doubtful (but not altogether impossible), influence from HEBBEN on ZIJN (for whatever underlying reason), then, might be an explanation for the occurrence of EM. Van Ginneken (1917: 145) gives as an example of an utterance by his subject Keesje 'Mag je emme', <Can you have>, where EMME is clearly an attempt at HEBBEN (often pronounced [ebə] in colloquial speech). If here the bilabial plosive /b/ can be transformed into a bilabial nasal /m/, then perhaps Kate's form EM is the result of a confusion between HEBBEN and ZIJN, where EM is a rendition of the underlying morph {heb} (/heb/), which of course cannot be pronounced as [heb] due to the devoicing rule (see section 7.2.1 above), and where as a 'solution' the final /b/ is rendered as the only type of voiced consonant that <u>can</u> occur in word-final position in Dutch, i.e. the corresponding nasal. At this point, however, no straightforward choice between the competing interpretations (i.e. transfer from English, or the phonetic argument on the basis of the confusion between ZIJN and HEBBEN) can be made, so utterances containing EM are in fact not unambiguously fully Dutch utterances. In the following, then, EM occurring in otherwise entirely Dutch utterances will be excluded from any discussion of Dutch ZIJN and English BE.

Finally, there is KEN [ken] to be accounted for. KEN only occurs in yes/no questions and is always followed by IK <I> or JIJ <you>. In Dutch, KEN does exist, but means KNOW. It is clear from Kate's utterances with KEN that she uses the form not in the meaning of KNOW, but in quite a different meaning: Kate uses KEN to ask permission to do something or to question the investigator on her willingness to do something, with the latter possibility occurring five out of the seven times that Kate uses KEN in an otherwise entirely Dutch utterance. In standard Dutch, it is possible to use a form of KUNNEN (KAN JE?, KUN JE?), often accompanied by a modal particle such as EVEN, to ask somebody to do something. However, this use does seem to be particular to business-like situations, and is a polite form of a command. Perhaps it is more common in informal situations to query someone's willingness to do something by using the modal WILLEN (again often accompanied by a modal particle). (These observations are entirely based on my own experiences as a native speaker of Dutch, and might not accurately reflect the 'objective' situation as it could be measured on the basis of extensive corpora of natural language use.) Kate does not use Dutch WILLEN in any other meaning than in the meaning of WANT, and so we might here be confronted with a 'lexical gap' so to speak, where querying someone's willingness to do something is not yet a lexically accessible notion in Dutch, whereas it is so in English: Kate does use CAN YOU? in querying someone's willingness to do something (but it occurs only six times in the whole period of observation). Since English CAN often translates into Dutch as KUNNEN, which has as the singular present form KAN (/kan/), Kate's use of KEN JIJ? in Dutch can best be seen as a phonetically adapted lexical transfer from English. The repaired utterance in example 3 below further exemplifies the connection between KEN and KUNNEN (and hence between KEN and CAN).

(3) 'Ken - kun je lie down?' (Age: 2;8,8) <Can - can you lie down?>
{inappropriate use of KEN [ken] repaired by appropriate choice of KUN [kyn]}

Since Kate's odd use of KEN may be unequivocally seen as a phonological adaptation of the English CAN, Dutch utterances with KEN used in the meaning of CAN will not be included in any discussion of Dutch KUNNEN or English CAN.

Table 7.3   *Verbs with morphemes from both English and Dutch as used by Kate*

Dutch infinitive morpheme {-en} added to an English UVF
* A: 'Wat zie je in 't bos?' <What do you see in the woods?>
  K: 'Ik zie boating in 't bos. Ik zeg ik ga [boudə] (<u>boden</u>) in 't bos.' (Age 2;7,17)
     <I see boating in the woods. I said I'm going boating in the woods.>
* K: 'Jij moogt niet [tətʃən] (<u>touchen</u>), okee.' (Age 2;7,17) <You can't touch, okay.>
* K: 'Beetje [kukə] (<u>cooken</u>).' (Age 2;9,0) <Cook a little bit.>
  A: 'Goed roeren, hé.' <Don't forget to stir well.>
* K: 'A-as jij wil kijk, dan dan zal jij-dan zal ik jou [telən] (<u>tellen</u>), okee?'
     (Age 3;3,16) (K and A are playing a hiding game)
     <I-if you want to look, then then you will-then I will tell you, okay?>
  A: 'Wablief? Watte?' <What? What?>
  K: 'Dan zal ik jou [telən] (<u>tellen</u>) eh?' (Age 3;3,16) <Then I will tell you hey?>

Dutch 3psg simple present morpheme {-t} added to an English UVF
* K: 'Paard [laikt] (<u>liket</u>) taart.' (Age 2;8,8) <Horse likes pie.>
* A: 'Wat is da? Da's een paard, he?' <What's that? That's a horse, right?>
  K: 'Jo.' (Age 2;10,13) <Yep.>
  A: 'Een paardje.' <A little horsie.>
  K: 'En en d-en da-en da die [muːft] (<u>movet</u>)!' <And and th-and tha-and that that moves!>
     (clearly looking for another word)
  A: 'Ja die beweegt! Die springt. Springt die? Springt het paardje?'
     <Yes it moves! It jumps. Does it jump? Does the little horsie jump?>
  K: 'Nee!' <No!>
  A: 'Nee? Wat doet het dan? Wat doet het paardje dan?--Loopt het paardje?'
     <No? What does it do then? What does the horsie do? --Does the horsie run?>
  K: 'Nee.' (Age 2;10,13) <No.>
  A: 'Nee? Wat dan wel?' <No? What *does* it do then?>
  K: '[muːft] (<u>Movet</u>!)' <Moves!>
  A: 'Movet? Ja....' <Moves? Well yes...>
* K: 'Maa jij moet ze-moet ze pakke! Als ik ze-a-als ik ze-ze <u>throwt</u>!' (Age 3;3,16)
     <Bu you have to-have to catch them! When I-w-when I throws them-them!>

Dutch imperative ending {-en} added to an English UVF
* K: '[iːtə] (<u>Eaten</u>).' (Age 3;0,17) <Eat.> (K has just given imaginary food to A)
* K: 'Look look! Look!! Look! [lukə] (<u>Looken</u>)! [lukə] (<u>Looken</u>) mum!' (Age 3;1,18)
  M: 'What's looken?'
  K: 'Look!'

Both EM and KEN, then, can be seen as phonological or phonetic adaptations of English verbs that are inserted into otherwise entirely Dutch utterances, although for EM, this is not the only possible interpretation. HEEF, on the other hand, is more likely than not a Dutch non-adult-like form constructed on the basis of a Dutch analogy, rather than as a phonetic adaptation of an English form.

We now turn to the discussion of a few language-ambiguous verb forms from the Mixed corpus that do not consist of a single morpheme but that are lexical items consisting of morphemes from both English and Dutch. The actual forms were tabulated in Table 5.2 part 3. in Chapter 5 but are again presented here in Table 7.3 together with their linguistic contexts.

Some of the English verbs used in the Mixed child utterances in Table 7.3 do not appear in their Dutch translation 'equivalents' but do occur in the English corpus (viz. LIKE, MOVE, THROW, BOAT). Of these, LIKE occurs both as an infinitive and as a finite verb, THROW also occurs as an infinitive and as a finite verb but much less frequently, MOVE occurs in the infinitive, -ing-form and the simple past, and finally BOAT only occurs as a gerund (with the {-ing} morpheme attached to [boud], which shows the American English tendency to voice consonants in intervocalic position). It is thus clear that Kate knows how to use these four verbs in an English context. When she transfers them to Dutch, she adapts the morphology to fit the Dutch system. TOUCHEN and TELLEN only appear in the data as 'mixed' items and thus we cannot know what status they have for the child, i.e. whether they are tagged for English or not. The remaining three verbs (EAT, LOOK, COOK) appear in their Dutch 'equivalents' as well and their occurrence within Mixed mainly Dutch utterances can probably best be explained as unrepaired slips of the tongue (see Chapter 10).

At any rate, it is clear that the conjugation systems of both languages are used appropriately, i.e. Dutch bound morphemes are always used within a largely Dutch utterance (or within a conversation that is largely Dutch), and never within otherwise entirely English utterances. Conversely, with the exception of a single utterance (see next sentence), English bound morphemes are never used within otherwise entirely Dutch utterances, but only within a discourse that is mainly English. The only one instance in the entire corpus of a possible transfer of an English bound morpheme to the Dutch system is given in example 4:

(4) 'Ik gaas dis snijden.' (Age 3;2,7)
   <I'm going to cut this>
      {non-adult-like addition of an {-s} morpheme to the Dutch verb
      stem GA in an otherwise mainly Dutch utterance (but note
      that DIS is a 'blend' of English THIS and Dutch DIT)}

The form GAAS could be interpreted as consisting of the stem GA of the Dutch verb GAAN <go> and the third person singular present tense English morpheme {-s}. This interpretation is possible since the Dutch verbal system does not contain an {-s} morpheme in any verb conjugation pattern. The {-s} morpheme does appear in the formation of some Dutch plurals, but it is unlikely that there is an influence from noun morphology on the class of verbs: although form class errors do occasionally occur in child language (e.g. De Vooys 1916, Maratsos 1982), they do not seem to constitute any major developmental strategy and show little systematicity. Hence the argument that influence from the English system is apparent here seems not too farfetched. Since, however, only one possibly 'mixed morphology' example was present in the corpus it cannot carry much weight in the global interpretation, especially also because there is yet an alternative interpretation, viz. that GAAS is not one word, but two, namely GA 'S, with 'S being the abbreviation of EENS, a particle meaning something like JUST (at least, in the context of example 4). [3] In this interpretation, there is no influence from English whatsoever.

Most of the evidence from lexical items consisting of morphemes from both English and Dutch, then, confirms the principle that was proposed earlier, viz. the **principle of morphological language stability**. This principle claims that the bilingual child exposed to two languages from birth in a fairly balanced fashion will always use the bound morphemes of the main language of the utterance once s/he has started to mark morphological distinctions. Morphemes do not 'travel' from one language to the other. Obviously, the very fact that in the entire corpus there were only a handful of verb forms which consisted of 'language-ambiguous' or 'dual-language' morphemes also confirms the principle of morphological language stability.

One might, though, see example 5 as a counterexample to the proposed principle. This, however, is not necessarily the case: the utterance starts in Dutch ('Hij gaat') and proceeds in English ('pyjamas bring'). One might expect BRINGEN since the overall structural pattern is Dutch rather than English (English word order would be: Subject/finite verb/non-finite verb/Direct Object). On the other hand, at the moment of uttering BRING, the utterance is clearly English, although the whole utterance is not mainly English or Dutch, but a 'true' Mixed utterance. The principle here is not a strong predictor. Had, however, the Direct Object been a Dutch word, the principle would definitely predict BRINGEN. Since again we are dealing with only one possible counterexample, the principle of morphological language stability can still stand.

(5) 'Hij gaat pyjamas bring.' (Age 3;0,6)
   <He's going to bring pyjamas.>
      {use of a Dutch modal which is not followed by a verb in the stem + {-en} form, but simply by a stem form (the 'stem' being an English UVF)}

There were no other instances in the corpus of verb forms with morphological shapes that did not unequivocally belong to just one language. So far, though, we have not presented any quantitative data concerning the frequencies of occurrence of the verb forms discussed above. Such quantitative data will be supplied after the analysis and discussion of the 'purely' Dutch and English VP's. We now turn to this analysis.

7.2.2.2 Morphologically unambiguous verb forms

Even though it was determined in the section 7.2.2.1 that on the free and bound morpheme levels very few instances could be found that showed the child's knowledge of the other language, it is still possible that in the use of morphologically unambiguous verb forms there is an influence from one language on the other. In order to examine this possibility, we shall take as our data base all the morphologically entirely Dutch or English VP's in the Dutch, English and Mixed corpora. Excluded, then, are VP's containing one of the morphologically ambiguous verb forms discussed in the previous subsection, as well as a few VP's in the Mixed corpus consisting of an English and a Dutch verb. (The only VP's in the Mixed corpus consisting of an English and a Dutch verb are some of the VP's mentioned in the previous subsection.) It must be emphasized again that VP's in Mixed utterances consisting of the language-indeterminate IS or S and a non-finite verb were considered to be wholly in the language of the non-finite verb: although IS and S are of course phonetically not language-indeterminate, the detail of the transcription does not allow the written forms IS and S in Mixed utterances to be assigned to any one language (see also later discussion).

Table 7.4 Kate's English verb forms [a]

	Affirm		Interrog [b]		Negative	
Lexical verbs						
SIMPLE PRESENT	UVF	215	UVF?	7	don't UVF	26
	WANNA	26	does UVF?	6	doesn't UVF	3
	UVF + {-s}	18	do UVF?	3		
			does? (tag)	2		
SIMPLE PAST	irregular	20	did UVF?	9	didn't UVF	4
	UVF + {-ed}	7	did + past	2		
	did UVF	1				
IMPERATIVE	UVF	101			don't UVF	10
	you UVF	11				
PRES. CONT.	simple present form of BE and UVF + {-ing}					36
HAVE						
SIMPLE PRESENT	have	24	have?	1	don't have	2
	has	4	does have?	1	doesn't have	1
SIMPLE PAST	had	1	did have?	2	didn't have	1
BE	**full**		**abbreviated**			
SIMPLE PRESENT	is	66	's	63		
	am	15	'm	45		
	are	28	're	9		
SIMPLE PAST	was	15				
	were	3				
VP's with a modal as finite verb						
SIMPLE PRESENT	modal (NOT) UVF			120		
	'LL + WILL + UVF			1		
	'LL + past			1		
Future time reference						
* the simple present form of BE + GOING TO/GONNA and UVF + {-ing}						48
* the present continuous form of a lexical verb						6
* 'LL + UVF						4
* non-adult-like use of 'LL + WILL + UVF						1
Other						
* non-adult-like use of 'LL + past						1

[a] The numbers here refer to the total number of occurrences of any one form in the entire corpus

[b] Affirm = affirmative; interrog = interrogative

In Table 7.4 the English data have been summarized (this table includes the relevant data from entirely English VP's in Mixed utterances). Since at this point the focus of interest is on the forms themselves rather than on Subject--finite verb agreement, this table differs in form from Table 7.1 in that the various verb forms are listed regardless of the Subjects they were combined with. Finite verbs occurring without an overt Subject are thus included as well. After each verb form the total number of occurrences for the entire English corpus is indicated. Under lexical verbs in the present, WANNA was tabulated separately, since it occurred fairly frequently and could not be 'squeezed into' the UVF vs. UVF + {-s} paradigm because of the presence of the phonetically reduced preposition 'to'.

In Table 7.4, abstraction was made of the particular functional uses of each verb. The data for HAVE, for instance, include use of HAVE as a modal, i.e. in the HAVE TO syntagm. Similarly, forms of BE include the occurrences of BE in copula usage, the present continuous forms and the BE GOING TO + ing-form constructions. This means that the figures for the various forms of BE and the figures for the uses of the present continuous overlap, with the former including the latter. A similar situation exists for the 'LL + UVF syntagm: although this syntagm occurs quite frequently throughout, its unambiguous use as a prediction about a future state of affairs occurs only four times. These four instances are included in the figure of 120 for the use of a modal followed by (NOT) UVF.

The data presented in Table 7.4 clearly show that most of Kate's English verbs have an adult-like form, both for the individual items as well as for their combinations: theoretically possible combinations of a form of HAVE with an ing-form, for instance, do not occur.

(6) 'What did you did?' (Age 2;10,5) <What did you do?>
    (asked when Kate's mother has hurt herself)
    {inappropriate use of finite past form of DO with a finite auxiliary form of DO}

Among the non-adult-like combinations, the first case concerns two utterances in which a form of DO is not followed by a UVF but by an irregular simple past form (see examples 6 and 7). On all other occasions, however (even in the few other cases where DID is used as an auxiliary), the auxiliary DO is combined with the appropriate UVF.

(7) 'What did you took me?' (Age 3;1,18) <Where did you take me?>
    {inappropriate use of finite past form of TAKE with a finite auxiliary form of DO}

In the non-adult-like utterances above, no influence from Dutch is apparent: there is no Dutch *'DEED + past form' syntagm. Rather we are here seeing a 'contamination' of the English interrogative syntagm 'DID UVF' and the declarative simple past form. Identical forms have been reported on for monolingual English-speaking children (see e.g. Hurford 1975, Maratsos and Kuczaj 1978). In fact, Hurford (1975: 300) mentions exactly the same utterance as shown in example (6) above, viz. 'What did you did?' as uttered by his daughter in the course of her third year. Maratsos and Kuczaj (1978) note that these cases of 'auxiliary overmarking', as they are called in the literature, occur in very low proportions, and rather than refer to some major developmental mechanism to account for these forms, Maratsos and Kuczaj strongly argue that these should be seen entirely as errors of performance. Whatever the reasons for the 'DID simple past' syntagm, then, it is clear that influence from Dutch is not one of them: if monolingual children produce exactly the same non-adult-like forms, any transfer argument loses ground (cf. our interpretation of HEEF above).

Instances of the present continuous and of the imperative only occur with lexical verbs, never with HAVE (even when used as a lexical verb) or BE.

The use of the modals entirely follows the adult English pattern: each modal auxiliary is followed by a UVF. There is certainly no undue influence from the Dutch system, where some modal auxiliaries may be used as main verbs. Two non-adult-like English combinations do occur, however (see examples 8 and 9). Since literal translations of these utterances into Dutch result in non-existent Dutch verb forms (*ZAL ZAL SPELEN and *ZAL WILDE/WOU), again these forms are most probably attributable to problems that Kate is encountering in learning the English system *per se* . Further comparisons between English and Dutch will be made after the presentation of the Dutch material, which is tabulated in Table 7.5.

(8) 'I'll just will play.' (Age 3;1,18) <I'll just play.>
 {inappropriate overmarking of the modal WILL and its use as a non-finite verb after 'LL}

(9) 'An-an-I-and she just listened and and I'll just wan-wanted to tell ?..?. I just said I want a way way way to the bath!' (Age 3;1,18)
(Kate is complaining to her mother about the investigator's 'unfair' treatment of her, but it is not clear quite exactly what Kate considered to be unfair: Kate had been riding her tricycle all the way to the bathroom at the other end of the long corridor and had met the investigator in the corridor) {inappropriate combination of the modal 'LL with the finite past form of WANT}

Table 7.5 *Kate's Dutch verb forms*

Lexical verbs					
SIMPLE PRESENT	stem				210
	stem + {-t}				201
	stem + {-en}				42
SIMPLE PAST	irregular non-adult-like				2
	irregular adult-like				1
PRESENT PERFECT	present form of HEBBEN + past participle				25
	present form of ZIJN + past participle				19
IMPERATIVE	stem + {-en}				46
	stem				23
	stem + {-t}				2
HEBBEN					
SIMPLE PRESENT	heb	53	heef		38
	heeft	6	hebben		2
SIMPLE PAST	had	1			
PRESENT PERFECT	present form of HEBBEN + gehad				1
ZIJN					
SIMPLE PRESENT	is	187	s		111
	zijn	37	ben		23
	bent	8			
SIMPLE PAST	was	12	waren		2
PRESENT PERFECT	present form of ZIJN + geweest				1
The modals					
SIMPLE PRESENT	modal verb (+ infinitive)				329
	modal verb + past participle		1		
Future time reference					
* simple present form of GAAN + infinitive					109
* ZAL + infinitive					10
Other					
* present form of ZIJN	and stem + {-en}				4
* present form of HEBBEN	and stem + {-en}				1
* present form of HEBBEN	and stem				1

As in Table 7.4 above, Table 7.5 does not distinguish between the various persons. After each verb form the total number of occurrences for the entire Dutch corpus is indicated. For each verb type or lexical item, forms have been arranged vertically in descending order of total frequency of occurrence. Abstraction was made of the particular uses of each verb. Thus, for instance, the form HEB refers to both lexical and auxiliary use of a form of HEBBEN. Similarly, forms of lexical verbs in the present include the occurrences of GAAN in inchoative constructions.

For the present perfect, eight constructions were included which could have been classified as consisting of a copula + Subject Complement in past participle form, but which might be actual present perfects as well (i.e., there was not enough information in the corpus to decide between the two possibilities). The forms of the past participles will be discussed separately when we present Table 7.6.

Contrary to English, the Dutch material does contain a number of non-adult-like individual forms. First there is, of course, the form HEEF, which was discussed earlier. Secondly Kate uses two non-adult-like simple past forms. These are *DOEDDE <doed> and *VONDE <founded>. In *DOEDDE [dudə] (adult form DEED /de:t/), an irregular paradigm is regularized, and the regular past morpheme {-de} is added to the stem DOE. Here, no influence from English is apparent. With *VONDE, which is combined with ZE <she>, a subject pronoun used to refer to Kate's mother, one might argue that Kate has inappropriately combined the adult form VOND with the plural morpheme {−en}, and that the past form *per se* is perfectly adult-like. Since only three past forms of lexical verbs occur (the third one being ZOCHT <sought, looked for>) we shall not discuss the matter further (but it is significant in itself that so few simple past forms occur - this point will be taken up again later). Thirdly, there are a number of past participles which are non-adult-like. Although no overt 'English' morphemes are used in these non-adult-like past participles (if there were, the forms would have been categorized as 'mixed'), a closer look at the actual items might reveal some influence from English after all. Table 7.6 lists all the Dutch past participles (the numbers after each type indicate how often that type occurred in the entire corpus). The fact that the total number of present perfect constructions is six tokens less than the total number (52) of past participles is due to the fact that a few past participles were repaired instances or repetitions of preceding forms. One of them was used with a modal auxiliary (see later discussion).

For the past participles, a distinction was made between irregular verbs (i.e. lexical verbs which do not get the regular simple past and/or past

The verb phrase 183

participle morphemes) and regular verbs (those that do). In addition, a separate class of 'transitional verbs' (Extra 1978) was distinguished. These lexical verbs are historically irregular but show a tendency towards regularization.

The non-adult-like forms in Table 7.6 all carry the first part of the discontinuous regular past participle morpheme, viz. {ge-} - a suffix consisting of a voiced or voiceless velar fricative (which we shall phonologically represent as /¥/) followed by a schwa, except for the non-adult-like form KOOMT [ko:mt] in which Kate has also used the 'wrong' suffix. For KOOMT no influence from English CAME [keim] is apparent, and since Dutch monolingual children also start their past participle productions by just adding a suffix to the stem without the {ge-} part (see e.g. Extra 1977, Tinbergen 1919), there is no reason for constructing an argument for influence from the English regular simple past formation paradigm. Since the partial {ge-} morpheme does not exist in English, no influence from English on any of the other past participles is apparent here. There is only one form which might partially be influenced by an English form, i.e. GEDRENK /¥ədreŋk/: the morpheme DRENK /dreŋk/ might be seen as a phonological adaptation of the English simple past form DRANK /dræŋk/. Conversely, one might argue that Kate 'knows' that she should apply a vowel change to the stem DRINK /driŋk/, but that she is not clear as to what shape that vowel change should receive (the adult form is GEDRONKEN /¥ədroŋkə/). This explanation, however, is unlikely, since none of Kate's other non-adult-like participles exhibit this type of phenomenon: some of them are not only 'wrong' because they use {-t} instead of {-en}, but also because they use as root the verb stem rather than a 'vowel-changed' root (viz. GEVLIEGD /¥ədvli:¥t/ instead of GEVLOGEN /¥əvlo:¥ə/, GEDRINKT /¥ədriŋkt/ instead of GEDRONKEN /¥ədroŋkə/). In GESCHIETEN and GEZOEKT Kate used a verb stem as root rather than a vowel-changed base but used the 'right' suffix (the adult forms are GESCHOTEN and GEZOCHT). There are also forms in which Kate only applies the 'wrong' suffix (viz. GEVALT instead of GEVALLEN, GEWAST instead of GEWASSEN). Then there are a few forms that are 'stopped short', i.e. they lack the final part of the discontinuous morpheme but are otherwise adult-like (viz. GEZEET instead of GEZETEN, GEKOOK instead of GEKOOKT, GEMAAK instead of GEMAAKT). There is one that uses an inappropriate root and lacks the final suffix (viz. GEVLIEG instead of GEVLOGEN). A sort of anomaly within this group of non-adult-like forms is GESPELEND, which takes as root the infinitive form. Again, though, as for all the others (except perhaps GEDRENK), the inappropriate forms operate within the formal boundaries of Dutch past participle formation: all contain {ge-}, and most contain a {-t} or {-en} suffix attached to a root in stem form (for the root, the child does not at this point create roots without formal similarities to the stem form of the verb - except for GEDRENK).

These inappropriate forms show that Kate has started to analyse Dutch regular past participle formation, rather than characteristics of English formal regularities. The occurrence of many adult-like Dutch past participles lends further evidence to the claim that Kate's Dutch past participle formation is guided from within the Dutch system rather than from within the English one.

Table 7.6 *Kate's Dutch past participles*

Adult-like	Irregular forms		Transitional		Regular	
	gedaan	7	gezien	2	getekend	2
	gebroken	2	gevangen	1	gebeurd	2
	gevlogen	1	gekomen	1	gekookt	2
	geweest	1	gevallen	1	gestopt	2
	gedronken	1			gemaakt	2
	gegeten	1			gepakt	2
	gekocht	1			geschilderd	1
	gehad	1			gekleurd	1
					verstopt	1
					geleerd	1
					gespeeld	1
TOTALS		15		5		17
Non-adult-like	forms					
	gezeet	2	gewast	2	gespelend	1
	gevlieg	1	gevalt	1	gekook	1
	gevliegd	1	koomt	1	gemaak	1
	gedrenk	1				
	gedrinkt	1				
	geschieten	1				
	gezoekt	1				
TOTALS		8		4		3

Not deducible from Table 7.5 is Kate's use (on two occasions only) of HEB with a past participle where BEN would have been required in adult usage and vice versa. On the whole, though, choice of the tense auxiliary is appropriate. Most certainly influence from English here for the two 'wrong' choices cannot be used as an explanation since Kate does not produce any present perfect forms in English; rather, an explanation for the two anomalous combinations must be sought in the intricacies of the Dutch adult system itself.

Kate's use of Dutch imperatives is mostly adult-like. Only twice do forms occur that are not standard, i.e. the stem + {-t} combination. Possibly this use derives from a pattern existing in the Antwerp dialect, where imperatives formed by adding {-t} to the verb stem of lexical verbs are quite common. Again, though, this explanation is doubtful, since Kate only hears the Antwerp dialect sporadically. It is quite clear, however, that the two stem + {-t} forms do not exhibit any influence from English. Since their frequency of occurrence is so minimal relative to adult-like usage, we are certainly not dealing with any strong acquisition strategy, and most probably the two forms are slips of the tongue. On the combinatorial level, Kate does not 'translate' her use of the English DON'T + UVF into Dutch: rather, she realizes Dutch prohibitions by means of the negative adverb NIET followed by the stem + {-en} form, as is fully adult-like. Never does she combine NIET with just a stem form to express a prohibition; this combination does not occur in adult Dutch either. Looking back at the English data (cf. Table 7.4), no instances can be found of the use of NOT + UVF to express a prohibition. In Kate's production of imperatives, then, again the limitations and possibilities of each language are used within their respective linguistic contexts.

At the end of Table 7.5 we find the last Dutch inappropriate forms. The inappropriateness here is not, as before, due to the forms themselves, but rather to the impossibility of their combination (from the adult point of view). In four of the six cases it can be argued that the syntagmatically non-adult-like combination of ZIJN and a infinitive is an early attempt at the ZIJN + AAN HET + infinitive construction (one of the 'durative' forms - see section 7.2.1). This interpretation fits the contexts of the four relevant utterances perfectly. On the other hand, one might contend that here there is an influence from English present continuous at work, with the {-ing} suffix replaced by a 'language specific' suffix {-en}. At this point no unambiguous choice between these two interpretations can be made. The made. The other two utterances would have been appropriate both meaningwise and formally if the non-finite parts of the VP's had been past participles (so GEZET instead of ZET and GEBAKKEN instead of BAKKEN). For these utterances no influence from English can be invoked as an explanation, but - as with KOOMT above - we are probably dealing with remnants of an earlier stage of past participle formation in which the first part of the discontinuous morpheme is not produced. Such use is reported on for monolingual Dutch acquisition both by Tinbergen (1919) and Extra (1977): in the early stages of past participle formation (which starts at around the age of two), the prefix {ge-} is usually absent; in a following stage, it is rendered as /ə/, and after this it is fully present. The suffixes {-en} and {-t}, while not always used appropriately, are always present in the early attempts at past participle formation (cf. Extra 1978). (These early renditions of 'past participles' in the form of stem + {-en} might, of course, not be past participles at all but 'unmarked' (Schaerlaekens 1977) or infinitive forms. The basis on which Extra (1977, 1978) decided that these forms were indeed past participles is not indicated. Similarly, BAKKEN above might be such an 'unmarked', infinitival form.)

In the English corpus, Kate uses the auxiliary DO in negative and interrogative sentences. In the Dutch corpus, no attempt to transfer this use from English occurs: there are no instances of DOEN used as an auxiliary. Conversely, the fact that in English DO-support is used in negative and interrogative clauses where the main verb is a lexical verb shows an absence of the Dutch pattern: in Dutch, Subject--finite verb inversion and the addition of NIET are enough in most cases to make a clause interrogative and negative respectively.

In the Dutch corpus, the only form of ZIJN that is abbreviated is the fully adult-like use of 'S. In fact, no other abbreviated forms of Dutch verbs occur. This closely follows adult usage. Conversely, the English data contain many abbreviated forms of BE as is possible in adult colloquial usage. Thus there is no underextension of abbreviated forms as might be expected if influence from Dutch on English were to be hypothesized. Again then, the data show no influence from the one language on the other.

Kate uses the English BE GOING TO + UVF construction rather than a theoretically possible GO + UVF construction that would be a close translation of the Dutch pattern. On the other hand, in Dutch Kate does not transfer the BE GOING TO + UVF construction from English.

A further clear difference between the English and the Dutch data is that in English Kate uses the simple past tense of lexical verbs, whereas lexical verbs in the past hardly ever occur in the Dutch corpus. Conversely, the Dutch corpus contains quite a number of present perfect forms. These are absent in the English corpus.

In both languages, Kate frequently expresses a desire, for things or actions. In Dutch, she makes use of the adult-like WILLEN + infinitive form or WILLEN followed by a Direct Object. In English, Kate uses the semantically virtually equivalent WANT TO (or the concatenation WANNA) + UVF or WANT followed by a Direct Object. There are no instances of *WILLEN TE + infinitive or of *WANT + UVF combinations, which might have been possible if the child were using grammatical rules from one language when using lexical items from the other. Note also that there is no 'confusion' between Dutch WILLEN (which mainly occurs in the form WIL [wil]) and the formally nearly identical English WILL ([wil]): Kate only uses Dutch WILLEN to express a desire or need, and English WILL only to indicate an intention or future state of affairs.

Syntagmatic use of the Dutch modals is mostly adult-like and exploits all the possibilities of the adult system: there is no 'underextended' use of the modals (i.e., only the modal + infinitive syntagm rather than also the modal + Direct Object combination without a non-finite verb) which might be predicted if transfer from the English pattern were seen to be paramount. There is one non-adult-like combination, however, when Kate uses the modal MOET and produces as a non-finite verb not the required infinitive form but a past participle. If the utterance in question had also contained the Dutch passive voice auxiliary WORDEN, it would have fitted the context perfectly. Since adult English does not allow for the construction *modal + past participle, and since such constructions do not appear in the English child data, certainly no influence from English on the anomalous MOET GESTOPT combination is apparent. As was pointed out before, the English data contain no instances of the use of a modal with a Direct Object, which would be possible if transfer from Dutch were an important acquisition strategy. Again, syntagmatic use is language-specific.

More comparisons between the Dutch and English data could be made, but always with the same result: apart from one or two doubtful cases, syntagmatic combinations of verb forms in VP's show no overlap between the two languages. In addition, the actual forms used in VP's are mostly relatable to each linguistic input system separately.

In order to further substantiate the latter conclusion, all the individual verb forms have been summarized in Table 7.7. This table contains only those data that can positively confirm or disconfirm the hypothesis put forward (cf. also Meisel i.p.). Thus, for instance, Kate's use of IS and 'S has been excluded: saying that these are used in a language-specific manner would be misleading, since in both adult systems these forms are present and both a language-specific and a non-language-specific route to acquisition would result in the same forms being used. Similarly, stems or UVF's of lexical verbs in the present used by themselves were not tabulated, since they are not marked by any distinctive language-specific morphemes in either language. One might argue, however, that in order to arrive at the Dutch stem forms, Kate must to some extent have analysed the infinitive, plural or third person singular forms. While this might indeed be the case, it is irrelevant to the present point of discussion.

In Table 7.7 a distinction was made between forms that were positively English or Dutch, and those that were not ('doubtful source'). A minimalistic interpretation was adopted for the 'doubtful source' items: although it was argued before that HEEF could best be seen as the result of an analysis on the child's part based on Dutch regular third person singular present tense formation, here again it was included with items that show a possibly 'mixed', i.e. non-separate development.

For non-lexical verbs, 60 tokens spread over three types are of the doubtful kind. Two thirds of those tokens concern HEEF. Note that neither EM, KEN or HEEF involve the transfer of morphological rules between languages: they may all be seen as phonological adaptations of lexical insertions (cf. Chapter 5).

More interesting for a possible refutation of the separate development hypothesis are the lexical verbs, which, unlike most of the non-lexical verbs, utilize morphological paradigms for their differentiation. Only forms containing bound morphemes were included, and formally similar items were collapsed across usages. Thus the Dutch stem + {-en} form, for instance, includes finite, imperative and non-finite use. The quantitative analysis clearly shows that most bound morphemes are attached to a root from the same language: only 1.6% of all morphologically marked lexical verb forms involve the use of a bound morpheme from language A attached to a root from language B. When lexical and and non-lexical verbs are

are taken together, only 4.5% of the items under consideration show an intertwining of Dutch and English forms. When HEEF is counted as a Dutch item, this percentage drops to 2.1%.

7.2.3 *Concluding remarks*
In conclusion, then, it has been sufficiently shown that Kate's verb phrase forms closely follow her two input languages, both as far as the production of individual verbs as their combination is concerned. It is thus methodologically acceptable to consider the English and Dutch systems separately. This will be done in the next two sections, where we shall look at Subject--finite verb agreement and at any developments in Kate's verb systems over time. In those two subsections we shall also make more detailed comparisons with findings from monolingual acquisition.

7.3 Kate's Dutch verb system
7.3.1 *Introduction*
In this section we shall look at Kate's use of Subject--finite verb agreement in Dutch and at changes in her production of Dutch VP's as time goes on.

In adult Dutch, all lexical verbs in the present tense (except HEBBEN) show a regular, productive paradigm. When the stem already ends in [t], however, the paradigm is neutralized in the singular. In the following analysis, then, we have excluded all lexical verbs whose stems end in [t] (except, of course, if this stem was followed by an {-en} morpheme): these forms cannot tell us anything about the acquisition of the paradigm. The analyses do not include VP's without an overt subject either, although this subject may have been elided in a fully adult-like manner.

In Chapter 6, comparisons with monolingual children were made at the end of the discussion of the findings from the present study. Since the data to be discussed here are much more diverse and complex in nature, comparisons will be made throughout the analysis of the material, and only a short summary in table form will be presented at the end.

We start by establishing that it makes sense to talk about Subject--finite verb agreement with reference to the corpus under consideration. Then we shall look at the conjugation of lexical verbs, HEBBEN and ZIJN, and lastly, at the conjugation of the modals. After this, we shall look at syntagmatic relationships within VP's and at the marking of past and future time reference.

Table 7.7 *A cross-linguistic comparison of Kate's verb forms* [a]

Copula, auxiliaries, modals

English source		Dutch source		Doubtful source	
can	81	moet/moe [b]	102	heef	38
am/m	60	wil	90	ken	14
are/re	37	kan	61	em	8
'll	27	heb	53		
have	25	mag	49		
was [wəz]	15	zijn	37		
has/shall	each 4	ben	23		
were/will	each 3	zal/was [was]	each 12		
would/may	each 2	moeten/bent	each 8		
'd/should	each 1	heeft	6		
wouldn't	1	kun	4		
had [hæd]	1	hebben/waren/willen	each 2		
		moogt/wilt/had [had]	each 1		

Lexical verbs

English source		Dutch source		Both D & E at once	
UVF + {-ing}	84	stem + {-en}	432	E UVF + {-en}	8
UVF + {-s}	18	stem + {-t}	204	E UVF + {-t}	3
VC UVF	15	{ge-} + stem + {-t}	23	D stem + {-s}	1
UVF + {-ed}	7	{ge-} + VC stem + {-en}	11	D {ge-} + E VC UVF	1
		{ge-} + stem + {-en}	7		
		{ge-} + frozen form [c]	3		
		{ge-} + VC stem	3		
		{ge-} + stem	3		
		{ge-} + infinitive + {-en}	1		
		koomt	1		

Calculations

Source	English	Dutch	Doubtful	TOTAL
non-lexical verbs	267 (33.4%)	472 (59.1%)	60 (7.5%)	799
lexical verbs	124 (15.0%)	688 (83.4%)	13 (1.6%)	825
TOTAL	391 (24.1%)	1160 (71.4%)	73 (4.5%)	1624

[a] VC UVF = Vowel Changed UVF; VC stem = Vowel Changed stem

[b] MOE is a phonetically reduced form of MOET which occurs in free variation with MOET; MOE is used in the Dutch spoken to Kate as well and thus is an adult-like form

[c] This is an adult-like, irregular form which cannot be broken down into a stem and suffix (e.g. GEKOCHT, GEHAD)

7.3.2 *Analyses and results*
7.3.2.1 Congruence

The notion of congruence, or the fact that verbs following a grammatical Subject should somehow be marked in relation to that Subject, is a fairly very early development in the acquisition of Dutch, although it is, of course, not present from the beginning. Frequently, young children in the 'two-word-stage' combine the Subject of a clause (or, perhaps more precisely, the constituent that expresses the agent of an action) with an 'infinitive' form of a verb, i.e. with a form of the verb that resembles the adult stem + {-en} form (Schaerlaekens 1977, Verhulst-Schlichting 1985). Often, this form is the only one that early verbs take (apart from a few exceptions). Very soon in the 'multi-word stage', however, the monolingual Dutch child begins to use other verb forms as well, such as the stem or stem + {-t} forms, which typically are placed immediately before or after the Subject (see e.g. the examples given in Tinbergen 1919 and de Haan 1986a; see also Extra 1977). As de Haan (1986a) has argued, though, by this point there is little trace of any systematic Subject--finite verb agreement: for instance, the child still often uses a singular Subject with a stem + {-en} form (see also Tinbergen 1919). In fact, it is not even clear whether the child at this stage operates with a general category of 'Verb' which is then divided up into 'finite' and 'non-finite' verbs. Rather, de Haan (1986a) has suggested that the child uses two semantically distinct 'form classes' (my term), where what is commonly described as a 'finite verb' is some sort of particle (de Haan uses the term 'Aux') indicating 'modality and/or time notions' (de Haan 1986a), and where what could be described as a 'non-finite verb lacking a finite verb' (my term - de Haan uses the term 'V') refers to elements (always in the stem + {-en} form) that denote actions. 'Aux' never occurs in sentence final position, while 'V' always does. Usually, any one utterance at this stage contains only V or Aux, but not both (except for utterances with GAAN + stem + {-en} used as an inchoative). de Haan explains how the child could come to develop a morphological verb marking system that unifies the earlier syntactically and morphologically disconnected 'Aux' and 'V' categories: "after noting the agreement relations between the subject and the 'auxiliary', the child constructs word-specific paradigms. Then the child discovers via segmentation procedures based on formal correspondences that this word variation is determined morphologically. The same procedures make it possible to establish that this variation in fact occurs cross-categorically. Consequently recategorization is necessary" (de Haan 1986: 10).

There is strong evidence in the Dutch data from Kate that she is well into this 'recategorization' stage: Subject--finite verb agreement is often adult-like, and when 'errors' occur, they are only very rarely due to the combination of a singular Subject with a stem + {-en} form. In fact, most stem + {-en} forms occur in the 'real' non-finite parts of Kate's Dutch VP's, i.e. in VP's that also contain a finite part. Subject-less utterances are quite uncommon: on the whole, whenever Kate produces a verb form that is not clearly an imperative, she uses a Subject. When the only verb in the clause is not an imperative and there is no overt Subject, we are usually dealing with an elided Subject that is perfectly clear from the linguistic and/or situational context. The resulting utterance is more often than not fully adult-like within the on-going discourse, and the verb form used clearly functions as a finite verb, i.e. it is made to agree with the covert Subject. Examples of utterances by the three-year-old boy whose language development Tinbergen (1919) reports on show that utterances containing a finite verb but no overt Subject appear in a monolingual child's speech production as well. Finally, Kate uses a host of different Subjects that are combined with a great number of different verbs. This does not mean that stereotyped, 'unanalysed' or 'gestalt-like' (Peters 1983) Subject--finite verb combinations do not occur, but since they are few in number as compared to combinations that clearly show rule-based production, the hypothesis that Kate is well into the 'recategorization' stage is not disconfirmed. In fact, it is quite a common finding in language acquisition studies in general that a small number of unanalysed forms exists side by side with forms that show the use of productive rule systems (see e.g. Tracy 1987).

The notion of congruence, then, seems to be fully established by the age of 2;8: more often than not, a finite verb is made to correspond to a Subject. This finding is in agreement with Tinbergen (1919), who writes that in the course of the monolingual child's third year the notion of congruence is fully present. Kate thus does not behave very differently from at least one Dutch monolingual child.

7.3.2.2 The conjugation of finite lexical verbs in the present

In this subsection we shall look at Kate's Subject--finite verb combinations which contain a lexical verb. Not included in the following analysis is the use of HEBBEN <have> as a lexical verb. Also excluded is the use that Kate makes of GAAN <go> as a tense auxiliary. This usage is very abundant, and nearly always adult-like as far as agreement goes (mostly IK GA <I go> or HIJ/HET GAAT <HE/IT GOES>). It is not inconceivable that in fact the use of GAAN is part of a memorized routine. Since the mostly adult-like combinations with a form of GAAN if analysed together with other lexical verbs might blur any major developments it was decided not to include auxiliary usage. Subject--finite verb combinations in which GAAN is used independently, however, are included in the analysis. Although this usage is frequent, it is believed that it is not by itself capable of masking any major developmental patterns.

The fact that the notion of congruence is present does not entail that the child always makes the 'right' choice of finite verb form. On the whole, though, Kate combines verbs with Subjects in an adult-like manner. While the absolute number of errors is quite small compared to the total of finite lexical verbs under consideration, very specific error patterns are apparent. Some of these are related to the fact that Kate does not yet fully know that plural Subjects must be combined with the stem+{-en} form: plural Subjects are seemingly randomly combined with stem+{-en}, stem+{-t} or just the stem forms (GAAN, however, always appears in the stem + {-en} form after a plural Subject - possibly this use is unanalysed, since most of the correct uses of a plural Subject with a stem+{-en} form involve the use of GAAN). Since Kate uses relatively few plural nouns in the whole of the corpus (see section 6.2 in Chapter 6), and since the plural personal subject pronouns WE <we> and ZE <they> hardly ever occur (and the second person plural subject pronoun JULLIE <you> not at all), one may hypothesize that she has not had much chance to develop any consistent conjugation pattern. On the other hand, the use of the stem+{-en} form in combination with a singular subject hardly ever appears, and when it does, one may interpret this as a remnant of a previous phase in acquisition, i.e. the time before the appearance of congruence. After all, to hypothesize influence from the plural conjugation pattern would make little sense in the light of the finding that no consistent adult-like conjugation pattern with plural Subject exists. Use of the stem+{-en} form as a finite lexical verb in the present, then, is mostly restricted to a small number of plural Subjects although occasionally it is combined with a singular Subject.

Tinbergen (1919) reports a highly similar situation for the speech production of his son Luuk, and suggests that Luuk often used singular verb forms with plural Subjects partially because of the formal similarity between the stem+{-en} present tense and the infinitive forms. Whatever the reasons for the observed findings, the data from Kate and those for a monolingual Dutch child run parallel here.

That Kate's uncertain and inconsistent use of plural lexical verbs in the present is not atypical when compared to monolingual children is further borne out by Verhulst-Schlichting's (1985) study of eight Dutch children's acquisition of verb forms: plural lexical verbs are not discussed in this study, implying that they did not occur with sufficient frequency to reach the 'productivity' criterion that Verhulst-Schlichting used as a basis for including verb constructions in her implicational acquisition-scale. Verhulst-Schlichting's (1985: 287-288) 'productivity' criterion was the following: a construction was considered to be productive if it occurred in three utterances within a sample, and if across these three utterances two lexically different verbs were used in the construction under consideration. Although Verhulst-Schlichting's 'productivity' criterion perhaps attributes too much knowledge to the child (the criterion is not very stringent), it does not seem surprising that, given the overall infrequency of plural nouns in children's language production around the age of three, plural lexical verbs were so rare that they were not even mentioned. Verhulst-Schlichting (1985) does mention the early use of the auxiliary GAAN in the plural which is usually correctly combined with a plural Subject (i.e. WE <we>). This finding corresponds with what was found for Kate (see above).

Rather a more frequent error pattern is the addition of the {-t} morpheme to the stem of the finite lexical verb when the Subject is IK <I> (see example 10). Quite clearly we are here seeing influence from the third person singular: most subjects in the third person singular are fully appropriately followed by a stem+{-t} form (only very occasionally is this {-t} missing). One could argue, however, that actually the second person singular might be the cause for the overgeneralized pattern. While the existence in the input of a second stem+{-t} form may well be a contributing factor, third person influence seems more straightforward as an explanation because of the general frequency in the corpus of third person singular Subjects (and concomitant stem+{-t} forms) and the low frequency of second person singular Subjects. Here it should be mentioned that more often than not, Kate appropriately supplies a {-t} to the stem when the finite verb follows the second person singular subject pronoun, but that she usually omits this {-t} when there is inversion. However, the limited number of combinations with JE or JIJ <you> as Subject does not allow us to draw any final conclusions about the extent to which the conjugation of the second person singular has been acquired. It is of interest to note that with none of the other persons is there any conjugation pattern to be discerned that is relatable to the relative placement of the Subject and finite verb: errors occur in either position, and there is no attempt to transfer the special conjugation pattern of the second person singular to any of the other persons (cf. Table 7.2).

(10) 'Ik valt in 't water'.' (Age: 3;0,11) <I falls in the water.>
 {inappropriate use of stem+{-t} in combination with IK <I>}

Again, the above patterns of Subject--finite verb combinations closely resemble those that occur in monolingual acquisition: the third person singular usually gets an an appropriate {-t} although occasionally it is absent; a rather more frequent error is the addition of a {-t} to the stem for the first person singular (Van Ginneken 1917, Tinbergen 1919, Extra 1977). (Verhulst-Schlichting 1985: 293 even goes as far as to suggest that the 'correct' usage of the stem and stem+{-t} forms posed no problems to her subjects once they had reached the 'productivity' criterion (see above). However, it is possible that the methodology used by Verhulst-Schlichting 1985, in which the focus was mainly on the appropriate use of various constructions, acted as a 'smoke-screen' so to speak, and that inappropriate Subject--finite verb combinations were simply not part of the 'productivity' criterion-oriented data base.)

Developmentally, there is little drastic change to be discerned. Errors occur throughout, and since the number of errors is quite low (barely 18% on a total of 236 combinations considered here, and this low percentage drops to 11% when all the Subject--finite verb combinations with GAAN as a finite verb and those with a stem ending in [t] are included), no statistical treatment is possible. There are no great shifts in the types of errors as time goes on either. Errors showing third person singular influence are the most frequent throughout. At the same time in development, then, adult and non-adult-like combinations exist side by side. In addition, the whole conjugation paradigm is not worked on to the same extent all at once: while the third person singular form seems to be more or less established, the overmarkings for the first person singular show that there is still quite a lot to be learned within the singular paradigm. The plural paradigm appears not to be acquired at all yet: here there is a clear experimenting with various forms, but again no drastic improvements or deteriorations take place during the course of the study. Again, the above findings correspond to the ones reported by Tinbergen (1919). Van Ginneken (1917: 155) also concludes that at the age of three, his subject's use of verb conjugation is by no means 'fabulous

("Alles te zamen is Keesje's vervoeging [...] op drie-jarigen leeftijd nog niet schitterend te noemen", ibid.).

The full evidence for the above findings for Kate has been tabulated in Table 15 in the Appendix. In Table 7.8 the various Subject--finite verb combinations are presented in summary form. The numbers here refer to the total number of occurrences of any one combination in the entire Dutch corpus.

An obvious point but one worth mentioning explicitly is that in the conjugation of lexical verbs in the present the child always uses the correct 'analogies' (Tinbergen 1919): only overgeneralizations from within the appropriate paradigm occur. There are no overgeneralizations across parts-of-speech or from within the form class of verbs. Thus vowel changed present tense forms do not appear, although vowel changes are possible in the simple past and past participle forms. [4]

The verb phrase 197

Table 7.8   *Kate's Dutch Subject--finite lexical verb combinations* [a]

		Stem	Stem+{-t}	Stem+{-en}	Totals
3psg		<u>9</u>	102	<u>4</u>	115
IK		55	<u>15</u>	-	70
3ppl		<u>1</u>	<u>7</u>	16	24
WE/WIJ		-	<u>4</u>	6	10
JIJ/JE	inversion	9	<u>1</u>	-	10
JIJ/JE no	inversion	-	6	<u>1</u>	7
TOTALS		74	135	27	236

[a] Instances of HEBBEN, GAAN as tense auxiliary and stems that end in [t] are not included; only present tense forms are tabulated; the non-adult-like forms are underlined

Both Schaerlaekens (1977) and Tinbergen (1919) mention that occasionally some monolingual children conjugate a lexical verb in the present by using a periphrastic form made up of a finite form of DOEN <do> and an infinitive (see also Schaerlaekens and Gillis 1987). No such constructions appear in Kate's speech production. This does not necessarily mean that we are dealing with a major point of difference: not all monolingual children use this DOEN-periphrasis, so if Kate does not use it either she is not behaving differently from at least some monolingual children.

7.3.2.3   The conjugation of HEBBEN

In contrast with the lexical verbs, the conjugation of HEBBEN does go through quite a well-delineated development. At the beginning of the study, all the forms of HEBBEN in the present are adult-like. Then, after the middle of the study, non-adult forms start to appear as well, while adult forms continue to be produced, but in proportionally smaller numbers. Table 16 in the Appendix tabulates all the relevant data, and Table 7.9 presents a summary (the totals in Table 16 and Table 7.9 do not all add up to the figures given in Table 7.5 above: forms of HEBBEN were not counted if they were combined with an English Subject, or if there was no overt Subject at all).

A typical error is shown in example 11:

(11) 'Heef jij da gezien?' (Age: 3;3,9) <Has you that seen?>
 {use of the non-adult-like form HEEF instead of HEB}

Table 7.9   Kate's conjugation of HEBBEN [a]

	HEB	HEEFT	HEEF	HEBBEN	Totals
IK	52	<u>2</u>	<u>26</u>	-	80
JIJ (inversion)	1	-	<u>6</u>	-	7
3 psg	-	4	-	-	4
WIJ	-	-	-	2	2
TOTALS	53	6	32	2	93

[a] The non-adult-like combinations are underlined

In the catalogue of forms above (subsection 7.2.2.1) we already discussed the possible source of the form HEEF: it was hypothesized that HEEF derives from the third person singular HEEFT which is misanalysed as consisting of a stem HEEF and a morpheme {-t}. The discussion of Kate's conjugation of lexical verbs (subsection 7.3.2.2) has shown that this morpheme {-t} is highly accessible to Kate: it occurs abundantly both in adult and non-adult-like Subject--finite verb combinations. The accessibility of the morpheme is further evident from the 'mixed' items MOVET, LIKET and THROWT (see Table 7.3 above): if Kate had no productive knowledge of the {-t} morpheme she would not be able to invent these forms (after all, she most probably has never heard these in the input). The hypothesis that HEEF derives from HEEFT is a bit problematic, however, because of the infrequency in the corpus of the form HEEFT: it occurs only six times, and on two of those occasions HEEFT is inappropriately combined with IK. Although it is possible of course that Kate produced many more forms of HEEFT when she was not being recorded, it can also be suggested that it may not be absolutely necessary for the child to produce a form in order for her to use it as a basis for (erroneous) analysis; simply hearing HEEFT might be enough for the child to start incorporating part of it in her speech production. It is also possible that due to assimilation phenomena the form HEEFT is not often actually produced as [he:ft] by the child's Dutch interlocutors, but as [he:f]. This is a matter for empirical investigation, and, if found to be realistic, the hypothesis that the child has construed HEEF on the basis of HEEFT becomes void - HEEF would then, of course, be an adult-like form. In monolingual acquisition, at least one child was also reported to abundantly use HEEF but hardly ever HEEFT. If HEEFT was used at all, it was combined with IK (Van Ginneken 1917: 154).

Although it might be possible that non-adult-like usage of HEBBEN is linked to whether HEBBEN is used as an auxiliary or as a lexical verb, no such link is evident.

The conjugation pattern of HEBBEN, then, shows an interesting phenomenon: frequent totally adult-like usage is drastically reduced in favour of a form that is probably based on the child's own creative construction. This suggests that the earlier correct forms were the result of rote-memorization. While for lexical verbs the stem+{-t} form happens to be productive, this is not the case for HEBBEN: at a later stage of development the child will have to completely revert to the earlier memorization strategy.

At age 3;4, the conjugation of HEBBEN has not at all been acquired: more than a third of all Kate's Subject--present form of HEBBEN combinations are non-adult-like. In addition, the range of subjects that HEBBEN combines with is very restricted: 86% of all instances of HEBBEN in the present follow IK. These findings contrast quite strongly with the ones for finite lexical verbs where a host of different Subjects was produced and where non-adult-like usage was much less frequent.

(12) Gerrit: 'Ik heeft geen ogen en geen mond.' (Age: 3;1)
    (Schaerlaekens 1977: 51)
    <I has no eyes and no mouth>
    {inappropriate combination of a first person singular pronoun with a third person singular form of HEBBEN}

Earlier on, it was mentioned that Dutch monolingual children use HEEF around the age of three. Examples from Tinbergen (1919) show that this form HEEF is used with IK (although perhaps not exclusively so: there is no information on this). Van Ginneken (1917) lists examples of (H)EEF being used with singular nouns as Subjects and with IK. Dutch monolingual children also combine HEEFT with IK: Schaerlaekens (1977) gives many examples of such inappropriate combinations (see e.g. example 12). Extra (1977) and Van Ginneken (1917) also mention this use. This suggests that the conjugation of HEBBEN is a problematic area in the acquisition of Dutch (see also Van Ginneken 1917: 154). Again, the bilingual data from Kate reflect this situation.

7.3.2.4 The conjugation of ZIJN

Kate's use of ZIJN in the present tense is mostly adult-like. Although plural Subjects are usually combined with the appropriate form ZIJN, occasionally they are followed by IS (examples of both these possibilities are mentioned by Tinbergen (1919), while Van Ginneken (1917) reports that Keesje mostly used the plural form ZIJN appropriately with plural Subjects), and on just two occasions there is evidence of overmarking when DA'S is followed by a plural subject and then by ZIJN. In these cases we are probably dealing with a remnant of an unanalysed form DA'S. In fact, the abbreviated form 'S usually occurs in combination with DA <tha(t)> or WA <wha(t)> : DA'S X <tha's X> and WA'S DA? <wha's tha?> are the main patterns in which 'S occurs.

Third person singular personal pronouns are usually followed by IS, rather than 'S (although use of 'S would be quite appropriate from the adult point of view). IS is never used with IK. Tinbergen (1919) also mentions that IK IS hardly ever occurs in his data. On two occasions, IS does appear inappropriately with the second person singular as in example 13 (this use is not mentioned by either Van Ginneken 1917 or Tinbergen 1919).

The form BEN is used quasi-exclusively (and appropriately) in combination with IK and also occurs once with the second person singular subject pronoun (the use of EM - cf. subsection 7.2.2.1 - does not compete with the use of BEN). Use of BENT with this second person singular pronoun is very infrequent, and BENT is once inappropriately used with IK. Rather than see this last case as due to influence from the second person singular form, it can be argued that there is again influence from the third person singular regular form with the {-t} morpheme. Tinbergen (1919) gives quite a number of examples of the combination IK BEN, but none of JIJ BENT or BEN JIJ. Of course it is possible that Tinbergen's subject used JIJ BENT and/or BEN JIJ and that this use was simply not reported on, but the detailed and quite thorough analysis by Tinbergen makes it more likely that these forms hardly ever occurred before his subject's third birthday and that this is why they were not mentioned. The main usage patterns of ZIJN in the present have been summarized in Table 7.10.

Though it might be possible that non-adult-like usage of ZIJN is linked to whether it is used as an auxiliary or as a copula, no such link is evident.

(13) 'Papa, waar is jij?' (Age: 3;3,16) <Daddy, where is you?>
{inapproriate use of the third person singular present tense form of BE in combination with a second person singular subject pronoun}

In the conjugation of ZIJN in the present, there is no developmental pattern to be observed: the few erroneous uses occur throughout, and there is no sudden appearance of new forms at any time.

Although most uses of ZIJN are adult-like, it cannot be concluded that the conjugation of ZIJN has been acquired. After all, 81% of all occurrences of ZIJN in the present concern IS or 'S, and apart from fairly regular use of BEN and ZIJN with the first person singular and the third person plural respectively, there is not enough quantitative evidence that the entire conjugation has been acquired. At best, one could say that Kate knows how to combine IK with BEN, and the third person plural and singular with ZIJN and IS or 'S respectively. Acquisition of the conjugation of ZIJN, then, appears to develop very much in a piecemeal fashion. Whether Kate resembles monolingual children as far as the actual forms goes is hard to say, due to lack of sufficient comparison material. It does seem to be the case, however, that the learning of the various present tense forms of ZIJN proceeds in a very slow item-by-item fashion in monolingual children, as it does in Kate (cf. Van Ginneken 1917, Tinbergen 1919).

Table 7.10 Kate's conjugation of ZIJN [a]

	IS/'S	BEN	ZIJN	BENT	Totals
3psg	258	-	<u>2</u>	-	260
3ppl	<u>4</u>	-	27	-	31
IK	-	22	-	<u>1</u>	23
JIJ (no inversion)	<u>1</u>	-	-	5	6
JIJ (inversion)	<u>2</u>	1	-	-	3
WE/WIJ	<u>1</u>	-	1	-	2
TOTALS	266	23	30	6	325

[a] Differences in total numbers of forms with the figures given in Table 7.5 are due to there being no overt Subject or due to the fact that Table 7.10 does not take into account multiple repetitions of a verb form with the Subject produced only once: a sequence such as 'hij is is is is is X' was counted as containing only one occurrence of HIJ IS (in cases of repairs, however, Subject--verb combinations are counted twice: 'hij's-is' would be counted once as an instance of HIJ'S and once as an instance of HIJ IS); the non-adult-like forms are underlined

7.3.2.5 The conjugation of the modals

For the conjugation of the Dutch modals we can be quite brief: apart from a few exceptions, Kate always uses modals appropriately. The actual forms used are: MAG, KAN, ZAL, KUN, MOE(T), WIL, WILLEN, MOETEN, WILT and MOOGT. The latter occurs only once, and while it is not part of standard colloquial usage, it is used in parts of Flanders in combination with the second person singular pronoun GIJ, another form of the second person singular frequently used in Flanders. Kate probably heard MOOGT from her baby-sitters and from her paternal grandparents, although her father always uses the standard form MAG in combination with JE. WILT is also used only once, namely in WILT JIJ? <do you want?>. This error is probably traceable to the adult form WILT GIJ? (common in standard Dutch spoken in Flanders). The standard form WIL JIJ? occurs seven times. Then twice the reverse happens, and Kate uses GIJ WIL instead of GIJ WILT. Here we are probably seeing an influence from the alternative JIJ WIL. On two occasions, KUN is combined with a singular subject NP, whereas KUN is only possible in the KUN JE? combination in standard adult usage (this use was not tabulated in Table 7.2. in subsection 7.2.1).

In total, then, there are only five non-adult-like combinations involving modals on a total of 330 opportunities for erroneous use. This does not mean that the conjugation of the modals has been fully acquired: again, acquisition probably proceeds in a piecemeal fashion. This is evidenced by the general infrequency of third person singular Subjects and plural Subjects used in combination with a modal (the plural forms WILLEN and MOETEN start to appear hesitantly only at the very end of the study). Usually, the Subject of any modal is the first person singular pronoun; second most frequent is the second person singular. There appears to be no influence whatsoever from the regular third person singular formation of lexical verbs: theoretically possible forms such as *KANT <*cans> or *MAGT <*mays> do not occur. Tinbergen (1919) also mentions only adult-like forms for the modals in the second half of his subject's third year, and Van Ginneken (1917) also reports that the non-adult-like addition of a {-t}-morpheme to a modal verb does not occur. Van Ginneken (1917) further notes that Keesje never uses modals in combination with a third person Subject. Again, then, the data from Kate closely correspond to findings from monolingual acquisition.

Since modals are all irregular in form, it can be argued that their conjugation will develop in a lexical-item-by-lexical-item fashion. ZAL, for instance, appears only towards the end of the study, and until ZULLEN (the plural finite form) has been learned as a separate lexical item, the conjugation of ZULLEN will not be complete. Although overgeneralizations based on the lexical verb paradigm may start to appear at a later stage, at this time in development there is no undue influence from the regular paradigm on the formation of modals.

As mentioned earlier, Subject--finite verb combinations with the tense auxiliary GAAN are nearly always adult-like. Although use of HIJ/HET/singular NP + GAAT is particularly frequent in the first three months of observation, while use of IK GA remains more constant over time, this variation in use is probably not very significant but due to normal variation in the topics talked about.

7.3.2.6 Syntagmatic relationships within VP's

Throughout the study, Kate uses many modals and the verb GAAN both as independent finite verbs and as auxiliaries. Whereas the use of GAAN as a tense auxiliary as compared to its use as a fully lexical verb varies quite considerably over time, with no clearly delineatable developmental pattern occurring, use of the modals does change over time. As was explained earlier, in many cases the use of just a Dutch modal by itself (i.e. without a non-finite verb) is nearly equivalent to its use with a non-finite part. Use of a modal with a non-finite part can be seen as formally more complex than use without it. In the Dutch corpus, there is a steady increase in the number of VP's with a modal and a non-finite part compared to those with just a modal verb (cf. Table 17 in the Appendix). This shows that Kate becomes more adept at manipulating more formally complex constructions as time goes on. From the beginning of the study onwards, however, Kate is already using some modals with a non-finite verb. The resulting VP's are always entirely adult-like. The data from Tinbergen (1919) again confirm this finding for monolingual acquisition.

All of the modals are at this stage of development only used as finite verbs although they can appear in the infinitive and past participle forms in the adult system as well. Modals used as non-finite verbs are not reported on in the monolingual literature either.

A point that is not explicitly mentioned by either Tinbergen (1919) or Schaerlaekens (1977) but that is clear from the examples they give is the fact that monolingual children use the appropriate syntagmatic relationships: modals combine with infinitives or Direct Objects, auxiliaries with past participles, finite lexical verbs appear on their own, with non-verbal complements or objects, the copula occurs with a Subject Complement etc. The same can be said for Kate: syntagmatic use of verbs is always adult-like: Kate has learnt much about what goes with what (not all the adult combinations are present yet), but maybe more importantly, she has learnt which combinations make no sense. Theoretical possibilities such as the combination of a finite lexical verb and an infinitive, for instance, do not occur. This point may be an obvious one, but it is highly significant: long before the morphological rules are learned, the child has apparently acquired the syntactic constraints operating on the combination of verbs. An explanation for this finding may lie in the fact that syntagmatic relationships are always present for direct perception: only short memory is required to hear what follows what. Morphological paradigms, on the other hand, are not that readily available: they can only be discovered after syntagmatically similar slots have been perceived to be filled by slightly differing forms. A lot more analysis and memory work is required for constructing morphological paradigms than for discovering syntagmatic relationships.

7.3.2.7 The expression of past time reference through the use of verb forms

The expression of past time reference through lexical verbs in monolingual Dutch children is first realized by means of the compound tense that combines an auxiliary (HEBBEN or ZIJN) and a past participle. Tinbergen (1919), Schaerlaekens (1977), Extra (1978) and Verhulst-Schlichting (1985) all state that the use of the simple past tense to refer to the past is a very late development. When the simple past does appear, it at first only has a modal rather than a temporal meaning: it does not refer to a condition in the past but to an imaginary, 'unreal' situation. This general picture is confirmed by the data from Kate: she uses the simple past form of a lexical verb only three times. Whenever she does so, reference is made to a hypothetical, 'pretend' situation. The past tense of the copula, however, usually refers to an actual event or state in a more or less distant point in time (an event that happened the day before or some days earlier). Usage seems to be purely temporal. Use of the compound present perfect tense compared with that of the simple past is much more frequent, and the present perfect is always used to refer to an action in the past. A resultative notion may be present as well, and usage is fully adult-like.

In the expression of past time reference through verbs a definite development can be discerned: up to the age of three, verb forms referring to a past time are quite infrequent in number. At the same time, the past participles used in that period are mostly adult-like. From the age of 3;2 onwards, there is a marked increase in the number of present perfects, and in addition Kate starts using many more non-adult-like past participles (the actual forms of these past participles can be found in Table 7.6 in subsection 7.2.2.2). While before the age of 3;2 nearly all of the past participles used were adult-like, irregular forms (transitional verbs are here seen as being a type of irregular verb), the sudden increase in the number of past participles produced also brings with it a diversification of the types of forms: both adult-like and non-adult-like irregular and regular forms are produced side by side. The findings presented here are tabulated in Table 18 in the Appendix.

The literature on monolingual acquisition reflects the above developmental pattern: in the second half of their third year, monolingual children start producing some past participles of irregular verbs in their adult forms. Later, the patterns for regular past participle formation are applied to strong verbs (that the full acquisition of past participle and simple past formation is a long drawn-out process that is not even completed by the age of 6 is for instance shown by van Driel, van Driel-Karthaus, Extra, Loffeld, van Peer and Peeters 1975). Although most of the literature on monolingual children does not state whether at the overgeneralization stage the child still produces correct irregular forms, a list of past participles used by Van Ginneken's subject Keesje before his third birthday (Van Ginneken 1917: 176) shows that Keesje used both overgeneralized and correct irregular forms at the same time in development (he even used overgeneralized and correct irregular forms of the same verb). The Dutch data from Kate, then, are consistent with the general developmental pattern that obtains for monolingual acquisition.

In subsection 7.2.2 above it was said that on the whole Kate's choice of the Dutch tense auxiliary is appropriate. No clear developmental pattern can be discerned here, i.e. there is not more or less frequent use of either HEBBEN or ZIJN as tense auxiliary as time goes on. In monolingual acquisition, the choice of the right auxiliary is not always successful but inappropriate choices are rare (Van Ginneken 1917, Tinbergen 1919). Schaerlaekens (1977) does not explicitly discuss the use of the auxiliary in the formation of the present perfect tense but in the examples she gives there are two instances of ZIJN used instead of HEBBEN (the bulk of the examples in which her subjects used a present perfect tense involve the appropriate choice of the tense auxiliary). Nowhere in the monolingual literature is there any mention of a major shift from the use of one auxiliary to the other. Again, then, the data from Kate resemble those for monolingual Dutch children.

It is clear that by the age of 3;4, Kate has only really started to learn how to refer to past actions by means of verb forms. Not only does she not fully control the formal means required for appropriate past participle formation, but in addition reference to the past through verbs is basically restricted to just one tense, i.e. the present perfect. The seeds for further development, however, have already been sown: the occasional past tense use of the copula may be the gateway through which single item reference to the past becomes possible. It may even be tentatively suggested that one of the possible reasons why the present perfect tense is an early development in Dutch rather than the simple past is that in the child's system there already is a single item verb form present, namely the present tense. Obviously, though, this cannot be the whole explanation:

presumably, the present perfect of lexical verbs is used much more frequently in the input than the simple past (of lexical verbs). This statement is partially supported by the finding that in a corpus of Dutch adult-to-adult conversation reported on by de Vriendt-de Man (1971), lexical verbs had a much higher chance of being used in the past participle than in the simple past form. [5] This finding is based on my own analysis of some of de Vriendt-de Man's (1971) figures: I took all her data for the "tweede hoofdvorm" (or simple past) on pages 199-201 and sifted out all the lexical verbs from the list. The total frequency of these was 625, or 28% of all the instances of the "tweede hoofdvorm" in the entire corpus. Secondly, I took the data for the "voltooid deelwoord" (or past participle) as presented on page 205 and extracted the non-lexical verbs ZIJN, HEBBEN and WORDEN from this list (modals did not occur in the past participle form - see de Vriendt-de Man 1971: 129-134). These non-lexical verbs in the past participle form accounted for 296 tokens on a total of 1888 instances of a past participle form, or 15%. This implies that lexical verbs accounted for 85% of all the past participles in the corpus. Obviously, the 57% difference between lexical verbs in the simple past (28%) and lexical verbs in the past participle form (85%) is quite substantial, and sufficiently shows that lexical verbs stand a much higher chance of occurring as a past participle than as a simple past. Since it is not clear whether the code "voltooid deelwoord" was applied to any verb in a past participle form or whether it was restricted to past participles as part of the present perfect, though, we cannot assume on the basis of the above calculations that lexical verbs stood a higher chance of being used in the present perfect rather than in the simple past.

Whether the frequency argument made above can actually hold up when it comes to caretaker-to-child speech, however, must unfortunately remain purely hypothetical at this point, due to the complete lack of information on the past verb forms that young Dutch children hear from

7.3.2.8 The expression of future time reference through the use of verb forms

From the beginning of the study Kate frequently uses the periphrastic form GAAN + infinitive to express that she is about to perform some action or to predict that something or someone is about to do something (i.e. GAAN + infinitive has an inchoative meaning here). The time of reference is either the immediate future (within seconds) or a more distant future (later in the day, or even some non-specified time within weeks). Towards the end of the study, ZULLEN (always in the form of ZAL + infinitive) is used as well; it expresses an intention to carry out an action in the future. Van Ginneken (1917), Tinbergen (1919) and Schaerlaekens (1977) write that around the age of three, the monolingual child often uses the form GAAN + infinitive to express an inchoative meaning. ZULLEN + infinitive appears rather later. Here again, then, there is a strong resemblance between the mono- and the bilingual data.

Both Van Ginneken (1917) and Schaerlaekens (1977) state that the expression of a future time through the use of verbs appears well before the expression of past time reference (again as far as the use of verbs is concerned), i.e. children already use the inchoative GAAN + infinitive from the first half of the third year onwards. Tinbergen's (1919) examples also show abundant use of GAAN + infinitive at that time. Since the data in the present study only start at the age of 2;7, they do not lend themselves to a comparison, but the fact that in the beginning of the study many verb forms referring to the future but very few referring to the past occur is certainly consistent with the findings from monolingual acquisition. Past verb forms, as was seen above, start to appear with some frequency only towards the end of the study.

7.3.3 *Recapitulation*

The preceding analyses have shown that in the development of the Dutch verb phrase, Kate is at the same time working on the conjugation of the present tense, the use of complex verb phrases combining two forms, the formation of the present participle and the congruence of Subject and finite verb for individual verb forms. Within this medley, some clear developmental changes take place. These mainly concern the beginning attempts to incorporate plural Subjects in the verb agreement system, the sudden 'misanalysis' of HEEFT as consisting of HEEF+{-t} by analogy with the highly productive stem+{-t} rule, the dramatic increase in the number of verb forms referring to a past event, the change from correct past participle formation to intensive experimenting, the more frequent appearance of a new element (ZAL) to refer to the future and the wider scope of the modals as they become more and more 'modal-like' by being increasingly used with a non-finite verb.

Table 7.11 *Kate's Dutch verb system and how it compares with findings from monolingual acquisition* [a]

	Kate	Monolingual acq.
Subject--finite verb combinations		
----notion of congruence	established	established
----adult and non-adult forms exist side by side	yes	yes
----most frequent error pattern for lexical verbs:		
IK + stem + {–t}	yes	yes
----occasional error pattern for lexical verbs:		
* singular Subject + stem + {–en}	yes	yes
* plural Subject NOT + stem + {–en}	yes	yes
----IK HEEF occurs regularly	yes	yes
Future time reference		
----GAAN + infinitive occurs first and abundantly	yes	yes
----ZAL + infinitive occurs later	yes	yes
Past time reference		
----mainly through present perfect	yes	yes
----use of auxiliary is mainly adult-like	yes	yes
----past participle formation:		
* first (and later) correct, irregular	yes	yes
* later correct, regular as well	yes	yes
and also incorrect, irregular	yes	yes
and also <u>incorrect, regular</u>	<u>yes</u>	no mention
* most frequent error is overgeneralization of regular paradigm	yes	yes
Miscellaneous findings		
----always the appropriate analogies	yes	yes
----syntagmatic relationships mostly adult-like	yes	yes

[a] I.e. in children around the age of three as reported on in the literature at large; the discrepancies between the findings for Kate and monolingual acquisition are underlined

Throughout the above analyses, comparisons were made with data from monolingual Dutch children. All these must remain rather vague and general, unfortunately. The main reason for this is that there are few or no exact quantitative data available on the acquisition of Dutch verbs for the age range that we are dealing with. With this limitation in mind, then, qualitative comparisons between monolingual children and a bilingual child show that in essence the bilingual child's production of Dutch VP's closely resembles that of monolingual Dutch children. This is certainly the case for the order in which verb forms are acquired. There is not much that can be said about the rate of acquisition, since no objective means of measurement exists on the basis of which this could be compared. However, similar forms seem to appear at around the same ages.

The above findings and how they compare with data from monolingual children have been summarized briefly in Table 7.11.

We now turn to an analysis of Kate's English verb system.

7.4 Kate's English verb system
7.4.1 *Introduction*

In this subsection we shall look at Kate's use of Subject--finite verb agreement in English and at changes in her production of English VP's as time goes on.

Adult English does not heavily rely on morphological verb marking: for most English finite lexical verbs, a two-way paradigm (zero marking and {-ed} form) expresses temporal and aspectual rather than person or number distinctions, with as conspicuous exception the third person singular, present UVF + {-s} form (cf. also Palmer 1974: 15). A general notion of Subject--finite lexical verb agreement, then, is not as central to the adequate formation of English VP's as it is in Dutch. Rather than learn a whole paradigm, the English speaker only has to remember to add an {-s} morpheme to the UVF when using a third person singular Subject. For the use of the copula, however, Subject--finite verb agreement assumes quite a lot more importance; then again for the modals it is of no significance whatsoever. A general notion of congruence, then, applicable to all finite verbs, is not a necessary prerequisite for English finite verb production. Rather, the child acquiring the English verb system need only memorize the various forms of BE and must learn to add {-s} to the UVF of lexical verbs in the present when the Subject is a third person singular (of course this is an oversimplified characterization of the actual task facing the child). Since, in this view, the presence of a general notion of congruence is not paramount for the production of finite lexical verbs in the present, we shall not try to prove that such a notion is available to Kate at the beginning of the study.

The following analyses do not include VP's without an overt Subject, although this subject may have been elided in a fully adult-like manner.

The verb phrase 211

As in the preceding section, comparisons with monolingual children will be made throughout the analysis of the material, and only a short summary in table form will be presented at the end.

We start by looking at the Subject--finite verb combinations that lexical verbs, HAVE, BE, DO and the modals enter into. After this, we shall look at syntagmatic relationships within English VP's and at the marking of past and future time reference.

7.4.2 *Analyses and results*
7.4.2.1 Subject--finite lexical verb combinations (present tense)

This section deals with Kate's Subject--finite verb combinations which contain a lexical verb in the present. Not included in the following analysis are the uses of HAVE and DO as lexical verbs, and the use of WANT in the WANT TO + UVF syntagm. As with the Dutch use of GAAN + infinitive, the use of WANT TO + UVF is very abundant (and always adult-like). WANT in this pseudo-auxiliary usage occurs almost exclusively in combination with the first person singular pronoun I.

More than a third of all the combinations considered in this subsection concern the use of WANT (used independently). Again, WANT occurs almost exclusively in combination with the first person singular pronoun I. On only one occasion is it combined with a third person singular Subject. In this case WANT is realized appropriately as WANTS. Of all the other lexical verbs in the present (so excluding all uses of WANT), 62% are used in combination with, again, the first person singular pronoun I.

Second most frequently occur combinations with the second person singular subject pronoun YOU. As example 14 shows, these combinations may express a command, which they often did (cf. Table 7.4 in section 7.2.2.2 above, in which YOU+UVF combinations expressing a command were subsumed under 'imperative', although actually these forms are ambiguous as to whether they are a simple present tense or an 'explicit' imperative - hence we shall refer to them as pseudo-imperatives).

Combinations with a UVF+{-s} form come third. The Subjects here are all in the third person singular (i.e., demonstrative pronouns, full noun phrases, IT, WHAT and once also SHE).

All the Subject--finite lexical verb combinations here are adult-like except two. On one of those occasions, IT is combined with just a UVF. However, this form is immediately repaired into a UVF+{-s} form (see example 15). On the second occasion, Kate is discussing an event that happened the day before at school, so one could argue that the error is due to the non-marking of the past tense rather than to the omitting of the {-s} morpheme (see example 16).

(14) 'You go on the floor.' (Age: 2;7,17)
    (Kate is ordering the investigator to lie down on the floor)
    {use of finite lexical verb in the present with YOU to express a command}
(15) 'Cause we have to be careful otherwise it break. So breaks.' (Age: 3;1,13)
    {repaired instance of non-adult combination of base form with a third person singular pronoun into an appropriate UVF + {–s} form}
(16) 'But-but but someone stop it.' (Age: 3;1,18)
    (Kate is referring to the fact that the day before, a teacher at school made a child stop talking)
    {inappropriate use of an unmarked verb form to refer to a past event}

Table 7.12 *Kate's English Subject--finite lexical verb combinations* [a]

	STEM	STEM + {-s}	Totals
I	141	-	141
YOU	31	-	31
3 p s g	2	16	18
TOTALS	174	16	190

[a] Instances of HAVE, DO and of WANT as an auxiliary are not included; only present tense forms are tabulated (including the pseudo-imperatives with YOU); the non-adult-like combinations are underlined

The general picture, then, is that most lexical verbs in the present occur in the UVF in combination with the first person singular pronoun I. Occasionally, a UVF is combined with the second person singular subject pronoun. Even less frequent are combinations involving a finite lexical verb and a third person singular. However, all these combinations except two are adult-like, i.e. instead of a UVF by itself, the form with {-s} is used. Plural subjects do not occur in combination with a lexical verb in the present. The data are summarized in Table 7.12., which shows the total number of occurrences of any one relevant combination in the entire English corpus.

Developmentally, there is some change to be discerned: although some UVF+{-s} forms are already present by Tape 2, most of these forms start to occur from the age of three onwards. Use of YOU and a UVF in clear declaratives (so not in pseudo-imperatives) also basically appears after

Kate's third birthday. Use of YOU+UVF in pseudo-imperatives already occurs in Tape 2. Combinations with I occur in great frequency throughout. These findings are tabulated in Table 19 in the Appendix.

Since most English Subject--finite lexical verb combinations are adult-like, including those with a third person singular as Subject, one might conclude that Kate has acquired the present tense formation paradigm. After all, Brown's (1973) 90% criterion for acquisition has been reached: in 99% of the 'obligatory contexts' (with all the methodological problems that this notion entails - see e.g. Fletcher 1979) Kate uses the appropriate verb form. However, this conclusion is premature: Kate uses a limited range of Subjects, and of those that she uses, one (viz. the personal pronoun I) strongly prevails. In addition, the absolute number of occurrences of the UVF+{-s} form is very small. Furthermore, the types of verbs that occur in this UVF+{-s} form are limited as well: the first few occurrences concern GOES (in fact, 7 out of 16 UVF+{-s} forms are GOES); only later does COMES get produced, and only from Kate's third birthday on do we find LOOKS, SAYS, BREAKS, WEIGHS, LIKES and WANTS (note that these forms are not restricted to one allomorph of {-s} but that Kate produces both the [z] and [s] allomorphs - but not yet [iz]). Whether in fact Kate has fully acquired the present tense formation paradigm, then, cannot be determined from the data available.

In naturalistic studies of monolingual English children there is very little information on the acquisition of Subject--finite lexical verb combinations in the present (see Keeney and Wolfe 1972 for an experimental study of agreement involving children between the ages of 3;0 and 4;11; a pragmatically oriented study of the use of the simple present by three-year-olds has been carried out by Gerhardt and Savasir 1986). Brown (1973) writes that the third person singular regular UVF+{-s} form is 'acquired' at stage V for his subjects Adam and Eve. If Brown's notion of 'obligatory context' is used, then Kate can be said to behave exactly like Adam and Eve (Kate is matched to these children since she has also reached Brown's Stage V - with an English MLU of 4.90 and an English upper bound of 22 at the age of 2;7,17, Kate easily reaches Brown's criterion for 'admission' to Stage V, viz. an MLU of 4.00 and an upper bound of 13 (cf. Brown 1973: 56)). The data from Kate further resemble those reported on by Brown (1973) and Bloom, Lifter and Hafitz (1980) to the extent that third person singular regular UVF+{-s} forms occurred quite infrequently, and certainly with much less frequency than gerunds and even verbs ending in

{-ed}. In addition, most of Kate's VP's involving just an unmarked verb form are stative verbs such as WANT and THINK. This again corresponds with the monolingual literature (see e.g. Bloom et al. 1980).

7.4.2.2   Subject--finite verb combinations with DO

DO as a finite verb occurs in a number of combinations, viz. with the pronouns I, YOU, SHE, HE, WE, THAT, THIS and on one occasion with a proper name as well. Usage is always adult-like. HE and SHE as a Subject occur only from the age of 3;1,6 onwards. The most frequent Subject combined with DO is the pronoun I. Combinations with other Subjects occur only sporadically. YOU and I with DO occur only in negatives, while questions with DO mainly involve third person singular Subjects (although DO WE? occurs twice).

Due to the general infrequency of forms with DO as a finite verb in the present there is little to be said about the question whether its conjugation has been acquired. In the section on the syntagmatic use of VP's we shall focus on the more interesting aspects of DO, viz. its auxiliary usage.

7.4.2.3   Subject--finite verb combinations with HAVE

The data for HAVE reflect the findings for the lexical verbs to the extent that, again, combinations with the pronoun I occur most frequently and combinations with YOU second most frequently. WE as a Subject occurs twice (for lexical verbs in the present, the Subject WE did not occur). The forms that HAVE takes are always adult-like: even on the rare occasions that HAVE is used with a third person singular Subject, we find the appropriate form HAS, which is never inappropriately used with another Subject.

Developmentally, there is not much to be reported on, except perhaps that WE in combination with HAVE occurs only from the age of 3;1,13 onwards. In general, HAVE as a finite verb in the present occurs quite infrequently (the data for HAVE are tabulated in Table 20 in the Appendix).

Due to the infrequent occurrences of HAVE and more specifically of HAS, it is not clear from the data whether the third person singular form HAS has been 'acquired', i.e. whether the child has formulated a 'third person singular > HAS' rule (rather than, say, an 'any person > HAVE' rule).

7.4.2.4 Subject--finite verb combinations with BE

BE behaves quite differently from the lexical verbs and HAVE: finite forms of BE occur with high frequency, and a great variety of Subjects is combined with a form of BE. Usually these combinations are fully adult-like. The three non-adult-like combinations are IS YOU (instead of ARE YOU) and twice the occurrence of THERE ARE + Subject Complement or gerund instead of THEY ARE. The IS YOU combination may be viewed as a simple production error, since the adult-like form ARE YOU (in questions) appears at the same time (although only 11 times in total). The use of THERE instead of THEY probably has to do with a confusion of the perceptually quite similar THERE and THEY forms (also, THERE occurs 33 times in the whole English corpus, while THEY occurs only 8 times).

On the whole, the AM/'M and IS/'S forms prevail (with their appropriate first and third person singular Subjects respectively). YOU and plural Subjects start to be combined with ARE/'RE with some frequency only from the age of 3;1,13 (Tape 14) onwards. The relevant data are tabulated in Table 21 in the Appendix.

In the above (and in Table 21) no distinction was made between the full and the abbreviated forms of BE in the present. However, it must be taken into account that their formal dissimilarity and the high frequency of abbreviated forms in declaratives in adult informal conversations (Crystal and Davy 1969) may cause the child to initially learn the full and the abbreviated forms not as basically interchangeable, but as quite distinct, unrelated elements (Fletcher 1981a). In order to approach this question, all English forms of BE were categorized according to whether they were abbreviated or full. Before we discuss the data, though, the following observations must be made: adult English provides three possible combinations for most Subjects, viz. Subject+full form of BE or Subject+ abbreviated form of BE in declaratives and negatives, and full form of BE+Subject in Y/N-questions (including question tags). [7] The Subjects that can occur in these syntagms are I, YOU, all third person singular and plural pronouns (including demonstratives not ending in [s] - THIS is always followed by IS, either in the form [iz] or [əz]), WE, and all singular and plural subject NP's. In WH-questions, the interrogative pronoun may be followed by either a full or abbreviated form of BE, whatever the Subject is. The third person singular, though, behaves differently from the other persons in that it is the only abbreviated form occurring after an interrogative pronoun that does not need to be syllabic (the abbreviated forms of AM and ARE still contain a schwa after a WH-word and thus are still quite different from the non-interrogative abbreviated forms, where Subject and 'M or 'RE are joined into one syllable). Finally, when HERE (or existential THERE) is the first word in the sentence either a full or an abbreviated form of BE may be used.

How does Kate manipulate these permutations? Above, it was noted that nearly all of Kate's combinations of a Subject with a finite form of BE in the present are adult-like, i.e. most Subjects are combined with a person and number appropriate form of BE. However, there is evidence that Kate underextends the possibilities of the adult system as far as her choice of full vs. abbreviated forms of BE goes. First, for pronominal Subjects (except THIS) there is a strong tendency for her to use only two combinations where the adult system allows three: Kate nearly always uses an abbreviated form of BE in a non-interrogative, and a full form in an interrogative clause (or a question tag). WH-questions that are not identity or naming questions and that have I or YOU as Subject contain a very full form of BE only (so [æm] and [a:r]), although, again, a reduced form would have been perfectly adult-like. More strikingly, non-interrogatives with a full form of BE, although they would be perfectly appropriate, are quite rare when the Subject is a pronoun. With a full NP as Subject, however, Kate's preference is for full forms of BE in non-interrogatives (a question with a full NP as Subject and with a full form of BE as finite verb occurs only once, viz. after WHERE). The evidence for these findings is summarized in Table 7.13.

The above findings suggest that Kate is not using a rule of the form <<use IS/'S and ARE/'RE when the Subject is in the third person singular or plural>>. Rather, Kate is apparently operating with a productive rule that allows her to appropriately choose IS or ARE when the Subject is a singular, respectively plural, full NP. However, at this stage there is little reason to assume that this use is connected with the use of 'S and 'RE after pronominal Subjects. This latter use is probably the result of rote-memorization: IT'S, THAT'S, SHE'S, HE'S, WE'RE and THEY'RE are more likely than not unanalysed routines at this stage of development. This hypothesis is corroborated by the fact that the full forms IS and ARE when combined with IT, THAT, SHE, HE, WE or THEY occur almost exclusively in interrogatives. In declaratives starting with THERE, THERE is always followed by 'S, but in one question tag, THERE follows IS.

Thus, the data do not show any sign that for the child 'S is a mere formal variant of IS. Rather, the two forms appear to be in complementary syntactic distribution. The same can be said of the pair AM/'M: again, Kate uses the abbreviated form in declaratives, whereas the full form appears almost exclusively in interrogatives. Note however that both full and abbreviated forms of BE carry the same 'functional load': in the present they both function as finite verbs, and there are no different usage patterns to be discerned depending on whether BE is used as a copula or as an auxiliary.

The evidence presented here not only shows that Kate has yet to construct a unified conjugation paradigm for BE, but also that a strong one form/one function strategy is being used: with pronominal Subjects, 'S, 'M and 'RE appear in declaratives, while IS, AM and ARE are virtually only used in interrogatives. However, this one form/one function strategy is starting to lose ground after the child's third birthday. This is evident from Kate's use of BE after interrogative pronouns in identity questions (see example 17): from the age of 3;1 onwards, Kate starts using full forms where before she was only producing abbreviated forms. (The existence side by side at the age of three of 'S and IS in WH-questions has also been noted by Fletcher 1985 in his study of a monolingual English child.) Although, admittedly, the number of occurrences showing this variation is very small (see the third part of Table 7.13), we may here be seeing the gateway through which it becomes possible for Kate to regard 'S and IS as two functionally equivalent forms, which then may allow her to discover that referring to third persons by means of pronouns is grammatically no different from referring to them by means of full NP's.

(17) 'What's that colour?' (Age: 2;7,17)
  {example of a WH-question to ask for identification. The form of BE (viz. 'S) is an abbreviated one}

Table 7.13 *Full vs. abbreviated forms of BE* [a]

Pronominal Subject, excluding THIS

	NON-INTERROGATIVE		Y/N Q	WH-Q [b]	Totals
	full	abbreviated	full	full	
1 p s g	2	46	5	7	60
HE/SHE/IT	3	23	7	-	33
2 p s g	1	3	6	5	15
THAT	-	11	3	-	14
3 p p l	-	2	2	-	4
1 p p l	-	2	-	-	2
TOTALS	6	87	23	12	**128**

Non-pronominal Subject, but including THIS

	NON-INTERROGATIVE		Totals
	full	abbreviated	
THIS	20	-	20
singular NP	16	4	20
plural NP	9	-	9
TOTALS	45	4	**49**

Subset of WH-questions [c]

			INTERROGATIVE		Totals
			full	abbreviated	
WHAT	'be'	singular	6	8	14
WHERE	'be'	singular	1	7	8
WHAT	'be'	plural	3	-	3
WHO	'be'	singular	-	1	1
TOTALS			10	16	**26**

[a] Not included are the three non-adult-like combinations (THERE ARE instead of THEY ARE and IS YOU) and utterances starting with HERE and THERE

[b] The question word here has Direct Object function only

[c] This subset consists of WH-questions where the question word is not the clause's Direct Object (most of these questions are identity or naming questions). Listed are the relevant question words and the following finite forms of BE

One question raised by the above findings concerns the reason <u>why</u> Kate has 'hit upon' the abbreviated forms after pronominal Subjects in non-interrogatives. After all, she might have equally well chosen full forms. Possibly a partial answer lies, again, in the type of input that Kate receives: Fletcher (1981a) has concluded from an informal analysis of the transcripts of Wells' data (see e.g. Wells 1985) that contracted forms of HAVE and BE prevail over full forms in language input to English monolingual children (there have been formal studies of the general use of auxiliaries in input to English-speaking children and their possible effects on auxiliary development (see e.g. Wells 1979; see also Richards 1986 for a short review and new findings), but as far as I know, there have been no formal studies of the use of contracted vs. full forms of HAVE and BE *per se* in input to children). It would be worthwhile to further explore this question, and to see whether in the input abbreviated forms are primarily used with pronominal Subjects, and full forms with full NP's. Before one embarks on such a study, however, it must first be examined to what extent the above findings from Kate correspond to what happens in other children learning English from birth onwards. At present, unfortunately, there is very little information on monolingual children's use of BE that could be used as a basis for comparing the data from the present study. Brown (1973: 268-269) devotes two pages to 'contractible' and 'uncontractible' forms of BE. If we assume that 'contractible' refers to abbreviated forms, and 'uncontractible' to full forms, [8] then it is clear that Kate behaves no different from the children Brown reports on: these children produced both 'contractible' and 'uncontractible' forms in both copula and auxiliary usage at Stage V of their language development (Brown 1973: 271), as does Kate.

Kuczaj in his study of the acquisition of full forms of BE notes that children "do not seem to learn all members of the copula or the auxiliary be class simultaneously" (Kuczaj 1981: 79). This finding is also confirmed by the data from Kate.

7.4.2.5 Subject --finite verb combinations involving the modals

For the conjugation of the English modals we can be quite brief: Kate always uses modals appropriately, i.e. she never adds any inflection to them. The actual forms used are (in descending order of overall frequency): CAN, 'LL, SHALL, WILL, WOULD, MAY, 'D, SHOULD and WOULDN'T. The latter three occur only once, and all of the others except CAN and 'LL occur only sporadically, so we shall not say anything about the kinds of Subjects that they combine with.

CAN and 'LL are both used most frequently with the first person singular pronoun I. With CAN, YOU is the second most frequently used Subject, while for 'LL, WE is the second most frequently used. Since third person singular and plural Subjects used in combination with a modal appear only sporadically, there is no clear evidence that the entire paradigm has been acquired. Although overgeneralizations based on the lexical verb paradigm or on the third person singular DOES or HAS forms may start to appear at a later stage, at this time in development there is no undue influence from the regular paradigm on the formation of modals. Such theoretically possible overgeneralizations are not, however, reported on in the monolingual literature. The monolingual literature furthermore does not discuss the 'conjugation' of the modals, and certainly non-adult-like forms such as *I CANS or *SHE MAYS are not reported on. It may thus be assumed that monolingual English children only produce adult-like forms, as does Kate.

The use of only the abbreviated form 'LL suggests that Kate has yet to learn that it is in fact a reduced form of WILL (WILL occurs only three times in the entire corpus). The fact that Kate uses 'LL rather than WILL is probably due to the great frequency of the reduced form vs. the full form in the input, although, again, this statement must remain purely hypothetical at this point due to lack of relevant empirical studies (but see Bellugi 1967 as referred to by Slobin 1985a).

Developmentally, there is some change to be observed in the combinations of CAN with a Subject. Although Kate uses both CAN and CAN'T after I and YOU from the beginning of the study onwards, as well as CAN followed by I or YOU, she only starts using CAN'T followed by I or YOU from the age of 3;2,7 onwards. These few instances of CAN'T I? and CAN'T YOU? are the only occurrences of negative Y/N-questions in the entire English corpus. This picture fits in well with Wells' (1985: 271) finding that in monolingual acquisition interrogatives containing a negative are very late to emerge (see also sections 8.2.2.2 and 8.2.2.4

7.4.2.6 Syntagmatic relationships within VP's

The modals are nearly always used appropriately, i.e. they are mostly followed by a UVF of a lexical verb, BE or HAVE. On two occasions, though, Kate produces non-adult-like combinations (see examples 8 and 9 in section 7.2.2.2 above). However, since only two syntagmatically inappropriate combinations with a modal auxiliary occur, we may be simply dealing with production errors rather than any new acquisition strategies. On a few occasions, CAN and 'LL are not followed by any non-finite verb form. In the two utterances with a 'hanging' 'LL form the reason is that the utterances are incomplete, i.e. Kate simply stops talking in the middle of her sentence (immediately after 'LL) and starts on a new

The verb phrase 221

unrelated sentence. In the 7 utterances with a 'hanging' CAN, the UVF has appropriately been ellipted (it might have appeared in one of Kate's preceding utterances or it may act as an elliptical reply to an adult's question - see e.g. example 18).

(18) K: Mommy I want to cut something else! (Age: 3;2,7)
 (Kate has been cutting up strawberries, or rather, she has been commandeering Annick to cut them up)
 M: Yeah, well just a minute darling! You may cut something else. Don't you worry. (then in a funny accent:) I shall give you something else and you may cut it up!
 K: An-an-an-an Annick can help me?
 M: She can indeed!
 K: Can indeed! (after a pause:) Mommy - mommy, Annick can help me.
 M: Ja ja. <Yeah yeah.>
 K: She can.
 {appropriate use of CAN with ellipted UVF}

Besides the 'pure' modals, Kate also uses HAVE as an auxiliary in HAVE TO. This use occurs from the age of 2;11,14 onwards. HAVE TO, when HAVE is the finite verb, is always appropriately followed by the UVF (so never by a gerund, for instance; the monolingual literature does not report on any such non-adult-like usage of HAVE TO either). Kate never uses HAVE as a tense auxiliary (furthermore, HAVE GOT does not appear in the data). This is again confirmed by the monolingual literature: Brown (1973) states that at Stage V, American English speaking children do not in general use HAVE as a tense auxiliary (but British children may - see e.g. Fletcher 1981a and also the discussion of past time reference later on).

Fletcher (1979) writes that the use of the modals is very frequent in monolingual children around the age of three (and under). The modals that appear most often are CAN and WILL (see also Wells 1979 - neither Wells 1979 nor Fletcher 1979 mention the use of 'LL, though).

The modals SHOULD, WOULD, MUST, COULD, SHALL and MAY are quite uncommon or even non-existent in children within Kate's age range (Wells 1979). Again, then, the data for Kate are comparable to those for monolingual children.

The fact that CAN occurs quite frequently and is formally used in an adult-like fashion does not mean that Kate already uses CAN in all its possible adult functions. Kate does not, for instance, use CAN in its epistemic sense of possibility of an action or state of affairs. Rather, in affirmatives she uses CAN to indicate a suggested action (both on somebody else's and her own part) or an ability. Kate uses CAN'T primarily to indicate inability or a prohibition. In interrogatives with the pronoun I as a Subject, Kate uses CAN to request permission, and with YOU as a Subject preceded by CAN, Kate is questioning the addressee's willingness to do something. This succinct overview of Kate's main uses of CAN shows great similarities with Fletcher's (1985) findings for his monolingual subject Sophie.

As was indicated in the section on the conjugation of lexical verbs (section 7.4.2.1), the verb WANT appears very frequently as a finite verb in the present. It is both used as a fully lexical verb and also as a sort of 'modal' auxiliary in the concatenative form WANT TO+UVF. WANT TO may here be realized as WANNA. In the corpus, WANT TO and WANNA appear to be in free variation, although WANNA starts to occur only from the age of 3;0,7 onwards, and just as suddenly disappears after the age of 3;1,26 (WANNA is always appropriately combined with a first or second person singular pronoun, and never with a third person Subject. This corresponds to adult American usage). WANT TO appears already from the very beginning of the study and continues to appear throughout, although during the period when WANNA appears, WANT TO occurs just once or twice, only to reappear in full force at the age of 3;2,7.

More interesting developments can be discovered from a comparison of the use of WANT as a lexical verb and as an auxiliary. Here we can see a parallel development to the one noted for the Dutch modals: in the Dutch corpus, there was a steady increase in the number of VP's with a modal and a non-finite part compared to those with just a modal verb (see section 7.3.2.6). Similarly, although both independent and auxiliary usage of WANT are present from the beginning of the study, there is a steady increase in the use of WANT as an auxiliary (see Table 22 in the Appendix), whereas the use of WANT as a lexical verb remains fairly stable, and strongly related to the general amount of talking per recording session. Use of WANT with a non-finite part can be seen as formally more complex than use without it. The data thus show that Kate becomes more adept at manipulating more formally complex constructions as time goes on.

Usually, use of WANT is fully adult-like. There are, however, two utterances in which the preposition TO of WANT TO is absent (once Kate uses I WANT+UVF and once she uses I DON'T WANT without TO).

Since most usage is appropriate, though, no great weight can be attached to these two non-adult-like utterances.

We now come to the discussion of Kate's use of DO. As a finite verb, DO appears most frequently as an auxiliary (it is used as a lexical verb in the present only three times). In the catalogue of forms section, it was noted that DON'T was used with a UVF quite frequently to express a prohibition. This usage is fully adult-like, but Kate also uses YOU DON'T+UVF at the beginning of the study to express a prohibition (these forms occur only at age 2;7,17). This use soon makes way for the DON'T UVF syntagm without YOU, though. On a few occasions Kate uses DON'T where CAN'T would have been more appropriate, as in example 19 (interestingly, Fletcher (1985: 129) has noted the inverse case: his monolingual subject Sophie once used CAN'T instead of the more appropriate DOESN'T). However, syntagmatically Kate's utterances with DON'T instead of CAN'T are perfectly adequate (as is the case for the YOU DON'T prohibitions as well). Auxiliary use of DO in the present, then, is fully adult-like, although not all the possibilities of the adult system are used (see the paragraph below).

(19) 'I don't hear anything!' (Age: 3;1,13)
  (Kate is saying that she cannot hear any sound coming from the cassette-recorder)
  {perhaps inappropriate use of DON'T instead of CAN'T}

DO as an auxiliary in the present appears both in negatives and interrogatives (including twice in tag-questions). An investigation of questions where DO could have been used but wasn't reveals that there are some cases where Kate does not use DO with a lexical verb. However, all these cases are limited to utterances in which DO or DO YOU are not necessarily present, i.e. where adults might also omit these elements (see e.g. example 20). Most of the lexical verbs here are WANT, the others are REMEMBER and THINK. It appears, then, that Kate is not only well on her way towards learning when and how the DO-periphrasis is used, but also when it is not (the use of DO in questions where adults would not use DO does not occur in the data although of course this does not mean that they did not occur when Kate was not being recorded). Alternatively, however, the omission of the lexical item DO as a question auxiliary (it only occurs twice as a question auxiliary in the entire corpus) might be seen as a result of the fact that the item DO is mostly used as a lexical verb (see

(see Table 7.14). A one form/one function strategy might, at least for some time, inhibit the productive use of the form DO as a meaningless, dummy auxiliary.

The very rare use of the item DO in questions is a first sign that the use of DO-support may be not yet be completely acquired. Furthermore, Kate does not use any form of DO for emphasis in declaratives (except in one utterance with DID where emphatic use of DID is fairly adult-like - see example 21). In addition, negative interrogatives with a form of DO are absent as well. The only data from the monolingual literature that could to some extent be compared to the ones above come from Fletcher's (1985) case study of Sophie, a monolingual British-English girl. At the age of three, when Sophie can be placed in Brown's (1973) Stage IV, she produced DO in both Y/N and WH-questions, as well as emphatic DOES in declaratives. The latter use does not appear at all in the Kate corpus, and DO appears only twice in Kate's questions. Sophie also used DIDN'T in WH-questions, whereas use of negative forms of DO in interrogatives is absent in Kate's English. Sophie did, like Kate, use DOES and DID in questions, and DOESN'T, DON'T and DIDN'T in non-interrogatives (see Fletcher 1985: 196). Because of the limitations of naturalistic, observational data, there is no way of knowing whether Kate's non-use of certain forms in comparison with Sophie is due to sampling, or is indicative of a gap in Kate's productive use. All the forms that Kate <u>does</u> use, however, also happen to appear in the speech production of a monolingual English child.

(20) 'Want some soup mommy?' (Age: 2;11,14)
    {appropriate use of WANT in a Y/N-question without DO support}
(21) M: Yesterday she knocked down that plant over there. And it was a real mess. But we cleaned it up, didn't we? It wasn't too serious. Mommy wasn't angry, was she?
    K: I did knock that plant over. (Age: 3;0,17)
    {use of emphatic DID+UVF}
    M: Yes, you certainly did!

There is a clear developmental picture as far as use of DO as an auxiliary is concerned (see Table 23 in the Appendix): up until the age of 3;1,6, the use of DO is quite infrequent. After this age there is a marked increase in the use of DO as an auxiliary, both in terms of frequency and in terms of the variety of syntactic contexts in which the auxiliary DO is used. The general increase in the use of DO as an auxiliary also brings with it the use of DO-support in the past in negatives and interrogatives. Usually, the non-finite part is in the appropriate UVF, but on two occasions, the non-finite part is a simple past form (see examples 6 and 7 in section 7.2.2.2 above). All the syntactic contexts in which forms of DO (except DOING) occur have been tabulated in Table 7.14.

Table 7.14 *The uses of DO* [a]

	Imperative		Finite			Non-Finite	Totals
	lexical	aux.	interrog. aux.	non-interrog. lexical	aux.	lexical	
DON'T	-	10	-	-	26	-	36
DO	2	-	2	3	-	14	21
DID	-	-	9	5	1	-	15
DOES	-	-	8	-	-	-	8
DIDN'T	-	-	-	-	4	-	4
DOESN'T	-	-	-	-	3	-	3
TOTALS	2	10	19	8	34	14	87

[a] Interrog. stands for 'interrogative', aux. stands for 'auxiliary'

Finally, interrogatives and negatives with the verb HAVE are nearly always formed with the help of DO. Kate is clearly following her mother's American usage patterns here.

DO as a dummy auxiliary is one of the first auxiliaries to emerge in English-speaking children (Wells 1979, 1985: 358). Similarly, Fletcher (1979) notes that in monolingual children (and, as he points out, in Leopold's English-German daughter Hildegard - see Leopold 1970, c. 1939-49) the auxiliary DO is used with regularity towards the end of the third year. Shortly after their third birthday (and also before), monolingual children start using past forms of DO in negatives and interrogatives (Fletcher 1979, 1981b). Again, then, there is a similarity between Kate and other children who are learning English from birth.

So far, we have said nothing about the use of BE as an auxiliary and the sorts of non-finite elements it is combined with. BE occurs quite frequently as an auxiliary (84 times in total). This auxiliary usage includes the use of BE in the present continuous and in the BE GOING TO+UVF syntagm. In the following, however, we shall only deal with the former (combinations of BE with GOING TO will be discussed in the subsection on the expression of future time reference).

When we leave out of consideration utterances without an overt Subject and use of the present continuous in lines of songs produced *verbatim*, we are left with only 28 instances of a complete present continuous tense. There are an additional three utterances in which an 'incomplete' present continuous occurs, i.e. in which a Subject is immediately followed by a UVF+{-ing} form. Since complete realizations of the present continuous far exceed incomplete ones, however, we may suggest that the syntagmatic form of the present continuous has been acquired, but this suggestion must remain tentative: after all, a total of 31 tokens is not a firm basis to draw any major hypotheses from. Monolingual English children use the BE+ UVF+{-ing} syntagm appropriately from the age of 2;6 onwards (Wells 1979).

Developmentally, there is a clearly noticeable change (see Table 24 in the Appendix): from the age of 3;0,11 onwards, the number of realizations of a complete present continuous tense suddenly increases (23 of the 28 tokens occur in the second half of the observation period).

(22) A: Wat doen wij nu? ?..? aan mama! Wat doe jij?
       <What are we doing now? ?..? to mommy! What are you doing?>
       (all addressed to Kate)
   K: We're eating soup! (Age: 3;0,11)
       (Kate addresses M who has just come in and tells her that she and the investigator are eating imaginary soup)
       {appropriate use of a present continuous tense to refer to an on-going (though imaginary) action}
   M: Eating soup? Is het lekker? <Is it good?>

Functionally, use of the present continuous is mostly adult-like. Kate always uses dynamic verbs in the non-finite {-ing} form (young American-English monolingual children use mainly dynamic verbs in UVF+{-ing} forms as well - see e.g. Brown 1973, Maratsos, Kuczaj II, Fox and Chalkley 1979, Bloom, Lifter and Hafitz 1980), and her present continuous tenses either refer to an on-going action in the present (see example 22) or to an action in the immediate or slightly more distant future (see example 23). On one of the occasions that the present continuous is used to refer to a future event (see example 24), Kate might have more appropriately used the WON'T+UVF syntagm, although this interpretation may not be the only possible one. On the whole, then, it appears that Kate is well on her way towards learning the functions of the present continuous tense. This is further lent support by the fact that in utterances with a lexical verb in the 'simple present' there appears only one in which a present continuous tense would have been more appropriate (see example 25).

(23) K: Hey mam, how am I going? (Age: 3;1,18)
<Hey mom, where shall I go/am I going?>
(Kate just went to get her tricycle)
M: Oh-
K: I'm going first to the bathroom.
{appropriate use of a present continuous tense to express an intended imminent action}

(24) K: I want pill! (Age: 3;0,6)
M: Well that's too strong. That's for later.
K: I want one now!!!
(Kate is screaming and has started to cry)
M: Well, you go in your room and cry about it because you're not gonna get one. OK?
K: Well then I'm just going to cry there and then I'm not getting one!
{possibly doubtful use of the present continuous}
M: That's true!

(25) K: I - I fly! (Age: 3;1,26)
(Kate is being lifted by the investigator and swung around in the air - this is a recurrent game which Kate greatly enjoys)
{inappropriate use of a UVF to express an on-going action}

It is clear from the preceding discussion that in general, Kate mainly uses the appropriate syntagmatic relationships: modals and DO as an auxiliary combine with UVF's (and not UVF+{-ing} forms, for instance), the auxiliary BE combines with UVF+{-ing} forms, finite lexical verbs appear on their own, with non-verbal complements or objects, the copula occurs with a Subject Complement etc. Theoretically possible but non-adult-like syntagms combining a finite lexical verb and a UVF, for instance, do not occur. It appears, then, that as in Dutch, Kate has learnt much about what goes with what. Not all the adult combinations are present yet, though: for instance, modals followed by HAVE+past participle do not occur. Fletcher (1985: 197) notes that monolingual children in the same range as Kate do not use these either.

Developmentally, Kate uses syntagmatically more complex VP's as time goes on: her third birthday marks the overall increase in the use of WANT, DO and the auxiliary BE+non-finite verb form combinations (excluding BE+GOING TO forms).

7.4.2.7 The expression of past time reference through the use of verb forms

The expression of past time reference through verbs in monolingual American-English children is first realized through the simple past tense (see e.g. Brown 1973, Bloom, Lifter and Hafitz 1980, Smith 1980). Researchers on monolingual acquisition agree that the use of the present perfect to refer to the past is a late development, but British-English children may start to use the present perfect form at an earlier age than their American counterparts (see e.g. Fletcher 1981a). This has been attributed to differences in the use of the simple past and the present perfect between American and British adult usage (Fletcher 1981a, Gathercole 1986). Kate was mainly exposed to American English, and her use of only the simple past corresponds to the usage patterns observed for monolingual American-English children. Like monolingual children, Kate uses past participles, but only in combination with the form IS or 'S. At this stage, these past participles are best considered as memorized lexical items rather than as forms arrived at through the application of a productive UVF+{-ed} rule. While the forms with 'S may be attempts at the present perfect (cf. Fletcher 1981a), there is no direct evidence in the data from Kate that this is definitely the case.

Developmentally, there is quite some change to be observed: although past forms are quite infrequent on the whole (62 tokens in total), most of them start to be used with higher frequency only from the age of 3;1,12 onwards (see Table 24 in the Appendix). Half of all the past forms occur at the age of 3;1,18 (recording session 15). At this age, we also see the completely novel use of a past continuous tense (see example 26), and even once of a future in the past (see example 27). Fletcher's Daniel also started to use past tenses more frequently after the age of three (Fletcher 1979). Daniel's first use of a past continuous also appeared (as was the case for Kate) at the age of 3;1 (Fletcher 1979).

(26) 'Those steps were going fast!' (Age: 3;1,18)
(Kate is talking about the moving escalator she saw at a visit to a museum the day before)
{appropriate use of past continuous tense to express a durative action in the past}

(27) 'Mrs. Rose wasn't gonna come.' (Age: 3;1,18)
(Kate is talking about her teacher who was not planning to come on a field trip and who stayed at the school)
{appropriate use of the past future WAS + GOING TO+UVF}

Functionally, use of Kate's past forms is largely adult-like. Her past forms refer to events that happened quite some time before, or to events that took place only seconds before speaking. Only once does a form occur that plainly refers to a past event but that is not morphologically marked for pastness (see example 16 earlier).

Table 7.15 *Kate's English past forms : types*

Regular
asked - moved - punished - stayed - wanted (5 types)

Irregular
ate - broke - did - fell - forgot - had - lost - said - took - was - were (11 types)

The forms that appear in the past are all adult-like (see Table 7.15), with the exception that the auxiliary DID is twice combined with a simple past form rather than a UVF only (see examples 6 and 7 in section 7.2.2.2 above). Both adult-like irregular and regular forms are present from the beginning of the study. On the basis of this evidence, one might conclude that Kate has fully acquired English simple past tense formation (after all, errors on the formation of individual items are non-existent). This hypothesis becomes doubtful, however, when we consider the monolingual literature: Cazden (1973) notes that irregular past forms are often used correctly by the child until (s)he starts to overgeneralize. Cazden adds that the temporary co-existence of the correct irregular form and the later overgeneralization based on the regular paradigm is common (see also Maratsos, Kuczaj II, Fox and Chalkley 1979 and Fletcher 1981a). According to Brown (1973) the past irregular is an early acquisition. This interpretation, however, has been challenged by Kuczaj (1977), who maintains that the irregular past is more difficult to acquire than the regular form. According to Kuczaj, regular past formation is fully acquired at age three while the irregular past tense is not acquired until the age of 4;6. In fact, older children and even adults may not always use the correct irregular forms (Bybee and Slobin 1982). Fletcher (1979) mentions that his subject Daniel used regular pasts and overgeneralized irregular verbs between the ages of 2;2 and 2;5. Other children may acquire regular past formation only much later, at age 4;0 for instance (see Brown 1973). The developmental picture in monolingual English children seems to be the following: initially, many correct irregular forms appear with here and there a correct regular form. Then a period sets in where regular past forms, irregular pasts with {-ed} added to the UVF, and irregular pasts with {-ed} added to the irregular past form all exist side by side. The transition between this and the preceding stage occurs anywhere in the third year. Only at about age 5 will most of the child's past forms be adult-like. It is clear that in the initial stage all the correct forms are a result of rote-memorization, i.e. they are syntactically unanalyzed (Kuczaj 1977).

When we return to the data from Kate, it seems hardly reasonable to suggest that at around the age of three, she has acquired all the necessary rules for English past formation. Findings from monolingual acquisition do not lend much support to this interpretation. Rather, it seems more plausible that Kate's past formation is still in the pre-analysis stage, and that her English past forms are mainly the result of lexical retrieval (partial acquisition of the regular rule may of course already be on its way). [9] This interpretation is further given support by the relatively low number of types that appear in the past form (only 16 in total).

7.4.2.8   The expression of future time reference through the use of verb forms

From the beginning of the study on, Kate frequently uses the periphrastic form BE + GOING TO + UVF to express that she is about to perform some action or (much less frequently) to predict that something or someone is about to do something. The time of reference is either the immediate future (within seconds) or a more distant future (later in the day, or even some non-specified time within weeks). Functional use of the BE + GOING TO + UVF combinations overlaps with that of the Dutch GAAN + infinitive periphrasis. Use of BE + GOING TO + UVF is also mentioned as a very frequent (and early) occurrence in the monolingual literature (cf. Wells 1979, Fletcher 1979, 1985).

A second means of referring to a future state of affairs is through the use of 'LL + UVF. When Kate uses the 'LL + UVF syntagm, she is often not only referring to a future state of affairs, but also to an intention to do something. Monolingual children also frequently use WILL + UVF in these functions (Fletcher 1979).

(28) 'I give some more!' (Age: 2;11,14)
   (Kate is about to give M some imaginary food)
   {inappropriate use of a UVF by itself rather than a combination with 'LL}

As was indicated above, Kate occasionally uses a present continuous tense to refer to a future event as well. This happens only 6 times in total. All the uses of verb elements to refer to a future time exhibit an adult-like form-function relation: however, unmarked verb forms to refer to a future event or a future intention also occur (see e.g. example 28). On all these occasions, the addition of 'LL would have been more appropriate. Although these non-adult-like uses are infrequent (only nine times in total) they do suggest that there is yet some way to go towards full acquisition of the expression of future time reference through verb elements. In the monolingual English literature there is no mention of the use of unmarked verb forms to refer to a future event. However, this does not mean that such forms do not occur (their general infrequency in the Kate corpus indicates that, while such forms might have been produced, they could have easily gone unnoticed).

7.4.3 *Recapitulation*

The preceding analyses have shown that in the development of the English verb phrase in the age period under consideration, it is not really the permutation and analysis of bound morphemes that is the centre of attention, but rather the expansion and elaboration of syntagmatic relations between VP elements. Where at the beginning of the study the realization of VP's is mainly limited to the use of the copula in the first and third person singular, the use of the BE GOING TO, CAN and 'LL + UVF syntagms and the use of unmarked verb forms in declaratives involving stative verbs and imperatives (the latter were not explicitly discussed in section 7.4.2 - suffice it so say here that imperatives are quite frequent, more than a third of them being instances of LOOK), the second half of the study - after Kate's third birthday - sees a sudden increase in the use of DO-support in interrogatives and negatives, in the number of verb forms referring to a past time, in the number of utterances containing a WANT TO + UVF syntagm, and in the number of utterances containing a present continuous tense. It is not the case, however, that these elements appear 'out of the blue': they are all already present at an earlier time, but in very small numbers. Development of each pattern, then, is fairly gradual, but the simultaneously increased use of various different patterns conspires to appear 'out of the blue': they are all already present at an earlier time, but in very small numbers. Development of each pattern, then, is fairly gradual, but the simultaneously increased use of various different patterns conspires to present a rather dramatic changing picture in Kate's English verb phrase use after the age of three.

Table 7.16 *Kate's English verb system and how it compares with findings from monolingual acquisition*

	Kate	Monolingual acq.
Subject-finite verb combinations		
----lexical verbs, HAVE, DO:		
* mostly adult forms	yes	? yes [a]
* UVF + {-s} occurs infrequently	yes	yes
----BE:		
* mostly adult forms	yes	? yes
* both full and reduced forms	yes	yes
Future time reference		
----BE + GOING TO and 'LL + UVF occur abundantly	yes	yes
Past time reference		
----only through simple past	yes	yes
----simple past forms are all correct	yes	yes
----mainly irregular and some regular past forms	yes	yes [b]
----first use of past continuous	at age 3;1	at age 3;1
----occasional use of DID-support in negatives and interrogatives	yes	yes
Periphrastic forms		
----early and frequent use of CAN and (WI)LL + UVF	yes	yes
----rare and later use of other modals	yes	yes
----present continuous:		
* syntagmatically appropriate use of BE+{-ing} form	yes	yes
* mostly functionally appropriate	yes	? yes
* {-ing} morpheme used with dynamic verbs only	yes	yes
* {-ing} morpheme attached to UVF only	yes	yes
----regular use of DO-support	yes	yes
----abundant and adult-like use of WANT TO + UVF	yes	yes
Miscellaneous findings		
----no aspectual auxiliary use of HAVE	yes	yes
----syntagmatic relationships mostly adult-like	yes	yes

[a] ? yes' means that no specific mention of this feature is made, but that examples shown as well as absence of reports to the contrary appear to confirm it

The verb phrase 233

Throughout the above analyses, comparisons have been made with data from monolingual English children. All these must remain rather vague and general, unfortunately. The main reason for this is that there are not many exact quantitative data available on the acquisition of English verbs for the age range that we are dealing with. Furthermore, the types of analysis carried out in the present study are not always to be found in the monolingual literature. With these limitations in mind, then, comparisons between monolingual children and a bilingual child show that in essence the bilingual child's production of English verbs very closely resembles that of monolingual English children: on the whole, similar forms seem to appear in approximately the same order and in the same age range.

The findings for Kate's English VP system and how they compare with data from monolingual children have been summarized briefly in Table 7.16.

7.5 The verb phrase: concluding remarks

When Fletcher (1979) takes Leopold's (1970, c. 1939-49) diary study from a German-English bilingual child as a basis for his discussion of the acquisition of the verb phrase in English, he is implicitly assuming that the development of a bilingual child's proceeds along two separate, language-specific paths. The present investigation of Kate's VP systems provides support for Fletcher's assumption: no evidence was found that in the VP productions of a bilingual child there is any major influence from one language on the other. Instead, the morphological make-up of individual verb forms used is entirely dependent on the language contexts in which they occur: bound morphemes of one language do not co-occur with bound morphemes from the other language within the same utterance, and errors in the choice of bound morphemes are determined intra- rather than inter-linguistically. These findings constitute further evidence for the principle of morphological stability, which was earlier found to be relevant in the production of noun phrase forms. Secondly, syntagmatic use within the VP is relatable to each language individually, even when non-adult-like syntagms appear. In addition, English and Dutch VP's form-function relationships are all traceable to English and Dutch respectively: there is no need to invoke influence from the other language in order to explain functional use.

This functionally language-specific use is most striking when all Kate's verb forms expressing past reference are considered: in English, Kate exclusively uses the simple past, whereas in Dutch she mainly uses the present perfect. Both the English simple past and the Dutch present perfect are used at the same time in development, although the Dutch present perfect can be said to be more formally complex than the English simple past. This suggests that formal complexity of linguistic forms is not in itself a determining factor in acquisition. Rather, given the need for the linguistic expression of a particular meaning, the input frequency of a particular form A relative to that of a competing form B within a particular language may play a decisive role in determining which of the two forms is the first to appear in a child's language production. In American-English input to young children, the simple past is used much more frequently than the present perfect in the same contexts (Gathercole 1986). In Dutch adult usage in general, the present perfect may be considered to be the most widely used form to refer to a past event by means of lexical verbs (see section 7.3.2.7). It appears, then, that within each language, Kate has chosen the "least marked linguistic form available in the input" (Gathercole 1986: 540). It is thus not necessarily instructive to try and determine order of acquisition of certain linguistic forms in terms of formal or cognitive complexity (see also Gathercole 1986), although the time at which expression of a particular semantic notion such as pastness occurs may well be highly dependent on a child's level of cognitive maturity. An example of this may be found in the fact that Kate's past verb forms, irrespective of language used, start to appear with much greater frequency than before at approximately the same time in both languages (compare Tables 18 and 24 in the Appendix). A further example concerns the general increase in syntagmatically more complex VP's at about the same time in both languages. The latter may be seen as the result of an increase in general cognitive processing abilities (but see also Chapters 9 and 10). The actual forms that these more complex structures take on, however, are in no immediate way traceable to such a general increase in processing capacity: they cannot but be the result of the inherent differences existing in the two types of input that the child is exposed to.

The separate development hypothesis is further lent support by the great similarity existing between Kate's handling of each of her two VP systems and monolingual English and Dutch children's VP productions. Apart from a few minor exceptions (cf. the use of EM and KEN), Kate is, in fact, behaving as two monolingual children in one (but see Chapter 11).

In the following chapter on the acquisition of syntax, it will have to be investigated whether the separate development hypothesis can be maintained in the area of syntactic development as well.

The preceding investigation of a young child's learning of the Dutch and English VP systems has further shown that development proceeds quite gradually: there is little evidence of categorical rule learning, although in some instances the child has already started to analyse (and overgeneralize) certain paradigmatic relationships. It does seem, however, that the learning of both syntagmatic and paradigmatic relationships largely takes place in a piecemeal, item-by-item fashion. Although at the age of 3;4, Kate already shows a quite sophisticated knowledge of the Dutch and English VP systems, she will have to start relying less on an item-by-item learning strategy in order to actively and appropriately use the many verb structures that at her present stage of development are still absent. By the age of 3;4, then, a firm verb-foundation has been laid, but a lot of time-consuming construction work is yet to be done.

Notes

1 Obviously, I am not pretending to give a formal definition of what a verb is here. An attempt at a more formal definition would probably lead to a treatise on its own, and is not necessarily relevant to the main topic under discussion, viz. language development. It should be noted that the characterization given is meant to be purely descriptive only: it does not in any way purport to say anything about what a verb category might actually 'mean' in the speaker's mind (if such a 'psychologically real' category can be said to exist at all).
2 We leave aside the question whether the child starts out with a general category 'VERB' that is later divided up into a component AUX and a component MAIN VERB, or whether the child starts out with two separate components AUX and MAIN VERB which are at a later stage 'unified' into a general category 'VERB' (see e.g. de Haan 1986a, 1986b).
3 I owe this suggestion to Prof. Sera de Vriendt (personal communication).
4 There is evidence, however, that while theoretically possible overgeneral- izations across parts-of-speech are extremely rare, they do occasionally occur: De Vooys (1916: 139), for instance, mentions the addition of the diminutive suffix to verb stems - in the adult system, this suffix can be added to nouns, adverbs and nominalized adjectives only.
5 S. de Vriendt (personal communication) has futhermore suggested that simple past forms of action-verbs occur quite rarely in spoken colloquial Dutch used in Flanders.
6 Snow, Arlman-Rupp, Hassing, Jobse, Joosten and Vorster (1976) in their study of three Dutch mother-daughter pairs do give some information on other types of verbs, though. They found, for instance, that present tense forms accounted for 94.5% of all the verbs in their data (unfortunately, however, there is no definition of what counted as a present tense and whether the figure given refers to only finite

forms or finite and non-finite verbs combined. It is not at all clear, then, whether the 5.5% non-present tenses were simple pasts, present perfects or even future forms).

7 In rapid colloquial speech, however, strongly reduced forms of IS and AM may also occur in Y/N-questions with HE and I as Subjects respectively, resulting in [zi] rather than the more careful [izi], and [mai] rather than the more careful [ðmai] or [æmai]. These uses, however, may be considered to be quite marked (there is no similarly reduced form for ARE YOU in Y/N-questions, although the realization of ARE YOU may still vary between [ð(r)ju] and [aː(r)ju]).

8 This assumption may not be the right one: Brown (1973) starts out with his discussion of 'contractible' and 'uncontractible' forms of BE on the basis of Labov's (1969) proposed principle that "Wherever SE [Standard English] can contract, NNE [Black English] can delete *is* and *are*, and vice versa; wherever SE cannot contract, NNE cannot delete *is* and *are*, and vice versa" (Labov 1969: 722). Although Brown does not specifically define his terms 'contractible' and 'uncontractible', after quoting from Labov he starts discussing 'contractibility'. It is thus possible that in Brown's terminology 'contractible' means: those forms of BE that can be contracted in standard English and that were actually contracted by his subjects (hence the allomorphs /m/, /s/, /z/ and /r/), and that 'uncontractible' means: those forms of BE in standard English that cannot be contracted (depending on their syntactic context) and that were not contracted by his subjects (hence the allomorphs /æm/, /iz/, /aːr/ and /biː/). If this interpretation is correct, then the data that Brown gives exclude the use of forms of BE where a contracted (i.e. abbreviated) form could have been used but was not (as in WHAT IS THAT?).

9 I owe this suggestion to Paul Fletcher (personal communication).

8 Syntactic analysis

8.1 Preliminaries

8.1.1 *Introductory remarks*

In the preceding section on morphology, it was established that Kate's use of bound morphemes and closed-class items such as articles, demonstratives and third person singular pronouns is largely language-specific. Apart from a few ambiguous errors which can be explained either developmentally from within the same language system or as being the result of knowledge of the other language, most errors (both over- and underextensions) can be interpreted by referring to elements existing within each language system separately. Correct usage can be traced back to each input system separately as well. For most of the aspects analysed, the data from Kate resemble those from monolingual children learning English or Dutch as their only language.

The present chapter will try to address the question whether this picture of separate development as found for morphology also holds in the area of syntax, which deals with "the way in which words are combined to form sentences" (Quirk, Greenbaum, Leech and Svartvik 1985: 43).

A first major section deals with word order. Secondly, we shall try to trace Kate's general syntactic development. In all parts of the analysis, only utterances that were fully transcribed are taken into account. In addition, only utterances with more than one constituent are analysed here. As in the chapters on morphology, comparisons will be drawn with reports on the language productions of monolingual children wherever possible.

8.1.2 *The syntactic codes*

For syntax, the coding system used is perhaps even more crucial to the shape of any later analysis than is the case for morphology. Whereas the terminology used for the components making up Dutch and English nouns, for instance, is not a matter of great debate among theoretical linguists, syntactic analyses in the literature widely differ in nature and the terminology used is often quite individualistic and not necessarily accepted by the community of linguists as a whole (compare, for instance, Matthews 1982, Hudson 1984, Halliday 1985, Chomsky 1986). Since the various terminological differences often also imply vast discrepancies in how language in general is approached, the choice of any particular syntactic framework for the descriptive analysis of child language has far-reaching consequences.

For the purposes of the present study, it was seen as paramount that the syntactic coding system to be used should capture the variations in the formal shapes of child utterances while not limiting ensuing analyses too much already from the start: in other words, a fairly neutral descriptive tool had to be devised, on the basis of which any explanatory theories could be implemented at a later stage.

With the above requirement in mind, it was decided that the most appropriate coding system would be one largely based on the European structuralist tradition. [1] More specifically, Quirk, Greenbaum, Leech and Svartvik's (1985) work was taken as the general framework for the syntactic codes. A major problem, of course, is that we are not only dealing with English, but with Dutch as well, and Quirk et al.'s work is specifically meant as a description of the English language only. However, it is possible to apply many of the general insights present in Quirk et al. (1985) to Dutch: in most cases, for instance, what would be called a Subject in English would also count as a Subject (or *onderwerp*) in Dutch. It is mainly when we get to those problematic 'little words' such as particles that the English terminology cannot be applied or does not adequately capture the syntactic characteristics involved.

In order to set up the syntactic coding system, then, Quirk et al.'s (1985) terminology and definitions were taken as a starting point. For each English term on the constituent level, we then looked for a Dutch term that would most closely express the content of the English term, and in coding the Dutch corpus we were led by the Dutch rather than by the English terminology (under the procedure followed here, of course, in most cases English and Dutch terms were interchangeable).

The Dutch terminology was taken from De Schutter and van Hauwermeiren (1983). Although this grammar-book does not actually belong to the structuralist tradition, but is rather eclectic in nature, with the major emphasis on a functional approach to language, it was chosen as a basis for the Dutch syntactic analyses because, just as Quirk et al. (1985) do, the authors have taken the valency of the verb (or *zinswerkwoord*) as the basis for their analysis. A second major reason for choosing De Schutter and van Hauwermeiren's (1983) work as a descriptive framework is that it offers a very useful, detailed description of a variety of word order phenomena in Dutch. This will be of great help when we analyse and discuss Kate's use of Dutch word order in section 8.2.

In order to further clarify the syntactic coding system, it is perhaps useful to go into a few issues in more detail.

A first major distinction was made between those utterances which formed sentences and those which did not (a 'sentence' is here defined in Quirk et al.'s (1985: 78) terms as "a grammatically autonomous unit"). 'Elliptical sentences in dialogue' (Quirk, Greenbaum, Leech and Svartvik 1985: 848) were not considered to be sentences, and thus were not assigned any further syntax code. These elliptical sentences typically consisted of one 'constituent' only, although the term 'constituent' here is not very precise: an immediate constituent in Quirk et al.'s terminology is a unit which forms the part "into which another unit is immediately divisible" (Quirk et al. 1985: 40). Elliptical sentences in dialogue are typically not divisible into other (syntactic) units. It should be added that the term 'elliptical sentences in dialogue' is not synonymous with 'a sentence with ellipsis'.

Utterances which did not form a sentence were given a 'Global code' Z, and, as said above, not coded any further. Utterances which did form sentences and thus consisted of more than one constituent were given one of four Global U codes: (1) the code UA if the utterance contained no negative particle or rising (question) intonation, not taking into account any tag questions, (2) the code UN if the utterance contained a negative particle but no rising (question) intonation, again not taking into account any tag questions, (3) the code UY if the utterance had at least one clause in it (but not a tag question) with rising (question) intonation and if this clause had the form of a Yes/No-question, and (4) the code UW if the utterance had at least one clause in it (but not a tag question) with rising (question) intonation and if this clause had the form of a WH-question.

Utterances which formed sentences (i.e., utterances which had received a Global U-code) were then assigned what we have called Structure codes. Quirk, Greenbaum, Leech and Svartvik (1985: 47) see the notion of 'sentence' as being a very indeterminate one (hence their vague definition above), and prefer to use an approach based on the clause-unit. In this approach, simple sentences (i.e. units consisting of a single independent clause) are seen as the "most central part of grammar" (Quirk et al. 1985: 47). Multiple sentences consist of more than one clause. For Dutch, the terms *enkelvoudige zin* and *samengestelde zin* coincide with the terms 'simple sentence' and 'multiple sentence' respectively. While no claims are made as to the exact nature of hierarchical relations, in the Structure codes a descriptive distinction was made between sentences consisting of a simple main clause resulting in a simple sentence, two co-ordinated main clauses (or *nevengeschikte zinnen*) forming a compound sentence, and sentences including at least one main clause and at least one subordinate clause (or *ondergeschikte zin*) forming a complex sentence. If an utterance contained two co-ordinated clauses and a subordinate clause, it was categorized as a complex sentence. Utterances consisting of a simple main clause and a tag question were given a separate code, but if tag questions were added to a complex or compound sentence, the sentence was coded as being just complex or compound (the fact that a tag question was present as well could easily be discovered by looking at the clause constituents, which were tagged for the type of clause they belonged to). A 'rest' category for sentences which did not fall in any of the preceding categories was included as well. Since the 'rest' category was not a major one in terms of frequency of occurrence (in fact, of all fully transcribed utterances only one per language had a Structure code 'rest'), it was unnecessary to subdivide it any further. It should be added that the occurrence of vocatives was irrelevant to the assignment of Structure codes: i.e. for instance, a simple sentence preceded by a vocative would still be given a simple sentence code.

Each word per sentence was coded for the nature of the constituent it belonged to, for the type of clause it was part of and whether the word was a repetition of a word in an adult's preceding utterance. Rather than present a list of the Constituent codes used here, we shall fill in more details about specific codes in the presentation of the analyses where necessary.

Finally, we were interested not only in the child's active use of clause and constituent elements, but also in the extent to which her use of syntax was adult-like or not. Hence Judgement codes were included, which give some indication about non-adult-like syntax. These latter codes are quite general in nature, and were only added in order to allow the easy separation of non-adult-like utterances for later manual analysis.

Throughout, we have used adult terminology. It should be emphasized again, though, that this does not imply that the child is attributed knowledge or awareness of the categories used: the terminology employed is meant to be purely descriptive (see also Crystal, Fletcher and Garman 1976: 62).

8.2 Word order

The basic word order patterns for Dutch and English are distinctly different (in the following, we abbreviate 'word order' as WO). It is generally agreed that English is an SVO language and that Dutch is an SOV language (see e.g. for English: Traugott 1972, Steele 1978, Comrie 1981; for Dutch: Koster 1974, Gerritsen 1980, de Haan 1986b). Furthermore, whereas Dutch has a very rigid '(finite) verb-second rule' which says that in main clauses one and only one constituent can precede the finite verb (see e.g. Jansen 1980), English has a much weaker 'verb-second rule' (see e.g. Stockwell 1981). Furthermore, Dutch contains a number of WO patterns defined by purely formal rules which seem not to be strongly guided by pragmatic conditions (see e.g. Jansen 1980), whereas the few possible variations in English WO are largely determined by variations in function (such as the distinction between declaratives and interrogatives).

How does Kate reflect these differences in her word order patterns? Can the separate development hypothesis be maintained? In order to approach these questions, we shall investigate the following areas: WO in declarative main clauses, WO in clauses containing a VP with at least two components, WO in subordinate clauses, questions and utterances with non-adult-like WO. Wherever possible, we shall draw comparisons with monolingual children's use of word order.

While there may obviously be many more elements present in a sentence besides Subject (S), Verb (V), Object (O), and finite verb, we shall mainly restrict ourselves to the relative order of only these four elements, except when we consider all of Kate's utterances with non-adult-like WO. Note that the term 'Verb' (with a capital and abbreviated as V) here refers to main verbs only. When there is but one element in the VP (by definition a finite verb), the 'Verb' constituent becomes empty (De Schutter and van Hauwermeiren 1983 explain this for Dutch, but the same situation holds for English). The term 'Object' here and in the following includes any constituent that together with the Subject is a necessary part of the sentence relation expressed by the Verb. Adverbials, for instance, are not usually part of the Object (for a clear overview of the Dutch constituents belonging to the Object part of a clause, see De Schutter and van Hauwermeiren 1983 - they call the Object part the 'obliek zinsdeel').

We shall first look at WO patterns in both languages separately, and afterwards compare the findings between them. The Mixed corpus will not be dealt with here.

8.2.1 *Dutch word order*
8.2.1.1 Declarative main clauses

De Schutter and van Hauwermeiren (1983: 182) mention two basic word order structures for Dutch declarative main clauses (see examples 1 and 2, which are both taken from De Schutter and van Hauwermeiren 1983: 182):

(a) **X - finite verb - S - O - (V)** and
(b) **S - finite verb - O - (V)**.

(The brackets around V indicate that this slot may be empty.) De Schutter and van Hauwermeiren define X as any part of the sentence ('zin') that is not a Subject or Verb. Their use of the term 'zin' here seems to coincide with our term 'clause', and assuming that this is indeed the case, it should be added that when a main clause (MC) is preceded by a subordinate clause there will be Subject--finite verb inversion in the MC (see the invented example 3). A subordinate clause, then, can act as an X-element as well. Note that the O-slot may be empty and any O-elements may be positioned in the X-slot (see the invented example 4). Co-ordinating conjunctions, interjections, the sentence adverbials JA <yes> and NEE <no> and 'vocatives' cannot trigger inversion though (see the invented example 5). When any of these elements precedes an X-element, it is the latter that 'takes control', and there will be inversion. When we consider sentences with declarative MC's, then, there are three main patterns that the child has to take into account:

(a@) **(Y) X - finite verb - S - (O) - (V)** , where X refers to any element within the MC that is not S, V or Y [see (c@)]
(b@) **S - finite verb - (O) - (V)** , where S is in the very first position in the entire sentence, and
(c@) **Y - S - finite verb - (O) - (V)** , where Y refers to co-ordinating MC's, co-ordinating conjunctions, interjections and vocatives.

It is of interest to note that in adult Dutch, the pattern (a@) is exceptionless: whenever there is fronting, there is Subject--finite verb inversion. There are limitations, however, on what types of elements can be fronted, one limitation being that the fronted element should carry a high thematic value (see e.g. Jansen 1980). One type of element that can never be fronted is the negative particle NIET <not> (for a more detailed description of the limitations and possibilities of fronting, see De Schutter and van Hauwermeiren 1983: 194-196). NIET (and phrases in which NIET occurs) must be placed between the finite and non-finite verb (see examples 1 and 4), or after the finite verb when there is no non-finite verb following it.

(1) Precies daarom heb ik haar brief niet beantwoord.
      X -   **finite verb - S   - O -   Negation -**   **V**
    exactly-that-why-have- I-her-letter-not-answered
    <That's exactly why I didn't answer her letter.>
(2) Ik had je vraag begrepen.
    S - finite verb   - O -   **V**
    I- had-your-question-understood
    <I had understood your question.>
(3) Als je traag praat kan ik je verstaan.
    X = subclause -   finite verb - S - O -   **V**
    when-you-slowly-speak-can-I- you-understand
    <I can understand you when you speak slowly.>
(4) Uw tafel heb ik nog niet gedekt.
    X =O -   finite verb - S - Negation -   **V**
    your-table- have-I-not-yet-laid
    <I haven't laid your table yet.>
(5) Mevrouw, uw tafel staat klaar.
    Y=vocative - S - finite verb   - O - (V=ø)
    madam- your-table-stands-ready
    <Madam, your table is ready.>

How does Kate reflect the patterns (a@), (b@) and (c@) in her production of declarative MC's? To approach this question we have culled out from the Dutch corpus all those utterances with a declarative MC containing at least an overt Subject and a finite verb. These utterances were then grouped according to the types of elements preceding the MC Subject. Three categories were distinguished: (i) the MC started with a Subject and this Subject was the first word in the utterance, (ii) the MC Subject was immediately preceded by a Y-element, and (iii) the MC did not start with a Subject, but the MC Subject was preceded by an X-element, whether this X-element followed a Y-element or not. Category (i) should exclusively exhibit pattern (b@), category (ii) pattern (c@) and category (iii) pattern (a@). Table 8.1 shows to what extent this is actually the case. (There are a handful of non-interrogative MC's which could not be placed in any of the categories (i), (ii) or (iii). These instances will be discussed when we look at all of Kate's utterances with non-adult WO).

In Table 8.2 all the lexical items filling the Y and X positions have been listed according to their syntactic functions.

Table 8.1   *Kate's word order patterns in Dutch declarative MC's* [a]

First element			SUBJECT (i)	Y (ii)	(Y) X (iii)	Totals
(a@) (Y) X	fin.verb S	OV	-	<u>1 %</u>	87 %	12 %
(b@) S	fin.verb	OV	100 %	-	-	66 %
(c@) Y S	fin.verb	OV	-	99 %	<u>13 %</u>	22 %
TOTALS			472 (67 %)	142 (20 %)	93 (13 %)	**707**

[a] Non-adult-like use is underlined; all percentages must be read vertically; the 'O' and 'V' slots may be filled or not; Table 8.1 does not take into account incorrect word orderings of elements outside the SOV kernel

It is clear that most of Kate's declarative MC's have fully adult word order (see examples 6, 7 and 8). The conspicuous exception concerns, not unexpectedly, MC's in which a fronted X-element precedes the Subject (although here again the majority of MC's exhibit adult-like WO). Occasionally, inversion is lacking here (see example 9), following the (c@) pattern (as indicated in Table 8.1), or, of course, the (b@) pattern. Because of the low number of MC's with non-adult-like WO even here, though, it can be suggested that Kate has near-complete knowledge of the inversion rule of pattern (a@). Strikingly, however, Kate has learned which elements do <u>not</u> trigger inversion: there is only one Dutch declarative MC in the entire corpus which shows inversion after a Y-element where it is inappropriate.

Another finding is that although utterances in category (iii) are in the minority (only 13% of all declarative MC's are preceded by an X-element), there is no striking underextension of this category. Furthermore, developmentally it is present in about the same proportion throughout. There is some developmental change to be noted, however, in the number of declarative MC's in category (ii): towards the very end of the study, their proportion increases drastically at the expense of MC's in category (i). This may be attributed to Kate's increased use of vocatives and co-ordinated MC's after the age of 3;3 (see also sections 8.3.2 and 8.3.3). Finally, declarative MC's with non-adult-like WO appear only up to the age of 2;11,14. After this, all declarative MC's have adult WO (at least as far as the relative placement of the elements in the SOV kernel is concerned). A detailed breakdown of all the relevant data may be found in Table 26 in the Appendix.

(6) 'Ik - ik wil vliegen met Annick'.' (Age: 3;3,9)
    S - finite verb - (O=ø) - V - Instrumental
   <I - I want to fly with Annick.>
     {appropriate use of pattern (b@) with a category (i) MC}
(7) 'Papa ik komt'.' (Age: 3;3,9)
    Y=vocative - S - finite verb - (O=ø) - (V=ø)
   <Daddy I's coming.>
     {appropriate use of pattern (c@) with a category (ii) MC}
(8) 'Twee vingers heb ik!' (Age: 2;10,13)
    X =O - finite verb - S - (V=ø)
   <I've got two fingers!>
     {appropriate use of pattern (a@) with a category (iii) MC}
(9) 'Nu hij gaat naar bed.' (Age: 2;9,0)
    X - S - finite verb - (O=ø) - (V=ø) - Adverbial
   <Now he's going to bed.>
     {inappropriate use of pattern (b@) or (c@) with a category (iii) MC}

A review of the lexical items filling the Y- or X-slots shows there to be quite a diversity in the sorts of elements that occur in these positions (Table 8.2). If, say, only Place Adverbials had been used to fill X-slots, we would have seen a clear underextension of the range of fronting possibilities. Such underextended use would not allow us to conclude that a general inversion rule was being applied. Both the diversity and the frequency of X-elements in the Dutch data, however, add further support to the hypothesis that Kate has near-complete knowledge of the inversion rule of pattern (a@).

A similar argument holds for the Y-elements: here the diversity covers a wide range of adult possibilities, and the general frequency of Y-elements is quite high.

Not shown in Table 8.2 is that it is mostly the lexical item NU which is responsible for the non-adult-like patterns ((EN) DAN comes second with three occurrences, and the other three words and phrases each occur only once). In fact, the lexical item NU 'travels' quite a lot in Kate's Dutch utterances, in that it occurs in all possible positions, often in a non-adult-like manner. Furthermore, its function is not always clear from the way in which Kate uses NU: she might have used NU as a Time Adverbial and hence a potential X-element, as is perfectly well possible in adult Dutch, or as an unstressed particle, as is equally possible in adult usage, and in which case NU could in fact be a Y-element. There is reason to believe that, at least for some time, Kate is using NU in a very idiosyncratic fashion, and our categorization of NU as a Time Adverbial and thus an X-element was perhaps an unwarranted interpretation. It is possible, then, that the occasional lack of inversion after NU is due to incomplete knowledge about what sort of a word NU is, rather than to incomplete knowledge of the inversion rule (pattern (a@)).

Table 8.2 *Y- and X-elements in Kate's Dutch declarative main clauses* [a]

Only a Y-element in first position

Pattern	Constituent	Specific lexical items
Y S fin.verb OV	CONJUNCTION	maar/en/want
	SENTENCE ADVERBIAL	ja/nee/ok
	INTERJECTION	allé/hee/oh
	VOCATIVE	papa/Annick/mammie/kindje
Y@ fin.verb S	SENTENCE ADVERBIAL	nee

An X-element in first position with or without a Y-element

Pattern	Constituent	Specific lexical items
X fin.verb SOV	TIME ADVERBIAL	(en) dan/(en) nu/ eerst/ 's avonds/vanmorgen
	DIRECT OBJECT	ditte/die/dat/fruitsap/woeps/ twee vingers
	PLACE ADVERBIAL	(en) daar/hier
	MANNER ADVERBIAL	zo/anders
X S fin.verb OV	TIME ADVERBIAL	nu/(en) dan/altijd/ op het klokken [b]
	PLACE ADVERBIAL	aan mijn vingertjes

[a] Non-adult-like use is underlined

[b] Our interpretation of the non-adult-like phrase 'op het klokken' as a time indicator may be entirely wrong, though

In the monolingual literature, there are only two studies which up to a certain degree could serve as a basis for comparison with the data described above.

The first study specifically addresses itself to the issue of the relative order of O and V in the spontaneous speech of a three- and a five-year-old and their parents (Leemans and Ramaekers 1982). However, in this study any discussion of Subject--finite verb order is a by-product of the analysis of the relative order of O and V, and thus the analyses and discussions as given by Leemans and Ramaekers are not immediately pertinent to the present study of Kate. Fortunately, though, Leemans and Ramaekers provide a full listing of all the utterances they used as the basis for their analyses in the Appendix to their work. These utterances comprise only those containing at least a Direct Object and a Verb, whether this Verb is in finite or non-finite form.

For purposes of comparison with the data from Kate, we reanalysed the material listed by Leemans and Ramaekers, restricting ourselves to the utterances produced by their three-year-old Flemish subject, Barbara. In the same way as we did for the data from Kate, we extracted from this material all the declarative MC's containing an overt Subject and a finite verb. 'Finite verb' was here defined as any verb that was not in the unmarked {-en} or past participle form for singular Subjects. For plural Subjects any unmarked verb form in a single-component VP was taken to be the finite verb. Using these criteria, we discarded from analysis 36 declarative main clauses that contained a singular subject (mostly IK <I>) and an unmarked verb form or a past participle. 34 of those were three-word utterances which from the adult point of view clearly lacked a finite verb, especially since the order of the S, O and V elements would not have to be changed to obtain an adult-like utterance, i.e. these 34 utterances had SOV order. There remain for analysis, then, 215 utterances with at least a Subject, Direct Object and a finite verb. Of those 215, 161 have a Subject or a Y-element in first position and the finite verb in second position. They thus follow the adult patterns (b@) and (c@) above. There is one utterance that violates the '(finite) verb-second rule' since it places both the Subject and the Place Adverbial HIER <here> before the finite verb. This utterance, then, is non-adult-like. Then there are 53 utterances which have an X-element at the beginning of the clause. 50 of those have appropriate Subject--finite verb inversion, and 3 of those do not. These findings have been briefly summarized in Table 8.3.

The elements occurring as X-elements in the Barbara corpus are the Direct Objects DANK U <thank you>/DAT <that (-one)>/DIE <that (-one)>/ANDER KOEKJE <other biscuit> and VOGELKE <little birdie>, the Time Adverbials or particles DAN/NU and SEFFES, and the Manner Adverbial ZO. These constituents also occur as X-elements in the Kate corpus (compare Table 8.2), often in exactly the same lexical shape.

Even though the Barbara corpus is much smaller and quite restricted in nature as compared to the data from Kate, the similarities between Kate and Barbara are obvious: they both use mainly adult-like Subject--finite verb order. In both sets of material, Subject--finite verb sequences prevail (rather than finite verb--Subject sequences). When an X-element is in first position, both Kate and Barbara use Subject--finite verb inversion in the majority of the cases. In addition, the elements occurring as X-element are similar for both girls.

Table 8.3 *Barbara's word order patterns in some declarative main clauses* [a]

First element	Subject or Y	X	Totals
inversion	-	94 %	23 %
no inversion	100 %	6 %	77 %
TOTALS	**162** (75 %)	**53** (25 %)	**215**

[a] These data are based on our own re-analysis of a corpus provided by Leemans and Ramaekers (1982); non-adult-like use is underlined

This comparison of a monolingual Dutch-speaking child and a bilingual English-Dutch child, then, has not found any significant differences between the two. Rather, both appear to use quite similar word order patterns in declarative main clauses.

The second of the two studies on Dutch monolingual acquisition that can be used as a basis for comparison is the one by Verhulst-Schlichting (1985). In this study, the main emphasis was on the morphosyntactic development of the VP, and in connection with this, some data on word order phenomena were discussed as well. It appears from this study that inverted word order in declarative MC's is a very early development in the speech of young Dutch children. When Dutch monolingual children are in the first half of their fourth year, they produce quite a number of inverted declarative MC's: on the average, 42.3% of all their declarative MC's are inverted. While this finding shows a qualitative similarity with the data from Kate, in that inverted declarative MC's are used by her monolingual peers in the same age range, the quantitative differences here are striking:

only 12% of all Kate's declarative MC's are inverted (see Table 8.1) vs. the 42.3% proportion for Dutch-speaking children living in the Netherlands. As Verhulst-Schlichting (1985) points out, the rather high proportion of inverted declarative MC's in her data is perhaps a reflection of the substantial proportion of inverted declarative MC's found in the spoken language of Dutch-speaking adults living in the Netherlands: on the average, about a third of these speakers' declarative MC's were inverted (de Vriendt-de Man 1971: 317). When we look at the data that de Vriendt-de Man (1971) gives for Dutch-speaking adults living in Belgium, the average proportion of inverted vs. non-inverted declarative MC's drops to a low 5% (de Vriendt-de Man 1971: 319). This number is much closer to the one found for Kate, and so the quantitative difference found between Kate's proportional use of inverted declarative MC's and that of monolingual Dutch-speaking children in the Netherlands may be due to frequency differences in the input as provided by adult speakers in Belgium vs. the Netherlands. Note that our re-analysis of the data from (Belgian) Barbara (see Table 8.3) support this hypothesis, in that the proportion of her inverted declarative MC's is much closer to the one found for Kate than to the average found for monolingual children growing up in the Netherlands.

Comparisons with Dutch-speaking monolingual children, then, show Kate to use similar types of word orders as her peers.

8.2.1.2 Clauses with a multi-component VP

In Dutch MC's with a VP consisting of more than just a finite verb, the non-finite verb(s) usually appear(s) as much towards the end of the clause as possible, although one constituent (very rarely more than one) may be placed after the final Verb (compare examples 10 and 11). Constituents following the non-finite verb usually are prepositional phrases, although it is not true that just any prepositional phrase can be placed after the Verb. In addition, subordinate clauses may follow the Verb. Very occasionally, single word Adverbials may occur in this position as well (for a more detailed account, see De Schutter and van Hauwermeiren 1983: 197-198). Unlike in English, however, the Direct Object must always precede the Verb (see example 12).

(10) Ze   wilde   niks aan haar moeder zeggen.
   S - finite verb - O - Indirect Object -   V
   she-wanted- nothing-to-her-mother-say
   <She didn't want to say anything to her mother.>
(11) Ze   wilde   niks zeggen aan haar moeder.
   S - finite verb - O -   V -   Indirect Object
   she-wanted-nothing-say-to-her-mother
   <She didn't want to say anything to her mother.>
(12) Hij   had   een mooie tafel gemaakt.
   S - finite verb -   O -   V
   he-had-a-beautiful-table-made
   <He had made a beautiful table.>

In order to see to what extent Kate reflects the adult Dutch system, all the Dutch MC's in the corpus containing a VP with more than just a finite verb were separated out. Note that both interrogatives and declaratives form the data base. Two major distinctions were then made between MC's ending in a non-finite verb and those not ending in a non-finite verb. The MC's ending in a non-finite verb are by definition adult-like (at least as far as the positioning of the non-finite verb is concerned). The MC's not ending in a non-finite verb were further divided up between those that were adult-like and those that were not. The results are shown in Table 8.4. Table 8.5 shows the types of elements that Kate placed after non-finite verbs in main clauses.

(13) 'Wil   jij nog eentje doen?' (Age: 3;2,7)
   finite verb - S -   O -   V
   want-you-other-one-do
   <Do you want to do another one?>
       {appropriate placement of non-finite verb in final position in an MC}

Table 8.4   *Kate's word order patterns in Dutch multi-component VP 's* [a]

Verb position	final	not final	Totals
adult-like	100 %	10	97 %
non-adult-like	-	7	3 %
TOTALS	240	17	257

[a] Non-adult-like use is underlined; all percentages must be read vertically

Although Table 8.4 clearly shows that Kate has learnt the basic Dutch rule which says that non-finite verbs should go as much towards the end of the main clause as possible (see example 13), it also shows that in those few cases where Kate ventures to divert from this basic WO pattern the resulting utterance has nearly as much chance of being adult- as non-adult-like (compare examples 14 and 15). In other words, Kate has no clear idea about the kinds of elements that can occur after the non-finite part of the VP, although there is a slight tendency for 'backed' elements to be prepositional phrases (see Table 8.5). The two utterances in which NIET<not> is inappropriately placed at the end of the MC both contain a second occurrence of NIET, i.e. in appropriate pre-non-finite verb position. The placement of a superfluous NIET at the very end of the clause may be an overgeneralization of the common pattern found in negative MC's with just a finite verb: there, NIET will usually be placed in clause-final position.

Developmentally, there is no clear picture to be noted: it is not the case that most of the MC's with an element following the final Verb occur only at the end of the study. Rather, such MC's occur very sporadically throughout, and further learning of the restrictions on the types of elements that can follow the final Verb will presumably be a very slow process indeed.

(14) 'Ik - ik wil   vliegen met Annick.' (Age: 3;3,9)
     S - finite verb - (O=ø) -   V - prepositional phrase
     I-I-want-fly-with-Annick
     <I want to fly with Annick.>
     {appropriate placement of prepositional phrase after non-finite verb in an MC}
(15) 'Jij mag   niet- niet   met mij stout zijn   niet!' (Age: 2;9,0)
     S - finite verb - Negation - Adverbial - O -   V - Negation
     you-can-not-not-with-me-naughty-be-not
     <You're not allowed to be naughty with me!>
     {inappropriate placement of negative particle after non-finite verb in an MC}

In conclusion, then, it appears that Kate has learnt that in Dutch, non-finite verbs are placed in final position. She is just starting to learn that this final verb can be followed by other constituents, but she has yet to discover exactly which elements can follow the final verb and which cannot.

Of all the 106 utterances with a Subject, Direct Object, finite and non-finite verb in the Barbara corpus (Leemans and Ramaekers 1982 - see section 8.2.1.1), only four do not have the non-finite verb in final position. In three of those cases, an Adverbial follows the Verb (as is possible in adult usage), and in the fourth utterance, the Direct Object is post-positioned, seemingly as an afterthought following a pause after the rest of the clause. Depending on the intonation pattern (about which we have no information), this utterance might have been fully adult-like.

Table 8.5 *The elements occurring after non-finite verbs in Kate's Dutch MC's* [a]

Adult-like

Item	Frequency
One prepositional phrase	8
TIME ADVERBIAL NU	1
Repetition of DIRECT OBJECT for emphasis after pause	1

Non-adult-like

Item	Utterance	Frequency
The negative particle NIET	* see example 15	2
	* 'Ik kan da nie doen nie.'	
DIRECT OBJECT	* 'Hij moet schieten de vogel.'	1
Prepositional phrase + TIME ADVERBIAL NU	* 'Ik moet gaan in de hoek nu.'	1
Two prepositional phrases	* 'Ik ga dansen met een kreuw op het boom.' [b]	1
Manner Adverbial ANDERS	* 'Ze moet staan anders.'	1
Particle inherently linked to Verb	* 'Ik wil gaan af!'	1

[a] For the non-adult-like cases, the relevant utterances have been listed in full
[b] 'Kreuw' [krøw], a non-existing word in standard adult Dutch, could be an attempt at Dutch 'kruis' <cross> or English 'crow', but these are just guesses

The data from Barbara, then, appear to indicate that she has learned that non-finite verbs are placed in final position. This was also the conclusion reached for Kate. Whether Barbara has learnt that in some circumstances a constituent (or subclause) can follow the final non-finite verb cannot be determined due to the lack of data that could be used to investigate this issue.

In all the examples given by Verhulst-Schlichting (1985) of main clauses with a multi-component VP, the non-finite verb is always in clause-final position.

Kate's preference for placing non-finite verbs in clause-final position, then, is also apparent in monolingual Dutch children.

8.2.1.3 Subordinate clauses

Dutch subordinate clauses (SC's) follow the WO patterns of MC's in that the relative order of Subject, Object and Verb is SOV, except in relative clauses with a fronted Object constituent and in some concessive and conditional clauses (see e.g. Gerritsen 1980). However, in most subordinate clauses the finite verb appears either immediately before or after the non-finite verb (see De Schutter and van Hauwermeiren 1983: 186-191 for a discussion of the restrictions on the freedom of choice here). In cases where there is no non-finite verb as in example 16, the finite verb appears at the very end of the SC (although some prepositional phrases may occur after the final verb).

(16) Ik wou   dat   ik   vijf miljoen dollar had.
     MC - connector - SC: S -   O -   finite verb
     I-wish-that-I-five-million-dollar-had
     <I wish (that) I had five million dollars.>

There is not much opportunity in the Dutch material for investigating whether Kate has acquired the above WO rules for subordinate clauses: there are only 22 fully transcribed SC's present in the entire corpus that contain at least a Subject and a finite verb. Most of those (17) have adult-like WO as far as the relative order of Subject, Object, and finite verb is concerned (see example 17). (Kate produces hardly any subclauses containing both a finite and a non-finite verb.) Three of the five non-adult-like SC's contain a Subject and a finite verb followed by an adverb which is intimately tied to the verb and should precede it (see example 18), this adverb being the separable part of a 'compound' (or 'samengesteld') verb (see De Schutter and van Hauwermeiren 1983). The fourth non-adult-like SC has full main clause WO [cf. pattern (b@) above], and the fifth one is inappropriate because the Direct Object was placed at the very end.

(17) 'Ik - ik ga slapen als-als-als het donker is   hé!' (Age: 3;3,9)
     MC -connector - SC: S -   O - finite verb -interj.
     I-I-go-sleep-when-when-when-it-dark-is-right
     <I-I-go to bed when-when-when it's dark, right?>
        {appropriate use of the finite verb in SC final position}
(18) 'As - as de poesetjes zijn   af, [2] dan kan ik gaan.' (Age: 3;3,9)
     connector - SC: S -   finite verb - adverb -   M C
     when-when-the ????? -are-off-then-can-I-go
     <When-when the ??? are off, then I can go.>
        {inappropriate use of the finite verb in SC pre-final position}

Because of the paucity of the material, it is probable that Kate has just started to learn the WO rules for Dutch subclauses. The fact that most of the few subclauses that do appear exhibit adult-like word order, however, suggests that strong influence from main clause word order may not be a necessary step in development. Verhulst-Schlichting (1985) has found that the few subclauses that her Dutch monolingual subjects used in the range from 3;0 to 3;6 always had the adult-like word order, in that the finite verb appeared in clause-final position. Here again, then, no major differences with Kate are apparent, although of course the few instances of subclauses in the Kate corpus are not a strong basis for comparison.

8.2.1.4 Questions

Dutch main clause interrogatives follow the basic word order of declarative MC's: the relative order of Subject, Object and Verb is always SOV. Most questions have Subject--finite verb inversion, with the exception of WH-questions in which the Subject is the question word (QW). Three distinct patterns obtain:

(d) **XQW - finite verb - S - (O) - (V)** + rising intonation, where XQW refers to any QW that is not in Subject position,
(e) **SQW - finite verb - (O) - (V)** + rising intonation, where SQW refers to the fact that the QW has Subject function and
(f) **finite verb - S - (O) - (V)** + rising intonation.

Patterns (d) and (e) occur in WH-questions (see examples 19 and 20), and pattern (f) is the one used in Y/N-questions (see example 21). Note that patterns (d) and (e) correspond with patterns (a@) and (b@) as defined in section 8.2.1.1. The word order pattern (f) can also occur in conditionals and optatives, but since these are probably not used very often in speech to children, it is reasonable to assume that in the child's Dutch input, pattern (f) is exclusively linked to interrogatives (when accompanied by rising intonation). It should be noted that in colloquial spoken styles some Y/N-questions can alternatively be expressed using an MC pattern (b@) produced with rising intonation [we shall refer to this as pattern (f2)]. This use, however, appears to be quite uncommon: de Vriendt-de Man (1971: 319) mentions that adult speakers of Dutch in Belgium use the intonation-only pattern (f2) in only 14% of their questions (the utterance may in these cases often be followed by 'hé?' <right?> or 'niet waar?' <isn't it?>).

(19) Waar   heb   je de bloemen gelegd?
   QW: Place - finite verb - S -   O -   V
      where-have-you-the-flowers-laid
      <Where did you put the flowers?>
(20) Wie   wil   de bloemen gaan halen?
   QW: S - finite verb -   O -   V
      who-wants-the-flowers-go-get
      <Who wants to go get the flowers?>
(21) Zijn   de bloemen   besteld?
   finite verb -   S -   (O=ø) -   V
      are-the-flowers-ordered
      <Have the flowers been ordered?>

In order to see to what extent Kate's Dutch questions make use of the patterns (d), (e) and (f) all full Dutch WH- and Y/N-questions were extracted from the corpus. 'Full' questions are those containing at least a finite verb and a Subject. These questions were then ordered according to whether they showed inversion or not. The results are presented in Table 8.6 (the figures per recording session are tabulated in Table 27 in the Appendix).

Table 8.6   *Kate's word order patterns in Dutch questions*

		WH-questions	Y/N-questions	Totals
XQW finite verb S (O) (V)	(d)	115	-	115
SQW finite verb (O) (V)	(e)	10	-	10
finite verb S (O) (V)	(f)	-	41	41
rising intonation only	(f2)	-	2	2
TOTALS		125 (74 %)	43 (26 %)	**168**

It is clear from Table 8.6 that all of Kate's Dutch questions are fully adult-like (see examples 22 and 23). Another finding is that the pattern (e) occurs very rarely in comparison with the patterns (d) and (f). Not shown in the table is that pattern (e) occurs mostly towards the end of the study, i.e. after the age of 3;1,18 (but see Table 27 in the appendix), and that it is always a *verbatim* repetition of an adult's preceding utterance when it occurs before this time. All this suggests that in fact pattern (e) is just starting to be acquired.

(22) 'Wil   jij nog een beker?'   (Age: 2;11,14)
    finite verb - S -   O -   (V=ø)
    want-you-other-one-beaker
    <Do you want another beaker?>
        {appropriate use of pattern (f) for a Y/N-question}
(23) 'Waar   is   de vis?'   (Age: 2;10,5)
    QW: Place - finite verb - S -   (O=ø) - (V=ø)
    <Where is the fish?>
        {appropriate use of pattern (d) for a WH-question}

Pattern (d), on the other hand, has firmly established itself: this is shown by its high frequency of occurrence, and also by the variety of WH-questions in which the QW is not the Subject (the full range of question words in Dutch WH-questions is presented in Table 8.7). If only one or two types of question words had appeared, one would have had to conclude that WH-question formation was not necessarily acquired. It is obvious, for instance, that early and frequent WH-questions that only appear in the form WA'S DA? <what's that?> are instances of frozen, unanalysed units which do not show productive rule-application. Not all the adult possibilities occur in the data at this point (for instance, WANNEER <when> is absent, as well as more complicated Place Adverbials such as IN WELKE ZAK <in which pocket>), but the three types of constituents that do regularly appear as question words show sufficient evidence of the application of WH-question pattern (d).

Although Y/N-questions appear much less frequently than WH-questions, there is little reason to suggest that pattern (f) has not been acquired: Y/N-questions are frequent enough, and are fully adult-like as far as their WO patterns are concerned. Although pattern (f2) would often be possible and appropriate, Kate hardly ever uses this pattern.

On the whole, then, the question inversion rule is well-established: it occurs frequently and is never lacking where it is necessary.

For comparisons with Dutch monolingual children we again refer to a re-analysis of the Barbara corpus in the Leemans and Ramaekers (1982) study. We extracted from this corpus all the questions with at least a Subject and a finite verb (note that because of Leemans and Ramaekers' own focus of analysis the corpus contains only utterances with at least a Direct Object and a Verb). The total number of questions in this (now very limited) corpus is 44, half of those being Y/N-questions and the other half WH-questions. All of these have appropriate Subject--finite verb inversion, except three WH-questions with a Subject as question word. In addition to the 44 questions with at least a Subject and a finite verb, there are two WH-questions with a Subject and an unmarked verb form but without inversion. These questions would have been fully adult-like had they contained a finite verb (in pre-Subject position) as well.

Table 8.7 *Syntactic functions of the question words occurring in Kate's full Dutch WH-questions*

Function	Lexical item	Frequency
Subject Complement	WAT <what>/WIE <who>	60
Place Adverbial	WAAR <where>	33
Direct Object	WAT <what>	20
Subject	WIE <who>	10
Subject Complement	HOE <how>	1
Adverbial of Reason	WAAROM <why>	1

These data, however limited they are, show a similar pattern to the ones obtained for Kate: at around the same age, Subject--finite verb question inversion seems to be established in both monolingual Barbara and bilingual Kate. Further supporting evidence that Kate's use of Subject--finite verb question inversion in Dutch follows that of monolingual children comes from Verhulst-Schlichting (1985), who reports that by the age of three, question inversion is quite well-established in Dutch monolingual children.

8.2.1.5 Non-adult word order in Kate's Dutch utterances

We end this analysis of word order in Kate's Dutch utterances by examining all the ones in which her use of WO is non-adult-like.

Utterances with non-adult-like WO appear quite infrequently, and are responsible for only a fraction (viz. 4.2%) of the total number of fully transcribed Dutch utterances with more than one constituent (i.e. 1103). For an overview of the data, see Table 8.8.

More than half of the 46 WO-errors have been discussed before. The remaining ones show a variety of error-sources. (It should be noted, though, that some of the utterances that were judged to have non-adult-like word order here may not be non-adult-like at all: Kate might in fact have heard some of these less-than-standard word orders used by some adults around her.)

Table 8.8   *Non-adult-like word order in the Dutch data*

Discussed in the previous sections	
* No inversion in MC with fronted X-element	12
* Inappropriate use of elements after non-finite verb in MC	7
* Verb not in final position in subclause	5
* Inversion in MC starting with a Y-element	1
TOTAL	**25**
Not discussed in the previous sections	
* Particle/Time Adverbial NU (AL) in final position in MC	7
'Ik moet in de hoek nu.' <I-must-in-the-corner-?now?>	
'Ik ben in de hoek nu al en ik ben niet leeuw.'	
<I-am-in-the-corner-?now?-?already?-and-I-am-not-lion>	
'Ik ben in de hoek nu al.' <I-am-in-the-corner-?now?-?already?>	
'Ik ga hier tussen nu.' <I-go-here-between-?now?>	
''t Is aan mij haar nu!' <It's-on-my-hair-?now?>	
'Maar het gaat niet regenen nu!' <But-it-goes-not-rain-?now?>	
'Jij komt er - je komt er niet aan nu hé?'	
<You-come-there-you-come-there-not-on-?now?-hey?>	
* Particle/adverb OOK in near final or final position in MC	3
'En da's de koe ook!' <And-that's-the-cow-too/also!>	
'Da's genoeg voor mij ook.' <That's-enough-for-me-also>	
'Ik heef kaas en en tofu ook hé!' <I-have-cheese-and-and-tofu-also-hey!>	
* Negative particle NIET not close enough to non-finite verb	2
'Ik kan niet het aan doen hé!' <I-can-not-it-on-put-hey!>	
'Nee, we gaan niet dat af doen!' <No-we-go-not-that-off-take!>	
* Inversion without X-element (in song)	2
'Gaat wij weg, ah, gaat wij weg!' <Goes-we-away-oh-goes-we-away!>	
* Time Adverbial NU after Place Adverbial rather than in front of it	1
'Ik gaat in de kreuws nu zitten!' <I-goes-in-the-?crows/cross?-?now?-sit!>	
* Subject in final position in MC	1
'Heeft een lange staart mijne.' <Has-a-long-tail-mine>	
* Fronting of negative particle NIET MEER	1
'Niet meer hij slaapt.' <No-more-he-sleeps>	
* Place Adverbial in front of Direct Object rather than vice versa	1
'Kindje, jij moet moet in mond stukjes doen.'	
<Baby-you-must-must-in-mouth-little pieces-do>	
* Particle ES (=EENS; approximate gloss here: for a change) after Direct Object rather than after finite verb in MC	1
'Maar ik ga zuurkool es doen.' <But-I-go-sauerkraut-for-a-change-do>	
* Two fronted elements in MC	1
'A - als jij ruste, a - als jij ruste, dan 's avonds gaan wij niet rusten hé?'	
<Wh-when-you-rest-wh-when-you-rest-then-at-night-go-we-not-rest-right?>	
* Particles TOCH OOK between Subject and finite verb	1
'Tomat toch ook vallen van de bomen!' <tomato-?but?-also-fall-from-the-trees!>	
TOTAL	**21**

Most of the errors as shown in the second part of Table 8.8 can be attributed to Kate's as yet rudimentary knowledge of the placement of 'little' words, i.e. particles and adverb-like elements. Especially the lexical item NU is a recurrent source of trouble. In fact, 16 of all the 46 utterances considered here involve the inappropriate placement of NU or the failure to treat NU as an inversion-triggering item. Errors involving the negative particle NIET account for a further five non-adult-like utterances, and the inappropriate placement of other particles accounts for yet another ten non-adult-like utterances.

More than two thirds of all the Dutch utterances with non-adult-like word order, then, are ascribable to insufficient knowledge of the use of particles. This is not surprising in the light of the fact that the placement of particles in Dutch is a highly elusive affair, the exact rules of which are not always clear even to linguists (see e.g. De Schutter and van Hauwermeiren 1983, Theissen 1984, de Vriendt and van de Craen 1986). An added difficulty for the lexical item NU is that it may be used both as a 'schakeringspartikel' <modal particle> (cf. de Vriendt and van de Craen 1986) and as a full temporal adverb.

The utterances with non-adult-like WO not involving the inappropriate placement of a particle exhibit no consistent pattern as far as the sources of the errors are concerned.

The above findings do not necessarily mean that all Dutch WO patterns have (nearly) been acquired: there are many particles and other sentence constituents that simply are not yet present in the child corpus at this point in development (see section 8.3.3 later on), and it is possible that as Kate starts using a larger variety of these, the number of WO errors will in fact go up rather than down. Word order in later subclauses may also become quite unstable as more different types of SC's will start to be introduced (for an overview of the types of Dutch complex sentences that get produced at a later stage of development, see van Ierland 1979). The data analysed here, however, show ample evidence that the basic relative placement of S, finite verb, O and V is quite well established by the age of three, both in questions and declarative MC's.

In the Barbara corpus (Leemans and Ramaekers 1982) there are 9 out of 261 (or 3.4 %) utterances which exhibit non-adult-like word order (261 is the total number of all declarative and interrogative MC's in the Barbara corpus containing a Subject, Direct Object and a finite verb). This low proportion reflects the one found for Kate.

8.2.1.6 Comparisons with Dutch monolingual children

In the literature on Dutch children surprisingly little attention has been paid to the acquisition of word order. There have been only three publications which have addressed themselves to the acquisition of Dutch word order from a syntactic perspective. The earliest one is a study by R. Klein (1974). Unfortunately, this study reports on a very small number of utterances (i.e. 44 for the younger child and 96 for the older one) by two children at ages (viz. 2;0 and 2;3) that are not comparable to the age range covered in the present study. Furthermore, the MLU values given by Klein (2.2 and 1.76) are much lower than the ones computed for Kate at the beginning of the present study (viz. 3.15). The data from the study by Klein, then, cannot be compared to the data from Kate.

A later study is the one by Leemans and Ramaekers (1982), which was frequently referred to in the previous subsections. As our re-analyses of some of Leemans and Ramaekers' data have indicated, there seem to be few, if any, discrepancies between the data for Kate and the speech productions of at least one Dutch monolingual child.

The most recent study is the one by Verhulst-Schlichting (1985), which was also referred to in the previous subsections. Comparisons with the data from Kate showed there to be no discernible qualitative differences between Kate's use of Dutch word order and that by her monolingual Dutch-speaking peers.

Other reports on the acquisition of Dutch hardly ever mention word order phenomena. In passing, Tinbergen (1919) notes that his three-year-old son Luuk occasionally has problems with the placement of NIET, which sometimes occurs at the very end of a main clause containing a two-component VP. A review of all the child utterances produced by Dutch-speaking children in the age range from 2;5 to 3;11 as printed in Van Ginneken (1917), Tinbergen (1919) and Schaerlaekens (1977) reveals that word order errors are very rare indeed. The declarative MC's preceded by an X-element (see section 8.2.1.1) all show Subject--finite verb inversion. There is no way of knowing, however, to what extent the authors whose work was consulted had it in mind to represent word order phenomena, and thus it is not at all clear to what extent the utterances given as examples of quite distinct phenomena can be taken as a basis to draw conclusions from in the area of word order. This area, then, is largely unexplored, and we can only tentatively say that the types of word orders occurring in child utterances as appearing in the work of Van Ginneken (1917), Tinbergen (1919) and Schaerlaekens (1977) are not very different from the types observed in the Kate corpus.

We now come to the analysis of the English data.

8.2.2 *English word order*
8.2.2.1 Declarative main clauses

Most English declarative MC's have SVO order (see example 24). There is, however, also the possibility of the order VSO. This order only occurs when the declarative MC starts with a fronted X-element, i.e. when an item X is in clause-initial position as the result of fronting, which Quirk, Greenbaum, Leech and Svartvik (1985) define as "the achievement of marked theme by moving into initial position an item which is otherwise unusual there" (Quirk et al. 1985: 1377). Such X-elements may or may not be topicalized, but their range is highly limited and for the most part appears to be restricted to formal levels of language that are far removed from the child's language world (see example 25). (Stockwell 1981 gives a clear overview of the possible (topicalized) X-elements in present-day English; see also Quirk et al. 1985: 1379-1381). Apart from fronted X-elements, there are other clause constituents (besides, of course, the Subject) which can be positioned at the very beginning of the clause. These, however, do not trigger Subject--finite verb inversion. We shall call such fronted constituents W-elements. Quite a wide range of units may be fronted in English declarative MC's (cf. Quirk et al. 1985: 1377-1378). In example 26, for instance, the fronted element is the Direct Object. As in the Dutch (c@) pattern (see section 8.2.1.1), Y-elements (i.e. vocatives, co-ordinating conjunctions, interjections and co-ordinating MC's) may precede the Subject without any ensuing inversion as well (see example 27). We thus find four possible declarative MC word order patterns in English:

(aa) **S - finite verb** - (V) - (O), where the Subject is in clause initial position,
(bb) **X - finite verb - S** - (V) - (O), where X is a fronted element triggering inversion,
(cc) **W - S - finite verb** - (V) - (O), where W is a fronted element not triggering inversion, and
(dd) **Y - S - finite verb** - (V) - (O), where Y is a non-fronted element.

In order to find out how Kate reflects these English WO patterns, all the declarative MC's containing at least an overt Subject and a finite verb were separated out from the English corpus. These declarative MC's were then divided up into four categories, viz. (i) the ones that started with a Subject, (ii) the ones that started with a Y-element, (iii) the ones that started with a W-element, and finally (iv) the ones that started with an X-element. It was then determined to what extent the first three categories exhibited appropriate Subject-before-finite verb order (i.e. without inversion), and whether the MC's in category (iv) had inversion.

(24) I   just   love baking cakes.
    S - Adverbial - finite verb - O
      {pattern aa}
(25) Hardly had   she sat down   whenhe started to cry.
    X - finite verb - S - V - (O=ø) co-ordinated clause
      {pattern bb}
(26) The cake I baked   myself, but the bread I bought.
    W=O - S - finite verb - S - co-ordinated clause
      {pattern cc}
(27) But I   never   said   I would!
    Y - S - Adverbial - finite verb - O= subordinated clause
      {pattern dd}

All the utterances analysed here contain fully adult-like WO as far as the relative placement of Subject and finite verb is concerned. The few utterances in category (iv) show the required inversion (see example 28), and the others appropriate Subject-before-finite verb order (see examples 29 to 31). Table 8.9 summarizes the data.

(28) 'Here   comes   the red-one!'   (Age: 3;0,17)
    X=Introductory Adverb - finite verb -   S -   (V=ø) - (O=ø)
      {appropriate use of pattern (dd) for a declarative MC starting with an X-element triggering inversion}
(29) 'This   is   my dress.' (Age: 2;7,12)
    S - finite verb - (V=ø) - O
      {appropriate use of pattern (aa) for a declarative MC starting with the Subject}
(30) 'Mommy   I   don't   need this.' (Age: 3;2,7)
    Y=vocative - S - finite verb -   V - O
      {appropriate use of pattern (bb) for a declarative MC starting with a Y-element not triggering inversion}
(31) ' Now   we   have   to eat the food.' (Age: 3;1,26)
    W=Time Adverbial - S - finite verb - V -   O
      {appropriate use of pattern (cc) for a declarative MC starting with a W-element not triggering inversion}

Syntactic analysis 263

Table 8.9 Kate's word order patterns in English declarative main clauses

Pattern					Frequency
/	Subject	finite verb	(V) (O)	(aa)	63.3 %
Y-element	Subject	finite verb	(V) (O)	(bb)	28.1 %
W-element	Subject	finite verb	(V) (O)	(cc)	5.1 %
X-element	finite verb	Subject	(V) (O)	(dd)	3.4 %
TOTAL					**409**

While the findings above strongly suggest that basic English WO is firmly established in Kate's language system around age three, there are a few indications that more subtle knowledge needs yet to be acquired. These indications are to be found in some clauses in category (ii), i.e. in those declarative MC's starting with a fronted constituent not requiring inversion. The actual elements that appear in the clause-initial position have been tabulated in Table 8.10 (for completeness' sake, the lexical items filling the X-elements in category (iv) clauses were included as well). It is clear from this table that Kate's W-fronting is quite odd at times: Kate uses fronted Direct Objects in situations where this would be pragmatically uncalled for from the adult point of view (see example 32). In the adult system, Direct Objects may be fronted if they form the marked theme of a clause (cf. Quirk et al. 1985: 1377). However, although fronting in general appears to be quite common in spoken English (cf. Quirk et al. 1985: 1377), fronting of Direct Objects may be seen as fairly unusual (Steele 1978, for instance, sees the fronting of Direct Objects as highly marked in present-day English). In the eight utterances in which Kate uses fronted Direct Objects, marked theme appears not to be applicable, although it must be admitted that in one or two cases, Direct Object fronting is used emphatically as an 'attention getter', which might be seen as fairly adult-like. Syntactically, though, the eight MC's with Direct Object fronting are entirely adult-like: it is the pragmatic constraints on the use of this type of fronting that still need to be fully acquired.

(32) 'Ice-show I see.' (Age: 2;7,17)
    (this utterance is an initiation and not a response to a question: out of the blue, Kate announces
        that she saw an ice-skating show - the event happened about a week earlier)
        {odd use of Direct Object topicalization}

Developmentally, there are few striking changes to be observed. The four declarative MC word order patterns are present throughout the study, and the ranking in their frequencies of occurrence is usually the same, although shortly after Kate's third birthday the proportion of utterances with an X-element suddenly increases. This increase dies down to almost nothing soon afterwards, however. At age 3;2,7, the proportion of utterances starting with a Y-element is suddenly much higher than before. This is mainly due to the increased use of the co-ordinating conjunction BUT used as an 'utterance initiator' at this time (see section 8.3.2 later on). The full data have been tabulated in Table 28 in the Appendix.

Table 8.10 *Clause-initial elements in Kate's English declarative main clauses*

W-element in first position

Constituent	Specific lexical items	Frequency
TIME ADVERBIAL or PARTICLE	(well) then/(and) then/ (and) now/on the seaside	13
DIRECT OBJECT	iceshow/that/(the/that) lollipop/ the yellow one/one last piece	8

X-element in first position

Constituent	Specific lexical items	Frequency
INTRODUCTORY ADVERBS	there/here	14

In the monolingual literature, there is very little information on the use of WO in English declarative MC's after the child has reached the multi-word stage. Wells (1985), however, provides a useful survey of all the syntactic patterns present in his extensive corpus of cross-sectional data from British-English children. It is clear from Table A18 in Wells' Appendix A that nearly all of the declarative clauses in his data as used by English children in the age period from 2;9 to 3;3 start with a Subject (presumably, Wells did not make a distinction between utterances with patterns (aa) and (bb) above). The few exceptions involve fronting of an Adverbial with or without ensuing Subject--finite verb inversion. These data, then, resemble the data for Kate. Wells' table does not show any fronting of Direct Objects. There are two possible explanations for this: either such fronting did not occur in Wells' material, or it did not occur with sufficient overall frequency to be included in his Table A18. Whether

Kate resembles monolingual children here, then, cannot be determined with certainty, although the rarity of Direct Object fronting in the Kate corpus does fit in with its (near?) absence in monolingual English children.

8.2.2.2 Clauses with a multi-component VP

In English MC's with a VP consisting of more than just a finite verb, the non-finite verb(s) usually appear(s) as close to the finite verb as possible (always following it), although some short, single word Adverbials (including the negative Adverbial NOT) may be placed immediately after the finite verb and the first ensuing non-finite verb (see examples 33 and 34). In case of Subject--finite verb inversion, however, the Subject--finite verb link takes precedence over the finite--non-finite verb link, with the result that the non-finite verb follows the finite verb--Subject--(NOT) sequence. Direct Objects follow the final non-finite verb (see example 35).

(33) She   had   told her mother.
     S - finite verb - V -   O
(34) She   had   not yet told her mother.
     S - finite verb - Negation - V -   O
(35) I   was   cleaning the kitchen when the phone rang.
     S - finite verb - V -   O -   subclause

Table 8.11 *Kate's word order patterns in English multi-component VP 's*

Group I	finite verb -(Subject)-----non-finite verb	78.6 %
Group II	finite verb - NOT----------non-finite verb	17.9 %
	finite verb - JUST --------non-finite verb	2.3 %
	finite verb - REALLY-----non-finite verb	.4 %
	finite verb - ALSO --------non-finite verb	.4 %
	finite verb - ALL ----------non-finite verb	.4 %
TOTAL		**229**

In order to see to what extent Kate reflects the adult English system, all the English MC's in the corpus containing a VP with more than just a finite verb were separated out. Both interrogatives and declaratives form the data base. Two major distinctions were then made between MC's in which a non-finite verb immediately followed the finite verb or a finite verb--Subject sequence (group I) and those in which this was not the case (group II). The MC's in group I are by definition adult-like (at least as far as the positioning of the non-finite verb is concerned). For the MC's in group II it was determined what kinds of elements intervened between the finite and the non-finite verb, and to what extent the placement of these elements was adult-like or not. The results are shown in Table 8.11.

All of Kate's MC's with a multi-component VP are fully adult-like as far as the positioning of the non-finite verb is concerned (see example 36). The elements intervening between the finite and the non-finite verb are all similar to ones that adults might use, with NOT occurring most frequently. Most of the clauses with NOT here are declaratives (see example 30 above): there are only four negative interrogatives (three Y/N-questions with CAN'T + non-finite verb, and one WH-question with full NOT).

(36) 'I'll put that in there, OK.' (Age: 2;7,12)
    {appropriate S - finite verb - V - O order in an MC with a two-component VP}

Developmentally, there seems to be a slight tendency for multi-component VP's to more frequently have an element in between finite verb and non-finite verb as time goes on. However, because of the small numbers involved no statistical tests can be carried out. The full data are tabulated in Table 29 in the Appendix.

Again, the monolingual literature provides little information about the relative placement of verb elements in multi-component VP's. Klima and Bellugi (1973) discuss the acquisition of negation in three American children. Most of the utterances with a multi-component VP that they give as examples of 'Period 3' in the development of negation look very much like the ones that Kate is producing. Unfortunately, no further comparisons can be drawn since Klima and Bellugi do not provide age or MLU indications. It can be deduced from Tables A18 and A19 in Wells (1985), however, that monolingual British-English children in the same age range as Kate always use the appropriate finite verb--non-finite verb WO, as does Kate (we interpreted Wells' use of the term 'aux' as equivalent to 'finite verb', and 'V' as equivalent to 'non-finite verb'). The only elements sometimes intervening between finite and non-finite verb are the Subject (in interrogatives) or the negative particle NOT (in declaratives). Other elements intervening between finite and non-finite verb are not listed, but again this does not necessarily mean that such structures did not occur: they may simply not have occurred frequently enough to be taken up in Wells' tables. On this latter point again, then, no real comparisons can be drawn with Kate, who did after all sporadically position an element other than NOT or the Subject between the finite and non-finite verb. It is striking, however, to what extent the proportion of Kate's clauses in group II compared to clauses in group I resembles the data given by Wells: in Wells' tables, 78.5 % of all the interrogative and declarative multi-verb component clauses used by children in the age range 2;9 to 3;3 are Group I clauses, while 21.5% are group II clauses. [3] This proportion is <u>identical</u> to the one found for Kate (cf. Table 8.11).

8.2.2.3 Subordinate clauses

English SC's completely follow the WO pattern (aa) of declarative MC's (see example 37), except in relative clauses with a fronted Object constituent: here the order becomes OSV (cf. pattern (dd) of non-interrogative MC's). The young child thus does not need to learn new ordering rules in order to produce English subclauses: pattern (aa) can immediately be transferred. Furthermore, English SC's with multi-component VP's follow exactly the same constraints as MC's with multi-component VP's.

(37) I would like to see you   if   you   can   find the time.
     MC   connector - SC: S - finite verb - V -   O

There is not much opportunity in the English material for analysing whether Kate has acquired the WO rule for SC's: there are only 27 fully transcribed SC's with an overt Subject and a finite verb present in the entire corpus. It could, furthermore, be argued that 13 of those are not 'real' SC's since they are not preceded by any subordinating conjunction and since they all could stand on their own without an accompanying MC. These 13 'subclauses' are all object clauses following I THINK, I HOPE and once also I SAID (see example 38). The only 'subclause' with non-adult-like WO is in fact one of those object clauses, and the error here is due to an inappropriate SOV ordering, although an alternative interpretation is that the clause is an incomplete one and has a Subject containing a demonstrative pronoun and a noun which is then followed by a finite verb and an 'ellipted' Subject Complement (see example 39). All the 14 'true' subclauses have adult-like WO (see example 40). This WO is usually SVO, although there are two relative clauses which have appropriate OSV order.

(38) 'I think   that one   is   finished.' (Age: 2;7,17)
     MC - no connector - SC: S -   finite verb - O
        {appropriate use of SVO order in a pseudo-subclause}

(39) 'I think   that ice-show   's.' (Age: 2;7,17)
    MC - no connector - SC: S -   O -   finite verb
        {probably inappropriate use of SOV order in a pseudo-subclause}
(40) 'What comes   if   we don't   brush our teeth?' (Age: 3;1,6)
    MC -   connector - SC: S - finite verb - V -   O
        {appropriate use of SVO order in a subclause}

The scarcity of the material here makes it impossible to say whether SC word order has been acquired or not. The fact that all the unambiguous cases have adult-like WO does indicate, however, that Kate is having little difficulty in appropriately transferring the WO patterns of declarative MC's.

Because of the scarcity of the material, comparisons with monolingual children make little sense.

8.2.2.4 Questions

English main clause interrogatives follow the basic WO of declarative MC's: the relative order of Subject, Verb and Object is always SVO. As in Dutch, most questions have Subject--finite verb inversion, with the exception of WH-questions in which the Subject is the question word (QW). Three distinct patterns obtain:

(ee) **XQW - finite verb - S - (V) - (O)**, where XQW refers to any QW that is not in Subject position,
(ff) **SQW - finite verb - (V) - (O)**, where SQW refers to the fact that the QW has Subject function and
(gg) **finite verb - S - (O) - (V)**.

Patterns (ee) and (ff) occur in WH-questions (see examples 41 and 42), and pattern (gg) is the one used in Y/N-questions (see example 43). Note that the patterns (ee) and (ff) correspond with patterns (dd) and (aa) above respectively (see section 8.2.2.1). Pattern (gg) is the only one that does not correspond to any other English WO pattern. It should be noted that in colloquial spoken styles some Y/N-questions can alternatively be expressed using an MC pattern (aa) produced with rising intonation only (so without DO-support - see the next paragraph). We shall call this pattern (gg2).

English questions are not only marked by their use of Subject--finite verb inversion in most cases, they also differ syntactically from declarative (affirmative) MC's in that they make use of DO-support whenever the VP contains just a main verb and no temporal, aspectual or modal auxiliary or copula (see example 41). Y/N-questions usually have rising intonation, and WH-questions may have so as well. In this section, however, we shall mainly focus on WO phenomena (further information on question formation can be found in section 8.3.1 later on).

(43) Where did you put the flowers?
    QW: Place - finite verb - S - V - O
(44) Who wants to go get the flowers?
    QW: S - finite verb - V - O
(45) Have the flowers been ordered?
    finite verb - S - V - (O=ø)

In order to see to what extent Kate's English questions make use of the patterns (ee), (ff) and (gg), all English WH- and Y/N-questions containing at least a Subject and a finite verb (or 'full' questions) were extracted from the corpus. These questions were then ordered according to whether they showed inversion or not. The results are presented in Table 8.12 (the figures per recording session are tabulated in Table 30 in the Appendix).

(44) 'Where 's the moonman?' (Age: 3;1,26)
    XQW - finite verb - S - (V=Ø) - (O=Ø)
    {appropriate use of Subject--finite verb inversion in a WH-question in which the QW is not in Subject position}
(45) ' Can I have some more?' (Age: 2;10,5)
    finite verb - S - V - O
    {appropriate use of Subject--finite verb inversion in a Y/N-question}

It is clear from Table 8.12 that all of Kate's English questions except two are fully adult-like (see examples 44 and 45). The two non-adult-like questions lack the appropriate Subject--finite verb inversion.

The first one (see example 46) is a WH-question with a third person singular pronoun and an abbreviated form of the copula. It is possible that in this utterance there is no Subject--finite verb inversion because of lack of complete control over the various forms of BE: there are no instances in the English corpus of WHAT IS + a third person singular pronoun, although there are a number of utterances where a WH-word is followed by AM or ARE and I or YOU (see section 7.4). Lack of control over Subject--finite verb inversion in general, then, is not a necessary reason for the non-adult-like WO here.

Table 8.12 *Kate's word order patterns in English questions*

		WH-questions	Y/N-questions	Totals
XQW finite verb S (V) (O)	(ee)	44	-	44
finite verb S (V) (O)	(gg)	-	41	41
rising intonation only	(gg2)	-	8	8
SQW finite verb (V) (O)	(ff)	3	-	3
XQWS finite verb (V) (O)		2	-	2
TOTALS		**49** (50 %)	**49** (50 %)	**98**

The second non-adult-like question (see example 47) is, again, a WH-question with a third person singular pronoun and an abbreviated form of the copula. However, the QW here is WHY?, which appears only very sporadically in the data (see Table 8.13) and may not yet be sufficiently 'known' as an inversion-triggering word. More significantly, though, apart from the possible contributing factor of lack of full control over the conjugation of BE, there is also the possibility that the presence of the negative particle NOT plays a role in the non-adult-like shape of the utterance under discussion: as was noted earlier (see section 8.2.2.2), negative questions appear only four times in the entire English corpus. Only one of those concerns a WH-question, viz. the non-adult-like one here. Limitations on processing abilities may make it impossible for Kate to appropriately combine Subject--finite verb inversion in a negative WH-question involving auxiliary usage of BE and the apparently quite novel question word WHY?. In Wells' (1985) data, negative interrogatives are only listed in his Table A19 for subjects at the age of 3;9. The very infrequent use of negative interrogatives by Kate suggests that she is not very different from her English peers here. Bellugi (1971) found that negative WH-questions were very rare in a three-year-old monolingual English child's speech production. The ones that did occur appeared in non-inverted form even when the child was using many inverted affirmative WH-questions.

(46) 'What   she   's   taking?' (Age: 3;0,17)
   XQW - S - finite verb - V
   {inappropriate lack of Subject--finite verb inversion in a WH-question in which the QW is not in Subject position}

(47) 'Why she 's not doing it again?' (Age: 3;1,26)
   XQW - S - finite verb - Negation - V - O - Adverbial
   {inappropriate lack of Subject--finite verb inversion in a WH-question in which the QW is not in Subject position}

Similar to the Dutch findings is that WH-questions with the QW in Subject position occur very rarely indeed. Y/N-questions with just rising intonation and without DO-support occur quite infrequently as well. The patterns (ee) and (gg), on the other hand, account for most of Kate's English questions.

The question words that appear in Kate's WH-questions differ widely as far as their syntactic functions are concerned (see Table 8.13) The lexical item filling these various functions more often than not is WHAT. WHERE occurs second most frequently. This coincides with the data for children in the age range from 2;9 to 3;3 presented by Wells (1985) in his Table A15. Tyack and Ingram's (1977) data on American children's WH-word production in the age range range from 3;0 to 3;5 also confirm the data for Kate.

Table 8.13 *Syntactic functions of the question words occurring in Kate's full English WH-questions*

Function	Lexical item	Frequency
Subject Complement	WHAT	16
Direct Object	WHAT	15
Place Adverbial	WHERE	9
Adverbial of Reason	WHY	3
Subject	WHO/WHAT	3
Object Complement	WHAT	2
Manner Adverbial	HOW	1

The finite verbs occurring in Kate's English WH-questions are the abbreviated copula 'S, ARE, DID, AM, WILL, IS, DOES, COMES and DO. While this range does not cover the entire range of possibilities in the adult system (most modals, for instance, are conspicuously absent, although they do occur quite regularly in declaratives), Kate's WH-questions do not show the prevalence of unanalysed patterns any more which is typical of earlier stages in (monolingual) acquisition (see e.g. Brown 1978). In Kate's Y/N-questions, there is also a wide variety of finite verbs that are placed before the Subject, viz. CAN, DOES, ARE,

SHALL, AM, IS, DID, CAN'T, SHOULD, and MAY (but not DO itself). Most of the auxiliaries in WH- and Y/N-questions as used by Kate are also present in the speech of Fletcher's (1985) subject Sophie at age 3;5,15 (see further section 8.3.1). [4]

Together with the findings that the Subject--finite verb inversion patterns (ee) and (gg) occur quite regularly and that there are only two cases in which Subject--finite verb inversion is lacking, the fairly wide variety of finite verbs in Kate's questions means that more likely than not, Subject--finite verb inversion has been acquired as a productive word order rule.

In the monolingual literature it is not quite clear at what point inversion in both Y/N- and WH-questions is fully acquired (Erreich 1984). Indeed, there seems to be quite some variation between children as to when they start producing fully adult-like question inversion in both types of interrogatives (or, more cautiously, there seems to be quite some variation in the findings as reported by various researchers - see Erreich 1984). For purposes of comparison with Kate, however, it is sufficient to find but one English monolingual child who produces inverted Y/N- and WH-questions at around the same time in development as Kate in order to obtain support for the separate development hypothesis. The more such children can be found, of course, the stronger the support will be. Bellugi (1971) reports that when her subject Adam had an MLU between 4.0 and 4.7 he produced both appropriately inverted Y/N- and WH-questions and very few non-inverted, non-appropriate WH-questions. Ingram and Tyack (1979) found that all the 21 American children aged 2;0 to 3;11 in their cross-sectional sample used inversion in both Y/N- and WH-questions. Only very rarely did non-adult-like lack of inversion in questions occur.

As far as word order in questions goes, then, Kate reflects the usage patterns produced by (at least some) monolingual English-speaking children.

8.2.2.5 Non-adult word order in Kate's English utterances

We end this analysis of word order in Kate's English utterances by examining all of the ones in which her use of WO is non-adult-like.

As in Dutch, utterances with non-adult-like WO appear quite infrequently, and are responsible for only a fraction (viz. 1.9 %) of the total number of fully transcribed English utterances with more than one constituent (i.e. 642). This count includes the six cases of 'odd' Direct

Object topicalization (see section 8.2.2.1 above), although these utterances do not show WO errors *per se* . For an overview of the data, see Table 8.14.

Three quarters of the 12 WO-errors have been discussed before (see the top part of Table 8.14). The remaining ones show different error-sources, but since there are only three of these, no general statements can be made.

Table 8.14 *Non-adult-like word order in the English data*

Discussed in the previous sections	
* Odd topicalization of a W-element in declarative MC's	6
* No Subject--finite verb inversion in a WH-question	2
* Probably inappropriate SOV order in a subclause	1
TOTAL	**9**
Not discussed in the previous sections [a]	
* Adverbial ALSO not in front of constituent that it has scope over	1
'I want also applejuice.'	
* Pronominal Direct Object at end of MC rather than closer to the finite verb	1
'Mama I'll give her later it!'	
* Adverbial FIRST after non-finite verb instead of between finite and non-finite verb or at the very end of the MC	1
'I'm going first to the bathroom.'	
TOTAL	**3**

[a] Under each case the relevant child utterance is listed in full

The above does not necessarily mean that all English WO patterns have (nearly) been acquired: there are a number of sentence constituents that are not yet present in the child corpus at this point in development or occur very infrequently (see section 8.3.3 later on), and it is possible that as Kate starts using a larger variety of these, the number of WO errors may in fact go up rather than down. The data analysed here, however, show ample evidence that the basic relative placement of S, finite verb, V and O is quite well established by the age of three, both in questions and declarative MC's.

In Wells' (1985) data, no non-adult-like WO patterns are apparent. A review of Fletcher's (1985) transcripts of his subject Sophie at ages 3;0,4 and 3;5,15 shows that she used only two utterances with non-adult-like WO, viz. at age 3;5,15. One error involves the misplacement of the Place

Adverbial HERE and the other concerns the misplacement of the verb particle UP. If English-speaking monolingual children around the age of three make WO errors at all, then, they seem to be very infrequent. This fits in with the findings for Kate's use of English WO.

Most of the work on sentential word order in studies of English children's language development has focussed on comprehension rather than production (see e.g. Bridges 1980, Lempert and Kinsbourne 1980, Slobin and Bever 1982). The little work that has been done on word order production beyond the two-word stage has mainly looked at Subject--finite verb word order in questions. The very fact, perhaps, that so little attention has been paid to word order phenomena in the monolingual literature at large may be an indication that word order is not a major source of trouble or difficulty in the English acquisition process. It appears not be a major trouble-spot for Kate either, and there are no obvious discrepancies between the bilingual data from Kate and data from monolingual children.

8.2.3 *A comparison between English and Dutch*

When we look at Kate's use of Subject and finite verb sequences only, there are quite some similarities to be found between her use of English and Dutch, as is shown in Table 8.15 below. In both languages, the Y--S--finite verb pattern appears exclusively in declaratives (this finding, however, is a rather direct result of the analyses conventions used in the preceding sections). The S--finite verb sequence with the Subject in clause-initial position is mainly associated with declaratives as well. Both the S--finite verb and Y--S--finite verb patterns appear quite regularly in both English and Dutch (together they account for 73% of all fully transcribed main clauses containing at least a Subject and a finite verb in the Dutch and English corpora). In both languages, WH-questions tend to be associated with the X/X@--finite verb--S pattern (X here refers to fronted elements triggering inversion in English, and X@ to fronted elements triggering inversion in Dutch). Furthermore, in both languages Kate reserves the finite verb--S sequence with the finite verb in clause-initial position for Y/N-questions. In fact, there is a strong tendency in both languages for inversion to occur mainly in interrogatives (see Table 8.16). Kate's non-inverted clauses are usually declaratives.

Syntactic analysis 275

Table 8.15 *Kate's English and Dutch use of Subject--finite verb sequences* [a]

Pattern	Syntactic form	English	Dutch
S--finite verb	declarative	96%	97.5%
	WH-question	1%	2%
	Y/N-question	3%	0.5%
TOTAL		**270**	**484**
Y--S--finite verb	declarative	100%	100%
TOTAL		**115**	**142**
X/X@--finite verb--S	declarative	24 ± 2%	41%
	WH-question	76 ± 2%	59%
TOTAL		**58**	**196**
finite verb--S	Y/N-question	100%	100%
TOTAL		**41**	**41**
W/X@--S--finite verb	declarative	91 ± 5%	<u>100%</u>
	WH-question	<u>9 ± 5%</u>	-
TOTAL		**23**	**12**

[a] Y in this table refers to clause-initial (but not fronted) elements both in English and Dutch;
W refers to clause-initial, fronted elements in English; the percentages are to be read vertically within each pattern; non-adult-like use has been underlined

There are not only similarities between English and Dutch, however. As is clear from Table 8.15, the X/X@--finite verb--S pattern in English is strongly associated with WH-questions, whereas in Dutch there is nearly a one in two chance that Kate uses this pattern in a declarative. This difference between English and Dutch becomes even starker when one considers the fact that in the Dutch corpus the X/X@--finite verb--S pattern appears nearly four times as often as in the English corpus. In addition, the X/X@--finite verb--S pattern accounts for 22% of all Kate's Dutch main clause patterns, whereas it accounts for only 11% of all her English main clause patterns (see Table 8.17). The differential status (or use) of the X/X@--finite verb--S pattern in Dutch vs. English is reflected in Kate's use of inversion: although it is true that in both languages there is a strong tendency for inversion to occur mainly in interrogatives (see Table 8.16), this tendency is much less pronounced in Dutch than it is in English (only 66% of inverted main clauses are interrogatives in Dutch, whereas the percentage is 86% for English).

A final difference between English and Dutch as it appears from the tables presented here concerns Kate's use of the W/X@--S--finite verb pattern. This pattern accounts for only 1% of all Dutch main clause word order patterns (see Table 8.17), whereas it accounts for 6% of all English main clause word order patterns. This finding, combined with the fact that the absolute number of English main clauses is much smaller than the one for Dutch, provides support for the conclusion that the status of the Dutch X@--S--finite verb pattern is much more peripheral than the status of the English W--S--finite verb pattern.

Table 8.16 *Kate's English and Dutch inversion patterns* [a]

Inversion		English	Dutch
	interrogative	86%	66%
	declarative	14%	34%
TOTAL		99	237
No inversion	interrogative	3%	2%
	declarative	97%	98%
TOTAL		408	638

[a] The percentages should be read vertically within each of the four major cells

What do the above findings mean for the separate development hypothesis? In order to approach this question it is instructive to examine what exactly could constitute evidence for or against this hypothesis.

Table 8.17 *The proportions of use of Kate's English and Dutch main clause WO patterns*

Pattern	English	Dutch
S--finite verb	53%	55%
Y--S--finite verb	23%	16%
X/X@--finite verb--S	11%	22%
finite verb--S	8%	5%
W/X@--S--finite verb	6%	1%
TOTAL	507	875

It is clear that only those areas in the adult language which contain different structures and forms can be used as a testing ground for exploring the validity of the separate development hypothesis (henceforth: SDH). Question inversion, then, is not an area that is of interest to this hypothesis:

the rules in English and Dutch are completely identical here. Subclause word order, on the other hand, is an area of crucial importance, but due to the scanty data here (see sections 8.2.1.3 and 8.2.2.3), no major conclusions can be drawn, although even the few data that are available suggest the absence of any strong influence from one language on the other.

The SDH can further be approached on the basis of word order in declarative MC's and in MC's with a multi-component VP. For declarative MC's, however, it is only the W/X@--S--finite verb and X/X@--finite verb--S patterns that can be compared, since here the adult rules are different for both languages (although some overlap exists between English X--finite verb--S and Dutch X@--finite verb--S patterns). Earlier in this section, we pointed out the different usage constellations of these patterns in English and Dutch, and it appears that Kate's English word orders here follow the limitations of the English adult system, and that her Dutch word orders follow those of the Dutch adult system.

Table 8.18 *Fronting in Kate's English and Dutch declarative main clauses* [a]

Pattern	English	Dutch
X/X@--finite verb--S	40 ± 3%	87%
W/X@--S--finite verb	60 ± 3%	13%
TOTAL	35	93

[a] Non-adult-like use has been underlined; percentages must be read vertically

This generalization, however, obscures the fact that Kate does occasionally use inappropriate X@--S--finite verb patterns in Dutch (cf. section 8.2.1.1). Could these non-adult-like patterns not be due to influence from the English W--S--finite verb pattern? In order to answer this question, we present all Kate's declarative MC's with fronting in Table 8.18. It is clear from this table that in English, W--S--finite verb patterns prevail over X--finite verb--S orderings, although not strongly so. In Dutch, on the other hand, appropriate X@--finite verb--S patterns strongly prevail over inappropriate X@--S--finite verb patterns. If influence from the English W--S--finite verb pattern on the latter is indeed a factor, it certainly is not a major one, since in 87% of the possible contexts for influence (i.e., when an X@-element is in clause-initial position), the influence does not materialize. Further evidence for the very low (or even absent) influence from English on Dutch here comes from the observation that at least one monolingual Dutch child also used inappropriate X@--S--finite verb patterns (see section 8.2.1.1). We can conclude, then, that the non-adult-like Dutch X@--S--finite verb patterns are most probably not due to influence from the English W--S--finite verb patterns. Furthermore, any influence from the Dutch X@--finite verb--S order on Kate's English declarative MC's with a fronted W-element is entirely absent.

It should be noted that influence from one language on another cannot only reveal itself through overgeneralizations (i.e. through the inappropriate use of a pattern from language A in language B), but also through underextended use. In the present case, underextended use of the X@--finite verb--S pattern might be predicted for Dutch, since this pattern is not a productive one in adult English (and certainly not in Kate's English). Although the pattern X@--finite verb--S only appears in 12% of all of Kate's declarative MC's (see section 8.2.1.1), this can hardly be called underextended (or avoided) use. Besides, the low frequency with which the said pattern appears in adult spoken Dutch (de Vriendt-de Man 1971) may be seen as a possible determinant of the frequency of use of this pattern by Kate (see section 8.2.1.1 - obviously, however, only data on input directed to the child can really be taken as a basis for the frequency argument). Influence from English on Dutch in the form of underextended use, then, is not entirely impossible, but appears to be unlikely.

We now turn to word order in main clauses with a multi-component VP. Again, we must consider only those cases which are distinct in both languages. Clauses with just a Subject, finite and non-finite verb, for instance, have the same Subject--finite verb--non-finite verb or finite verb--Subject--non-finite verb order in both adult Dutch and English, and cannot serve as a basis for testing the SDH. In addition, if negative particles or certain short, single word Adverbials and particles are present, the orders are again identical in both languages. In order to investigate the SDH then, we can only investigate those main clauses containing a Subject, finite and non-finite verb, and a minimum of one other constituent Z that is not a particle or a short, single word Adverbial that can be placed in front of the non-finite verb in English (and in Dutch). Since our analyses in sections 8.2.1.2 and 8.2.2.2 earlier were not specifically geared towards comparing Dutch and English, we present additional data in Table 8.19.

The data base for Table 8.19 consists of all MC's with at least a Subject (S), a finite verb (Vf), a non-finite verb (VNF), and a constituent Z that is not an optionally present particle or short, single word Adverbial (A). Note that Table 8.19 starts looking at word order patterns only once a Subject or finite verb is encountered. Thus, for instance, a question of the form QW=Direct Object--finite verb--Subject--non-finite verb--Place Adverbial was simply coded as an instance of a <S--Vf>--(A)--VNF--Z pattern.

Table 8.19 reveals that in nine out of ten cases, Dutch and English relevant MC's with a multi-component VP have completely different word order, with the English patterns all following the adult English order, and the Dutch most frequent pattern reflecting the basic order in adult Dutch. Already, this big difference shows an absence of any major influence from one language on the other. We cannot be too premature in our interpretation, however, since there are still the 17 Dutch utterances following the <S--Vf>--(A)--VNF--Z pattern to be accounted for. This pattern is the only one possible in English, but the pattern is marginally possible in adult Dutch as well (see section 8.2.1.2). The question then is whether Kate is following the English pattern or the Dutch one.

Table 8.19 *A comparison of Kate's English and Dutch main clauses with a multi-component verb phrase* [a]

Pattern		English	Dutch
<S--Vf> -- (A) --	VNF --Z	100 %	10 %
<S--Vf> -- (A) --Z--	VNF	-	90 %
TOTAL		**183**	**170**

[a] <S--Vf> indicates that Subject and finite verb may occur in inverted or non-inverted order

In the 10 cases where Kate uses the Dutch <S--Vf>--(A)--VNF--Z pattern appropriately, it cannot be ascertained whether she is in fact taking the Dutch adult pattern as a basis, rather than the English one: here we are faced with data that cannot constitute evidence either for or against the SDH. The 7 clauses in which Kate uses the Dutch <S--Vf>--(A)--VNF--Z pattern inappropriately, however, might well be seen as the result of a transfer of the English <S--Vf>--(A)--VNF--Z pattern, although it can be argued (as we did in section 8.2.1.2) that incomplete knowledge of the types of clause elements that can follow a Dutch non-finite verb may play a role as well. At this point, the bilingual data do not allow any unambiguous choice between the two possible interpretations. In addition, we lack evidence from monolingual acquisition which could provide a basis for a more informed choice. However, even if it is conceded that in fact Kate's Dutch <S--Vf>--(A)--VNF--Z patterns (and especially the non-adult-like ones) follow the English <S--Vf>--(A)--VNF--Z pattern, this influence is clearly very marginal, since most of Kate's Dutch clauses considered here follow the order possibilities of Dutch. Influence from Dutch on English cannot be detected.

There is no evidence at all that Kate underextends either the Dutch or English WO patterns in clauses with a multi-component VP: in order for Kate to underextend any WO pattern here, she would have to simply not use any multi-component VP's in any one language. This, clearly, does not happen.

We must conclude from the preceding that the acquisition of word order patterns that are different in the two adult systems proceeds in a language-dependent manner: no major cross-linguistic over-generalizations or underextensions can be discerned. This means that the separate development hypothesis, which was found to be of great relevance in the area of morphology, also holds in a crucial area of syntax.

A second major conclusion is that from an early age on, Kate uses purely syntactically motivated word orders that are particular to each of her languages. While fronting itself may be pragmatically motivated, the ensuing Subject--finite verb inversion in Dutch is a purely syntactic operation (compare also Meisel 1986: 151). Both the Object-final and Object-middle positions of English and Dutch respectively in Kate's MC's with a multi-component VP are syntactically defined and target-language specific. That the one order (viz. SOV) should be more 'natural' than the other (viz. SVO), as has been claimed by Yau (1979), is certainly not evident from the data here: from the beginning of the study, both SVO (for English) and SOV (for Dutch) appear abundantly, without any noticeable underextension of the SVO pattern in English or overgeneralization of the SOV pattern from Dutch to English (as might be predicted on the basis of Yau 1979).

Although Kate is already in too advanced a stage at the beginning of the study to allow an investigation of her word order patterns in early multi-word utterances, the data that are available suggest that even though at an earlier stage, word orders may have been primarily semantically and/or pragmatically defined (see e.g. Bates and MacWhinney 1982), the "syntactic mode of processing" (Meisel 1986) becomes of major importance very early on. This syntactic mode is definitely strongly established by the age of 2;7.

The importance of syntactic vs. semantic-pragmatic bases for early word order production has also been emphasized by other researchers. Meisel (1986) in his study of two young French-German simultaneous bilingual children strongly argues even for the <u>primacy</u> of the "syntactic mode of processing" (his term) [5] and found that from the beginning of the multiword stage (and, he claims, even shortly before this), his bilingual subjects already used German and French word order patterns that closely followed the structural possibilities of each language separately. Meisel concludes from this that "acquiring the syntactic system of a language is a learning task in its own right" (Meisel 1986: 158). Kaltenbacher (1987), in her longitudinal study of a German monolingual child, also argues for the hypothesis that the child uses formal rather than semantic or pragmatic strategies in the very earliest word-combinations: she did not find any orders that did not conform to the ordering possibilities existing in the adult input. Finally, Weist and Witkowska-Stadnik (1986) have convincingly shown that there is no one-to-one mapping in Polish children's early word-combinations of semantic role and syntactic position. Rather, they argue that syntactic processing is evident from the very start, and that "the dominant word order in the child's language will be the same as the adult's" (Weist and Witkowska-Stadnik 1986: 373) (see also Weist 1983).

Our two conclusions, then, that Kate's use of word order develops separately for each of her two languages and that syntactically motivated word orders appear from the beginning of the study are clearly interdependent: it can be hypothesized that the use of a syntactic mode of processing is at the root of the separate development of English and Dutch word order. It is partially because the child attends to the purely formal aspects of the input that she is able to produce two closed language systems from very early on.

8.3 General syntactic development

The aim of the present section is to provide an outline of Kate's general syntactic development. There will be little emphasis on the separate development hypothesis (SDH) here, since on the whole, except for word order phenomena, the similarities between Dutch and English in the types of syntactic constituents and clause structures are much more noticeable than any differences. Differences do exist, of course, but are probably only relevant to acquisition after the pre-school stage.

In the literature on monolingual acquisition, it has been shown that the three-year-old already has much control over the manipulation of most clause constituents, and is on the brink of gaining control over the combination of elements at clause level (cf. for English: Crystal, Fletcher and Garman 1976, Wells 1985; for Dutch: Bol and Kuiken 1987, 1988). Furthermore, most of the clause types such as declarative, interrogative and imperative (Quirk, Greenbaum, Leech and Svartvik 1985: 78) open to the adult speaker are also available to the monolingual three-year-old (cf. for English: Crystal et al. 1976, Wells 1985; for Dutch: Bol and Kuiken 1987, 1988). The following analyses will mainly be geared towards examining to what extent these findings are also applicable to bilingual Kate.

We shall take the syntactic coding system (cf. 8.1.2) as a basis for the data analysis. As in the section on word order, we shall restrict ourselves to the English and Dutch corpora.

8.3.1 *The Global codes*

First there are the one-constituent utterances to be considered (i.e. those with a Z-code). Although these are not very interesting syntactically, since by definition they do not encode any syntactic relationships, it may well be instructive to see whether their frequency changes over time. Wells (1985), for instance, found that one-constituent utterances steadily decreased in number (and in proportion to other types of utterances) as his British subjects grew older (see his Table A18). In order to investigate whether this finding is also reflected in the Kate corpus, the sum was taken of all the utterances with a Z-code and all the utterances with a U-code (UA, UN, UY and UW - for definitions, see section 8.1.2). Then the proportions represented by each of these sums were computed per recording session. The results can be seen in Table 31 in the Appendix.

Neither in the Dutch nor in the English data is there any major increase or decrease to be observed in the proportions of utterances with a Z-code over time: there are changes to be noted, but these appear to be fairly random. There is, however, a substantial difference between the Dutch and English data in that in Dutch, one-constituent utterances appear more frequently than utterances with more than one constituent, whereas in English the reverse picture obtains. Furthermore, the difference between the proportions of use of utterances with a Z-code vs. those with a U-code is far greater in English than it is in Dutch (for Dutch, U-codes appear in

43% of all utterances and Z-codes appear in 57% of all utterances; for English, U-codes appear in 64% of all utterances and Z-codes appear in 36% of all utterances).

The meaning of the above findings is not straightforward: the decrease in one-constituent utterances noted by Wells (1985) is not apparent in the Kate corpus, and why there should be the great quantitative differences between Dutch and English is a mystery. It is not inconceivable, though, that differences in the conversational styles of the Dutch and English interlocutors may have had an influence on these differences. This is a matter for further investigation.

More interesting should be the analysis of Kate's use of the various types of U-codes by themselves (note that in the following, proportions are always based on the total number of fully transcribed English or Dutch utterances with a U-code). A detailed developmental picture of the data can be found in Table 32 in the appendix.

In both the English and the Dutch corpus, affirmatives (i.e. utterances with a code UA) occur most frequently throughout, although as time goes on, dips and hills occur in a seemingly random fashion. In both languages, negatives (utterances with a code UN) are the second most frequent, but are used much less frequently than affirmatives. The developmental picture for negatives is much the same as it is for affirmatives. The proportions of affirmatives and negatives are very similar in both languages: in English, 71% of all utterances with a U-code are affirmatives. In Dutch, the percentage is 69%. In English, 11% of all utterances with a U-code are negatives, while in Dutch the percentage is 15%.

The above similarities sharply contrast with the data for interrogatives (i.e. utterances with a code UY or UW): although the total proportion of interrogatives is virtually the same in both languages (18% for English and 16% for Dutch), the types of interrogative structures differ quite considerably in use. In English, Yes/No-questions appear most frequently, although the pro-portional difference with WH-questions is small (10 vs. 8%). In Dutch, the reverse is true: here, WH-questions are by far the most prominent, and the proportional difference with Yes/No-questions is relatively great (12 vs. 4%). (Note that the total numbers for questions here are slightly higher than the ones given in sections 8.2.1.4 and 8.2.2.4. This is because in those sections only questions containing an overt Subject and a finite verb were included, whereas in the present section all questions are taken into account.)

Why there should be this difference between both languages is not clear. However, some of the literature on maternal speech to young children gives some clues about the possible causes of the difference observed here. Snow, Arlman-Rupp, Hassing, Jobse, Joosten and Vorster (1976) found that Dutch mothers when addressing their children in the age range of 1;6 to 3;2 used WH-questions almost three times as often as Y/N-questions (the exact figure is 2.67). Interestingly, this is exactly the same proportion as found for Kate: on a total of 177 fully transcribed Dutch questions, 72% are WH-questions and only 28% are Y/N-questions. This means that there are 2.6 WH-questions for each Y/N-question in the Dutch corpus. Matters become even more intriguing when data from American mothers addressing their daughters at the age of 2;3 are compared to the English data in the Kate corpus: Furrow, Nelson and Benedict (1979) found that on the average, mothers used slightly more Y/N-questions than WH-questions (on the average, 16 out of 100 utterances were in the form of Y/N-questions, and 15 out of 100 utterances were in the form of WH-questions). A nearly identical relationship is apparent in the English Kate corpus: Kate used slightly more Y/N-questions than WH-questions (on a total of 116 fully transcribed English questions, 45% are WH-questions and 55% are Y/N-questions).

The striking similarities here between Dutch mothers' and Kate's use of Dutch questions, and between American mothers' and Kate's use of English questions, combined with the fact that the English frequency data are very different from the Dutch ones, provides a strong basis for the hypothesis that input frequencies are of major importance in determining the child's proportional use of WH- vs. Y/N-questions. Obviously, though, this statement will have to be substantiated by further research investigating the properties of the input used by Kate's interlocutors. However, since mothers speaking the same language have not been found to greatly differ as far as their use of investigated structures is concerned (see e.g. Snow 1977), it is not expected that there would be statistically significant differences between the data reported on in the literature and data based on an analysis of the speech addressed to Kate.

Developmentally, the English data show that Kate starts using interrogatives in full force only from Tape 8 onwards. At this point, however, she uses mainly Y/N-questions. WH-questions start to appear with sustained higher frequency only from Tape 14 onwards. In the Dutch data, on the other hand, WH-questions appear in high frequencies from Tape 1 onwards, with sudden deep dips and high mountain passes. Y/N-questions come in markedly later (i.e. starting from Tape 5).

Table 8.20 *Kate's use of novel verb forms in English and Dutch interrogatives* [a]

WH-questions

Age	Lexical verb with or without a non-modal auxiliary	Copula or modal
2;7,12		(D) 's
2;7,17		(D) is
		(E) 's
2;9,0	(D) stem/ stem in {-t}/ stem + {-en}	
2;10,5	(D) stem + {-t}	
	(E) are + GERUND/ did + PAST	
2;10,13	(D) heb	(D) was/zijn
2;10,28	(E) am + GERUND	(E) will/is
		(D) wil
3;0,11	(E) do (by itself)	
	(D) stem + {-t} + {-en}	
3;0,17	(E) 's + GERUND	
3;1,6	(E) does + UVF/(E) UVF + {-s}	
3;1,13	(E) do + UVF	
3;1,18	(E) did + UVF	
3;1,26	(E) 's not + GERUND	
	(D) PRESENT PERFECT	
TOTAL	(D) 7 (E) 10	(D) 5 (E) 3

YES/NO-questions

Age	Lexical verb with or without a non-modal auxiliary	Copula or modal
2;7,17	(E) UVF	(E) can
2;10,5		(D) kan
2;10,13	(D) stem	(D) kun
2;10,28	(D) stem+ {-en}	
2;11,14	(E) does + UVF	(D) mag/is/wil
3;0,17		(E) are/shall
3;1,12	(D) stem + {-t}	
3;1,13	(E) did + UVF	(E) am/is
3;1,18	(E) are + GERUND	(E) can't
3;1,26		(E) should
3;2,7	(E) is + GERUND	(E) may
3;3,16	(D) heef	
TOTAL	(D) 4 (E) 5	(D) 5 (E) 8

[a] (D) refers to novel use in the Dutch corpus, (E) to novel use in the English corpus; non-adult-like use has been underlined

It could be argued that the general earlier appearance of Dutch interrogatives means that Dutch question formation is being acquired earlier than it is in English. In order to investigate this possibility, we tabulated each novel use of a verb form per question type in terms of its occurrence over time. In this tabulation (see Table 8.20), we distinguished between VP's that contained a modal verb (whether this modal was combined with another verb form or not) or a copula, and between those that did not. The latter were listed in the column 'Lexical verb with or without a non-modal auxiliary'.

Although there are obviously differences between the Dutch and English data as presented in Table 8.20 (for instance, there are four different copula forms used in Dutch WH-questions, but only two in English; another example concerns IS as used in Y/N-questions: it appears three months earlier in Dutch than in English; on the other hand, negative questions occur only in English), there is little evidence to suggest that on a general level, Dutch question formation is being acquired prior to English. In fact, the similarities between Dutch and English are quite striking: in both languages, modal auxiliaries tend to be used in Y/N-questions rather than in WH-questions. Conversely, the use of the copula in WH-questions is firmly established much earlier than it is in Y/N-questions. Furthermore, novel uses of lexical verbs without a modal auxiliary are concentrated in the WH-questions rather than in the Y/N-questions. There is also a strong tendency for lexical verbs without a modal auxiliary to first appear in WH-questions (this is particularly clear for the occurrence of the present continuous in English).

Novel use of verb forms by itself, however, may not be enough of a basis to settle the issue of the earlier acquisition of Dutch question formation. Perhaps there is a qualitative difference between the types of question words used in WH-questions that accounts for the developmental quantitative differences between English and Dutch. In order to investigate this possibility, we tabulated all novel uses of question words in terms of their occurrence over time. The results are shown in Table 8.21.

Table 8.21 shows that in the beginning of the study, Kate's use of question words is identical in both languages: only the interrogative pronouns WAT/WHAT and WAAR/WHERE occur, and the first pair is used as Subject Complement or Direct Object only (see examples 48 through 51). Tape 6 at the age of 2;10,13 sees the appearance of three new Dutch question words. All three constitute immediate repetitions of question words as used by the interacting adult in the previous turn, so the fact that two of these question words do not appear in their English equivalent until Tape 15 (i.e. at the age of 3;1,18), and that the third one does not appear at all, is probably not very significant (see also the earlier discussion of Kate's use of question words in sections 8.2.1.4 and 8.2.2.4). In the twenty-day period encompassing Tapes 12 to 16 (i.e. between the ages of 3;1,6 and 3;1,26), Kate produces 'old' question words in new syntactic functions, and also comes up with the new lexical items WHO, HOW, WAAROM and WHY. To say that the use of question words is being acquired earlier in Dutch makes little sense here: this claim would have to be substantiated by, for instance, the use of WAT and WIE in many different syntactic positions at a time when WHAT and WHO are used in only very restricted contexts. Other acceptable evidence would be the use of many different question words in Dutch simultaneously with the use of only one or two question words in English. As it stands, neither type of evidence has been found.

(48) 'Wa's dat?' (Age: 2;7,12) <Wha's that?>
{interrogative pronoun WAT used as a Subject Complement in a Dutch WH-question}
(49) 'What are you doing?' (Age: 2;10,5)
{interrogative pronoun WHAT used as a Direct Object in an English WH-question}
(50) 'Waar is mijn suiker nu al?' (Age: 2;9,0) <Where is my sugar now already?>
{interrogative pronoun WAAR used as a Place Adverbial in a Dutch WH-question}
(51) 'Where's the inside?' (Age: 2;7,17)
{interrogative pronoun WHERE used as a Place Adverbial in an English WH-question}

Combined with the results from the investigation above of novel verb forms in Kate's questions, then, the results reported on in the previous paragraph indicate that there are no significant qualitative differences between Kate's use of English and Dutch interrogatives that support the hypothesis that Dutch question formation is ahead of English question formation (on another level, though, there are of course significant qualitative differences between Kate's English and Dutch questions, in that in either language, Kate uses the quite distinct means employed in question formation available in the separate input systems - see also section 7.2 in Chapter 7). The quantitative differences that sparked off the qualitative investigation, we must conclude, are most likely discourse-related: Kate simply happened to use many more Dutch questions than English ones in the early recording sessions.

Before going on to a discussion of the Structure codes, a comparison of Kate's use of utterances with a U-code with Wells' (1985) frequency data offers some intriguing results.

Table 8.21 *Kate's use of novel question words in WH-questions* [a]

Age	Question word		Syntactic function
2;7,12	(D) WAT		Subject Complement
2;7,17		(E) WHAT	Subject Complement
		(E) WHERE	Place Adverbial
2;9,0	(D) WAAR		Place Adverbial
	(D) WAT		Direct Object
2;10,5		(E) WHAT	Direct Object
2;10,13	(D) WIE		Subject
	(D) HOEVEEL		Direct Object
	(D) HOE		Subject Complement
3;1,6		(E) WHAT	Subject
3;1,3		(E) WHAT (modifying)	Subject Complement
3;1,18	(D) WAT	(E) WHO	Subject
		(E) HOW	Manner Adverbial
3;1,26	(D) WAAROM	(E) WHY	Adverbial of Reason

[a] (D) refers to novel use in the Dutch corpus, (E) to novel use in the English corpus; novel use here does not only refer to the use of different lexical items, but also to use in different syntactic functions

In his Table A17, Wells (1985) lists the relative frequencies of various 'Mood Options' as present in his cross-sectional data. He explains on page 266 that 'Moodless' utterances were not included in this Table (unfortunately, though, we have not been able to find a clear definition of what Wells counted as a 'Moodless' utterance). In our coding system, no 'Moodless' code was included. A further difference between Wells' coding and ours is that he coded one-constituent utterances as having a 'Mood' as well (Declarative, Imperative, *Wh*-Interrogative, Polar Interrogative, Polar Interrogative (Intonation only), Declarative + Tag, Tag alone). Yet another difference with the coding system for the present study (as the above listing of Wells' Mood options shows) is that Imperatives were not coded separately in the syntactic coding system. This was for the simple reason that imperatives (at least as expressed by verbs) were already coded for in the morphological coding system. Even with all these differences, however, it was still felt that a comparison between Wells' data and the

(English) data from Kate might be useful. In order to draw such a comparison we conflated our UA and UN codes (Wells did not distinguish between these), and retained the separate UY and UW codes, which coincide with Wells' Polar Interrogative and Polar Interrogative (Intonation only) on the one hand and with his *Wh* -Interrogative code on the other. Wells' Declarative, Imperative, Declarative + Tag and Tag alone were then taken together to be compared with the conflation of the UA and UN codes used in the present study. On the quantitative level, we took into account all the data as presented by Wells (1985) in his Table A17 for the ages of 33, 36 and 39 months: we added up the three frequencies per Mood option, then organized these sums in one of three categories DECLARATIVE, YES/NO-QUESTION and WH-QUESTION and computed the proportions represented by each (it must be noted that Wells' Mood option frequency data are already proportional to some degree: they represent x out of 1000 utterances for the entire corpus obtained from the whole sample of approximately 60 children at a particular age - see Wells 1985: 18-30 and 227). From the Kate data, we computed the proportions of each of the categories DECLARATIVE, Y/N-QUESTION and WH-QUESTION as based on the total number of English utterances with a U-code. The results of these manipulations are shown in Table 8.22.

Table 8.22 *Kate's use of declaratives and interrogatives as compared to data from British children* [a]

Kate corpus		
Code	Category	Proportion
UA+UN	DECLARATIVE	82 %
UY	YES/NO-QUESTION	10 %
UW	WH-QUESTION	8 %
Wells corpus		
Code	Category	Proportion
Declarative, Imperative, Declarative + Tag and Tag alone	DECLARATIVE	82 %
Polar Interrogative and Polar Interrogative (Intonation only)	YES/NO-QUESTION	10 %
Wh -Interrogative	WH-QUESTION	8 %

[a] The data from British children here are taken from Wells (1985: Table A17)

The striking resemblance (in fact, the identical values) of the two proportions is clear. The importance of the similarity cannot be exaggerated, though, since the figures are based on slightly different coding decisions and rather more different numerical data. Nevertheless, the resemblance remains and must be accounted for. At this point, however, possible explanations can only be guessed at. Although Wells himself (1985: 267) comments on the quite stable relative proportions of the various Mood options by the age of 45-48 months, he does not attempt to explain the finding. (My own calculations for the combined ages of 42, 45 and 48 months show the proportions as they appear in Table 8.22 to be virtually identical, while the values for the ages of 24, 27 and 30 months are slightly different, with DECLARATIVES accounting for 87%, Y/N-QUESTIONS for 6% and WH-QUESTIONS for 7% of all the utterances taken into account. Again the figures here are based on the data in Table A17 given by Wells 1985.) That an American-Belgian bilingual child growing up in a different culture should show exactly the same proportions, however, leads one to believe that some general phenomenon pertinent to the organization of discourse interaction is at work here. The fact that the proportions of interrogative vs. non-interrogative utterances in Kate's use of Dutch and English are virtually identical may be seen as support for this (highly tentative) hypothesis. Only more data (including badly needed quantitative data on Dutch monolingual children) and a closer examination of the corpora available can provide us with a better basis for approaching this hypothesis. The issue certainly seems to be an area worthy of more investigation.

We close this subsection by pointing out that on the qualitative level, Kate is producing types of clauses that her monolingual peers around the age of three employ as well: both English- and Dutch-speaking children produce affirmative and negative clauses, and a range of Y/N- and WH-Questions (see e.g. Crystal, Fletcher and Garman 1976 for English; Bol and Kuiken 1987, 1988 for Dutch).

8.3.2 *Clauses*

Both in the Dutch and the English corpora, simple sentences are by far the most frequent (see Table 33 in the Appendix). Quantitative data for English-speaking children in the same age range show the same result (Wells 1985). Unfortunately, quantitative data about the use of various clause types for Dutch-speaking children are lacking. In the Kate corpus, there is no clear development to be discerned: the one utterance/one clause link remains quite strong throughout. Examples 52 and 53 show some typical simple sentences.

(52) 'Ik wil ook een kussen.' (Age: 2;7,17)
 I-want-also-a-cushion
 <I also want a cushion.>
 {example of a Dutch simple sentence}
(53) 'I want that lollipop mommy!' (Age: 2;10,5)
 {example of an English simple sentence}

Besides simple sentences, Kate uses some compound and complex sentences as well (see examples 54 through 57). [6] Monolingual Dutch- and English-speaking children also use these constructions around the age of three (cf. for Dutch: Bol and Kuiken 1987, 1988; for English: Fletcher 1985). It could be argued that in the Kate corpus, compound and complex sentences start to appear with some regularity earlier in English than in Dutch (see Table 33 in the Appendix), but the 'earlierness' of English here is not very pronounced. Partly this is because the proportion of compound and complex sentences is quite minimal on the whole (this finding is comparable to what has been reported in the literature on English-speaking children - see e.g. Wells 1985; in the literature on Dutch-speaking children quantitative data are unavailable). In both languages, compound sentences appear quasi-simultaneously with complex sentences. This seems also to be the case for English-speaking children (see e.g. Crystal, Fletcher and Garman 1976: 76-77; Wells 1985: 195, Table A18). For Dutch, it can be inferred from Bol and Kuiken's (1987) description that Dutch-speaking children also start to use complex and compound sentences at approximately the same time in development. In the following we shall go into some of the formal characteristics of Kate's complex and compound sentences in more detail.

(54) 'Ik ga nu zitten en nu werken.' (Age: 2;9)
 I-go-now-sit-and-now-work
 <I am going to sit down now and to work now.>
 {example of a Dutch compound sentence}
(55) 'You have to stand and come back to wash!' (Age: 2;11,14)
 {example of an English compound sentence}

(56) 'Omdat ik kan nie z-, kan nie zien da,als zij - is zo, is zo allemaal stof!'
   (Age: 3;3,9)
   because-I-can-not-s-can-not-see-that-when-she-is-so-is-so-everybody-dust
   <Because I can't see that when there's so much dust!>
      {example of a Dutch complex sentence with the main clause ellipted}
(57) 'I hope I like them.' (Age: 2;10,5)
      {example of an English complex sentence}

In the Dutch corpus, the clause connectors EN <and> and MAAR <but> are first used mainly to introduce simple sentences. It is much later (viz. at the age of 3;2,7) that there starts to be more regular use of a clause connector as a 'true' co-ordinating conjunction, linking two clauses within one utterance. Note that not all of Kate's Dutch compound sentences include a co-ordinating conjunction: Kate also occasionally juxtaposes two clauses without using any conjunction, as in example 58.

(58) 'Da's nie de ezel, da's de koekelekoe.' (Age: 3;1,26)
   <That's not the donkey, that's the rooster.>
      {example of a Dutch compound sentence without a co-ordinating conjunction}

The clause connector EN occurs regularly from the very beginning of the study. At the same time that it starts to get used more frequently as a 'true' co-ordinating conjunction, the clause connector MAAR appears, but mainly only in the 'utterance introducer' function. EN continues to be used in this function as well, but much less frequently so. Only once or twice (and then only in the final tape, at age 3;3,16) is MAAR used to link two co-ordinating clauses. The clause connector ALS <if/when> emerges at the same time as MAAR, and does not appear until the age of 3;2,7. It occurs only as a 'true' subordinator, except in one utterance where it is used as an 'utterance introducer'. When the first clause of a complex sentence is a subclause introduced by ALS, Kate frequently uses DAN <then> as the first word of the main clause following it. The clause connectors WANT <since> and OMDAT <because> each occur only once in the entire corpus of fully transcribed Dutch utterances. Only the clause connectors EN, MAAR and ALS, then, are fairly productive by the end of the study. The reader can find a summary of the major points mentioned here in Table 8.23.

Bol and Kuiken (1987) report that EN is the first clause connector to be used by monolingual Dutch children. After EN, MAAR starts to be used as well, and subordinating conjunctions start to be used at the same time as

MAAR. These developments take place during the period from 3;0 to 3;6. Unfortunately, Bol and Kuiken do not mention in what types of clauses EN and MAAR occur. As an example of the first subordinating conjunctions to appear in children between the ages of 3;0 to 3;6, Bol and Kuiken only specifically mention OMDAT, which occurs only once in the Kate corpus. Does this mean that Kate does not resemble Dutch-speaking children here? The answer here is negative, since Van Ginneken (1917: 252) reports that the first subordinating conjunction to appear in his Dutch-speaking subject was ALS, in the realizations [a], [as] and [als]. Kate also uses ALS as the first subordinating conjunction to occur productively, and her realizations of this conjunction also take the form of [a], [as] and [als]. Thus she resembles at least one monolingual Dutch child.

Finally, it should be mentioned that nearly all of Kate's Dutch subclauses are conditional or temporal adverbial clauses introduced by ALS. Only four times do other subclauses occur, and two of those have the form 'Klaar denk ik' <ready-think-I> (Age: 2;10,13). KLAAR here is an elliptical object clause without a clause connector, and the whole sentence is fully adult-like (two non-elliptical alternatives might be: 'het is klaar denk ik' <it-is-ready-think-I> or 'ik denk dat het klaar is' <I-think-that-it-ready-is>). Note that 'Klaar denk ik' only appeared as an immediate repetition of the adult's preceding turn. The little information that there is on Dutch children's early subclauses seems to indicate that these are quite restricted, and that object clauses do not occur. Since there is no indication that Kate uses object clauses productively, we again find no discrepancies between her speech production and that of her monolingual Dutch-speaking peers.

The available comparison data, then, show that Kate's use of clause connectors, complex and compound sentences in Dutch is highly similar to that reported on with regard to monolingual Dutch-speaking children. Developmentally, there is a clear change to be observed: complex and compound sentences start to appear with some regularity only at the very end of the study.

Kate's use of English clause connectors is virtually identical to that observed for Dutch, except that there are differences in the ages at which new connectors and new functions occur. As was the case in the Dutch data, not all compound sentences contained a co-ordinating conjunction: some simply consisted of two juxtaposed clauses, as in example 59.

In the English corpus, the first syntactic function of the clause connector AND is to introduce simple sentences. Although AND is strongly present from the very beginning of the study, it starts to get regularly used as a 'true' co-ordinating conjunction as well only from the age of 2;10,28. This is 4 months earlier than the regular co-ordinating use of the Dutch equivalent EN. The clause connector BUT appears much later than AND: it occurs regularly only from the age of 3;1,12 onwards, and is mainly used in the 'utterance introducer' function, except perhaps in one utterance at the age of 3;1,26, when 'true' co-ordinating use is also a possible interpretation. Even in this case, however, BUT still appears in utterance-initial position. Note that BUT appears a month earlier than its Dutch pseudo-equivalent MAAR (see above), but that the syntactic use that Kate makes of either is identical. The clause connector IF emerges with some regularity at virtually the same time as BUT, namely at the age of 3;1,6. It occurs only as a 'true' subordinator, except in one utterance where it is used as an 'utterance introducer'. IF appears a month earlier than its Dutch pseudo-equivalent ALS, but the syntactic use that Kate makes of either is identical. The clause connectors SO, 'CAUSE and WHEN each occur only three times in the entire corpus of fully transcribed English utterances. There is a once-off occurrence of the relative pronoun WHICH at age 2;7,12, but this form is an immediate repetition of part of the interacting adult's previous turn. Only the clause connectors AND, BUT and IF, then, are fairly productive by the end of the study. The major points mentioned here have been summarized in Table 8.23.

Table 8.23 *Kate's use of clause connectors* [a]

Age	Utterance introducer	Co-ordinating use	Subordinating use
2;7,12	(D) EN/(E) AND		
2;10,28		(E) AND	
3;1,6			(E) IF
3;1,12	(E) BUT		
3;2,7	(D) MAAR	(D) EN	(D) ALS

[a] Only lexical items and uses occurring more than three times in the entire English or Dutch corpus have been included; cells for BUT/IF and MAAR/ALS were only filled once these forms were starting to be used regularly, i.e. when they were found at least once in three consecutive recordings containing at least 20 utterances per relevant language.

(59) 'Bu's not scream, bu's just bu!' (Age: 3;1,18)
(uttered after Kate had been reprimanded by her mother when she had yelled 'Bu!!' [by] several times very loudly. Kate's mother had told her not to scream)
{example of an English compound sentence without a co-ordinating conjunction}

In the literature on English-speaking children, it is reported that AND occurs quite some time before any other clause connectors (Crystal, Fletcher and Garman 1976, Fletcher 1985, Wells 1985). According to Crystal et al. (1976: 76), BUT starts to be used in the same age period that AND is used in its 'true' clause-coordination function (i.e. between the ages of 3;0 and 3;6). Unfortunately, however, no data are presented on the usage patterns of BUT. Such data are absent in Fletcher (1985) and Wells (1985) as well, although the few utterances in which Fletcher's (1985) subject Sophie uses BUT at the ages of 3 and 3;6 are very similar to the ones Kate is producing, i.e. BUT is used as an 'utterance introducer'. In his large study of English children, Wells (1985: 172) found that IF and BUT are co-emergent. The same holds for the data from Kate.

In section 8.2 on word order, we only briefly touched on the subject of Kate's use of subclauses. Even though subclauses appear very infrequently in either language, the differences between the two languages in the use of subclauses is quite striking: whereas in Dutch Kate uses almost exclusively subclauses introduced by ALS, her English subclauses show a larger variety (this was already hinted at in section 8.2.2.3). It was also offered as a suggestion in that section that many of Kate's English subclauses were not really subclauses, since they lacked subordinating conjunctions (or relative pronouns). However, in the present discussion we shall treat these 'pseudo-subclauses' (the term we used in section 8.2.2.3) as examples of 'true' subclauses, since this is how they would be described if they had been produced by an adult speaker. No claim is made, however, about the hierarchical status of these subclauses in the child's linguistic system. At the present time, we aim to be descriptive only. The types of English subclauses and their time of first occurrence are briefly summarized in Table 8.24.

The types of English subclauses as produced by Kate are quite similar to the types reported on for English monolingual children (cf. Limber 1973, Fletcher 1985).

The available comparison data, then, show that Kate's use of clause connectors, complex and compound sentences in English is highly similar

The acquisition of two languages from birth: a case study

to that reported on for monolingual English-speaking children. Developmentally, complex and compound sentences gain more ground as time goes on.

Finally, we shall briefly discuss Kate's use of tag questions. As noted earlier in the explanation of the syntactic coding system (see section 8.1.2), sentences with tag questions were only coded as such if a tag was attached to a simple sentence. In other cases, the 'compound sentence' or 'complex sentence' code prevailed (since complex and compound sentences were analysed manually after their automatic separation from the rest of the corpus, any tags occurring in them were easily recognized).

Table 8.24 *Kate's English subclauses* [a]

Age	Type/Example	Frequency
2;7,12	* Relative clause without a relative pronoun 'Give me the lollipop I want!' (Age: 2;10,5)	3
2;7,17	* Object clause without THAT after or before I THINK, I HOPE or I SAID 'I think the blue one is finished now.' (Age: 2;7,17)	16
2;11,14	* Relative clause with a relative pronoun 'This what you have to need!' (Age: 2;11,14)	2
3;1,6	* Conditional clause 'If the seat is broken you can't get in it!' (Age: 3;1,18)	7
3;1,12	* Embedded object clause after WANT 'She doesn't want me to take her book!' (3;1,12)	2
3;1,26	* Temporal clause 'Mammy where am I gonna go when you're away?' (Age: 3;2,7)	2
TOTAL		32

[a] The bold face age indications indicate when a particular type of subclause first occurred; one example of a particular subclause is given per type; the subclauses in each example have been underlined; the frequencies cover the entire English corpus

In the Dutch corpus, tags appear quite frequently (more frequently than compound and complex sentences taken together) and were always of the form 'hé?' (see example 59). This form is fully adult-like, and 'real' tag questions as they are used in English (i.e. consisting of at least an auxiliary and a pronoun) are virtually non-existent in Dutch.[7] The data thus show no trace of any influence from English on Dutch. Conversely, there is no influence from Dutch on English to be discerned: Kate does occasionally use OK or HEY as a tag, as is also possible in adult usage. However, these one-word tags are quite infrequent: if there were any influence from Dutch at work, one would at least expect to find many more instances of them in the English corpus (especially since they are sometimes allowable in adult English usage as well). On the other hand, even if these short tags had appeared more consistently in the English data, this would not necessarily have indicated influence from Dutch: American children have been found to produce these short tags quite regularly long before they use the 'full' tag questions (Brown and Hanlon 1970: 15). In the Kate corpus, some full tag questions very hesitantly start to occur from the age of 3;1,6 onwards. They have a variety of forms, and are always used quite appropriately (see example 60).

(59) 'Eerst moet ik mij-mijn groenten opeten hé?' (Age: 3;3,16)
    first-must-I-m-my-vegetables-up-eat-right
    <First I have to eat my vegetables, don't I?>
    {adult-like use of Dutch 'tag'}
(60) 'It weighs a lot, does it?' (Age: 3;1,18)
    (this utterance was uttered when Kate saw her mother carry a teapot)
    {adult-like use of English 'tag'}

Comparisons with data from Dutch-speaking children cannot be made since there are no comparable data. In the English literature, there has been somewhat more interest in the use of question tags (see e.g. Brown and Hanlon 1970, Fletcher 1985, Wells 1985). The data reported on English-speaking children reveals there to be quite a difference between American and British subjects. Full tag questions appear much later in American vs. British children: American children appear not to use them in any regular fashion until the age of 3;6 or even 4;0 (Brown and Hanlon 1970). If Kate is seen to use question tags only sporadically and relatively late as compared to her British peers (cf. Wells 1985), then, this is probably attributable to the fact that most of her English language input is American rather than British.

In conclusion we can say that Kate's use of clause types reflects that of monolingual children in the same age range. Furthermore, Kate's clause system is slowly changing and becoming more diversified as she grows older, although any developments that take place are gradual and can only be captured by means of a highly detailed analysis.

8.3.3 Constituents

Wells (1985: 188) states that in his data there was a very large number of different structural patterns to be observed. The same is true for Kate: there is a surprisingly small number of patterns that appears more than twice or three times in the entire corpus, and this is true of both the English and the Dutch material. There are only six structures (types) that occur 10 times or more in the entire Dutch corpus, only two such structures that occur 10 times or more in the entire English corpus (for a listing, see Table 8.25). This means that in effect the type/token ratio for sentence structures is very low. Since there is this high variability and comparative lack of stereotype in the actual shape of strings, it was decided that a constituent analysis would be more elucidating than a string analysis, which would have to consist of a pure listing of most of the strings (note that in the following, again only fully transcribed utterances with a U-code will be discussed).

Table 8.25 *Structure types appearing at least 10 times*

Dutch corpus
  (1) Subject--Intransitive Verb--Intransitive Verb
  (2) Subject--Intransitive Verb--Adverbial [a]
  (3) Subject--Intransitive Verb--Place Adverbial
  (4) Place Adverbial--Intransitive Verb--Subject
  (5) Subject Complement--Copular Verb--Subject
  (6) Subject--Copular Verb--Subject Complement

English corpus
  (1) Subject--Monotransitive Verb--Direct Object
  (2) Monotransitive Verb--Direct Object

[a] An Adverbial is an optionally present Adverbial that is not a Time, Manner or Place Adverbial

In both the English and the Dutch material, the number of constituents per clause remains fairly constant over time and vacillates around an average of 2.7 (English) and 2.6 (Dutch) constituents per clause. The ranges here are between 2.4 and 3.1 for English, and between 2 and 2.9 for Dutch (these numbers take into account only recordings at which Kate produced more than 10 clauses for either Dutch or English). This means that on the whole, English clauses consist of slightly more constituents than Dutch clauses. The full data have been presented in Table 34 in the Appendix.

The main development for Dutch and English respectively that Bol and Kuiken (1987) and Crystal, Fletcher and Garman (1976) see on the clause level between the ages of 2;6 and 3;0 is the appearance of clauses with more than 4 elements. Kate uses such clauses in the same age period (in the English corpus, utterances with six constituents appear from the age of 2;7,17 onwards and in the Dutch corpus they appear from the age of 2;10,13 onwards. Dutch utterances with five constituents appear from the age of 2;9 onwards).

In both languages, Subjects and Verbs are the most central elements: most of Kate's clauses contain at least both a Subject and a Verb. Direct Objects, Place Adverbials and Subject Complements (in this order) are the next most frequently occurring clause constituents, but they appear markedly less consistently and less often that either Subjects or Verbs: only a quarter of all English and Dutch clauses contains at least a Direct Object, Place Adverbial or Subject Complement. There is some difference between Dutch and English, though: on the average, English Direct Objects occur once per two clauses, and English Place Adverbials and Subject Complements each occur only once per four clauses. Dutch Direct Objects, Place Adverbials and Subject Complements each occur once per three clauses. Time Adverbials, Manner Adverbials, other optionally present Adverbials and Indirect Objects appear only on the periphery (i.e. in one out of 20 clauses on the average). Again, though, there is a clear difference between Dutch and English, in that Dutch Indirect Objects are virtually non-existent, and really appear only in the final three recordings, whereas English Indirect Objects are used more frequently, and appear fairly regularly from the beginning of the study, although in very small numbers. Only in English are there Object Complements and Prepositional Objects, but these are used very rarely indeed, and only occur from the age of 3;1,12 onwards. Absent in either language are Obligatory Subject and Object Adverbials (see Quirk, Greenbaum, Leech and Svartvik 1985).

Rather than present a table giving the percentages of particular constituents used per clause, we thought it would be clearer to list the proportions represented by each constituent per recording, regardless of the number of clauses used. This list can be found in Table 35 in the Appendix. In this table, we have separated out the various types of verbs (Monotransitive, Intransitive, Copular, Ditransitive and Complex

Transitives). The proportions in Table 35 are based on the total number of constituents per recording. Not included in this table are Vocatives, Clause connectors and Sentence Modifiers. Constituents which could not be clearly defined were excluded from Table 35 as well.

Whereas Table 35 confirms the overall similarities in constituent use between Kate's two languages, it clearly shows some significant differences as well. One of these concerns Kate's use of Monotransitive Verbs. These occur far more frequently in English than in Dutch (17.8% of all clause constituents in English vs. only 10.8% of all clause constituents in Dutch). This difference in relative frequency is consistent throughout: a Wilcoxon matched pairs signed-ranks test based on the proportion of Monotransitive Verbs per clause for recording sessions containing at least 21 clause constituents (tokens) for each language reveals a highly significant difference between both languages for the entire course of the study (T=1; N=11; $p < .005$). Associated with this finding is that English Direct Objects are proportionally much more strongly represented than Dutch Direct Objects: although non-adult-like ellipsis of a Direct Object does occur occasionally in either language, Kate usually produces a Direct Object when she uses a Monotransitive Verb, and since Monotransitive Verbs appear much more frequently in English than in Dutch, the higher relative frequency of English vs. Dutch Direct Objects is but a natural outcome of this. A second highly significant difference concerns Intransitive Verbs: Kate uses many more of these when speaking Dutch than when speaking English (again a Wilcoxon test found high statistical significance at the $p < .005$ level with T=1 and N=11; *mutatis mutandis*, the basis for the test was the same as for Monotransitive Verbs).

Reasons for the observed differences between Dutch and English here are more likely than not directly related to the types of interactions that Kate entered into with her Dutch interlocutor on the one hand and her English interlocutor on the other: expressions of needs and desires were much more frequent when Kate was addressing her mother, with the concomitant high frequency of I WANT + NP constructions and variations (see also the two string types that appeared 10 or more times each above - cf. Table 8.25). Conversely, the activities that Kate was engaged in with the Dutch interlocutor were mostly play activities, often involving the manipulation of toy animals and the concurrent description of the types of actions carried out upon or by these toy animals.

In both languages, Place Adverbials appear quite regularly and are, with the exception of WHERE?/WAAR?, THERE/DAAR and HERE/HIER, virtually always in the form of a prepositional phrase. In fact, most prepositional phrases in the corpus tend to be place indications (but note the main exceptions below). Time Adverbials almost exclusively consist of the lexical items NOW/NU or THEN/DAN. More specific, precise time indications come in quite late in both English and Dutch, and have very unstable meanings. It should be noted that the precise meaning of the Dutch NU was not always clear, and that in those cases where doubt existed whether NU was actually used as a time indication, it was coded as a Sentence Modifier on the syntactic level (and a particle on the morphological level). Most Dutch Manner Adverbials take the form ZO <like this>, and the English ones LIKE THIS or LIKE THAT (here we have prepositional phrases not used as Place Adverbials). The other optionally present Adverbials (Other Adverbials or OA's) consist of a variety of forms, the most frequent of which are instrumental or comitative prepositional phrases (a distinction between the two possibilities is often hard to draw. This may be not only because we are dealing with child language, but because of the often indeterminate boundaries between these two possibilities in the adult system - see e.g. Meys 1975). Following Quirk et al. (1985), the English adverbs ONLY, ALSO, JUST and the like were coded as OA, whereas the Dutch pseudo-equivalents of these forms (e.g. ALLEEN, OOK) were coded as Sentence Modifiers. This probably explains why the relative frequency of Dutch Other Adverbials in Table 35 is much less compared to that of English OA's. Dutch particles (other than negative particles) occurred 53 times in the entire corpus, and 33 of those instances (or 62%) occurred in Tape 4. These 33 mainly had the form NU or NU AL. There are no data on monolingual Dutch children's use of particles or Sentence Modifiers (Bol and Kuiken 1987, it appears, coded these as Adverbials) so we cannot compare the data from Kate with monolingual acquisition. It is clear, though, that the variety of particles as produced by Kate is quite small, and that on the semantic and pragmatic levels a lot is yet to be learned.

Most of Kate's English Ditransitive Verbs consist of the lexical item GIVE (i.e. 19 out of 27 tokens), and all her Indirect Objects are pronominal. Furthermore, most Ditransitive Verbs are imperatives. This may suggest that Indirect Object constructions are not quite established yet, and are the result of unanalysed, stereotyped routines rather than of productive rules. Again, though, Kate strongly resembles monolingual English children here: Wells (1985: 197) reports as the first construction with an Indirect Object (IO) to emerge the string <S + V + IO + O>, in which the Indirect Object precedes the Direct Object (O). This order also appears in the Kate corpus, and is in fact the only one. Wells (1985) does not list any other order for Indirect Object and Direct Object either. Whether's Kate's virtually non-existent use of Indirect Objects in Dutch is similar to what happens in Dutch-speaking children cannot be ascertained due to the lack of comparative material.

It was noted above that all Kate's English Indirect Objects are pronominal. There is a very strong tendency for both English and Dutch Subjects to be pronominal as well. Non-pronominal Subjects account for only 11.6% of all English Subjects, and 17.5% of all Dutch Subjects. There are no clear developmental changes to be observed in the proportions of pronominal vs. non-pronominal Subjects in either language. The situation is different for Direct Objects: in Dutch, pronominal and non-pronominal Direct Objects occur throughout in more or less the same 50/50 proportion, whereas in English there is a fairly strong tendency for Direct Objects to be non-pronominal, although this tendency is not nearly as strong as the tendency for English Subjects to be correlated with one type of form: more than a quarter of all Direct Objects is pronominal. Although there are strong ups and downs in the proportions of English pronominal vs. non-pronominal Direct Objects per recording session, no clear developmental pattern is apparent.

Finally, the use of Vocatives needs to be discussed briefly. Comparisons here with data from monolingual children are impossible, since these are lacking. However, it did seem curious to find that Kate starts using Dutch Vocatives only towards the very end of the study (i.e. in the final three recording sessions), whereas in English they are strongly present already from Tape 5 (at the age of 2;10,5) onwards. It is not at all clear why the quantitative use of Dutch and English Vocatives should be so different (there are also only 25 Dutch Vocatives but a grand total of 174 English ones): they are extra-clausal elements with exactly the same status in both languages. Although these Vocatives do not add to the structural complexity of utterances, they do raise MLU counts and appear to add to the discourse complexity of the child's language production. This is only speculation, of course, but perhaps it is a point worthy of more investigation.

Developmentally, major shifts in the types or proportions of clause constituents are not discernible, although there is a slight tendency for the least frequent constituents to start appearing mainly after the age of 3;1. We can confirm Crystal, Fletcher and Garman's (1976) finding that by the age of three, the main structural elements have been 'acquired' and are firmly established. Although Crystal et al.'s (1976) statement was meant only for English, it holds up for Dutch as well, and Kate uses structures that appear in Bol and Kuiken's (1987) profile chart for the age periods from 2;6 to 3;0 and 3;0 to 3;6. On the other hand, phrase structure at this age "is by no means so fully developed" (Crystal et al. 1976: 75). This is confirmed in the data from Kate as well: as was discussed in chapters 6 and 7 on the Noun Phrase and the Verb Phrase respectively, there are quite a few developments to be discerned in the number and variety of elements constituting an NP or a VP, and this development is far from completed by the end of the study.

We have here come to the end of our analysis of Kate's use of syntactic categories. Although Ellipsis codes were included in the coding system and although we fully agree with Crystal et al. (1976) that the appropriate use of ellipsis highly depends on the extent of the child's syntactic knowledge, we maintain that ellipsis is a phenomenon which primarily needs to be tackled on the discourse level, with of course ample cross-referencing to purely syntactic phenomena. Since a discourse analysis is beyond the scope of the present study, Kate's use of ellipsis will not be discussed in any detail. Suffice it to say in the most general terms that Kate's use of ellipsis was mostly fully adult-like, although 'odd' ellipsis did occur throughout in both languages. The converse of elliptical utterances, namely utterances containing elements redundant in the on-going discourse, can also best be discussed within a discourse analysis.

A very small percentage of Kate's utterances was syntactically non-adult-like on other levels besides that of word order and the use of ellipsis. Since the sources of the 'errors' here were nearly as many as the number of syntactically non-adult-like utterances, an analysis would be quite pointless. The lack of any systematicity in the errors and their low number shows that there is probably no all-encompassing acquisition strategy to be discerned here that would be relevant to the acquisition of syntax as a whole. It is perhaps best to consider the utterances under discussion as slips of the tongue.

8.3.4 Conclusion

The preceding analyses and discussions have shown that in her use of both Dutch and English, Kate closely resembles three-year-old monolingual children speaking either language as far as the use of sentence types, clause types and clause constituents is concerned. This finding, compared with the fact that many quantitative and qualitative differences exist between the data for both languages, strongly suggests that Kate's general syntactic development proceeds in a language-dependent manner.

After her third birthday, Kate's syntactic system has clearly diversified and become much more complex than before, with the advent of different interrogative structures, complex and compound sentences, English tag questions and 'peripheral' clause constituents. By the end of the study syntactic development is by no means complete, though: for instance, interrogatives consisting of two clauses or more are virtually non-existent, the variety of complex and compound sentences is highly restricted, as is the variety of Adverbials. Furthermore, there is very little use or demonstrated productive control of Prepositional Objects, Object Complements and Indirect Objects, and Obligatory Adverbials do not appear at all. These limitations are, presumably, highly dependent on the types of verbs that the child uses, and as she grows older and as her vocabulary increases, her use of verbs requiring Prepositional Objects, Object Complements, Indirect Objects, and Obligatory Adverbials will increase, and thus also her use of these required constituents: no further drastic structural changes in the child's system are needed to incorporate these elements. Certainly considerations of length, which play such an important role in earlier stages of acquisition (see e.g. Brown 1973, Wells 1985), have become insignificant by the age of 3;4, with the child effortlessly producing clauses with six or more constituents.

Notes

1 This approach is - either implicitly or explicitly - taken by many other researchers in child language as well (see e.g. Crystal, Fletcher and Garman 1976, Fletcher 1985, Bol and Kuiken 1987).
2 POESETJES appears to be a child neologism, the meaning of which could not be discerned. AF, although translated as 'off' in example 19, may also be interpreted as 'finished/ready'. In both interpretations AF is placed inappropriately.
3 These figures were arrived at by adding up the following: (I) all the figures given by Wells (1985) in his Tables A18 and A19 for declarative and interrogative clauses containing an auxiliary aux and a main verb V for the ages of 33, 36 and 39 months. The total yield of this was 207 tokens; (II) all the figures given by Wells

(1985) in his Table A18 for declarative clauses containing an auxiliary aux followed by a negative adverbial and a main verb V for the ages of 33, 36 and 39 months. The total yield here was 57 tokens. It was then computed what percentages 207 and 57 constituted on an average total of 264 per 3000 clauses with a multi-component VP as used by Wells' subjects in the age range of 2;9 to 3;3 inclusive (all Wells' figures are averaged across all children per age group. The basis for each averaged figure per age group is 1000 utterances).

4 Sophie uses negative forms of DO in questions, though, as well as past tenses (of verbs other than DO). These do not appear in the data from Kate, but of course non-occurrence can never be an argument for 'non-acquisition'.
5 But see our objections to this view of 'primacy' in section 2.2.6 of Chapter 2.
6 It must be noted here that, following Matthews (1982: 182 ff.) and Brown (1973), sentences containing a WANT TO + UVF construction in which both WANT and the verb expressed in the UVF have the same Subject were coded not as consisting of a clause with WANT and an embedded clause as Wells (1985: 190) did, but as consisting of a catenative construction involving one clause only.
7 Dutch speakers may use the tag IS HET NIET? or WAS HET NIET? <is it not?/was it not?> consisting of a finite verb and a pronoun (as well as a negative particle) which can be used without any clear restrictions as far as the preceding finite verb goes. These tag are very much set phrases, however.

9 The morphological and syntactic analyses: a recapitulation

Chapters 6, 7 and 8 have shown that in Kate's language production, her two languages form two separate, closed systems which exercise very little (if any) influence on each other on the morphosyntactic level. Thus, the Separate Development Hypothesis has been confirmed (see further chapter 11).

Another major finding is that Kate's third birthday marks a turning point in her linguistic development in general: in both languages, structures start to appear that were absent before, or initially rare patterns start to appear more frequently. It seems as if the child is suddenly much more intensively occupied with the formal aspects of language and their possibilities than before: language as a "formal problem space" (Karmiloff-Smith 1979) is much more at the centre of attention once Kate is into her fourth year. In order to show this more clearly, we have collated all the evidence in chapters 6, 7 and 8 that unequivocally indicates a change in any subsystem that Kate is in the process of acquiring (see Table 9.1).

Table 9.1   *Changes in Kate's language production after her third birthday* [a]

THE NOUN PHRASE

English

* appearance of natural gender pronouns	6.1.2.2
* noticeable increase in the number of plural nouns	6.2
* increased syntagmatic complexity of NP's	6.5

Dutch

* noticeable increase in the number of plural nouns	6.2
* increased syntagmatic complexity of NP's	6.5
* more inappropriate uses of independent pronouns	6.1.2.1

Main conclusions from the morphosyntactic analyses 307

WORD ORDER

English

* increase in the number of declarative main clauses with order
    Y - S - Verb finite - REST   8.2.2.1

Dutch

* increase in the number of declarative main clauses with order
    Y - S - Verb finite - REST   8.2.1.1
* WH-questions with Subject as question word appear mainly after 3;1   8.2.1.4

THE VERB PHRASE

English

* more UVF + {–s} and YOU + UVF forms   7.4.2.1
* appearance of WE HAVE   7.4.2.3
* YOU/Plural Subjects+ARE/'RE combinations occur more consistently   7.4.2.4
* appearance of full forms of BE in WH-questions   7.4.2.4
* short appearance of WANNA and increased use of WANT TO + UVF   7.4.2.6
* increase in use of DO as an auxiliary   7.4.2.6
* increase in use of the present continuous   7.4.2.6
* highly increased use of past verb forms   7.4.2.7

Dutch

* appearance of non-adult-like forms of HEBBEN   7.3.2.3
* continued increase in syntagmatic complexity of VP's   7.3.2.6
* highly increased use of past verb forms   7.3.2.7
* appearance of non-adult-like past participles   7.3.2.7
* appearance of ZULLEN for future reference   7.3.2.8

GENERAL SYNTACTIC DEVELOPMENT

English

* 'old' question words used in new syntactic functions   8.3.1
* general increase in the use of questions   8.3.1
* appearance of new question words   8.3.1
* clause connectors BUT and IF appear in full force from 3;1 only   8.3.2
* increased use of complex and compound sentences   8.3.2
* more tag-questions   8.3.2
* Object Complements and Prepositional Objects are new   8.3.3
* 'peripheral' clause constituents are new   8.3.3

Dutch

* 'old' question words used in new syntactic functions	8.3.1
* clause connector EN used as real co-ordinating conjunction	8.3.2
* clause connectors ALS and MAAR first appear at 3;2	8.3.2
* complex and compound sentences are new	8.3.2
* Indirect Objects and Vocatives are new	8.3.3
* 'peripheral' clause constituents are new	8.3.3

[a] Every 'item' is followed by the section number in which it was discussed; the term 'appearance' in this table means 'first appearance';

It is quite striking that the many changes in Kate's two language systems take place at the same time. Furthermore, there are hardly any wide-ranging changes in her language production in the time between the beginning of the study and shortly after Kate's third birthday. So although the actual 'contents' of Kate's speech production is quite language-specific, there appears to be a mechanism at work here that concerns both languages at once. Now obviously, as Kate is getting older, she is also maturing on the cognitive level. Might it not be that general cognitive development here leads to changes in behaviour in general, including the quite drastic changes in linguistic behaviour? Even if an empirically motivated answer to this complex question were possible, a positive answer would still not be very illuminating, since it would be quite vague (after all, the question is very broad).

Perhaps we can learn more from a less ambitious question: is there any other type of behaviour that could give us an insight into the reasons for the changes in Kate's speech production (and thus perhaps serve as a possible link between these observed changes and any non-observable cognitive developments)? According to Eve Clark, "children change their language by relying on a monitoring system" (Clark 1982: 191). As most crucial evidence for this she sees the child's use of self-initiated repairs, which are the clearest sign that the child is trying to co-ordinate his/her production with his/her memory representations for words and utterances heard from adults (Clark 1982: 190). On the basis of these suggestions, then, an analysis of Kate's self-initiated repairs should provide us with a starting point to approach the question of what might have triggered the changes in Kate's use of both English and Dutch after the age of three. An analysis of other kinds of behaviour that can be called metalinguistic might also lend us greater insight into the possible causes of the changes observed. We shall examine these possibilities in Chapter 10.

10 Metalinguistic behaviour

10.1 Introductory remarks

As suggested in Chapter 9, metalinguistic behaviour may be an important contributing factor in any changes taking place in a child's linguistic system(s) during acquisition. If this hypothesis is at all valid, the material from Kate should show an increase or a change in metalinguistic behaviour slightly before or simultaneously with the changes observed in her speech production in general. Since metalinguistic behaviour presumably is the outcome of general metacognitive development (see e.g. Clark 1982), one would not expect to see any language-specific metalinguistic behaviour; rather, increases or changes in metalinguistic behaviour should occur independently of whether Kate is using Dutch or English. [1]

In the following, we shall proceed by first analysing any signs of metalinguistic behaviour as it presents itself in the corpus. After discussing issues pertaining to this metalinguistic behaviour itself, we shall come back to the hypothesis above.

Possible signs of metalinguistic behaviour as they appear in the corpus are spontaneous (or self-initiated) repairs, elicited (or other-initiated) repairs, sound-play, hesitations, self-repetitions and explicit metalinguistic statements. How exactly these phenomena can be seen as signs of metalinguistic behaviour will be discussed where relevant (see also section 10.6).

10.2 Spontaneous repairs

Spontaneous repairs are speaker-initiated self-corrections. The term 'correction' reflects the fact that the speaker changes something to an utterance (in the course of its production), presumably in order to improve on it in some way or other. The 'improvement' may or may not result in a formally or referentially more appropriate utterance.

In the coding of the corpus, spontaneous repairs were given the code 'corr1' when any part of an utterance (even a phone) was retraced and changed, either by modification or addition, or a combination of these (see example 1). The code 'corr1' was also used when there was no re-tracing, i.e. when there was no 'backtracking' to an earlier point of the utterance (van Wijk and Kempen 1985). In these cases, there was definitely a repair, however, since the speaker (Kate) started producing an utterance, paused before the intonation contour was completed, and continued with the utterance with an addition to the part uttered before the pause, or with a clause apparently unrelated to the (mostly incomplete) clause uttered before the pause. These repaired utterances without retracing are non-retracing repairs (van Wijk and Kempen's 1985 terminology). In our data, non-retracing repairs mostly concerned what we shall call 'changes in sentence plan' (see later).

(1) 'Da's - da zijn yellow and red.' (Age: 2;9,0)
    <That's - those are yellow and red.>
    {Mixed utterance in which a singular copula form is modified into a more appropriate plural copula form}

Repairing is usually seen as the result of *monitoring* one's speech production (see e.g. Laver 1973, Clark 1978, Hagen 1981, Nooteboom 1980, Levelt 1983). In the literature, monitoring has been found to operate in Dutch (Hagen 1981, Levelt 1983), German (Nooteboom 1980) and English (Clark and Andersen 1979). This suggests that monitoring is a language-independent mechanism. If this is indeed the case, then there should be no substantial differences between Kate's use of repairs in either language. If there is any particular language effect this should be revealed by both a quantitatively and qualitatively differential use of repairs per language. In order to investigate the issue, we start by looking at Kate's quantitative use of spontaneous repairs.

Table 36 in the Appendix shows the percentages of English and Dutch spontaneous repairs used by Kate as related to the total number of English and Dutch utterances respectively. It also shows the spread of Dutch and English repairs over time as compared to the total number of Dutch and English repairs.

Spearman rank correlation tests were used to explore the relation between the number of English repairs and the number of English utterances per recording session as well as the relation between the number of Dutch repairs and the number of Dutch utterances per recording session. The same level of significance was found for both these relations:

Dutch rho: .632; English rho: .692; p < .005 in both cases (one-tailed). In both cases there was a positive correlation: the more English was spoken, the more English repairs were produced and the more Dutch was spoken, the more Dutch repairs were used. Thus, there is a strong tendency for Kate to use more repairs in either language depending on how many utterances she produces in that language per recording session. However, there is at the same time a clear developmental picture to be observed: 68.6% of all Dutch repairs occur in the final three sessions (i.e. between the ages of 3;2,7 and 3;3,16), and 70.6% of all English repairs occur in the final six recording sessions (i.e. between the ages of 3;1,13 and 3;3,16). One might object that these results are a natural outcome of Kate speaking more in either language in these final recording sessions: after all, it was said earlier that the more Kate speaks, the more repairs she produces. This counterargument does not hold for either language: for Dutch, there are quite a few recording sessions before Tape 17 in which Kate produced very many utterances (at least as many as in each of Tapes 17, 18 and 19), but in which the proportion of utterances containing a repair is much smaller than for Tapes 17, 18 and 19. In the English material 70.6% of all repairs appear in the span of two months at the end of the study. Furthermore, until Tape 14 English repairs occur only sporadically (in 5 out of 13 recording sessions only), but from Tape 14 onwards they occur in each recording session with more than three English utterances. All this very clearly shows a developmental pattern. At virtually the same time in both languages, then, Kate produces many more spontaneous repairs than she did before. Another similarity between Dutch in English is that the overall proportions of Dutch and English repairs as compared to the total number of Dutch and English utterances are nearly identical: of all English utterances, 3.7% were repaired, and of all Dutch utterances 3.8 % were repaired.

The above findings warrant the conclusion that the quantitative use of repairs is language-independent: proportionally there are as many repairs in Dutch as there are in English, and repairs start to be used more frequently at virtually the same time in both languages.

We now turn to a detailed analysis of the types of repairs used.

A distinction was made between five major types of spontaneous repairs: lexico-semantic repairs, morpho-lexical repairs, morphological repairs, syntactic repairs, and phonological repairs. Lexico-semantic repairs are repairs that change the referential meaning of open-class items or that add an open-class item to an utterance after part of it has been retraced (see example 2). Morpho-lexical repairs are repairs that change the referential meaning of closed-class items or that add an closed-class item to an utterance after part of it has been retraced (see example 3). Morphological repairs substitute or add bound morphemes or closed-class items after a retracing procedure, but without any change in referential meaning (see example 4). Syntactic repairs involve a retracing of certain words or constituents and a rewording using different word order, or alternatively, syntactic repairs constitute what we have called changes in sentence plan. These repairs have the effect that the final utterance seems to consist of one incomplete clause which is stopped short, only to be followed by a second clause which in most cases bears no connection with the first incomplete one (see example 5). Often a complete change of intonation is observed after the 'break' between the 'two' utterances. Typically, changes in sentence plan constitute non-retracing repairs (see earlier). Phonological repairs change or add phonemes on the level below that of bound morphemes; also included here are completions of words after a retracing procedure (see example 6). Table 10.1 lists the overall distribution of the five types of repairs per language (note that a 'rest' category was added: there were some repairs which could not unambiguously be classified in any of the other types of repairs).

(2) 'De mama gaat ook - de leeuw gaat ook slapen.' (Age: 2;9,0)
<The mommy is also going to - the lion is also going to sleep.>
{lexico-semantic repair: the noun head of an NP is substituted by another noun}

(3) 'Jij jij moet de moet de - de jouw jouw voeten zo doen.' (Age: 3;2,7)
<You you have to put the - the your your feet like this.>
{morpho-lexical repair: the article DE <the> is substituted by the possessive pronoun JOUW <your>}

(4) 'I am - I'm on a horse!' (Age: 3;0,6)
{morphological repair: the full copula is substituted by a contracted form}

(5) 'Nee nee ik zie - maar die's op - op de counter in de keuken!' (Age: 3;3,9)
<No no I see - but that-one's on - on the counter in the kitchen!>
{syntactic repair (change in sentence plan): Mixed utterance consisting of a first unfinished utterance followed by an utterance that has little to do with the first one}

(6) 'Ik ke - ik ken ander liedje zingen!' (Age: 2;10,13)
<I ca - I can sing other song!>
{phonological repair: the incomplete form KE <CA> is substituted by the complete form KEN <CAN>}

In both English and Dutch, phonological and morpho-lexical repairs are the two most frequently occurring types of spontaneous repairs. For the syntactic, lexico-semantic and morphological repairs there is quite some variation within each language, although due to the small total number of English repairs, any quantitative differences with Dutch are difficult to interpret. Quite significant, however, is that in both languages the five types of repairs are present without there being any clear underuse of any one type. Qualitatively, then, spontaneous repairs of the same nature occur in both languages, although not necessarily in equal proportions.

Table 10.1 *Types of spontaneous repairs*

	English	Dutch
1. Phonological	$27 \pm 2\%$	35.0 %
2. Morpho-lexical	$29 \pm 2\%$	18.5 %
3. Syntactic	$10 \pm 2\%$	16.5 %
4. Morphological	$20 \pm 2\%$	15.0 %
5. Lexico-semantic	$12 \pm 2\%$	10.0 %
6. Other	$2 \pm 2\%$	5.0 %
TOTALS	41	102

How do the data above compare with data from monolingual children?

For Dutch, there is but one study which could to some extent be taken as a basis for comparison.[2] This study looks at self-corrections and false starts in the spontaneous speech productions of 4- and 7-year-old Dutch children (Anonymous, 1982). Since many of the coding and analysis procedures in this study were different from the ones in the present study, not many comparisons can be drawn. When we take the four-year-olds' morpho-lexical repairs (see page 29 of the report), however, there are notable similarities with the data from Kate: pronoun and auxiliary substitutions were the most frequent in this category, and preposition substitutions appeared quite frequently as well. Further comparisons are impossible.

In the literature on English-speaking children, researchers have paid rather more attention to the use of spontaneous repairs by children (see e.g. Clark and Andersen 1979, Iwamura 1980, Cazden, Michaels and Tabors 1984, Shatz and Ebeling 1987). For purposes of comparison we shall take the Clark and Andersen (1979) study as a basis (of the four studies quoted, the latter most closely resembles the present study as far as data collection is concerned).

Clark and Andersen (1979) found that in the spontaneous repairs by the two older children in their study (in the age range from 2;8 to 3;7,14) phonological repairs occurred least frequently. This is the converse of what was found for the English Kate corpus, in which phonological repairs were the second most frequently occurring type of repair. Clark and Andersen (1979) further found that lexical repairs constituted by far the major type of repair in their material. In the material from Kate, the comparable lexico-semantic repairs came only fourth in frequency. Although some of the examples that Clark and Andersen (1979) give of lexical repairs suggest that they included in this category some of the repairs we subsumed under morpho-lexical repairs, the proportional differences remain quite high. In the Clark and Andersen (1979) material, morphological repairs (which are more or less a combination of our morpho-lexical and morphological repairs) occurred less frequently than syntactic repairs. Again, the data from Kate are different: morpho-lexical and morphological repairs combined certainly appear much more frequently than syntactic repairs. It is possible, of course, that due to the very small number of English repairs in the Kate material we do not have a firm enough basis to quantitatively compare the data with other, more substantial, corpora. Whatever accounts for the quantitative differences, however, it is quite significant that Kate produces very similar types of repairs as compared to at least two other monolingual English-speaking children. This similarity does not only reveal itself on the general level of the five categories (or Clark and Andersen's 1979 four categories), but also on a more detailed level. Within their morphological repairs, Clark and Andersen (1979) found that pronoun substitutions were quite common. The same is true of Kate. Additions of a copula and repairs to tense and aspect were fairly frequent as well. Kate also used these kinds of repairs. There are not only qualitative similarities but also differences between the Clark and Andersen (1979) study and the data from the present study: the greater part of syntactic repairs in the English Kate corpus involves what we have called changes in sentence plan. Clark and Andersen (1979) do not mention this type of repair, but they do mention another one which we have categorized as belonging to the kind of repair under discussion, namely a switch in the choice of the Subject: "this type of repair involved the child's starting out with one particular noun phrase, pausing, picking up a new noun phrase as the subject, producing the verb and then inserting the original subject as the object of the current utterance" (Clark and Andersen 1979: 6). In our data there is only one instance that comes close to this kind of repair. We thus are confronted with a discrepancy between findings which is probably explicable by sampling limitations (it is also possible, of course, that Clark and Andersen (1979) simply did not code for changes in sentence plan, which are non-retracing repairs, but that they took into account retracing repairs only).

As far as comparisons with monolingual children are possible, then, there is some evidence that Kate largely produces the same types of repairs as monolingual children do in the same age range; however, there are quantitative differences in the extent to which use is made of the various types.

Earlier on it was noted that repairs are made by the speaker when a need is felt to somehow 'improve' the original wording of an utterance. Are in fact most repairs 'improvements' or not? This question poses the methodological problem of finding some adequate measure of what counts as an improvement. Normative judgements cannot be avoided here but perhaps the danger of subjectivity can be diminished if we give precise definitions of the norms used. In coding the spontaneous repairs made by Kate, five kinds of judgements were applied:

(a) The repair can be considered as formally or referentially more appropriate than the repaired part of the utterance:
  * 'formally' here refers to elements of structure and grammar.
    If the repair is formally closer to what an adult might say, it is judged formally more appropriate
  * 'referentially' here points to elements of meaning.
    If the repair more closely approximates a particular state of affairs than if the repair had not been made, the repair is considered referentially more appropriate
(b) The repair can be considered as formally or referentially less appropriate than the repaired part of the utterance: see (a) for explicitation
(c) The repair can be considered to be formally and referentially as appropriate as the repaired part of the utterance: see (a) for explicitation
(d) The repair cannot be coded in terms of more or less appropriate: in this case the repair has very little connection with the original attempt and as such cannot be compared to it in any way (this is particularly the case for repairs involving a change in sentence plan)
(e) The repair cannot be coded at all: in this case the entire utterance makes very little sense and hence the final structure cannot be evaluated.

Table 10.2 shows the proportions for each rating.

Table 10.2 *Improvement rating of Kate's spontaneous repairs*

	English	Dutch
a. More appropriate	58.5 ± 2 %	60.0 %
b. Less appropriate	5.0 ± 2 %	3.0 %
c. No change	14.5 ± 2 %	15.0 %
d. Irrelevant	19.5 ± 2 %	17.0 %
e. No rating possible	2.0 ± 2 %	6.0 %
TOTALS	41	102

The first and quite striking finding from Table 10.2 is that the proportions of the various ratings are highly similar across Kate's two languages. This again suggests that some mechanism is at work that is independent of a particular language, but that is relevant to 'Language' in a general sense (we shall not attempt to define what exactly this might be, and leave it open to the reader to speculate). A second major finding is that more than half of all repairs are more appropriate than the original attempt. They constitute true self-corrections: their supposed aim is achieved.

Quite a large percentage of repairs cannot be judged in terms of more or less appropriate (see rating 'd. Irrelevant'). Most of these repairs constitute a change in sentence plan (see our working definition of rating (d) above). One might well argue, actually, that these repairs are not repairs at all, since there is no apparent connection between the original and the 'repair', but then it is clear that changes in sentence plan occur whenever an urgent thought in the mind of the speaker supersedes another one to the extent that it is given priority of expression (to the detriment of the previous one). From the speaker's point of view this surely means an 'improvement', a closer connection between what she wants to express and what is actually said. For the hearer, certainly, the first part of the utterance is no more or less appropriate formally or referentially than the second part.

Repairs not involving a change in the level of 'appropriateness' occur third most frequently. These repairs are, so to speak, useless from the adult hearer's point of view. However, the fact that a repair is made (even to a form or word that is perfectly appropriate already from the adult point of view) shows that there is a concern on the child's part to try and improve on what she has just said (adults may also repair utterances which from the listener's point of view are perfectly adequate to start with - see e.g. Levelt 1983). The repair mechanism thus offers an opportunity for learning (see also Hagen 1981). Gradually, as the child becomes more certain of particular words and structures, she will realise that they are not to be repaired. Other aspects that the child is not sure of will be repaired. There thus is a constant flux of the types of elements that get repaired. Repairing itself will persist throughout adulthood (Laver 1973, Nooteboom 1980), but the types of repairs an adult makes might be quite different from the types of repairs a child makes (Levelt 1983, for instance, lists a number of repairs made by his adult subjects that do not occur in the Kate corpus).

Finally, repairs that resulted in a less appropriate utterance were very uncommon.

On the whole, then, Kate uses the repair mechanism in a constructive fashion, i.e. to render an utterance more appropriate by putting it into a form that is closer to (or that she assumes is closer to) what she hears adults say around her, or by re-structuring an utterance to accommodate a novel thought. The fact that so few repairs actually result in a less appropriate utterance means that most of the time, Kate has a fairly good idea of what are possible forms in the languages she hears spoken around her.

Kate does not repair all her own non-adult-like utterances, but only some (adults do not always repair their speech errors either - see e.g. Levelt 1983). Clark and Andersen (1979) suggest that children mainly repair those elements they are currently trying to learn. While many of the morphological and morpho-lexical repairs in the Kate corpus do reflect areas that we know the child is actively working on in the period studied, such as pronouns, articles, verb agreement (in Dutch), past reference and auxiliary usage (cf. Chapters 6, 7 and 8), there are many more areas that Kate is actively working on and that are not repaired. Furthermore, not all non-adult-like uses of elements that are occasionally repaired are in fact repaired: for instance, there are still examples of non-adult-like verb agreement where Kate does not repair her choice of verb form. Why this situation should exist is not quite clear, but we can speculate by suggesting that perhaps there is a threshold of learning which has to be reached before particular repairs can be made. After all, in the execution of a repair quite a lot of knowledge is required: typically, two forms are compared to each other. This means that these forms are seen as related to one another. In order for the child to feel the need to repair form A, she must be quite certain that A is not acceptable. This kind of elaborate knowledge is only possible after extensive experience with form A in varied circumstances. In order to find a more acceptable form B, the child must have a clear memory representation of this form B, and must thoroughly know form B to be in some way related to form A so that B can become a substitute for A. Again, quite detailed knowledge of form B is necessary, and this kind of knowledge is only possible after extensive experience with form B in a variety of circumstances.

In this line of reasoning, then, it is not the forms that a child is currently trying to learn, but the forms that the child has recently (or less recently) been trying to learn that will stand a chance of being repaired. One clear example of this is Kate's rather frequent repairing of IK <I> into JIJ <YOU> or *vice versa* : there are only one or two examples in the entire corpus of pronoun reversal involving the first and second person singular subject pronouns. Usually, Kate uses IK and JIJ quite appropriately (and also abundantly). Both IK and JIJ, then, seem to have been acquired. What Kate has perhaps just discovered, however, is the relationship between the two. This novel discovery possibly has triggered off the occurrence of the slips-of-the-tongue (i.e. the inappropriate uses of IK or JIJ) which are then repaired into more appropriate forms (see e.g. the collection of papers in Fromkin 1978 for research on slips-of-the-tongue in adults).

All this must remain purely speculative, though, and more data and more detailed investigations are needed to examine the validity of the above suggestions.

10.3 Elicited repairs

Prompted or elicited repairs are repairs made on request by the participant in the interaction and take place within the following three-term discourse frame:

(1) Turn 1: speaker A: original utterance
(2) Turn 2: speaker B: request for clarification (RC)
(3) Turn 3: speaker A: response to the RC in the form of an utterance that is a repaired version of the original utterance

Langford (1981) sees four steps in 'clarification sequences'. While his suggestion is certainly a valid one, we thought that a three-term sequence was sufficient as a frame in which to study elicited repairs. After all, should the third term of the sequence yet be followed by another request for clarification (rather than an indication that the child's response to the request for clarification had been adequate), then the third term here becomes a new first term in another three-term sequence.

A request for clarification forces the child to reflect on what she is saying and how she is saying it (Clark 1978). As such, it is a prompt for metalinguistic behaviour. Since the very occurrence of an elicited repair highly depends on the presence of a request for clarification, it is possible that the form of this RC has an influence on the response it meets with. As a first step for analysis, then, it is important to distinguish between various types of RC's. A three-way distinction (see below) captures most of the variety present in the corpus. Note that the corpus here consists not of Kate's utterances, but of utterances by her interlocutors.

(1) Type I:
these RC's consist of 'What?', 'Huh?', 'Wablief?' (Dutch), 'Watte?' (Dutch) and the like (Käsermann and Foppa 1981 call Type I RC's 'unspecific questions')

(2) Type II:
these RC's are loosely based on the child's original utterance and may consist of a short question about part of the original utterance (e.g. 'A what?'; 'Wa gaat-ie doen?' < What is he going to do?>) or of a question that is the interrogative form of the child's utterance (see example 7)

(3) Type III:
these RC's repeat part or exactly whole of the child's utterance in a questioning tone (see example 8). It may be the case that the adult repeats (part of) the child's utterance but 'corrects' it in the process (see example 9)

Responses to requests for clarification may not always be in the form of a repair or modification of the original utterance (for such a modification, see example 10). It is possible that the child simply pays no attention to the interlocutor's RC and continues with the interaction as if the RC had not existed. Another possibility is that the child repeats her original utterance without repairing it in any way (see example 7). It is also possible for the child to respond to an interlocutor's RC by an acknowledgement (see examples 8 and 9). This one would largely expect to be the case after Type III RC's, which are uttered in a questioning tone. Such an acknowledgement may also be accompanied by an expansion of the child's original utterance. Also counted as an acknowledgement were the few instances where Kate repeated the adult's RC in a questioning tone. In Table 10.3 we have listed the four types of RC's in relation to the types of responses they met with.

Table 10.3 *Kate's responses to requests for clarification* [a]

	Type I RC	Type II RC	Type III RC	Totals
Repaired response	65 ± 1 %	59 ± 4 %	-	52 (48%)
No change	11 ± 1 %	9 ± 4 %	7 ± 4 %	11 (10%)
No attention	4 ± 1 %	-	-	2 (2%)
Acknowledgement	20 ± 1 %	32 ± 4 %	93 ± 4 %	44 (40%)
TOTALS	60	22	27	**109**

[a] The percentages must be read vertically

(7) Kate: Ik ga weg! <Im going away!> (Age: 2;9,0)
    Adult: Ja ga je weg? <Really are you going away?>
    Kate: Ik ga weg! <Im going away!>
(8) Kate: You have a green-one? (Age: 2;7,17)
    Adult: A green-one?
    Kate: Hm.
(9) Kate: Heb appeljuice in [be:nət]. (Age: 2;10,13)
    <Have applejuice in [be:nət].>
    Adult: In [be:nət]?... In uwen beker? <In [be:nət]?... In your beaker?>
    Kate: Ja. <Yes.>
(10) Kate: Der is de mama nu al. (Age: 2;9,0)
    <There is the mommy now already.>
    Adult: Mm?
    Kate: De mama is nu al hier. <The mommy is now already here.>

As can be seen from Table 10.3 most of the RC's (55%) are of Type I. The two other types are more or less equally divided among the remainder. What interests us more, however, is Kate's response patterns. Most Type I and Type II RC's are met with a response in which Kate modifies her original utterance. Not surprisingly, nearly all Type III RC's are met with an acknowledgement, with or without an expansion of the original utterance. A more or less similar proportion of all responses to the three types of RC's constitutes the exact repetition of the original utterance. Only on two occasions does Kate not respond to a request for clarification: she is thus highly sensitive to the dynamics of the interaction, and is actively engaged in communication. The two instances in which

Kate does not respond to an RC may be seen as instances of miscommunication.

In their study of 22 children's reactions to requests for clarification, Anselmi, Tomasello and Acunzo (1986) also found that their subjects mostly responded to requests for clarification and hardly ever ignored them. Our data differ from those of Anselmi et al. (1986), however, in the types of responses given to Type I and Type II RC's (their 'neutral' and 'specific' queries respectively): Anselmi et al. (1986) found that their subjects mainly responded to a Type I RC by simply repeating their original utterance (our category 'No change'), whereas a Type II RC was most often met by a repaired response. No such link is evident in the Kate corpus, but it is well possible that any main effect here has gone unnoticed due to the comparatively few clarification sequences in the Kate corpus (only 82 for Type I and II RC's combined), whereas presumably Anselmi et al.'s (1986) corpus was a lot larger (no absolute figures are given, however).

In Table 10.3 one out of two reactions to an RC constitutes a repaired response. Gallagher's (1977) data for English monolingual children confirm this finding. The question is, what types of elicited repairs did Kate produce?

Repetitions of part of the original utterance (whether in response to a type I or type II RC) account for 38.5% of all repaired responses. In these repairs Kate is doing what Fox and Routh (1975) asked their subjects to do i.e. 'just say a little bit of this': when in a type II RC a particular constituent is questioned, Kate is able to supply the information desired and thus shows some knowledge of sentence and constituent structure. Word order is hardly ever repaired. About a quarter of all prompted repairs are phonological repairs involving modifications of individual phones, volume level or stress pattern. Other kinds of modifications constitute 32.6% of all elicited repairs. The most frequent changes here concern pronouns and verbs (these are morpho-lexical repairs - see section 10.2) and content word substitutions (these are lexical repairs - see also section 10.2). These types of changes also occurred in Kate's spontaneous repairs. Note however that morphological repairs do not appear as elicited repairs, only as spontaneous repairs. This is perhaps because elicited repairs are "repairs for the listener" (Clark and Andersen 1979) rather than "repairs to the system" (ibid.), as spontaneous repairs tend to be.

In the preceding, we have examined elicited repairs and other responses to RC's irrespective of whether they were expressed in English or Dutch. After all, responses to RC's are triggered by the interlocutor, and even if we did find significant differences between both languages in the types of response patterns, these differences would not necessarily be due to the child using language-dependent response strategies: they might very well be linked to the particular individual interacting with the child (that there may be such an 'interactant' effect was found by Anselmi et al. 1986: children in their study tended to respond differently in clarification sequences depending on whether they were talking to their mothers or to an investigator - this effect was found within one language only). Two sequences that would never occur in monolingual children, however, are the following (see examples 11 and 12):

(11) Kate: Nog! Once more time. (Age: 2;7,17) <Again! Once more time!>
   {English utterance addressed to Dutch interlocutor}
   Investigator: Nog ene keer? <One more time?>
   Kate: Ja, ene keer. <Yes, once.>
   {elicited repair in which a previously English utterance is changed into Dutch}
(12) Investigator: Blauw! <Blue!>
   Kate: Jij white!! (Age: 3;0,11) <You white!>
   {Mixed utterance consisting of a Dutch personal pronoun followed by an English colour term}
   Investigator: Wablieft? <What?>
   Kate: Jij wit! <You white!>
   {elicited repair in which a previously English lexical item is changed into Dutch, resulting in a Dutch utterance consisting of a Dutch personal pronoun followed by a Dutch colour term}

Examples 11 and 12 are the only clarification sequences involving a repaired response that constitute a change in language. Both times Kate was speaking to a person she usually uses Dutch with. Her use of English thus was less appropriate than the use of Dutch might have been. In switching to Dutch in her response to the adult's RC, Kate made her utterance sociolinguistically more appropriate.

We shall now examine whether Kate responds differently to a clarification request depending on whether her original utterance (OU) was formally adequate to start with or not. An utterance is here defined as formally adequate if it could pass as an adult utterance, and as formally inadequate if it could not. The findings are tabulated in Table 10.4.

As Table 10.4 shows, Kate does seem to treat formally adequate and formally inadequate OU's differently: responses to RC's after formally adequate OU's stand a two in four chance of being repaired, whereas responses to RC's after formally inadequate OU's stand a three in four chance of being repaired. In addition, formally adequate OU's are changed less often than formally inadequate OU's. There is some evidence, then, that Kate is more aware of the need to repair formally inadequate utterances than formally adequate ones. One might predict that in the course of development the slots for 'changed formally adequate' and 'unchanged formally inadequate' utterances will become virtually empty, since as knowledge of the structure of language develops, an awareness that formally adequate utterances need not be repaired (but rather expanded or repeated) will become more pronounced, as well as the realisation that a hearer's comprehension might be greatly improved if all formally inadequate utterances are repaired. At this stage of development such an awareness is well under way but its results are possibly hampered by doubts as to what constitutes a formally adequate or inadequate utterance: in other words, doubt may still exist as to which structures are part of accepted usage and which are not.

Table 10.4 *Kate's responses to requests for clarification as dependent on the formal adequacy of the original utterance (OU)*

	OU: formally adequate	OU: formally inadequate
Repaired response	$55 \pm 1\%$	$70 \pm 2.5\%$
No change	$24 \pm 1\%$	$15 \pm 2.5\%$
No attention	$3 \pm 1\%$	-
Acknowledgement	$18 \pm 1\%$	$15 \pm 2.5\%$
TOTALS	68	41

Like an adult, the three-year-old under observation is able to remember the utterance she is asked to clarify and the specific request made. She then is able to classify the particular RC and on the basis of this classification she can narrow down the range of possible responses (after having decided she should respond at all of course). She is then able to draw on her knowledge of possible structures and to compare her original utterance with these possibilities. In finally responding she is guided by her choice of various options. Whether her response to the RC will be more adequate than her original utterance will highly depend on her knowledge of possible structures.

The cognitive steps outlined above were ordered sequentially but probably all these steps take place at once. Their operation is guided by the monitor, which is also at work with spontaneous repairs (Clark 1978). We shall come back to a further discussion of the monitor in our concluding remarks.

10.4 Metalinguistic statements

In this section we shall not be dealing with the use that Kate makes of lexical items such as WORD, MEAN, SPEAK and the like as Slobin (1978) did in his study of the emergence of language awareness in his daughter. Rather, we shall be concerned with Kate's direct statements about language and corrections of the language use of others (or comments about it). There are not many instances of these in the material available, but the few that are present are certainly noteworthy (Clark 1978 treats comments on language use as being different from corrections of others whereas here we have subsumed the latter under the main heading of metalinguistic statements. Both, however, according to Clark, "can only stem from a growing awareness [of language]" Clark 1978: 25).

We will proceed in chronological order rather than divide among categories. The first explicit correction of others occurs in Tape 4 at the age of 2;9 (see example 13).

(13) Investigator: Zitten er rozijntjes in de pudding?
    <Are there any little raisins in the pudding?>
    Kate: Nee rozijntjes zijnen. (Age: 2;9) <No little raisins big sins.>
    Investigator: Rozijnen? <Raisins?>
    Kate: Ja! <Yes!>

The point here is that Kate seems to object to the investigator's use of the diminutive. The word ROZIJN <raisin>, however, consists of one morpheme to which the plural ending {-en} can be added or the diminutive ending {-tje} (+ {-s} in the plural). A correction of ROZIJNTJES <little raisins> should thus be ROZIJNEN rather than just *ZIJNEN, which is nonsensical. Kate shows that she has not grasped the morphological make-up of the lexical item ROZIJN, but the important thing is that she insists on correcting A's use of ROZIJNTJES, hence indicating some differential treatment of the {-en} and {-tje} morphemes.

It is clear that Kate is monitoring the investigator's speech production and trying to change it in a case where she thinks this is necessary.

(14) Investigator: Wie is daar? O dag madam, hoe is't met u vandaag?
    <Who is there? O hello madam, how are you today?>
    Kate: Jij bent raar! .(Age: 3;0,17) <You are funny/strange!>

In example 14 Kate explicitly comments on the investigator's use of unusual language: the investigator does not normally address Kate with MADAM <madam>, nor does she use the politeness formula <how are you today?>. Kate noticed this (or at least she has noticed a difference from what is usual) and shows this by commenting on it.

Example 15 contains a very explicit comment on language:

(15) Father: Aah!
    Kate: Aah! (Age: 3;1,13)
    Father: OK.
    Kate: OK.
    Mother: (laughs)
    Kate: He's speaking French!
    Mother: Then he would say Ça va! instead of OK!

It is unclear why Kate would correlate OK (often used by all members of the family in both English and Dutch) with 'speaking French'. More likely than not Kate does not really know what 'French' exactly is. More important, though, is that Kate is taking her father's speech as an object that can be discussed. In order to do this she must possess some degree of awareness of language as a reality by itself.

Example 16 again involves a correction of what an adult said.

(16) Kate: Bu!! (loud noise) (Age: 3;1,18)
    Mother: Hey, don't scream!
    Kate: Bu!!Bu!! No! Bu's not scream, bus just bu!

Here Kate comments on what she perceives to be different (BU versus screaming) and corrects her mother when the latter does not seem to make this distinction. In order to make this correction a certain reflection on the meaning of screaming is necessary, and a reflection on the meaning of a word can be seen as forming part of an awareness of language.

In extract 17 Kate scolds her mother for using a particular word in Dutch incorrectly.

(17) Investigator: Zal ik de tafel dekken? <Shall I lay the table?>
Mother: Ja. First afdekken en dan - (laughs) <Yes. First lay off and then - >
Kate: Afdekken??? .(Age: 3;1,26) <Lay off???> (in a reprimanding tone)
Mother: Afdekken -da's nie een woord hé? <Lay off- thats not a word, is it?
Investigator: Nee. <No.>

Here Kate is monitoring speech going on around her, and not addressed to her. When she notices a discrepancy between what she hears and what she knows of Dutch she makes a comment, although it still is in a rudimentary form. Kate more likely than not would not be able to explicitly tell her mother 'That's not a word in Dutch'.

The next extract (see example 18) shows Kate correcting her mother's use of a preposition.

(18) (Kate's mother is asking Kate what she did with her clothes when she went to the bathroom)
Kate: First the pants. (Age: 3;1,26)
Mother: Yeah.
Kate: And - and then like this!
Mother: Then you - then you'd sit the dress down, so first you put your pants down and then you put the dress down? Is that what you did?
Kate: No put the p - the pants up!
Mother: Up! Jaaa! Of course.

In example 19 Kate reprimands her mother for saying something that presumably she regards as being inappropriate. This reprimand shows an awareness of language to the extent that language as an object is something that can be judged.

(19) Mother: Oh futs!
Kate: Oh futs! Mommy don't say oh futs! (Age: 3;2,7)

In example 20 Kate is protesting against being called 'rhubarb':

(20) Mother: Hi rhubarb!
Kate: I'm not rhubarb! (Age: 3;2,7)
Mother: Oh? Who's rhubarb then?
Kate: Nobody!

In her answer 'nobody' Kate may be considered to know that a person cannot be named 'rhubarb'. A certain degree of awareness of what people can be named is apparent here.

In example 21 Kate notices a difference between what she knows to be the bellybutton's name and what her father is saying. She explicitly comments on this and corrects her father (she probably has not realised that her father has been teasing her). This type of statement in which first a form is negated and then the form that is felt to be more appropriate is given is quite different from simply naming something. In naming no reflection on the name as such is needed; in correcting others on the use of names their speech must be monitored and comparisons must be drawn between one's own knowledge of forms and the forms that one hears. This requires a high degree of awareness of the forms as such.

(21) Father: Wat een nagel in die buik! <What a navel in that belly!>
   (i.e. Kate's belly)
   Investigator: Ja! Goh! Bijna zo groot als de neus!
   <Yeah! Gosh! Nearly as big as the nose!>
   Father: Ja! Een nagelneus. <Yes! A navelnose.>
   (the investigator and Kate's father are teasing Kate)
   Kate: Nee da's nie nagelneus das alleen de navel! (Age: 3;3,9)
   <No that's not navelnose thats only the navel!>
   Father: Alleen de navel. OK. Alleen de navel.
   <Only the navel. OK. Only the navel.>

In connection with the previous example (we briefly stray from our chronological order here) it may of interest to note that, quite regularly, Kate corrects the use of a particular word by her interlocutor (see example 22). Usually, however, these instances concern cases where Kate herself has used an inappropriate word, and is then corrected by the adult but insists on her original word, after which the adult gives the conventional label, perhaps accompanied by an explanation of why this label rather than the one that Kate used is the right one. After such an explanation or simple insistence on a different label by the interlocutor, Kate usually accepts the 'new' word as being what she should use. We are here dealing with mini-discussions on appropriate words for specific referents. The child is monitoring the speech of her interlocutor and comparing it with what she knows about the languages she speaks. With each correction by the adult, Kate has to let go of her earlier idea of what the name of a specific thing was. In accepting the adult's suggestion, Kate implicitly accepts the arbitrariness of the relation between an object and the form used to refer to it. As such, her behaviour can be seen to show some degree of awareness of language.

(22) Investigator: En wie is da? <And who is that?>
   (Kate and the investigator are looking at a picture book and

naming the pictures in it; the investigator is pointing at a cow)
Kate: Po - a pig! (Age: 2;11,14)
Investigator: Neu!! Da. <No!! That.>
Kate: Ja!!! Da! <Yes!!!! That!>(in a insisting voice while pointing at a cow)
Investigator: D_at is het varken. <Th_at's the pig.> (while pointing at a pig)
Kate: Nee, d_as de varken! <No, th_at's the pig!> (while pointing at a cow)
Investigator: Nee, dat is de k_oe! <No, that's the cow!>
Kate: Dat is de koe! (accepting the investigator's label)
Investigator: Ja. <Right.>

In the following extract (see example 23) Kate is constantly correcting a phonetic aspect of the investigator's speech.

(23) Investigator: Wat hebt al - heb't gallemaal gespeeld mé Rapali?
    <What kinds of games did you play with Rapali?>
Kate: Rupali! (Age: 3;3,16)
Investigator: Mm? Alleen maar eh - . <Mm? Only just eh - .>
Kate: Pali!
Investigator: Bali?
Father: R_upali!
Investigator: R_upali?
Father: Ja. t Is R_upali, nie Rapali. <Yes. Its Rupali, not Rapali.>
Investigator: Oh pardon. <Oh sorry.>
Father: Dit wil zij - <This is what she wants - >
Investigator: Mm.
Kate: Ehm!
Father: - ter kennis brengen. < - to tell you.>
Father: (to Kate) Hé, 't is toch R_upali da ze heet é, nie R_apali. R_upali.
    <Right? Her name is Rupali, isn't it, not Rapali. Rupali.>
Kate: (acknowledges)
Father: Dat dacht ik ook. <That's what I thought.>

Here Kate corrects the investigator's 'Rapali' into 'Rupali', the name of a favourite friend at school. A little later the following exchange occurs (see example 24):

(24) Investigator: Rapali ook? <Rapali also?>
Kate: Eh! (Age: 3;3,16) (strongly reprimanding tone)
Investigator: Rupali ook? <Rupali also?>
Kate: Ja. <Yes.>
Investigator: Mm.
Kate: Nie Rapali! <Not Rapali!>
Investigator: Nee! Zeg het's voor mij. Ik kan da nie goe.
    <You're right. Could you say it for me? I can't say it properly.>
Kate: Rupali.
Investigator: Rupali.

In this extract it is very clear that Kate is attending to the form of the interlocutor's utterances and that there is a concern on her part that her friend's name be pronounced the way she thinks it should be. An awareness that pronunciation makes a difference seems to be present. Again two forms are compared with one another, one is found lacking and another one is chosen as being preferable.

In the following and last extract, however, Kate shows that she is aware of language use to quite a high degree (as is the case for the name 'Kate', all Christian names are pseudonyms):

(25) Investigator: Jij noemt papa toch ook soms Robert, hé?
 <You sometimes call daddy Robert, don't you?>
Kate: Nee pappie! (Age: 3;3,16) <No daddy!>
Investigator: Pappie - ja, OK. En hoe noem - hoe noem jij mama?
 <Daddy - right, OK. And what do you call mommy?>
Kate: Sue! (in high voice)
Investigator: Sue! (imitates Kate) Nee! (laughs) <No!>
Kate: Ja! <Yes!>
Investigator: Nee! Jij zegt mammie! Mam'a! Zo doe jij.
 <No! You say mommy! Mommy! Thats what you do.>
Kate: Nee ik doet - soms - Sue! (again high voice) Su-ue?
 <No I sometimes does Sue!>
Investigator: Ja? <Really?> (surprised)
Kate: Ja! <Yes!>
Investigator: Hohohoho! En wa zegt mama dan?
 <And what does mammy say then?>
Kate: OK! (in high funny voice)

In this sequence Kate responds to questions about her language use in other situations. Whether what she says is true or not is not very important: more telling is her ability to reflect upon language use. Language is taken as an objective reality and discussed as such: here we are truly dealing with metalinguistic statements.

In retrospect, then, metalinguistic statements by Kate fall in the following categories:

(1) Correcting others:
 - morphology (example 13)
 - word meaning/labelling (examples 16, 17, 18, 20, 21)
 - pragmatics (example 19)
 - phonology (examples 23, 24)

(2) Commenting on language use:
   - style (example 14)
   - particular language used (example 15)
   - naming (example 25).

Since 11 out of the 12 clear instances of metalinguistic statements listed occur after Kate's third birthday we can confirm Eve Clark's (1978) finding for monolingual children that 'explicit comments on language seem to begin around the age of three' (Clark 1978: 22). The English-German bilingual girl Joanna reported on by Clyne (1987), on the other hand, already made quite explicit comments on language use soon after her second birthday. Whether Joanna was precocious or whether Kate's use of such comments was a bit 'delayed' in comparison with other bilingual children cannot be determined for lack of sufficient comparison material.

10.5 Hesitations and self-repetitions

Although Clark (1978) suggests that 'repeated attempts at a word in the presence of a listener should be labeled as repairs' (Clark 1978: 30) we have not labelled self-repetitions and hesitations as repairs since no need for self-correction is apparent in these.

In our material, hesitations and self-repetitions occur on all linguistic levels. Their occurrence remains fairly constant throughout the study and there is no differential use of hesitations depending on language used (see section 5.1 in Chapter 5); however, we shall not analyse them in any detail. Suffice it to point out that in self-repetitions linguistic items are repeated and the utterance completed without any change to the items that were repeated. Obviously some monitoring of one's on-going speech is required here and concomitantly some awareness of the units of language (in order to be able to repeat chunks of one's utterances one must have some idea of what constitutes an acceptable chunk). In our material the following categories were repeated quite frequently:

- single words of all types
- word groups forming a single constituent or Subject--finite verb or Verb--Direct Object combinations
- first phonemes of morphemes.

10.6 Other metalinguistic behaviour

In his discussion of the emergence of language awareness in his young daughter, Slobin (1978) mentions her babbling in foreign sounds and her inventions of words of her own. Kate, also, frequently engaged in these: her parents noticed that Kate would often utter Gujarati-like sounds. This they did not find surprising since the preschool Kate went to had quite a number of children from Bombay who spoke Gujarati with one another. Some of Kate's word inventions include *POEDEN (Dutch; an action probably referring to something to do with flying in the air) and *POKKELEN (Dutch; an action probably referring to a particular type of tickling). When Kate utters strange sounds she often laughs very strangely or affectedly, sometimes as if she is embarrassed or as if she is engaging in something very private and mysterious. Once in a while a conversation similar to the following one would occur (see example 26):

(26) Kate: Papa! (Age: 3;3,9) <Daddy!>
 Father: Ja-a! <Ye-es!>
 Kate: [pikasəlabeinawan] ! (very matter of fact tone) <= ???>
 Father: Aja? Daar zeg je nu eens iets Kate.
  <Oh really? You don't say so, Kate.>
 Investigator: Da verstaan wij nie. <That we don't understand.>
 Father: Nee. <No, we don't.>
 Investigator: Wa betekent da? <What does that mean?>
 Kate: [wataʃu:wa] ! Wa is da nu? (laughs strangely)
  <= ???. What could that be?>
 Investigator: Ja, wat is da? <Right, what could that be?>
 Kate: [ka:ka:jo:ja:] [ka:ka:jo:j] - ! (laughs) <= ???>
 Investigator: [ka:ka:jo:ja:] ? <= ???>
 Kate: [ka:ka:jo:ja:] ! (laughs) <= ???>
 Father: Aja. Dat zal dan wel hé. <Right, well, I guess so.>
 Investigator: Spreekt Rap - <Does Rap speak - >
 Kate: [ka:ka:jo:ja:] <= ???>
 Investigator: Spreekt Rapali zo? <Does Rapali speak like that?>
 Kate: Rupali! <Rupali!>
 Inves'tigator: Rupali?
 Kate: k Weet het nie. <I dont know.>
 Investigator: Spreekt die zo?<Does she speak like that?>
 Kate: Ja. (whispered) <Yes.>

Whether Kate was correct in saying that her Indian friend Rupali speaks in words like [ka:ka:jo:ja:] we shall never know. Kate's laughing after she has uttered the strange sounds would seem to indicate that Kate is giving these words (sounds) a special place, that they are not 'normal'. Thus an awareness of their strangeness seems to be present.

10.7 General discussion and conclusion

The main impetus behind the present chapter was the search for a possible reason for the quite drastic changes in Kate's two language systems after the age of three. Have we found such a possible reason? The answer here can at best be: 'perhaps'. Indeed, we did find changes in types of behaviour that we have labelled 'metalinguistic', such as spontaneous repairs and explicit comments on or corrections of other people's speech productions (not all researchers, though, would concede that spontaneous repairs constitute a type of metalinguistic behaviour - see e.g. Hakes 1982). Such changes clearly took place after Kate's third birthday. However, while there is a strong correlation between these changes in signs of metalinguistic behaviour and the changes in Kate's language production in general, the one is not necessarily a driving force behind the other; instead, it is possible (and even probable) that there is a symbiotic relationship between the two types of behaviour, without there being any uni-directional and decisive influence from the one on the other. The latter possibility, of course, cannot be excluded, but the data in the present study do not allow any direct causal relationship to be observed.

This rather disappointing result - which, admittedly, could have been predicted at the outset, notwithstanding the theoretical possibility that indeed metalinguistic abilities are a crucial factor in children's language development as suggested by Clark (1982) - does not mean, I believe, that this chapter has been a waste of time and effort. On the contrary, it has taught us more about the capability of the young language-learning child to use that mechanism which is at the root of any further metalinguistic abilities, viz. the monitor.

Lindsay and Norman (1977) see the 'monitor' as a cognitive mechanism that "oversees the operations, deciding when they are productive and when they are not, exercising an overall guidance to the operation of the [cognitive] system" (Lindsay and Norman 1977: 367). The monitor can focus its attention on all types of behaviour, including language behaviour. As such, monitoring is "een cognitieve strategie gericht op het bewaken van een op optimale communicatie gerichte taalproductie of - in gevallen waar geen directe communicatie in het geding is - van de specifieke, niet-communicatieve doelen van de taalproductie (bijvoorbeeld bij taalleer- of taalreflectie-taken)" (Hagen 1981: 42). [3] How do we see the role of the monitor in the various characteristics of Kate's speech production that we labelled 'metalinguistic'? In answering this question, we shall proceed from cases where we assume that there is little monitoring going on to cases where the monitor is considered to be of crucial importance.

Sound-play can be seen as involving perhaps just a little bit of monitoring, in the sense that vocal sounds are played with for their own sake. To what extent we are actually dealing with any metalinguistic behaviour here, however, is not clear: perhaps sound-play is pre-metalinguistic behaviour. When sound-play and 'nonsense' are emitted in the presence of interacting individuals, any ensuing embarrassment on the child's part may be seen as a first sign that (s)he has some notion of what is appropriate in the communicative context and what is not. It is here that the 'little bit of monitoring' comes in. It should be added, though, that sound-play is not necessarily inappropriate within the communicative context, and that its level of appropriateness will very much depend on the interlocutor's attitude to it. Children are sensitive to this, and will be delighted (and quite surprised) to hear an adult engage in sound-play and nonsense. This delight and surprise is a further sign that sound-play and nonsense are somehow experienced as 'different' from 'normal' speech. For any such experience to take place, some monitoring is required.

In hesitations, the speaker shows a lack of control or a slowness in processing (i.e. producing) an utterance. Rather than the monitoring of already produced speech, hesitations and self-repetitions may be seen as the result of monitoring one's speech production before it is realized. Monitoring here, then, is very much connected with the speech production process, and gives the speaker a chance to better plan the rest of the utterance by 'holding off' for a while. The speaker, in other words, has some time to consider the rest of the utterance by inserting a pause, a term like 'eh', and a self-repetition.

In spontaneous repairs, one's own speech is looked upon as something that can be changed, either in order to be more easily understood or to be more appropriate in terms of linguistic structure. The monitor needs to be quite sophisticated here since it needs to have access to detailed information about the regularities that govern speech production at any particular stage of development. For sound-play no such access was necessary and neither was there for hesitations. In spontaneous repairs, steps are retraced when a (linguistic) action is not satisfactory; this situation can be likened to e.g. the case where one starts up a car but one's foot slips off the accelerator by accident and by this time the car has stalled so one has to start it up all over again, this time paying more attention to what one is doing. This can happen on a very automatic level (so for instance without an interruption of the conversation one is having with one's passenger). Yet one must have an idea of what the total action should look like and this is where monitoring comes in.

In elicited repairs the monitor must be able to function at the request of an outside source. The temporal distance between one's (linguistic) actions and the products of reflecting on them (the repairs) is quite large. The monitor is highly sophisticated since it is now not only able to monitor productions of one's own system but also signals coming from another individual.

In correcting others, one's own productions are irrelevant: what is monitored is speech from another individual that is not necessarily related to anything one has said oneself; incoming signals are compared to one's knowledge of the relevant linguistic structures and when a discrepancy is found a corrective response is the result. The monitor is highly sophisticated (more so than with elicited repairs) since it must be able to immediately guide the hearer's attention to the relevant part of his linguistic knowledge. This guiding is only necessary when the monitor notices something odd, i.e. something that does not correspond with the knowledge the monitor user has: thus the monitor itself possesses a very sophisticated knowledge of what its owner knows.

In comments on language use the distance between using a body of knowledge and reflecting upon it is greatest. This is the level where a certain degree of consciousness of one's actions becomes apparent. Language is lifted out of concrete situations and is discussed *in abstracto*. The distance between one's actions and one's reflection upon them is very great. The monitor is extremely sophisticated here. Although Kate shows the beginnings of such sophisticated monitor use, she is not yet able to be as explicit in her comments on language use as the Dutch-speaking five-year-old in the following extract from my unpublished data:

(27) David: Ik eet het. (Age: 36)
<Im eating it.>
(uttered <u>before</u> the speaker was about to eat a pear)
(David is an adult learner of Dutch whose first language is English)
Liesbeth: Hij zegt: ik eet het, maar ge moet zeggen: ik ga het opeten.
(Age: 5;6)
<He says: Im eating it, but you have to say: Im going to eat it.>

The roots for such explicit comments, however, are firmly present soon after the age of three.

The picture that emerges is one of a cognitive mechanism that is highly *dynamic* in nature since it is constantly shifting its attention to fulfil the increased needs of the learner (various changes in children's metalinguistic abilities over time are the clearest evidence for this - see e.g. Berthoud-Papandropoulou 1978, Clark 1978, Januschek, Paprotté and Rohde 1979, Sinclair 1982, Hoppe and Kess 1983, Rogers 1983, Konefal and Fokes 1984). The monitor becomes more and more sophisticated as time goes on in the sense that it becomes more and more able to distance itself from the operations it is overseeing towards a position from where these can be 'observed' best.

It is only through the workings of the monitor that an awareness of language can develop (see also Marshall and Morton 1978): awareness of something (whether conscious or not) implies a distance of sorts, the opportunity to view something as a whole (in this case anything pertaining to language) and reflect on it. This distance is provided by the monitor. Since the finesse, nature and focus of the monitor are shifting all the time, presumably as a result of the constant flux of all cognitive systems as a whole, concomitant features such as awareness of language will change as well. Thus both the monitor and awareness of language are highly dynamic concepts.

Although the child under observation in this study is a bilingual child we have not focused on this aspect except in order to show that it was safe to speak of the development of metalinguistic abilities in general rather than the development of metalinguistic abilities in a particular language.

Several researchers have claimed that experience in a bilingual environment may positively influence rate of metalinguistic development (Slobin 1978, Saywitz and Wilkinson 1982). Such claims must remain suggestions at this point, however, since no comparisons have taken place between monolingual and bilingual children that could unequivocally settle the issue (but see Cummins 1978a and Galambos and Goldin-Meadow 1983).

The fact that the metalinguistic abilities discovered in Kate appear to be language-independent implies that use of the monitor is so as well. This conclusion fits in well with theories of bilingual processing (see e.g. Obler and Albert 1978) and with theories of language awareness in monolinguals (see e.g. Clark 1978, Marshall and Morton 1978, Clark and Andersen 1979). In the latter theories, however, empirical evidence for the hypothesis that there is a general, language-independent mechanism such as the monitor which provides a basis for the development of language awareness is conspicuously absent: after all, data from monolinguals cannot logically provide any evidence for any language-independent bases for behaviour. The bilingual child, on the other hand, offers the ideal testcase for hypotheses in this area. Although the relevant data reported on in the present study have been rather limited on the quantitative level (see primarily section 10.2 on spontaneous repairs), they do support the language-independent and hence probably universal nature of the monitoring mechanism. Much more evidence is needed, however, to investigate this intriguing issue in more depth.

Notes
1 It has also been claimed that metalinguistic abilities have an influence on metacognitive abilities (see e.g. Pratt and Grieve 1980; on metacognition, see e.g. Flavell 1979).
2 There is another study (Hagen 1981) in which self-corrections as used by Dutch-speaking children are discussed. However, in this study there was no sub-analysis of the types of spontaneous repairs produced, and the data were collected by means of a production task. Hence, neither the data nor the analysis are really comparable to the data for Kate.
3 Approximate translation: 'monitoring is a cognitive strategy oriented towards ensuring that language production serves an optimal communication, or, in non-communicative contexts, monitoring is a cognitive strategy controlling specific, non-communicative goals of language production (as for instance in language learning or language reflection tasks)'.

11 Findings and implications

In Chapter 3 we introduced two hypotheses about the acquisition process in young bilingual children exposed to two languages from birth in a separate fashion: the separate development hypothesis, which proposes that a bilingual child's morphosyntactic development proceeds along separate, non-intersecting lines for each language, and the transfer theory, which proposes that morphosyntactic development in the one language is carried over into the other. When in Chapter 3 we discussed the possible empirical bases on which to approach either hypothesis, it was pointed out that for each of the languages that the child was exposed to we would need a corpus of child utterances consisting of lexical items from one language only. In the present study investigating the speech production of a young Dutch-English bilingual girl, Kate, two such sets of data were present: we collected a substantial number of utterances containing both only Dutch and only English lexical items. Thus, we were able to address the question whether and to what extent Kate's two languages were developing separately as far as morphosyntactic features go.

In the analyses of Kate's use of morphology and syntax (cf. Chapters 6, 7 and 8) we were trying to find positive evidence for the separate development hypothesis. Such evidence was abundant: in all aspects of language use investigated that provided unambiguous opportunities for discovering either the presence or the absence of inter-linguistic interaction, we were able to show that Kate's developing morphosyntactic knowledge of Dutch could not function as a basis for her speech production in English, or vice versa. Instead, Kate mostly used Dutch morphosyntactic devices when producing utterances with only Dutch lexical items, and English morphosyntactic devices when producing utterances with only English lexical items. Furthermore, not only were the morphosyntactic devices themselves usually relatable to only one language, they were also used in a language-specific manner. Therefore, I believe it has been convincingly demonstrated that the Separate Development Hypothesis accurately describes a major part of Kate's bilingual acquisition process. In stating this, I am claiming that the morphosyntactic development of a pre-school child regularly exposed to two languages from birth which are presented in a separate manner proceeds in a separate fashion for both languages. Inter-linguistic interaction in this case, then, is considered to be peripheral at best, and certainly not a fundamental aspect of the bilingual child's acquisition process. Thus the transfer theory can be rejected.

As far as was possible using the available literature, we drew comparisons between Kate's Dutch speech production and that of monolingual Dutch-speaking children and between Kate's English speech production and that of monolingual English-speaking children. In most of the cases investigated, Kate was found to use English and Dutch in the same way as the monolingual children reported on.

Thus it seems that Kate can, so to speak, be seen as two monolingual children in one. This generalization does not, however, accurately and fully capture Kate's linguistic capabilities. After all, Kate is able to alternate languages both at and within utterance boundaries (see Chapter 5), a type of behaviour that is considered to be typical of bilinguals anywhere: Hasselmo (1972), for instance, sees the very use of Mixed utterances (or 'code-switching', as he calls it) as constituting "an aspect of a bilingual's competence" (Hasselmo 1972: 261). Poplack (1980) goes as far as to suggest that code-switching, i.e. the "alternation of two languages within a single discourse, sentence or constituent" (Poplack 1980: 583), is "a sensitive indicator of bilingual ability" (Poplack 1980: 581). Furthermore, she sees code-switching as the "skilled manipulation" (Poplack 1980: 601) of a bilingual's two languages. This skill, Poplack says, is, amongst others, shown by a smooth transition between elements of either language. Such smooth transition is also noticeable in Kate's production of Mixed utterances: these are not marked by an unusual number of false starts, hesitations, or lengthy pauses. Similarly, Kate's changes in language choice (i.e. at utterance boundaries) are fluent and in no way distinct from her use of consecutive utterances in the same language. According to Poplack's criteria, Kate is a skilled code-switcher.

The metaphor of Kate as a 'double monolingual', then, is a reductionist and simplistic one. Kate is, for all intents and purposes, already fully bilingual by the age of 2;7 (i.e., at the time that formal data collection began): in producing speech, she uses phonological, lexical and morphosyntactic elements drawn from two input systems, and secondly, within one and the same discourse she is able to rapidly and fluently alternate between Mixed, English and Dutch utterances. [1] In these alternations, Kate is guided by a sophisticated sociolinguistic knowledge of her interlocutors.

Although Kate usually expresses herself adequately and although she can verbally communicate a wide range of messages, she does not yet quite speak like the people around her. When we consider her use of English and Dutch as separate systems, it is clear that at the age of 3;4 (i.e. around the time of the last data collection session), Kate still has a lot to learn about the morphosyntax of both these languages. When we look at Kate's behaviour that is considered unique to bilinguals, we also see that Kate still has some things to learn: a few 'insertions' in Kate's Mixed utterances involve elements which would not normally be inserted into Mixed utterances by adult bilinguals, and Kate occasionally addresses a monolingual speaker either in a Mixed utterance or in a language that this speaker is not really familiar with. This is not usually done by adult bilinguals (cf. e.g. Baetens Beardsmore 1982).

It was hypothesized that Kate would increasingly come to resemble both older monolingual speakers of either language and bilingual speakers in general thanks to the development of metalinguistic knowledge. We investigated this hypothesis by looking at various possible behavioural signs of such metalinguistic knowledge (see Chapter 10), but while we could not find any counterevidence for the hypothesis, we did not really find any unambiguous positive evidence for it either.

Finally, we briefly return to the three major questions in the field of BFLA as discussed in Chapter 2. The first of these concerned the issue of eventual language differentiation vs. independent development of a bilingual child's languages from the very beginning of speech production. In the exploration of Kate's language development we have not addressed this issue: whether Kate went through a 'language separation' phase cannot be determined, since already from the beginning of the study onwards (i.e. at age 2;7) she was capable of producing utterances in both languages that fully conformed to adult usage in either. Hence, her languages were already 'separated' (but see section 2.2.2 in Chapter 2 for a critique of the use of this term). Since we did not study Kate from the time that she started to produce speech, we were in no position to address the converse of the differentiation hypothesis, viz. the Independent Development Hypothesis.

The second question raised in Chapter 2 was whether bilingual children's language development in their two languages proceeds along similar lines as in monolingual children acquiring only one of these. In the most general of terms, and limiting our answer to morphosyntactic aspects and some signs of metalinguistic behaviour, we can say that the development of language does appear to run parallel in our bilingual subject and monolingual children.

Thirdly, there was the question of whether there is a link between the fashion in which the input systems are presented to the child and the way in which the child develops his two languages (see section 2.2 of Chapter 2). This question, again, has not been empirically investigated in the present study, and must remain fundamentally unanswered.

In the following we shall explore some implications of what we see as the most significant finding of the empirical study presented in this book, namely the confirmation of the Separate Development Hypothesis.

In our analysis of the Kate corpus, we did not initially treat the data as consisting of basically two closed sets. After all, it remained to be investigated whether such a treatment would be valid. In any future analyses of similar data, and in any re-analyses of the Kate corpus, however, one could quite acceptably start by first examining most of the morphosyntactic developments within Dutch only, and then proceed to look at English (or vice versa of course). In the descriptions of the input systems there would be no need for cross-references to the other language. In addition, a separate analysis method would require no comparisons between the child's English and Dutch speech productions. Instead, the two input systems and their separate development by the child would be seen as fully independent from one another on the morphosyntactic level, and both in the description of the input systems and in that of the child's speech productions formal elements within each system could be related and compared to other such elements within the same system.

In effect, such a method would most closely reflect the actual acquisition process: since Kate's speech production can be adequately described in language-specific terms, this suggests that she is approaching each of her two languages as closed sets with their own internal structures.

Such a highly language-specific approach can only take place if very close attention is paid to the input - in the bilingual child's case, to the two separate input systems. After all, the language-specific formal elements used by the bilingual child are correlatable <u>solely</u> to the input systems that the child is exposed to.

This is not to imply that there is a direct, one-to-one relationship between the environment's input and the child's output. Rather, the child's mind acts as a creative agent on the two input systems, filters them, manipulates them and transforms them. However, in so doing, the bilingual child keeps the two systems virtually completely separate, thereby retaining a very close connection with either one of the input systems. Thus, it is in the first place the concrete realities of two specific languages that guide the bilingual three-year-old in her development, rather than, for instance, general principles of learning applicable to Language in the abstract. More likely than not, such general principles do operate, but if so, they apparently are not that strong that they can cross language boundaries. Instead, they are held captive, so to speak, by the particular system that the child is trying to learn. On the process level, we can thus speculate that rather than a single-storage model with two outputs it is a dual-storage model in which each store leads to its own output that is a realistic metaphor.

The bilingual child's close attention to the input and her concomitant unfailing reflection of it can be seen as a result of the seemingly all-important drive that presumably underlies the bilingual acquisition process, namely the child's need to speak like the people around him.

A second finding of the present study was that the bilingual child's morphosyntactic development in either language closely reflects the morphosyntactic development in her monolingual peers. This suggests that in each of her languages the bilingual child is following similar acquisition strategies as monolingual children - or indeed, vice versa. Since here there is much similarity and little difference between the bilingual and the monolingual child, it is perhaps not unreasonable to assume that the fundamental approach to the language acquisition task is also highly similar in both. This has brought us back to our claim in Chapter 1 that findings from bilingual children are relevant to theoretical concerns in the field of child language in general.

Phrasing the implications of the present study's findings concerning a bilingual child in more general terms, we believe that this study has provided strong support for a theory of language acquisition that sees the child's attention to the concrete linguistic reality that he lives in as central to the acquisition process: the language-learning child's main guiding force is to speak like the people around him. In trying to do this, the child actively manipulates, analyses and organizes the 'data' that he has gathered through closely attending to the language(s) spoken around him. This manipulation, analysis and organization, however, does not exist *ab initio* or *ex nihil* , but is engrafted onto the concrete material the child is working with, i.e. the specific language(s) he is trying to learn.

Thus, the present study has highlighted the language-specific nature of morphosyntactic development.

The proposal that language-specific factors are of great importance in the acquisition process is by no means new. Karmiloff-Smith (1979) and Bowerman (1985), for instance, strongly emphasize the significant influence in development of the specific structural (and semantic) properties of the language the young child is exposed to. On the basis of Quiche acquisition data, Pye (1987) also concludes that children "demonstrate a remarkable sensitivity to the unique properties of the language they are attempting to learn" (Pye 1987: page 10 in MS). Mills suggests that "the course of acquisition is linked closely to the structural properties of the language concerned" (Mills 1986a: 31), basing her argument on a comparative study of monolingual children's learning of the English and German natural gender rules.

In the field of monolingual acquisition, however, such claims about the importance of language-specific or input-related developments must, I believe, remain tentative. After all, there are too many possibly confounding factors that might play a role when one compares different children acquiring different languages (cf. Chapter 1). Studies of bilingual first language acquisition, however, can be used to disentangle these factors. The available data on bilingual children that could be used to address the theoretical issue of the relative importance of language-specific factors in acquisition support the claims mentioned in the previous paragraph: both the research presented here and the work done by Meisel (1985, 1986, i.p.) would seem to confirm that indeed morphosyntactic development is a highly language-specific process.

Since the study presented in this book was a case study of a single child, its results are not necessarily generalizable to other children. Nevertheless I hope to have indicated a fruitful direction for further investigations of bilingual children's language development. My main hope, however, is that researchers in the field of monolingual acquisition research will come to realize the wealth of insights that the study of bilingual children can offer them.

Notes
1 We have no intention here of defining what the term 'bilingual' means in general (for a review of possible characterizations and some of the problems involved, see e.g. Baetens Beardsmore 1982), or of giving a view of what might constitute minimal criteria for the definition of this term. We are simply giving one possible characterization which seems to adequately sum up the situation at hand.

References

Aldenhoff, Jules, 1979. 'Ein Beispiel für die Entwicklung deutsch-französischer Zweisprachigkeit eines Kleinkindes in einem sprachlichen Uebergangsgebiet'. In: Nelde, ed., 1979: 133-147.

Appel, René, 1984. Immigrant children learning Dutch. Sociolinguistic and psycholinguistic aspects of second-language acquisition. Dordrecht: Foris Publications.

Anonymous, 1982. Zelfverbetering en valse starts. Unpublished manuscript. Amsterdam: Universiteit van Amsterdam.

Anselmi, Dina, Michael Tomasello and Mary Acunzo, 1986. Young children's responses to neutral and specific contingent queries. Journal of child language 13: 135-144.

Arnberg, Lenore, 1979. Language strategies in mixed nationality families. Scandinavian journal of psychology 20: 105-112.

Arnberg, Lenore, 1981. Early childhood bilingualism in the mixed-lingual family. Summary. Linkœping Studies in Education Dissertations No. 14, Linköping University, Dept. of Education.

Arnberg, Lenore, 1987. Raising children bilingually: the pre-school years. Clevedon: Multilingual Matters.

Baetens Beardsmore, Hugo, ed., 1981. Elements of bilingual theory. Brussels: Vrije Universiteit Brussel.

Baetens Beardsmore, Hugo, 1982. Bilingualism: basic principles. Clevedon: Tieto Ltd.

Baetens Beardsmore, Hugo and Roland Willemyns, eds., 1981. Linguistic accommodation in Belgium. Brussels pre-prints in linguistics. Brussels: Vrije Universiteit Brussel.

Bain, Bruce, 1976. Verbal regulation of cognitive processes: A replication of Luria's procedures with bilingual and unilingual infants. Child Development 47: 543-546.

Barrett, Martin, 1983. 'The early acquisition and development of the meanings of action-related words'. In: Seiler and Wannenmacher, eds., 1983, 191-209.

Bates, Elizabeth and Brian MacWhinney, 1982. 'Functionalist approaches to grammar'. In: Wanner and Gleitman, eds., 1982, 173-218.
Bellugi, Ursula, 1971. 'Simplification in children's language'. In: Huxley and Ingram, eds., 1971, 95-117.
Bergman, Coral Rhodes, 1976. 'Interference vs. independent development in infant bilingualism'. In: Keller, Teschner and Viera, eds., 1976, 86-96.
Bergman, Coral Rhodes, 1977. Problems in the developmental psycholinguistics of bilingualism: language acquisition and language use. Unpublished Ph.D. thesis. San Diego, CA: University of California.
Berkele, Gisela, 1983. Die Entwicklung des Ausdrucks von Objektreferenz am Beispiel der Determinanten. Eine empirische Untersuchung zum Spracherwerb bilingualer Kinder (Französisch/Deutsch). Unpublished thesis: University of Hamburg.
Berman, Ruth, 1979. The re-emergence of a bilingual: a case study of a Hebrew-English speaking child. Working papers on bilingualism 19: 157-180.
Berman, Ruth, 1986. 'A crosslinguistic perspective: morphology and syntax'. In: Fletcher and Garman, eds., 1986, 429-447.
Berthoud-Papandropoulou, Ionna, 1978. 'An experimental study of children's ideas about language'. In: Sinclair et al., eds., 1978, 55-64.
Bloom, Lois and Margaret Lahey, 1978. Language development and language disorders. New York: John Wiley and Sons.
Bloom, Lois, Karin Lifter and Jeremie Hafitz, 1980. Semantics of verbs and the development of verb inflection in child language. Language 56: 386-412.
Bol, Gerard and Kuiken, Folkert, 1986. Het gebruik van pronomina bij kinderen van een tot vier. Toegepaste taalwetenschap in artikelen 24: 47-58.
Bol, Gerard and Folkert Kuiken, 1987. The development of morphosyntax in Dutch children from one to four. Belgian journal of linguistics 2.
Bol, Gerard and Folkert Kuiken, 1988. Grammaticale analyse van taalontwikkelingsstoornissen. Unpublished Ph. D. dissertation, University of Amsterdam, Amsterdam.
Bowerman, Melissa, 1985. 'What shapes children's grammar?'. In: Slobin, ed., 1985b, 1257-1320.

Brainerd, Charles and Michael Pressley, eds., 1982. Verbal processes in children. Progress in cognitive development research. Berlin: Springer Verlag.
Breston, A.F.L., 1970. The Arabic language today. London: Hutchinson University Library.
Bridges, A., 1980. SVO comprehension strategies reconsidered: the evidence of individual patterns of response. Journal of child language 7: 89-104.
Brown, Roger, 1973. A first language. The early stages. Cambridge, Massachusetts:Harvard University Press.
Brown, Roger, 1978. 'The development of WH-questions in child speech'. In: Bloom, ed., 1978, 239-253.
Brown, Roger and Camille Hanlon, 1970. 'Derivational complexity and order of acquisition in child speech'. In: Hayes, ed., 1970, 11-53.
Bubenik, Vit, 1978. 'The acquisition of Czech in the English environment'. In: Paradis, ed., 1978, 3-12.
Bybee, Joan and Dan Slobin, 1982. Rules and schemas in the development and use of the English past tense. Language 58: 265-289.
Cazden, Courtney, 1973. 'The acquisition of noun and verb inflections'. In: Ferguson and Slobin, eds., 1973, 226-240.
Cazden, Courtney, Sarah Michaels and Patton Tabors, 1984. 'Spontaneous repairs in sharing time narratives: the intersection of metalinguistic awareness, speech event and narrative style'. In: Freedman, ed., 1984.
Chesterfield, Ray and Ray Pérez, 1981. Dual language acquisition among Hispanic preschoolers in bilingual settings. The bilingual review/La revista bilingüe 8: 20-27.
Chiat, Shulamuth, 1978. The analysis of children's pronouns: an investigation into the prerequisites for linguistic knowledge. Unpublished Ph.D. dissertation, University of London 1978.
Chiat, Shulamuth, 1986. 'Personal pronouns'. In: Fletcher and Garman, eds., 1986, 339-355.
Chomsky, Noam, 1986. Knowledge of language. Its nature, origin and use. New York: Praeger.
Chukerman, Amy, Mitchell Marks and John Richardson, eds., 1983. Papers from the Nineteenth Regional Meeting. Chicago: Chicago linguistic society.

Chun, Judith Anne, 1978. 'Selected processes in second language acquisition'. In: Nickel, ed., 1978, 93-107.

Clark, Eve, 1978. 'Awareness of language: some evidence from what children say and do'. In: Sinclair et al., eds., 1978, 17-43.

Clark, Eve, 1982. 'Language change during language acquisition'. In: Lamb and Brown, eds., 1982, 171-195.

Clark, Eve, 1985. 'The principle of contrast: a constraint on language acquisition'. In: MacWhinney, ed., 1985.

Clark, Eve and Elaine Andersen, 1979. Spontaneous repairs: awareness in the process of acquiring language. Papers and reports on child language development 16: 1-12.

Clark, Eve and Herbert Clark, 1977. Psychology and language: an introduction to psycholinguistics. New York: Harcourt Brace Jovanovich.

Clark, Eve and Barbara Hecht, 1982. Learning to coin agent and instrument nouns. Cognition 12: 1-24.

Clyne, Michael, 1987. '"Don't you get bored speaking only English?" Expressions of metalinguistic awareness in a bilingual child'. In: Steele and Threadgold, eds., 1987, 85-103.

Collins, W., ed., 1979. Children's language and communication. Hillsdale, N.J.: Lawrence Erlbaum Associates.

Comrie, Bernard, 1981. Language universals and linguistic typology. Syntax and morphology. Oxford: Basil Blackwell.

Crystal, David, 1974. Review of Roger Brown's A first language. Journal of child language 1: 289-334.

Crystal, David and Derek Davy, 1969. Investigating English style. London: Longman.

Crystal, David, Paul Fletcher and Michael Garman, 1976. The grammatical analysis of language disability. A procedure for assessment and remediation. London: Edward Arnold.

Cummins, James, 1978a. Bilingualism and the development of metalinguistic awareness. Journal of cross-cultural psychology 9: 131-148.

Cummins, James, 1978b. 'Sensitivity to non-verbal communication as a factor in language learning'. In: Nickel, ed., 1978, 109-117.

de Haan, Ger, 1986a. A theory-bound approach to the acquisition of verb placement. Unpublished manuscript. Utrecht: University of Utrecht.

de Haan, Ger, 1986b. De rol van morfologie en syntaxis in de ontwikkeling van het werkwoord. Glot 9: 28-41.

De Houwer, Annick, 1987. Two at a time: an exploration of how children acquire two languages from birth. Unpublished Ph.D. thesis. Brussels: Vrije Universiteit Brussels.

de Jong, Eveline, ed., 1979. Spreektaal. Woordfrequenties in gesproken Nederlands. Utrecht: Bohn, Scheltema & Holkema.

De Jonghe, H. and W. De Geest, 1985. Nederlands, je taal. Van In: Lier.

De Schutter, G. and P. van Hauwermeiren, 1983. De structuur van het Nederlands. Malle: De Sikkel.

Deuchar, Margaret and Angeles Clark, 1987. 'Infant bilingualism: are there two voicing systems?'. In: Proceedings of the 1987 Child Language Seminar, University of York, York, 1-12.

Deutsch, Werner, ed., 1981. The child's construction of language. London: Academic Press.

Deutsch, Werner and Frank Wijnen, 1985. The article's noun and the noun's article: explorations into the representation and access of linguistic gender in Dutch. Linguistics 23: 793-810.

De Vooys, C., 1916. Iets over woordvorming en woordbetekenis in kindertaal. De nieuwe taalgids 10: 93-100/128-141.

de Vriendt, Sera, to appear. Nederlands in Nederland en in Vlaanderen. To appear in Neerlandica Wratislaviensia, Wroclaw, Poland.

de Vriendt, Sera and Piet van de Craen, 1986. Over plaatsingsmogelijkheden van schakeringspartikels. Interdisciplinair tijdschrift voor taal- en tekstwetenschap (TTT) 6: 101-116.

de Vriendt-de Man, M.J., 1971. Frequentie van woorden en structuren in spontaan gesproken Nederlands. Brussel: Didier.

Dodson, Carl, 1981. 'A reappraisal of bilingual development and education: some theoretical and practical considerations'. In: Baetens Beardsmore, ed., 1981, 14-27.

Dominicy, Marc, ed., 1980. Linguistics in Belgium 5. Brussels: Didier Hatier.

Donaldson, Margaret, Robert Grieve and Chris Pratt, eds., 1983. Early childhood development and education. Readings in psychology. Oxford: Basil Blackwell.

Dore, J., M. Franklin, R. Miller and A. Ramer, 1976. Transitional phenomena in early language acquisition. Journal of child language 3: 13-28.

Doyle, Anna-Beth, Mireille Champagne, Norman Segalowitz, 1978. 'Some issues in the assessment of linguistic consequences of early bilingualism'. In: Paradis, ed., 1978: 13-20.
Ellul, Sonia, 1978. A case study in bilingualism. Code-switching between parents and their pre-school children. Cambridge: Huntington Publishers Ltd.
Elwert, W. T., 1959. Da zweisprachige Individuum. Ein Selbstzeugnis. Mainz: Akademie der Wissenschaften und Kultur.
Erreich, Anne, 1984. Learning how to ask: patterns of inversion in *yes-no* and *wh-* questions. Journal of child language 11: 579-592.
Extra, Guus, 1977. 'Taalontwikkeling'. In: Taaldidactiek aan de basis, Groningen: Nijmeegse Werkgroep.
Extra, Guus, 1978. Eerste- en tweede-taalverwerving. De ontwikkeling van morfologische vaardigheden. Muiderberg: Coutinho.
Fantini, Alvino, 1978a.' Bilingual behavior and social cues: case studies of two bilingual children'. In: Paradis, ed., 1978, 283-302.
Fantini, Alvino E., 1978b. Emerging styles in child speech: case study of a bilingual child. The bilingual review/La revista bilingüe 5: 169-189.
Ferguson, Charles and Dan Slobin, eds., 1973. Studies of child language development. New York: Holt, Rinehart and Winston.
Fillmore, Charles, Daniel Kempler and William Wang, eds., 1979. Individual differences in language ability and language behavior. New York: Academic Press.
Flavell, John, 1979. Metacognition and cognitive monitoring. A new area of cognitive-developmental inquiry. American psychologist 34: 906-911.
Fletcher, Paul, 1979. 'The development of the verb phrase'. In: Fletcher and Garman, eds., 1979, 261-284.
Fletcher, Paul, 1981a. Description and explanation in the acquisition of verb-forms. Journal of child language 8: 93-108.
Fletcher, Paul, 1981b. Verb-form development: lexis or grammar?. Paper presented at the second International Congress for the Study of Child Language, Vancouver, August 1981.
Fletcher, Paul, 1985. A child's learning of English. Oxford: Basil Blackwell.
Fletcher, Paul and Michael Garman, eds., 1979. Language acquisition. Cambridge: Cambridge University Press.
Fletcher, Paul and Michael Garman, eds., 1986. Language acquisition (second edition). Cambridge: Cambridge University Press.

Fox, Barbara and Donald Routh, 1975. Analyzing spoken language into words, syllables, and phonemes: a developmental study. Journal of psycholinguistic research 4: 331-341.

Freedman, S., ed., 1984. The acquisition of written language: revision and response. Norwood, N.J.: Ablex.

French, Ann, 1987. No want [ə] play in [ə] 'garden/'play in [ə] hòuse [ə] bike/: some early strategies for dealing with function words. In: Proceedings of the 1987 Child Language Seminar, University of York, York, 67-80.

French, Peter and Margaret MacClure, eds., 1981. Adult-child conversation. London: Croom Helm.

Fromkin, Victoria, ed., 1980a. Errors in linguistic performance. Slips of the tongue, ear, pen, and hand. New York: Academic Press.

Fromkin, Victoria, 1980b. 'Introduction'. In: Fromkin, ed., 1980a, 1-12.

Furrow, David, Katherine Nelson and Helen Benedict, 1979. Mothers' speech to children and syntactic development: some simple relationships. Journal of child language 6: 423-442.

Galambos, Sylvia and Susan Goldin-Meadow, 1983. 'Learning a second language and metalinguistic awareness'. In: Chukerman et al., eds., 1983, 117-133.

Gallagher, Tanya, 1977. Revision behaviors in the speech of normal children developing language. Journal of speech and hearing research 20: 303-318.

Gathercole, Virginia, 1986. The acquisition of the present perfect: explaining differences in the speech of Scottish and American children. Journal of child language 13: 537–560.

Geerts, G., W. Haeseryn, J. de Rooij and M.C. van den Toorn, 1982. Algemene Nederlandse Spraakkunst. Groningen: Wolters-Noordhoff.

Gerhardt, Julie and Iskender Savasir, 1986. The use of the simple present in the speech of two three-year-olds: Normativity not subjectivity. Language in society 15: 501-536.

Gerritsen, Marinel, 1980. 'An analysis of the rise of SOV patterns in Dutch'. In: Traugott et al., eds., 1980, 123-136.

Gillis, Steven, 1984. De verwerving van talige referentie. Unpublished Ph.D. thesis. Antwerpen: Universitaire Instelling Antwerpen.

Greenberg, J.H., ed., 1978. Universals of human language. Volume 4: Syntax. Stanford: Stanford University Press.

Grosjean, François, 1982. Life with two languages. An introduction to bilingualism. Cambridge, Massachusetts: Harvard University Press.

Grossman, R., L. San and T. Vance, eds., 1975. Papers from the parasession on functionalism. Chicago: Chicago Linguistic Society.

Hagen, A., 1981. Standaardtaal en dialectsprekende kinderen. Een studie over monitoring van taalgebruik. Muiderberg: Dick Coutinho.

Hakes, David, 1982. 'The development of metalinguistic abilities: what develops?'. In: Kuczaj, ed., 1982, 163-210.

Hakuta, Kenji, 1978, c. 1974. 'A report on the development of the grammatical morphemes in a Japanese girl learning English as a second language'. In: Hatch, ed., 1978, 133-147.

Halliday, M.A.K., 1985. An introduction to functional grammar. London: Edward Arnold.

Harding, Edith and Philip Reilly, 1987. The bilingual family. A handbook for parents. Cambridge: Cambridge University Press.

Harrison, Godfrey and A. Piette, 1980. Young bilingual children's language selection. Journal of multilingual and multicultural development 1: 217-230.

Hasselmo, Nils, 1972. 'Code-switching as ordered selection'. In: Scherabon Firchow, Grimstad, Hasselmo and O'Neill, eds., 1972, 261-280.

Hatch, Evelyn, ed., 1978. Second language acquisition. A book of readings. Rowley, MA: Newbury House.

Hayes, John, ed., 1970. Cognition and the development of language. New York: John Wiley and Sons.

Hoffman, Charlotte, 1985. Language acquisition in two trilingual children. Journal of multilingual and multicultural development 6: 479-495.

Hoffman, Charlotte, and Francisco Ariza, 1979. Bilingualism in a two year old child. Polyglot 1, No. 2.

Hofmans, Mark. 'Hebben of zijn en de deverbalisering van de modale werkwoorden in het Nederlands'. In: Dominicy, ed., 1980, 81-97.

Hoppe, Ronald and Joseph Kess, 1983. The acquisition of metalinguistic abilities. Rassegna italiana di linguistica applicata 15: 105-120.

Huang, Joseph, and Evelyn Hatch, 1978. 'A Chinese child's acquisition of English'. In: Hatch, ed., 1978, 118-131.

Hudson, Richard, 1984. Word grammar. Oxford: Basil Blackwell.

Huerta, Ana, 1977. The acquisition of bilingualism: a code-switching approach. Sociolinguistic working paper number 39. Austin: University of Texas.

Hurford, James, 1975. A child and the English question formation rule. Journal of child language 2: 299-301.

Huxley, R. and E. Ingram, eds., 1971. Methods and models in language acquisition. New York: Academic Press.

Hyltenstam, Kenneth and Loraine Obler, eds., 1989. Bilingualism across the lifespan. Cambridge: Cambridge University Press.

Ianco-Worrall, A.D., 1972. Bilingualism and cognitive development. Child development 43: 1390-1400.

Idiazabal, Itziar, 1988. First verbal productions of a bilingual child learning Basque and Spanish simultaneously. Analysis of the noun phrase. Paper presented at the First Hamburg symposium on multilingualism, Hamburg, September 1988.

Imedadze, N.V., 1960. K psikhologicheskoy prirode rannego dvuyazychiya. Vopr. psikhol. 6: 60-68.

Imedadze, Natela and D. Uznadze, 1978, c. 1967. 'On the psychological nature of child speech formation under condition of exposure to two languages'. In: Hatch, ed., 1978: 33-37.

Ingram, David and Dorothy Tyack, 1979. Inversion of Subject NP and Aux in children's questions. Journal of psycholinguistic research 8: 333-341.

Iwamura, Susan, 1980. The verbal games of pre-school children. London: Croom Helm.

Jansen, Frank, 1980. 'Development in the Dutch left-dislocation structures and the verb-second constraint'. In: Traugott et al., eds., 1980, 137-149.

Januschek, F., W. Paprotté and W. Rohde, 1979. 'The growth of metalinguistic knowledge in children'. In: Van de Velde and Vandeweghe, eds., 1979, 243-254.

Jarovinskij, Alexandr, 1979. On the lexical competence of bilingual children of kindergarten age groups. International Journal of Psycholinguistics 6-3 [15]: 43-57.

Jekat, Susanne, 1985. Die Entwicklung des Wortschatzes bei bilingualen Kindern (Frz.-Dt.) in den ersten vier Lebensjahren. Unpublished Master's Thesis. Hamburg: University of Hamburg, Dept. of Romance Languages.

Jisa, Harriet, 1987. Quand papa était loin: l'importance du contexte linguistique chez les bilingues précoces. Paper presented at the Colloque contacts de langues: quels modèles?, Nice, September 1987.

Kagan, Jerome, 1984. The nature of the child. New York: Basic Books.

Kaltenbacher, Erika, 1987. Production strategies and the acquisition of German word order. Paper presented at the Fourth International Congress for the Study of Child Language, Lund, Sweden, 1987.

Karmiloff-Smith, Annette, 1979. A functional approach to child language. Cambridge: Cambridge University Press.

Käsermann, Marie-Louise and Klaus Foppa, 1981. 'Some determinants of self correction: an interactional study of Swiss-German'. In: Deutsch, ed., 1981, 77-104.

Keeney, Terrence and Jean Wolfe, 1972. The acquisition of agreement in English. Journal of verbal learning and verbal behavior 11: 698-705.

Keller, G.D., R.V. Teschner and S. Viera, eds., 1976. Bilingualism in the bicentennial and beyond. New York: Bilingual Press/Editorial Bilingüe.

Kessler, Carolyn, 1971. The acquisition of syntax in bilingual children. Washington: Georgetown University Press.

Kielhöfer, Bernd and Sylvie Jonekeit, 1983. Zweisprachige Kindererziehung. Tübingen: Stauffenberg Verlag.

Klein, Rudolf, 1974. Word order: Dutch children and their mothers. Publikaties van het instituut voor algemene taalwetenschap 9. Amsterdam: Universiteit van Amsterdam.

Klima, Edward and Ursula Bellugi, 1973. 'Syntactic regularities in the speech of children'. In: Ferguson and Slobin, eds., 1973, 333-353.

Konefal, Joanne and Joann Fokes, 1984. Linguistic analysis of children's conversational repairs. Journal of psycholinguistic research 13: 1-11.

Koster, Jan, 1975. 'Dutch as a SOV language'. In: Kraak, ed., 1975, 165-177.

Kraak, A., ed., 1975. Linguistics in the Netherlands 1972-1973. Assen: Van Gorcum.

Kuczaj, Stan, 1977. The acquisition of regular and irregular past tense forms. Journal of verbal learning and verbal behaviour 16: 589-600.

Kuczaj, Stan, 1981. The acquisition of copula and auxiliary BE forms. Papers and reports on child language development 20: 78-83.

Kuczaj, Stan, ed., 1982. Language development. Volume 2. Hillsdale, New Jersey: Lawrence Erlbaum Associates.

Labov, William, 1969. Contraction, deletion, and inherent variability of the English copula. Language 45: 715-762.

Lamb, Michael and Ann Brown, eds., 1982. Advances in developmental psychology. Volume 2. Hillsdale, New Jersey: Lawrence Erlbaum Associates.

Langford, David, 1981. 'The clarification request sequence in conversation between mothers and their children'. In: French and MacClure, eds., 1981, 159-174.

Lanza, Elizabeth, 1987. Code-mixing and code-switching in the bilingual infant's discourse. Paper presented at the Fourth International Congress for the Study of Child Language, Lund, Sweden, 1987.

Lattey, Elsa, 1981. 'Individual and social aspects of bilingualism'. In: Baetens Beardsmore, ed., 1981, 48-65.

Laver, John, 1973. 'The production of speech'. In: Lyons, ed., 1973, 53-75.

Lee, Victor, ed., 1979. Language development. London: Croom Helm.

Leemans, Margaretha and Brigitte Ramaekers, 1982. De volgorde van Subject-Object-Verbum in Nederlandse kindertaal. Unpublished Master's Thesis. Leuven: Katholieke Universiteit Leuven.

Lempert, H. and M. Kinsbourne, 1980. Preschool children's sentence comprehension: strategies with respect to word order. Journal of child language 7: 371-379.

Leopold, Werner, 1953. Patterning in children's language learning. Language learning 5: 1-14.

Leopold, Werner, 1970, c. 1939-49. Speech development of a bilingual child. A linguist's record. 4 Volumes. New York: AMS Press.

Leopold, Werner, 1978, c. 1954. 'A child's learning of two languages'. In: Hatch, ed., 1978, 24-32.

Levelt, Willem, 1983. Monitoring and self-repair in speech. Cognition 14: 41-104.

Limber, John, 1973. 'The genesis of complex sentences'. In: Moore, ed., 1973, 169-185.

Lindholm, Kathryn, 1980. 'Bilingual children: some interpretations of cognitive and linguistic development'. In: Nelson, ed., 1980, 215-266.

Lindholm, Kathryn and Amado Padilla, 1978a. Child bilingualism: report on language mixing, switching and translations. Linguistics 211: 23-44.

Lindholm, Kathryn and Amado Padilla, 1978b. Language mixing in bilingual children. Journal of child language 5: 327-335.

Lindholm, Kathryn, Amado Padilla, and Arturo Romero, 1979. Comprehension of relational concepts: use of bilingual children to separate cognitive and linguistic factors. Hispanic journal of behavioral sciences 1: 327-343.

Lindsay, Peter and Donald Norman, 1977. Human information processing. An introduction to psychology. New York: Academic Press.

Linnakylä, Pirjo, 1980. Hi Superman: what is most functional English for a Finnish five-year-old. Journal of pragmatics 5: 508-513.

Lipski, John, 1978. 'Code switching and the problem of bilingual competence'. In: Paradis, ed., 1978: 263-277.

Lowenthal, F., F. Vandamme and J. Cordier, eds., 1982. Language and language acquisition. New York: Plenum Press.

Lyons, John, ed., 1973. New horizons in linguistics. London: Penguin.

Lyons, John, 1977. Semantics. Volume 2. Cambridge: Cambridge University Press.

MacWhinney, Brian, ed., 1985. Mechanisms of language acquisition. Hillsdale, New Jersey: Lawrence Erlbaum Associates.

Maratsos, Michael, 1982. 'The child's construction of grammatical categories'. In: Wanner and Gleitman, eds., 1982, 240-266.

Maratsos, Michael and Stanley Kuczaj, 1978. Against the transformationalist account: a simpler analysis of auxiliary overmarking. Journal of child language 5: 337-345.

Maratsos, M., S. Kuczaj II, D. Fox and M. Chalkley, 1979. 'Some empirical studies in the acquisition of transformational relations: passives, negatives, and the past tense'. In: Collins, ed., 1979, 1-11.

Marshall, John and John Morton, 1978. 'On the mechanics of Emma'. In: Sinclair et al., eds., 1978, 225-239.

Martinez Jr., J. L. and R. H. Mendoza, eds., 1984. Chicano Psychology. Orlando: Academic Press.

Matthews, P.H., 1982. Syntax. Cambridge: Cambridge University Press.

McClure, Erica, 1977. 'Aspects of code-switching in the discourse of bilingual Mexican-American children'. In: Saville-Troike, ed., 1977, 93-115.

McClure, Erica, and Jim Wentz, 1975. 'Functions of code switching among Mexican- American children'. In: Grossman, San and Vance, eds., 1975, 421-432.

McLaughlin, Barry, 1978. Second-language acquisition in childhood. Hillsdale, NJ: Lawrence Erlbaum Associates.

McLaughlin, Barry, 1984. Second-language acquisition in childhood: Volume 1. Preschool children second edition. Hillsdale, NJ: Lawrence Erlbaum Associates.

Meisel, Jürgen, 1985. Les phases initiales du développement de notions temporelles, aspectuelles et de modes d'action. Étude basée sur le langage d'enfants bilingues français-allemand. Lingua 66: 321-374.

Meisel, Jürgen, 1986. Word order and case marking in early child language. Evidence from simultaneous acquisition of two first languages: French and German. Linguistics 24: 123-183.

Meisel, Jürgen, i.p. 'Early differentiation of languages in bilingual children'. Manuscript as prepared for and now published as a chapter in Hyltenstam and Obler, eds., 1989.

Métraux, Ruth, 1965. A study of bilingualism among children of U.S.-French parents. The French Review 38.

Meys, W.J., 1975. 'The English comitative. A doubtful case?'. In: Kraak, ed., 1975, 178-186.

Mikès, Melanija, 1967. Acquisition des catégories grammaticales dans le langage de l'enfant. Enfance 967: 289-298.

Mikès, M. and P. Vlahovic, 1966. Razvoj gramatickih kategorija u decjem govoru. Prilozi proucavanju jezika II. Novi Sad.

Miller, J., 1981. Assessing language production in children: experimental procedures. London: Edward Arnold.

Mills, Anne, 1985. 'The acquisition of German'. In: Slobin, ed., 1985b, 141-254.

Mills, Anne, 1986a. Acquisition of the natural-gender rule in English and German.Linguistics 24: 31-45.

Mills, Anne, 1986b. Review of T. Taeschner's The Sun is Feminine. Linguistics 24: 825-833.

Mills, Anne, 1986c. The acquisition of gender. A study of English and German. Berlin: Springer-Verlag.

Moore, T.E., ed., 1973. Cognitive development and the acquisition of language. New York: Academic Press.

Nelde, Peter, ed., 1979. Deutsch als Muttersprache in Belgien. Wiesbaden: Franz Steiner.

Nelson, Katherine, Leslie Rescorla, Janice Gruendel and Helen Benedict, 1978. Early lexicons: what do they mean? Child development 49: 960-968.

Nelson, Keith, ed., 1980. Children's language. Volume 2. New York: Gardner Press.

Nickel, G., ed., 1978. Psycholinguistics. Stuttgart: Hochschul Verlag.

Nooteboom, Sieb, 1969. The tongue slips into patterns. Nomen: 114-132.

Nooteboom, Sieb, 1980. 'Speaking and unspeaking: detection and correction of phonological and lexical errors in spontaneous speech'. In: Fromkin, ed., 1980, 87-95.

Nuckle, Lucie and Kerry Lappin, 1982. Sur la notion d'erreur et de développement linguistique chez de jeunes bilingues. In: Pupier et al., eds., 1982, 63-87.

Obler, Loraine K. and Martin L. Albert, 1978. 'A monitor system for bilingual language processing'. In: Paradis, ed., 1978, 156-164.

Olmsted, D., 1971. Out of the mouth of babes. The Hague: Mouton.

Padilla, Amado and Ellen Liebman, 1975. Language acquisition in the bilingual child. The bilingual review/La revista bilingüe 2: 34-55.

Padilla, Amado and Kathryn Lindholm, 1984. 'Child bilingualism: the same old issues revisited'. In: Martinez Jr. and Mendoza, eds., 1984: 369-408.

Palmer, Frank, 1974. The English verb. London: Longman.

Paradis, Michel, ed., 1978. Aspects of bilingualism. Columbia, South Carolina: Hornbeam Press.

Parisi, D., and F. Antinucci, 1973. Elementi di grammatica. Turin: Boringhieri.

Peters, Ann, 1983. The units of language acquisition. Cambridge: Cambridge University Press.

Pfaff, Carol, 1985. The problem of plurifunctionality in bilingual language acquisition. Papers and reports on child language development 24: 95-103.

Poplack, Shana, 1980. Sometimes I'll start a sentence in Spanish Y TERMINO EN ESPANOL: toward a typology of code-switching. Linguistics 18: 581-618.

Porsché, Donald, 1983. Die Zweisprachigkeit während des primären Spracherwerbs. Tübingen: Gunter Narr Verlag.

Pratt, Chris and Robert Grieve, 1980. The role of language awareness in cognitive development. Education research and perspectives 7: 69-79.

Pupier, Paul, Kathleen Connors, Kerry Lappin, Wendy Greene and Lucie Nuckle, eds., 1982. L'acquisition du français et de l'anglais chez des petits enfants de Montréal. Québec: Gouvernement du Québec.

Pye, Clifton, 1986. The acquisition of syntax in Quiche Mayan. Paper presented at the Fourth International Congress for the Study of Child Language, Lund, Sweden, 1987.

Quirk, Randolph and Sidney Greenbaum, 1973. A university grammar of English. London: Longman.

Quirk, Randolph, Sidney Greenbaum, Geoffrey Leech and Jan Svartvik, 1985. A comprehensive grammar of the English language. London: Longman.

Redlinger, Wendy, 1979. Early developmental bilingualism: a review of the literature. The bilingual review/La revista bilingüe 6: 11-30.

Redlinger, Wendy and Tschang-Zin Park, 1980. Language mixing in young bilinguals. Journal of child language 3: 449-455.

Richards, Brian, 1986. Yes/No questions in input and their relationship with rate of auxiliary verb development in young children. Proceedings of the 1986 Child Language Seminar, University of Durham, Durham.

Rijpma, E., and F. Schuringa, 1971. Nederlandse spraakkunst. Groningen: Wolters-Noordhoff.

Rogers, Sinclair, 1983. 'Self-initiated corrections in the speech of infant-school children'. In: Donaldson et al., eds., 1983, 75-82.

Ronjat, Jules, 1913. Le développement du langage observé chez un enfant bilingue. Paris: Champion.

Rosansky, Ellen, 1976. Methods and morphemes in second language acquisition. Papers and Reports on Child Language Development 12: 199-212.

Saunders, George, 1980. Adding a second native language in the home. Journal of multilingual and multicultural development 1: 113-144.

Saunders, George, 1982. Bilingual children: guidance for the family. Clevedon: Multilingual Matters.

Saunders, George, 1988. Bilingual children: from birth to teens. Clevedon: Multilingual Matters.

Saville-Troike, Muriel, ed., 1977. Linguistics and anthropology. Georgetown University Round Table on Languages and Linguistics. Washington: Georgetown University.

Saywitz, Karen and Louise Cherry Wilkinson, 1982. 'Age-related differences in metalinguistic awareness'. In: Kuczaj, ed., 1982, 229-250.

Schaerlaekens, Anne-Marie, 1977. De taalontwikkeling van het kind. Een oriëntatie in het Nederlandstalig onderzoek. Groningen: Wolters-Noordhof.

Schaerlaekens, A. M. and S. Gillis, 1987. De taalverwerving van het kind. Een hernieuwde oriëntatie in het Nederlandstalig onderzoek. Groningen: Wolters-Noordhoff.

Seiler, Thomas and Wolfgang Wannenmacher, eds., 1983. Concept development and the development of word meaning. Berlin: Springer-Verlag.

Shatz, Marilyn and Karen Ebeling, 1987. "What are bicycle call means?". Child initiated learning behaviors in the third year. Paper presented at the Fourth International Congress for the Study of Child Language, Lund, Sweden, 1987.

Sinclair, Anne, 1982. 'Children's judgments of inappropriate speech acts'. In: Lowenthal et al., eds., 1982, 273-281.

Sinclair, A., R. Jarvella and W. Levelt, eds., 1978. The child's conception of language. Berlin: Springer-Verlag.

Slobin, Dan, 1973. 'Cognitive prerequisites for the development of grammar'. In: Ferguson and Slobin, eds., 1973, 175-208.

Slobin, Dan, 1978. 'A case study of early language awareness'. In: Sinclair et al., eds., 1978, 45-54.

Slobin, Dan I., 1985a. 'Crosslinguistic evidence for the language-making capacity', in Slobin, ed., 1985b, 1157-1256.

Slobin, Dan I., ed., 1985b. The crosslinguistic study of language acquisition. Hillsdale, N.J.: Lawrence Erlbaum Associates.

Slobin, Dan, 1985c. 'Introduction: Why study acquisition crosslinguistically?'. In: Slobin, ed., 1985b, 3-24.

Slobin, Dan and Thomas Bever, 1982. Children use canonical stentence schemas: A crosslinguistic study of word order and inflections. Cognition 12: 229-265.

Smith, Carlota, 1980. The acquisition of time talk: relations between child and adult grammars. Journal of child language 7: 263-278.

Smith, Madorah, 1935. A study of the speech of eight bilingual children of the same family. Child development 6: 19-25.

Smith, Neilson, 1973. The acquisition of phonology. A case study. Cambridge: Cambridge University Press.

Smout, H., 1980. Het Antwerps dialect. Antwerpen/Amsterdam: Standaard.

Snow, Catherine, 1977. 'Mothers' speech research: from input to interaction'. In: Snow and Ferguson, eds., 1977, 31-49.

Snow, C., A. Arlman-Rupp, Y. Hassing, J. Jobse, J. Joosten and J. Vorster, 1976. Mother's speech in three social classes. Journal of psycholinguistic research 5: 1-20.
Snow, Catherine and Charles Ferguson, eds., 1977. Talking to children. Language input and acquisition. Cambridge: Cambridge University Press.
Snow, C., N. Smith and M. Hoefnagel-Höhle, 1980. The acquisition of some Dutch morphological rules. Journal of child language 7: 539-553.
Sridhar, S. and Kamal K. Sridhar, 1980. The syntax and psycholinguistics of bilingual code mixing. Studies in the Linguistic Sciences 10: 203-215.
Steele, Ross and Terry Threadgold, eds., 1987. Language topics. Essays in honour of Michael Halliday. Amsterdam: John Benjamins.
Steele, Susan, 1978. 'Word order variation: a typological study'. In: Greenberg, ed., 1978, 585-623.
Stockwell, Robert, 1981. On the history of the verb-second rule in English. Paper presented at ICEHL II, Odense, April 1981.
Stoops, Yvette, 1980. Introduction to Smout 1980.
Swain, Merrill, 1972. Bilingualism as a first language. Unpublished Ph.D. thesis. Irvine, CA: University of California.
Swain, Merrill, and Mari Wesche, 1975. Linguistic interaction: case study of a bilingual child. Language sciences 37: 17-22.
Tabouret-Keller, Andrée, 1963. l'Acquisition du langage parlé chez un petit enfant enmilieu bilingue. Problemes de psycholinguistique 8: 205-219.
Taeschner, Traute, 1983. The sun is feminine: A study on language acquisition in bilingual children. Berlin/Heidelberg: Springer.
Templin, Mildred, 1957. Certain language skills in children. Their development and interrelationships. Minneapolis: The University of Minnesota Press.
Theissen, S., 1984. De semantisch-syntactische valentie van enkele connecterende adverbiale partikels. In: Van der Auwera and Vandeweghe, eds., 1984, 89-101.
Tinbergen, D., 1919. Kinderpraat. De nieuwe taalgids 13: 1-16/65-86.
Tracy, Rosemarie, 1987. The acquisition of verb placement in German. In: Proceedings of the 1987 Child Language Seminar, University of York, York, 81-94.
Traugott, Elizabeth, 1972. A history of English syntax. New York: Holt, Rinehart and Winston.

Traugott, Elizabeth, Rebecca Labrum and Susan Shepherd, eds., 1980. Papers from the fourth International Conference on Historical Linguistics. Amsterdam: John Benjamins.

Tsushima, William and Thomas Hogan, 1975. Verbal ability and school achievement of bilingual and monolingual children of different ages. Journal of educational research 68: 349-353.

Tyack, Dorothy and David Ingram, 1977. Children's production and comprehension of questions. Journal of child language 4: 211-224.

Van de Craen, Piet, 1982. Sociale linguïstiek. Bouwstenen voor een interaktionele linguïstiek op hermeneutische grondslag. Unpublished Ph.D. dissertation. Brussel: Vrije Universiteit Brussel.

Van de Velde, M. and W. Vandeweghe, eds., 1979. Sprachstruktur, Individuum und Gesellschaft. Volume 1. Tübingen: Niemeyer Verlag.

Van der Auwera, Johan and Willy Vandeweghe, eds., 1984. Studies over Nederlandse partikels. Antwerp papers in linguistics 35. Antwerpen: Universitaire Instelling Antwerpen.

van Driel, H., I. van Driel-Karthaus, G. Extra, M.L. Loffeld, J. van Peer and A. Peeters, 1975. Morfologische differentiatie in kindertaal: de ontwikkeling van het werkwoordensysteem. Manuscript: Katholieke Universiteit Nijmegen.

Van Ginneken, Jacques, 1917. De roman van een kleuter. Malmberg: Nijmegen.

van Ierland, Margreet, 1979. Complex sentences in the spontaneous speech of four to eight year olds. Paper presented at the MPGPP/NIAS Child Language Conference, June 1979, Nijmegen.

van Ierland, Margreet, 1983. Loont tellen in taal? Een pleidooi voor meer kwantitatieve taalkunde vanuit taalverwervings-onderzoek. Gramma 7: 269-280.

van Wijk, Carel and Gerard Kempen, 1985. A dual system for producing self-repairs in spontaneous speech. Evidence from experimentally elicited corrections. Unpublished manuscript. Nijmegen: University of Nijmegen.

Verhulst-Schlichting, Liesbeth, 1985. De ontwikkeling van het werkwoord: plaats, vorm, type. Interdisciplinair tijdschrift voor taal- en tekstwetenschap (TTT) 5: 285-298.

Verlinden, An, 1987. Woordfrequentie in de input en de lexicale verwerving van het kind. Unpublished Master's thesis. Antwerpen: Universitaire Instelling Antwerpen.

Vihman, Marilyn May, 1981a. A developmental perspective on code-switching: conversations between a pair of bilingual siblings. Paper presented at the Second International Congress for the Study of Child Language, Vancouver, 1981.

Vihman, Marilyn, 1981b. Phonology and the development of the lexicon: evidence from children's errors. Journal of child language 8: 239-264.

Vihman, Marilyn May, 1985. Language differentiation by the bilingual infant. Journal of child language 12: 297-324.

Vihman, Marilyn May and Barry McLaughlin, 1982. 'Bilingualism and second language acquisition in children'. In: Brainerd and Pressley, eds., 1982, 35-58.

Vila, Ignasi and Javier Zanón, 1986. Learning to regulate joint action. Paper presented at the Developmental Psychology Section Conference, University of Exeter, September 1986.

Vogel, Irene, 1975. One system or two: an analysis of a two-year-old Romanian-English bilingual's phonology. Papers and reports on child language development 9: 43-62.

Vogel, Irene, Rita Harder, Allard Jongman, Dik Nagtegaal, Els den Os, Aimé vanReydt, Vera Slockers, 1980. De ontwikkeling van de Nederlandse morfologie. Unpublished manuscript. Amsterdam: Universeit van Amsterdam.

Volterra, Virginia and Traute Taeschner, 1978. The acquisition and development of language by bilingual children. Journal of Child Language 5: 311-326.

Wagner-Gough, Judy, 1978, c. 1975. 'Comparative studies in second language learning.' In: Hatch, ed., 1978, 156-171.

Wanner, Eric and Lila Gleitman, eds., 1982. Language acquisition. The state of the art. Cambridge: Cambridge University Press.

Weist, Richard, 1983. The word order myth. Journal of child language 10: 97-106.

Weist, Richard and Katarzyna Witkowska-Stadnik, 1986. Basic relations in child language and the word order myth. International journal of psychology 21: 363-381.

Wells, Gordon, 1979. 'Learning and using the auxiliary verb in English'. In: Lee, ed., 1979, 250-270.

Wells, Gordon, 1985. Language development in the pre-school years. Cambridge: Cambridge University Press.

Wells, Gordon, 1986. 'Variation in child language'. In: Fletcher and Garman, eds., 1986, 109-139.
Wijnen, Frank, 1984. De mentale representatie van grammaticale geslachten bij kinderen tussen 4 en 9 jaar. Unpublished Master's Thesis. Utrecht: Rijksuniversiteit Utrecht.
Willemyns, Roland, 1981. 'Interaction of dialect and standard language: the case of Netherlandic-speaking Belgium'. In: Baetens Beardsmore and Willemyns, eds., 1981, 22-44.
Wong-Fillmore, Lily, 1979. 'Individual differences in second language acquisition'. In: Fillmore, Kempler and Wang, eds., 1979, 203-228.
Yau, Shun-Chiu, 1979. Natural word order in child language? International journal of psycholinguistics 6: 21-43.

Appendix

Table 1 *Kate's utterances: language preserving or not?* [a]

TAPES:	1	2	3	4	5	6	7	8	9	10	11	12	13	14	15	16	17	18	19	TOTAL
A. English [b]																				
E/MME-E %	60.0	*27.7*	-	-	*93.7*	-	*64.5*	*71.0*	*90.3*	*80.4*	*94.6*	*90.6*	*94.1*	*97.4*	*97.6*	*93.7*	*97.9*	*33.3*	*16.7*	*81.0*
E/MME-not E %	40.0	72.3	100	100	6.3	100	35.5	29.0	9.7	19.6	5.4	9.4	5.9	2.6	2.4	6.3	2.1	66.7	83.3	19.0
Kate's English utts. =	10	112	9	2	79	2	62	62	31	46	74	32	34	114	125	95	94	3	12	998
B. Dutch [c]																				
D/MMD-D %	95.3	*97.6*	100	100	*96.4*	100	100	*99.0*	*97.9*	100	100	*94.9*	100	100	84.2	*98.5*	*99.3*	100	100	99.2
D/MMD-not D %	4.7	2.4	-	-	3.6	-	-	1.0	2.1	-	-	5.1	-	-	15.8	1.5	.7	-	-	.8
Kate's Dutch utts. =	43	166	18	362	139	515	171	210	47	74	20	39	48	4	19	134	135	252	370	2766

[a] In all of the following tables, totals that are very small (under 20) are printed in italics; it is acknowledged that of course percentages involving totals less than 100 are in effect meaningless. Any percentages involving generally low totals, then, are simply presented to facilitate an easier reading of the data, and to indicate the most general of trends
[b] E/MME-E stands for English and Mixed mainly English utterances either in response to English or to an English speaker and E/MME-not E for English and Mixed mainly English utterances not in response to English or to an English speaker
[c] D/MMD-D stands for Dutch and Mixed mainly Dutch utterances either in response to Dutch or to a Dutch speaker and D/MMD-not D for Dutch and Mixed mainly Dutch utterances not in response to Dutch or to a Dutch speaker

Table 2 *Kate's utterances as a function of addressee and/or language addressed in*

TAPES:	1	2	3	4	5	6	7	8	9	10	11	12	13	14	15	16	17	18	19	TOTAL
A. Kate addressing a Dutch speaker or responding to Dutch [a]																				
E/MME-not E %	8.9	33.3	33.3	-	3.6	*4*	11.4	8.0	6.1	10.8	16.7	7.5	4.0	42.9	15.8	4.3	1.5	*.8*	*2.6*	6.5
D/MMD-D %	91.1	66.7	66.7	*99.5*	96.4	99.6	88.6	92.0	93.9	89.2	83.3	92.5	96.0	57.1	84.2	95.7	98.5	99.2	97.4	93.5
utts.to D =	45	243	27	364	139	517	193	226	49	83	24	40	50	7	19	138	136	254	380	2934
B. Kate addressing an English speaker or responding to English [b]																				
D/MMD-not D %	25.0	*11.4*	-	100	*6.3*	-	-	*4.3*	3.4	-	-	*6.5*	-	-	*2.4*	2.2	1.1	-	-	2.7
E/MME-E %	75.0	88.6	-	-	93.7	-	100	95.7	96.6	100	100	93.5	100	100	97.6	97.8	98.9	100	100	97.3
utts.to E =	8	35	-	*1*	79	-	40	46	29	37	70	31	32	111	125	91	93	1	2	830

[a] E/MME-not E stands for English and Mixed mainly English utterances not in response to English or to an English speaker and D/MMD-D stands for Dutch and Mixed mainly Dutch utterances either in response to Dutch or to a Dutch speaker
[b] D/MMD-not D stands for Dutch and Mixed mainly Dutch utterances not in response to Dutch or to a Dutch speaker and E/MME-E for English and Mixed mainly English utterances either in response to English or to an English speaker

Table 3 Kate's mixed utterances as a function of addressee [a]

TAPES:	1	2	3	4	5	6	7[b]	8	9	10	11	12	13	14	15	16	17	18	19	TOTAL
A. Kate addressing a bilingual Dutch speaker																				
MMD to bil.D	–	52.2	62.5	66.7	–	73.7	55.6	31.3	20.0	46.7	14.3	100	–	–	50.0	50.0	71.4	80.0	66.7	54.9
Dutlsh to bil.D %	100	23.9	37.5	33.3	100	26.3	44.4	62.5	80.0	46.7	57.1	–	100	100	50.0	50.0	28.6	20.0	26.7	36.8
MME to bil.D %	–	23.9	–	–	–	–	–	6.3	–	6.7	28.6	–	–	–	–	–	–	–	6.7	8.3
(A) Mixed to bil.D =	3	46	8	12	1	19	9	16	5	15	7	2	2	–	4	2	7	15	30	204
Proportion (A) %	6.3	18.0	26.7	3.3	.7	3.6	4.5	7.0	9.3	16.5	30.4	4.9	3.8	14.3	19.0	1.4	5.0	5.8	7.7	6.8
Tot.Utts. to bil.D =	48	255	30	368	138	522	199	228	54	91	23	41	52	7	21	141	139	257	391	3005
B. Kate addressing a monolingual English speaker [c]																				
MME to monol.E	–	–	–	–	–	–	–	100	66.7	100	–	–	77.8	–	85.7	60.0	80.0	100	–	65.9
Dutlsh to monol.E %	–	–	–	–	100	–	–	–	33.3	–	–	–	11.1	–	14.3	40.0	20.0	–	–	19.5
MMD to monol.E %	100	100	–	–	–	–	–	–	–	–	–	–	11.1	33.3	–	–	–	–	–	14.6
(B) Mixed to monol.E=	1	3	–	–	1	–	1	3	2	–	–	3	–	7	5	5	1	–	–	41
Proportion (B) %	12.5	8.8	–	–	1.2	–	2.6	5.5	7.1	–	11.8	9.7	–	6.2	3.9	5.6	1.1	–	–	4.9
Tot.Utts. to monol.E=	8	34	0	0	82	0	38	55	28	36	76	31	32	113	127	90	92	1	0	843

[a] Non-language-specific utterances are excluded in the counts; MMD stands for a Mixed mainly Dutch utterance and MME for a Mixed mainly English utterance; utts. stands for utterances and Tot. for Total

[b] bil.D stands for a bilingual Dutch speaker (a bilingual who uses mainly Dutch with Kate, viz. A and F); Proportion (A) is the percentage of Mixed utterances to a bil.D as based on the total number of utts. to a bil.D per tape

[c] monol.E stands for a monolingual English speaker, viz. M; Proportion (B) is the percentage of Mixed utterances to a monol.E as based on the total number of utts. to a monol.D per tape

Table 4 *Types of insertions in Kate's Mixed utterances*

TAPES:		1	2	3	4	5	6	7	8	9	10	11	12	13	14	15	16	17	18	19	TOTAL
NOUN inserts	%	16.7	44.4	12.5	25.0	50.0	33.3	60.0	47.4	37.5	53.3	44.4	80.0	100	20.0	25.0	50.0	37.5	60.0	72.4	46.4
ADJECTIVE inserts	%	16.7	12.7	12.5	37.5	-	27.8	-	10.5	37.5	13.3	11.1	-	-	-	16.7	10.0	-	6.7	3.4	12.3
MORE THAN 1 insert	%	16.7	12.7	12.5	-	-	16.7	10.0	-	12.5	13.3	11.1	-	-	40.0	25.0	20.0	-	13.3	-	10.7
VERB inserts	%	-	7.9	25.0	37.5	-	11.1	-	5.3	-	-	16.7	-	-	-	25.0	-	37.5	-	13.8	10.0
ADVERB inserts	%	-	6.3	-	-	-	-	-	21.1	-	13.3	5.6	-	-	-	8.3	10.0	-	-	3.4	5.4
PREPOSITION inserts	%	-	-	37.5	-	-	11.1	30.0	5.3	-	-	-	-	-	-	-	-	-	-	-	3.4
Remaining inserts	%	50.0	15.9	-	-	50.0	-	-	10.5	12.5	6.7	11.1	20.0	-	40.0	-	10.0	25.0	20.0	6.9	11.9
TOT.MIXED UTTERANCES=		6	63	8	8	2	18	10	19	8	15	18	5	2	5	12	10	8	15	29	261

Table 5 *Occurrence of tokens of the parts of speech in the full corpus*

TAPES:		1	2	3	4	5	6	7	8	9	10	11	12	13	14	15	16	17	18	19	TOTAL
VERBS	%	18.4	23.4	23.1	25.1	21.7	21.2	17.5	19.8	25.4	26.6	23.3	24.8	28.4	25.0	27.2	22.1	24.2	23.2	21.9	23.2
PRONOUNS	%	22.4	21.5	14.9	17.1	22.6	19.6	21.9	18.1	23.9	23.6	21.0	21.2	19.4	20.9	19.6	18.2	21.7	18.3	22.0	20.3
NOUNS	%	11.4	14.3	14.9	11.0	20.8	11.4	16.8	19.6	10.7	14.8	17.0	17.4	17.5	10.2	12.6	14.1	14.5	13.3	12.9	14.0
ADVERBS	%	6.6	5.7	9.9	13.8	6.3	9.4	13.8	8.6	11.3	7.2	6.0	5.1	4.1	10.8	7.2	10.4	9.5	8.9	9.0	8.9
PREPOSITIONS	%	7.9	7.0	11.6	4.0	2.4	4.8	2.9	3.7	7.0	9.5	9.1	12.5	9.6	6.8	7.5	6.0	7.1	6.3	4.6	6.1
ARTICLES	%	5.3	8.6	14.0	7.2	9.1	6.8	5.6	9.3	4.8	5.1	6.9	3.5	4.6	2.4	4.0	4.4	3.7	4.3	3.5	5.8
ADJECTIVES	%	9.2	7.6	5.0	3.4	2.6	5.4	5.5	7.0	7.3	5.1	8.3	2.9	4.9	7.9	4.2	6.9	3.6	5.3	4.5	5.4
OTHER	%	18.9	11.9	6.6	18.4	14.5	21.3	16.0	13.7	9.6	8.3	8.5	12.5	11.5	16.1	17.8	17.9	15.7	20.4	21.5	16.3
TOTAL TOKENS	=	228	1464	121	1381	572	1359	549	895	355	433	519	311	366	660	1074	653	1053	1179	1471	14643

Table 6 Overt syntactic gender marking in complex Dutch singular noun phrases [a]

TAPES:	1	2	3	4	5	6	7	8	9	10	11	12	13	14	15	16	17	18	19	TOTAL
A. The use of DE vs. HET																				
DE used as article =	2	15	4	72	14	56	6	23	1	2	5	2	1	-	4	12	5	20	13	256
HET used as article =	-	4	2	3	1	5	1	-	-	3	-	1	1	-	1	-	-	1	1	24
B. Non-neuter head noun																				
a. Appropriate choice of determiner and/or modifier																				
DE NOUN =	1	11	4	67	14	42	6	17	-	2	4	-	-	-	3	12	3	19	9	214
DIE NOUN =	1	-	-	3	1	1	2	1	-	-	-	-	-	-	-	-	3	5	3	17
(EEN) adj+ {-e} NOUN=	-	3	-	-	-	2	1	1	-	-	-	3	-	-	-	-	1	1	2	13
DE adj+ {-e} NOUN =	-	-	-	1	-	-	-	-	-	-	1	-	-	-	-	-	-	-	-	2
appropr. non-neuter =	2	14	4	71	15	45	7	18	-	2	5	3	-	-	3	12	6	25	14	246
b. Inappropriate choice of determiner and/or modifier																				
EEN adj NOUN =	-	-	-	-	-	1	-	-	-	-	-	-	1	-	1	-	-	3	-	5
HET NOUN =	-	-	-	1	-	-	-	-	-	-	-	-	-	-	1	-	-	1	1	3
DEES/DA(T)/DIT NOUN =	-	-	-	-	-	-	1	1	-	-	1	-	-	-	-	-	-	1	1	3
DIE adj NOUN =	-	-	-	-	-	-	-	-	-	-	-	-	-	-	-	-	-	1	-	1
inappropr.non-neuter=	-	-	-	1	-	1	1	1	-	-	-	-	1	-	1	-	-	5	1	12
NON-NEUTER REFERENCE=	2	14	4	72	15	47	8	19	-	2	5	3	1	-	4	12	6	30	16	258
C. Neuter head noun or adjective used as head referring to a neuter noun																				
a. Appropriate choice of determiner and/or modifier																				
HET NOUN =	2	4	2	2	1	5	1	-	-	3	-	1	1	-	-	-	-	-	1	21
DA(T) NOUN/NDIM =	2	1	-	-	1	1	-	2	-	-	-	1	-	-	-	-	-	1	2	8
adj NOUN/NDIM =	-	1	-	-	1	3	-	1	-	-	-	-	-	-	-	2	-	-	-	8
EEN adj NOUN/NDIM =	-	-	-	1	-	1	-	1	-	-	-	-	-	-	-	1	2	-	2	8
appropr. neuter =	2	5	2	3	3	10	1	4	-	3	-	1	1	-	-	2	2	1	5	45
b. Inappropriate choice of determiner and/or modifier																				
DE NOUN/NDIM =	1	4	-	-	-	13	-	6	1	-	-	2	-	-	1	-	1	1	3	34
DIE NDIM =	-	-	-	-	-	-	-	1	-	-	2	-	-	-	1	-	-	3	-	6
adj+e NOUN/NDIM =	-	-	-	-	-	3	-	-	-	-	-	-	-	-	-	-	1	-	-	3
DE adj+e NOUN =	-	-	-	-	-	1	-	-	-	-	-	-	-	-	-	-	1	-	-	2
EEN adj+e NDIM =	-	-	-	-	-	-	-	1	-	-	-	-	-	-	-	-	-	-	-	1
inappropr. neuter =	1	4	-	1	-	17	-	8	1	-	2	2	-	-	1	-	2	4	3	46
NEUTER REFERENCE =	3	9	2	4	3	27	1	12	1	3	2	3	1	-	1	2	4	5	8	91

[a] Fully Dutch noun phrases from Mixed utterances are included here; all included adjectives are changeable

Table 7 *Development in the appropriate use of overt syntactic gender marking in complex Dutch noun phrases?* [a]

TAPES:	1	2	3	4	5	6	7	8	9	10	11	12	13	14	15	16	17	18	19	TOTAL
appropr. choice =	4	19	6	74	18	55	8	22	-	5	5	4	1	1	3	14	8	26	19	291
inappropr. choice =	1	4	-	2	-	18	1	9	1	-	2	2	1	-	2	-	2	9	4	58
complex NP's gender =	5	23	6	76	18	73	9	31	1	5	7	6	2	-	5	14	10	35	23	349

[a] appropr. choice means that determiners and modifiers are used in an adult-like fashion; inappropr. choice means that determiners and modifiers are not used in an adult-like fashion; complex NP's gender stands for Dutch noun phrases that show overt syntactic gender marking

Table 8 *The marking of gender by means of pronouns* [a]

TAPES:	1	2	3	4	5	6	7	8	9	10	11	12	13	14	15	16	17	18	19	TOTAL
A. Dutch third person singular pronouns and independent demonstratives																				
HIJ 3psg =	1	1	-	35	1	35	7	2	4	1	-	1	-	-	-	-	1	-	1	39.0
HET/'T Impro =	2	2	-	-	-	5	1	1	1	1	-	2	-	-	3	-	1	18	5	20.5
DA/DAT demproI =	-	-	-	3	4	5	4	4	1	-	-	-	-	-	1	-	4	5	3	15.2
DIE demproI =	-	3	-	1	4	4	4	4	-	-	-	2	-	-	-	1	6	1	5	12.9
ZE/ZIJ 3psg =	-	1	-	2	2	8	1	1	2	-	-	2	-	-	-	-	-	-	3	6.2
HEM persI =	-	-	-	-	-	-	-	1	-	-	-	-	-	-	-	1	-	-	6	2.4
ZIJN possD =	1	-	-	1	-	3	1	1	-	-	-	-	-	-	-	-	-	-	-	1.4
DIT demproI =	-	-	-	1	1	-	1	-	-	-	-	1	-	-	-	-	-	-	-	1.0
DITTE demproI =	-	-	-	-	-	1	-	-	-	-	-	-	-	-	-	-	-	-	-	.5
DEZE demproI =	-	-	-	-	-	1	1	-	-	-	-	-	-	-	-	-	-	-	-	.5
HAAR possD =	-	-	-	-	-	-	1	-	-	1	-	-	-	-	-	-	-	-	-	.5
PRONOUN GENDER TOT. =	2	8	-	42	8	57	6	8	9	3	-	6	1	-	4	1	11	24	20	210
B. English third person singular pronouns and independent demonstratives																				
IT Impro =	3	2	-	-	3	1	7	1	3	5	8	4	2	10	6	4	1	-	-	38.9
SHE 3psg =	-	-	-	-	-	-	-	-	-	-	9	1	2	-	12	2	2	-	5	18.8
THAT demproI =	1	3	-	-	4	-	1	4	3	2	3	1	1	-	1	1	-	-	3	16.1
THIS demproI =	-	3	-	-	-	-	1	1	-	-	2	2	-	3	-	-	6	-	5	12.1
HE 3psg =	-	-	-	-	-	-	-	-	-	-	-	1	1	2	1	-	3	-	6	5.4
HER persI or possD =	-	-	-	-	-	-	-	-	-	1	-	2	3	1	1	1	-	-	-	5.4
HIS possD =	-	-	-	-	-	-	-	-	-	-	1	1	-	-	1	-	-	-	1	2.0
HIM persI =	-	-	-	-	-	1	-	-	-	-	-	-	-	-	2	-	-	-	-	1.3
PRONOUN GENDER TOT. =	4	8	-	-	7	1	6	6	6	8	24	11	9	16	23	7	12	-	1	149

[a] Pronouns referring to actions or inanimates are excluded; 3psg = third person singular subject pronoun; Impro = impersonal pronoun; demproI = independently used demonstrative pronoun, persI = independent personal pronoun not in subject function; possD = modifying possessive pronoun; DA and DAT were combined since not much difference seemed to exist between either. The same goes for HET and 'T; all figures with decimal points are proportions, all other figures are absolute numbers; all figures with decimal points are proportions, all other figures are absolute numbers

Table 9 Animate vs. inanimate reference as marked by means of pronouns [a]

TAPES:	1	2	3	4	5	6	7	8	9	10	11	12	13	14	15	16	17	18	19	TOTAL
A. Dutch																				
TOTAL ANIMATE =	-	2	-	34	3	53	1	4	1	1	-	3	1	-	-	1	2	-	6	54.4
TOTAL INANIMATE =	2	5	-	7	3	5	4	4	8	2	1	4	-	-	3	-	9	26	13	45.6
ANIM/INAN REFERENCE =	2	7	-	41	6	58	5	8	9	3	-	6	1	-	3	1	11	26	19	206
B. English																				
TOTAL INANIMATE =	4	8	-	-	7	1	6	6	7	7	16	8	3	14	7	5	7	-	-	71.6
TOTAL ANIMATE =	-	-	-	-	-	-	-	-	-	1	8	2	6	3	15	2	5	-	-	28.4
ANIM/INAN REFERENCE =	2	7	-	41	6	58	5	8	9	3	-	6	1	-	3	1	11	26	19	206

[a] The totals here do not precisely add up to the totals in Table 8 because in the case of repairs and hesitations only the second pronoun used was counted here, whereas in Table 8 all occurrences are included

Table 10 Errors in the choice of gender pronouns and independent demonstratives

TAPES:	1	2	3	4	5	6	7	8	9	10	11	12	13	14	15	16	17	18	19	TOTAL
A. Dutch																				
HET/'T NON-NEUTER =	-	1	-	1	-	-	-	-	-	-	-	-	-	-	3	-	-	2	5	12
DA/DAT NON-NEUTER =	-	-	-	-	-	-	-	1	-	-	-	-	-	-	1	-	-	-	4	6
DA PLURAL REFERENCE =	-	-	-	-	2	-	1	-	-	-	-	-	-	-	-	-	-	-	1	4
HIJ NEUTER =	-	-	-	2	-	-	-	-	-	-	-	-	-	-	-	-	-	-	-	2
DIE NEUTER =	-	-	-	-	-	1	-	1	-	-	-	-	-	-	-	-	-	-	-	1
TOTAL D ERRORS =	-	1	-	3	2	1	1	1	-	-	-	-	-	-	4	-	-	2	10	25
B. English																				
IT PLURAL REFERENCE =	-	-	-	-	-	-	2	-	-	-	1	-	-	1	-	-	-	-	-	4
THAT PLURAL REF. =	-	1	-	-	-	-	1	-	-	1	-	-	-	-	-	-	-	-	-	3
TOTAL E ERRORS =	-	1	-	1	-	-	3	-	-	1	1	-	-	1	-	-	-	-	-	7

Table 11 Dutch corpus: independent vs. modifying use of DAT/DA/HET/'T/DIE/DEZE/DIT/DITTE [a]

TAPES:	1	2	3	4	5	6	7	8	9	10	11	12	13	14	15	16	17	18	19	TOTAL
independent use =	1	2	-	4	5	6	7	8	9	-	-	1	5	-	1	2	1	18	36	81.7
modifying use =	7	18	-	13	17	55	14	19	7	4	-	5	5	1	2	3	23	50	13	18.3
modifying use =	1	3	2	5	2	7	1	5	-	3	2	1	2	-	-	-	4	15	-	
ALL USES =	8	21	2	18	19	62	15	24	7	7	2	6	7	-	2	3	27	65	49	344

[a] All decimal figures represent proportions, all the others absolute numbers

Table 12 *Plural nouns* [a]

TAPES:	1	2	3	4	5	6	7	8	9	10	11	12	13	14	15	16	17	18	19	TOTAL
A. The proportion of plural nouns in relation to the number of utterances per tape																				
a. English plurals =	-	-	-	-	3	-	4	-	1	2	8	8	1	14	7	5	9	1	3	75
b. E+MME utts. =	18	12	10	2	85	2	64	62	37	48	90	42	41	122	176	98	96	3	12	1153
c. a as % of b =	-	8.3	-	-	-	-	6.3	-	2.7	4.2	8.9	19.0	2.4	11.5	4.0	5.1	9.4	33.3	25.0	6.5
d. Dutch plurals =	-	11	-	15	3	16	7	6	1	4	2	1	6	-	-	6	20	26	25	150
e. D+MMD utts. =	55	172	22	362	141	519	172	211	47	75	21	41	48	7	26	139	142	254	370	2824
f. d as % of e =	-	6.4	-	4.1	2.1	3.1	4.1	2.8	2.1	5.3	9.5	2.4	12.5	-	-	4.3	14.1	10.2	6.8	5.3
g. ALL PLURAL NOUNS =	-	23	-	15	3	16	11	6	2	6	10	9	7	14	7	11	29	27	28	225
h. E+D+M utts. =	77	334	35	368	228	526	240	284	88	130	117	84	91	131	207	240	240	260	391	4071
i. g as % of h =	-	6.9	-	4.1	1.3	3.0	4.6	2.1	2.3	4.6	8.5	10.7	7.7	10.7	3.4	4.6	12.1	10.4	7.2	5.5
B. The proportion of plural nouns per tape in relation to the total number of plural nouns																				
English plurals (75)%	-	16.4	-	-	-	-	5.5	-	1.4	2.7	11.0	11.0	1.4	16.4	9.6	6.8	12.3	1.4	4.1	100
Dutch plurals (150) %	-	7.3	-	10.0	2.0	10.7	4.7	4.0	.7	2.7	1.3	.7	4.0	-	-	4.0	13.3	17.3	16.7	100
All plurals (225) %	-	10.2	-	6.7	1.3	7.1	4.9	2.7	.9	2.7	4.4	4.0	3.1	6.2	3.1	4.9	12.9	12.0	12.4	100

[a] E+MME utts.refers to all English and mainly mixed English utterances, D+MMD utts.to all Dutch and mainly mixed Dutch utterances and E+D+M utts.to all English, Dutch and Mixed utterances; the 3 numbers between brackets are the totals in rows a, d and g respectively and represent the bases for the proportions in part B

Table 13 *NP's with an adjective as head*

TAPES:	1	2	3	4	5	6	7	8	9	10	11	12	13	14	15	16	17	18	19	TOTAL
DUTCH =	–	–	1	4	2	5	–	3	3	1	1	–	1	1	3	1	2	2	2	19
ENGLISH =	3	20	2	–	–	–	4	–	–	–	10	–	1	7	–	3	–	–	–	61

Table 14 *Common nouns in combination* [a]

	TAPES:	1	2	3	4	5	6	7	8	9	10	11	12	13	14	15	16	17	18	19	TOTAL
DUTCH																					
def article/noun	%	25.0	36.5	66.7	53.0	53.6	47.7	21.1	30.0	16.7	30.0	30.8	25.0	15.4	–	62.5	41.4	12.5	24.5	19.3	35.9
zero article/noun	%	12.5	27.0	22.2	20.9	25.0	17.7	42.1	22.5	16.7	50.0	30.8	41.7	57.7	–	37.5	31.0	37.5	40.8	20.5	27.2
pronoun/noun	%	37.5	6.3	–	11.9	10.7	5.4	2.6	10.0	16.7	20.0	15.4	8.3	11.5	–	–	13.8	15.6	11.2	33.7	12.5
indef article/noun	%	25.0	22.2	11.1	7.5	0.0	12.3	18.4	25.0	33.3	0.0	0.0	0.0	3.8	–	–	0.0	3.1	7.1	16.9	12.1
adjective/noun	%	–	4.8	–	3.7	3.6	13.8	15.8	3.7	–	–	7.7	25.–	7.7	–	–	10.3	9.4	11.2	3.6	7.5
indef art/adj/noun	%	–	3.2	–	.7	3.6	2.3	–	5.0	16.7	–	7.7	–	3.8	–	–	–	9.4	4.1	4.8	2.7
def art/adj/noun	%	–	–	–	1.5	3.6	.8	–	3.7	–	–	7.7	–	–	–	–	–	6.3	–	–	1.2
adv or adj/adj/noun	%	–	–	–	.7	–	–	–	–	–	–	–	–	–	–	–	–	6.3	–	1.2	.5
pron/adj/noun	%	–	–	–	–	–	–	–	–	–	–	–	–	–	–	–	3.4	–	1.0	–	.2
ALL COMBINATIONS	=	8	63	9	134	28	130	38	80	6	20	13	12	26	–	8	29	32	98	83	808
ENGLISH																					
zero article/noun	%	–	11.1	–	100	24.5	–	42.9	7.7	21.4	34.8	28.6	21.7	35.3	39.5	21.9	20.0	28.6	100	71.4	26.1
def article/noun	%	20.0	30.2	66.7	–	55.1	–	3.6	3.8	7.1	43.5	5.7	17.4	11.8	10.5	32.8	35.0	17.9	–	28.6	24.3
pronoun/noun	%	40.0	22.2	–	–	10.2	–	3.6	0.0	14.3	13.0	17.1	39.1	17.6	23.7	15.6	20.0	17.9	–	–	16.3
indef article/noun	%	40.0	11.1	33.3	–	8.2	–	17.9	50.0	42.9	0.0	22.9	13.0	29.4	–	10.9	5.0	3.6	–	–	14.0
adjective/noun	%	–	6.3	–	–	2.0	–	7.1	26.9	–	4.3	11.4	8.7	–	10.5	9.4	5.0	21.4	–	–	8.5
indef art/adj/noun	%	–	9.5	–	–	–	–	3.6	3.8	14.3	–	2.9	–	5.9	10.5	6.3	15.0	7.1	–	–	5.6
adv or adj/adj/noun	%	–	4.8	–	–	–	–	7.1	7.7	–	–	8.6	–	–	5.3	–	–	–	–	–	2.7
def art/adj/noun	%	–	4.8	–	–	–	–	14.3	–	–	4.3	2.9	–	–	–	–	–	3.6	–	–	2.2
pron/adj/noun	%	–	–	–	–	–	–	–	–	–	–	–	–	–	–	3.1	–	–	–	–	.4
ALL COMBINATIONS	=	5	63	3	2	49	–	28	26	14	23	35	23	17	38	64	20	28	4	7	449

[a] def article/noun = a definite article followed by a noun; adjective/noun = a noun without determiner or modifier; pronoun/noun = a noun preceded by a pronoun; indef article/noun = an indefinite article followed by a noun; adjective/noun = a noun preceded only by an adjective; indef art/adj/noun = an indefinite article followed by an adjective and a noun; adv or adj/adj/noun = an adverb or adjective followed by an adjective and a noun; def art/adj/noun = a definite article followed by an adjective and a noun; pron/adj/noun = a pronoun followed by an adjective and a noun;

Table 15 *Dutch subject--finite lexical verb combinations* [a]

TAPES:	1	2	3	4	5	6	7	8	9	10	11	12	13	14	15	16	17	18	19	TOTAL
A. Adult-like combinations																				
singularNP(VFPr)stt =	2	2	1	15	4	21	1	1	–	1	–	–	1	–	–	1	1	7	3	60
1psg(VFPr)stem =	3	8	–	14	1	11	–	3	1	2	–	–	1	–	–	1	–	2	9	55
3psg(VFPr)stt =	–	–	–	14	1	23	1	–	–	–	–	–	1	–	–	1	–	1	–	42
3ppl(VFPr)stn =	–	–	–	1	–	11	–	–	–	–	–	–	–	–	–	–	–	–	–	13
(VFPr)stem 2psg =	–	–	–	1	–	–	1	–	–	1	–	2	1	–	–	–	2	2	1	9
1ppl(VFPr)stn =	–	–	–	–	–	–	1	1	–	1	–	1	1	–	–	–	1	1	1	6
2psg(VFPr)stt =	–	–	–	–	–	–	–	1	–	1	–	1	–	–	–	–	–	1	3	6
pluralNP(VFPr)stn =	–	–	–	–	–	1	–	–	–	–	–	–	–	–	–	–	–	1	–	3
TOTAL ADULT-LIKE USE=	5	10	1	44	6	68	3	5	1	6	–	3	3	–	–	2	3	17	17	194
B. Non-adult-like combinations																				
1psg(VFPr)stt =	–	–	–	3	1	3	1	–	–	2	–	–	–	–	–	–	–	2	2	14
singularNP(VFPr)stem=	–	–	–	2	–	1	1	–	–	–	–	–	1	–	1	–	–	2	1	8
pluralNP(VFPr)stt =	1	–	–	–	1	2	–	–	–	–	–	–	1	–	–	–	–	2	–	7
1ppl(VFPr)stt =	–	–	–	–	–	4	–	–	–	–	–	–	–	–	–	–	–	–	–	4
singularNP(VFPr)stn =	–	–	–	1	–	–	–	–	–	–	–	–	–	–	–	–	–	1	–	2
3psg(VFPr)stn =	–	–	–	–	–	–	–	–	–	1	–	–	–	–	–	–	–	–	1	2
(VFPr)stem 3psg =	–	–	–	1	–	–	–	–	–	–	–	–	–	–	–	–	–	–	–	1
(VFPr)stt 1psg =	–	–	–	–	1	–	–	–	–	–	–	–	–	–	–	–	–	–	–	1
(VFPr)stt 2psg =	–	–	–	–	1	–	–	–	–	–	–	–	–	–	–	–	–	1	–	1
2psg(VFPr)stn =	–	–	–	–	–	–	–	–	–	–	–	–	–	–	–	–	–	1	–	1
pluralNP(VFPr)stem =	–	–	–	–	–	–	–	–	–	–	–	–	–	–	–	–	–	1	–	1
TOTAL NON-ADULT USE =	1	–	–	7	4	10	2	–	–	3	–	–	1	–	1	–	–	9	4	42
C. Adult-like vs. non-adult-like use																				
TOTAL ADULT-LIKE USE%	83.3	100	100	86.3	60.0	87.2	60.0	100	100	66.7	–	100	75.0	–	–	100	100	65.4	81.0	82.2
TOTAL NON-ADULT USE %	16.7	–	–	13.7	40.0	12.8	40.0	–	–	33.3	–	–	25.0	–	100	–	–	34.6	19.0	17.8
TOT. ADULT/NON-ADULT=	6	10	1	51	10	78	5	5	1	9	–	3	4	–	1	2	3	26	21	236
D. Non-adult-like use: error analysis																				
stem + (-t) %	–	–	–	42.9	100	90.0	50.0	–	–	66.7	–	–	100	–	–	–	–	44.4	50.0	63.4
stem %	–	–	–	42.9	–	10.0	50.0	–	–	–	–	–	–	–	100	–	–	33.3	25.0	24.4
stem + (-en) %	100	–	–	14.3	–	–	–	–	–	33.3	–	–	–	–	–	–	–	22.2	25.0	12.2
TOTAL NON-ADULT USE =	1	–	–	7	4	10	2	–	–	3	–	–	1	–	1	–	–	9	4	42

[a] This table tabulates the use of Dutch subjects in combination with fully Dutch lexical verbs in the present. Excluded are: all stems ending in 't', all forms of HEBBEN, all forms of GAAN when it is used as a tense auxiliary; except for the combinations with a 2psg pronoun, all combinations listed abstract from the exact orderings observed (e.g. '1psg(VFPr)stem' refers to combinations in which the subject pronoun either followed or preceded the finite verb); (VFPr) = finite verb form, present tense; stem, stt and stn stand for stem, stem + (-t) and stem + (-en) forms; 1psg, 2psg and 3psg stand for first, second and third person singular subject pronoun; 1ppl and 3ppl stands for first and third person plural subject pronoun

Table 16 *The conjugation of Dutch HEBBEN*

TAPES:	1	2	3	4	5	6	7	8	9	10	11	12	13	14	15	16	17	18	19	TOTAL
A. ADULT-LIKE COMBINATIONS
ik heb =	-	3	-	17	-	20	-	1	-	2	-	-	-	-	-	2	2	2	3	52
3psg heeft =	-	-	-	-	-	-	-	2	-	-	-	-	-	-	-	-	-	-	2	4
wij hebben =	-	-	-	-	-	-	-	-	-	-	-	-	-	-	-	-	1	-	1	2
heb jij =	-	-	-	-	-	1	-	-	-	-	-	-	-	-	-	-	-	-	-	1
ADULT-LIKE HEB/HEEFT=	-	3	-	17	-	21	-	3	-	2	-	-	-	-	-	2	3	2	6	59
B. NON-ADULT-LIKE COMBINATIONS
ik heef =	-	-	-	-	-	-	-	6	-	3	-	-	-	-	-	1	3	8	5	26
heef jij =	-	-	-	-	-	-	-	-	-	-	-	-	-	-	-	-	-	2	4	6
ik heeft =	-	-	-	-	-	-	-	-	-	-	-	-	-	-	-	-	-	-	2	2
NON-ADULT HEEF/HEEFT=	-	-	-	-	-	-	-	6	-	3	-	-	-	-	-	1	3	10	11	34
C. ADULT-LIKE vs. NON-ADULT-LIKE USE
ADULT-LIKE %	-	100	-	100	-	100	-	33.3	-	40.0	-	-	-	-	-	66.7	50.0	16.7	35.3	63.4
NON-ADULT HEEF/HEEFT%	-	-	-	-	-	-	-	66.7	-	60.0	-	-	-	-	-	33.3	50.0	83.3	64.7	36.6
TOTAL HEBBEN present=	-	3	-	17	-	21	-	9	-	5	-	-	-	-	-	3	6	12	17	93

Table 17 *Kate's independent vs. auxiliary use of Dutch modals* [a]

TAPES:	1	2	3	4	5	6	7	8	9	10	11	12	13	14	15	16	17	18	19	TOTAL
auxiliary use %	33.3	42.9	57.1	59.5	12.5	54.5	80.0	81.3	100	50.0	100	100	33.3	-	50.0	83.3	62.3	72.9	83.5	67.8
independent use %	66.7	57.1	42.9	40.5	87.5	45.5	20.0	18.8	-	50.0	-	-	66.7	-	50.0	16.7	37.7	27.1	16.5	32.2
indep. vs. aux. use=	3	21	7	37	8	22	5	16	1	2	1	1	3	-	2	6	53	48	91	329

[a] The percentages at the recording sessions where there were more than 10 modals have been underlined: only these figures can start to show any preference for either independent or auxiliary usage

Table 18 *Past reference in the Dutch corpus* [a]

TAPES:	1	2	3	4	5	6	7	8	9	10	11	12	13	14	15	16	17	18	19	TOTAL
A. PAST REFERENCE THROUGH THE USE OF DUTCH VERB FORMS: DEVELOPMENT
past reference	-	6.1	-	6.1	-	1.5	3.0	-	4.5	-	-	4.5	9.1	-	1.5	6.1	6.1	27.3	25.8	66
B. ADULT VS. NON-ADULT DUTCH PAST PARTICIPLE FORMATION
adult past part.%	-	100	-	75.0	-	100	-	-	100	-	-	-	100	-	100	50.0	50.0	80.0	50.0	71.2
non-adult past part.%	-	-	-	25.0	-	-	-	-	-	-	-	-	-	-	-	50.0	50.0	20.0	50.0	28.8
all past participles=	-	5	-	4	-	1	-	-	2	-	-	-	3	-	1	4	4	15	12	52

[a] The figures in part A include the use of HEBBEN with stem or stem + (-en) form; the percentages in part B. must be read horizontally

Table 19 *English subject--finite lexical verb combinations* [a]

TAPES:	1	2	3	4	5	6	7	8	9	10	11	12	13	14	15	16	17	18	19	TOTAL
I + UVF =	-	40	2	-	25	-	15	13	15	1	7	1	2	6	5	7	2	-	-	141
you + UVF =	-	3	-	-	-	-	-	1	1	4	5	1	-	3	9	2	1	-	-	20
3psg + UVF + {-s} =	-	3	-	-	-	-	-	1	-	2	5	1	-	2	1	-	1	-	-	16
you + UVF (imperat.) =	-	5	-	-	1	-	-	-	-	-	2	-	-	-	1	-	2	-	-	11
3psg + UVF =	-	-	-	-	-	-	-	-	-	-	-	-	-	1	1	-	-	-	-	2
ALL COMBINATIONS =	-	48	2	-	26	-	15	14	16	7	14	2	2	12	17	9	6	-	-	190

[a] This table tabulates the use of English subjects in combination with fully English lexical verbs in the present. Excluded are: all forms of HAVE and DO and all forms of WANT when it is used as an auxiliary; UVF = unmarked verb form; Imperat. = Imperative; 3psg = third person singular subject (here not necessarily a pronoun)

Table 20 *English subject--HAVE combinations* [a]

TAPES:	1	2	3	4	5	6	7	8	9	10	11	12	13	14	15	16	17	18	19	TOTAL
I HAVE =	-	3	-	-	-	-	-	1	-	-	1	-	-	-	1	2	-	-	-	7
I HAVE TO + UVF =	-	-	-	-	-	-	-	-	-	1	2	2	-	-	-	-	-	-	-	6
you HAVE TO + UVF =	-	-	-	-	-	-	-	1	-	-	2	-	-	-	2	1	-	-	-	6
you HAVE =	-	2	-	-	-	-	-	-	-	-	1	-	-	-	-	-	-	-	-	3
name/she/he HAS =	-	-	-	-	-	-	-	-	1	-	1	-	-	1	-	-	-	-	-	3
we HAVE TO + UVF =	-	-	-	-	-	-	-	-	-	-	-	-	-	1	-	1	-	-	-	2
sg full NP HAS TO =	-	-	-	-	-	-	-	-	1	-	-	-	-	-	-	-	-	-	-	1
(DO) you HAVE? =	-	1	-	-	-	-	-	-	-	-	-	-	-	-	-	-	-	-	-	1
USE OF HAVE AS VFPr =	-	6	-	-	-	-	-	3	2	1	5	3	-	2	3	4	-	-	-	29

[a] This table tabulates the use of English subjects in combination with HAVE in the present (both lexical and modal use are included); name/she/he HAS = a name, or SHE or HE used with HAS; sg full NP = singular subject that is not a pronoun or a name

Table 21 *English subject--BE combinations* [a]

A. A catalogue of combinations

TAPES:	1	2	3	4	5	6	7	8	9	10	11	12	13	14	15	16	17	18	19	TOTAL
3psg IS/'S =	1	30	-	-	3	-	4	2	4	2	13	8	2	30	19	7	3	-	-	128
1psg AM/'M =	1	14	-	-	2	1	1	1	6	3	3	-	1	6	8	4	9	-	-	60
2psg ARE/'RE =	-	-	-	-	2	-	-	1	-	1	3	-	-	-	7	-	1	-	-	15
3ppl ARE/'RE =	-	1	-	-	-	-	-	-	-	-	-	-	1	5	5	-	-	-	-	12
1ppl'RE =	-	-	-	-	-	-	-	-	-	1	-	-	-	-	1	-	2	-	-	4
there ARE =	-	-	-	-	-	-	-	-	-	-	-	-	-	2	-	-	-	-	-	2
2psg IS =	-	-	-	-	-	-	-	-	-	-	-	-	1	-	-	-	-	-	-	1
USE OF BE AS VFPr =	2	45	-	-	7	1	5	4	10	7	19	8	5	43	40	11	15	-	-	222

B. Use of the forms ARE and 'RE [b]

	1	2	3	4	5	6	7	8	9	10	11	12	13	14	15	16	17	18	19	TOTAL
you/plural + ARE/'RE=	-	3.0	-	-	6.1	-	-	3.0	-	6.1	9.1	-	3.0	21.2	39.4	-	9.1	-	-	33

[a] This table tabulates the use of English Subjects in combination with BE in the present (both copula and auxiliary use are included). The figures for ARE/'RE are slightly different from those given in Table 7.4 of section 7.2.2 in Chapter 7 since Subject-less utterances were not included
[b] The figures in part B. are percentages of the total number of occurrences of Subject--finite verb combinations involving ARE/'RE

Table 22 *Use of WANT as auxiliary* [a]

TAPES:	1	2	3	4	5	6	7	8	9	10	11	12	13	14	15	16	17	18	19	TOTAL
WANT as auxiliary =	3.1	3.1	-	-	3.1	-	3.1	7.7	3.1	1.5	10.8	4.6	16.9	4.6	3.1	13.8	18.5	-	3.1	65

[a] The decimal figures are percentages of the total number of tokens

Table 23 *Use of DO as auxiliary* [a]

TAPES:	1	2	3	4	5	6	7	8	9	10	11	12	13	14	15	16	17	18	19	TOTAL
DO as auxiliary =	-	6.3	-	-	6.3	-	-	4.8	-	3.2	1.6	11.1	12.7	14.3	25.4	-	12.7	-	3.2	63

[a] The decimal figures are percentages of the total number of tokens

Table 24 *Realizations of the English present continuous* [a]

TAPES:	1	2	3	4	5	6	7	8	9	10	11	12	13	14	15	16	17	18	19	TOTAL
future action/event =	-	1	-	-	-	-	-	-	1	-	-	-	-	-	3	-	1	-	-	6
ongoing action =	-	-	-	-	1	-	1	1	1	4	2	2	1	4	1	4	1	-	-	22
ALL PRESENT CONT. =	-	1	-	-	1	-	1	1	1	4	2	2	1	4	4	4	1	-	-	28

[a] No percentages were given because of the very small number of occurrences

Table 25 *English past forms* [a]

TAPES:	1	2	3	4	5	6	7	8	9	10	11	12	13	14	15	16	17	18	19	TOTAL
past forms =	-	6.5	-	-	6.5	-	4.8	-	1.6	-	3.2	-	11.3	8.1	46.8	1.6	9.7	-	-	62

[a] The decimal figures are percentages of the total number of tokens

Table 26 *Kate's Dutch declarative main clauses* [a]

TAPES:	1	2	3	4	5	6	7	8	9	10	11	12	13	14	15	16	17	18	19	TOTAL
A. Element in first position is the Subject (category i)																				
S finite verb (O) (V) =	6	38	4	119	12	87	11	36	7	18	1	6	6	-	1	11	27	43	39	472
B. Element in first position is a Y-element not triggering inversion (category ii)																				
correct no inversion=	-	6	1	12	1	5	4	16	3	1	2	1	1	-	1	3	8	25	50	141
incorrect inversion=	-	1	-	-	-	-	-	-	-	-	-	-	-	-	-	-	-	-	-	1
FIRST ELEMENT IS Y =	-	7	1	12	1	5	4	16	3	1	2	1	1	-	1	3	8	25	50	142
C. Element in first position is an X@-element triggering inversion (category iii)																				
correct inversion =	1	2	-	14	3	23	-	3	1	-	3	-	1	-	-	-	3	15	12	81
incorr. no inversion=	-	-	-	6	-	5	-	-	-	-	-	-	-	-	-	-	-	-	12	12
FIRST ELEMENT IS X@ =	1	2	-	20	3	28	-	4	1	-	3	-	1	-	-	-	3	15	12	93
D. Dutch main clause declaratives: first overview																				
correct word order %	100	97.9	100	96.0	100	95.8	100	98.2	100	100	100	100	100	-	100	100	100	100	98.2	
incorrect word order%	-	2.1	-	4.0	-	4.2	-	1.8	-	-	-	-	-	-	-	-	-	-	1.8	
E. Dutch main clause declaratives: second overview																				
Subject first %	85.7	80.9	80.0	78.8	75.0	72.5	73.3	64.3	63.6	94.7	16.7	75.0	75.0	-	50.0	78.6	71.1	51.8	38.6	66.7
Y-element first %	-	14.9	20.0	7.9	6.3	4.2	26.7	28.6	27.3	5.3	33.3	25.0	12.5	-	50.0	21.4	21.1	30.1	49.5	20.1
X@-element first %	14.3	4.3	-	13.3	18.8	23.3	-	7.1	9.1	-	50.0	-	12.5	-	-	-	7.9	18.1	11.9	13.2
TOTAL DMC's NON-INT.=	7	47	5	151	16	120	15	56	11	19	6	8	8	-	2	14	38	83	101	707

[a] For an explanation of the symbols Y and X@, please refer to the section 8.2.1.1 in Chapter 8; DMC's NON-INT. = Dutch non-interrogative main clauses; (O) (V) means that either O or V (or both) may be absent

Table 27 *Kate's Dutch interrogative main clauses*

TAPES:	1	2	3	4	5	6	7	8	9	10	11	12	13	14	15	16	17	18	19	TOTAL
A. Y/N-QUESTIONS																				
finite verb S O V =	–	–	–	2	2	6	4	6	1	1	–	–	1	–	–	1	8	7	1	41
rising intonation =	–	–	–	–	1	–	–	1	–	–	–	–	–	–	–	–	–	–	–	2
B. WH-QUESTIONS [a]																				
QW finite verb S O V=	3	3	–	7	16	40	9	3	2	7	–	2	1	–	1	2	2	8	9	115
S finite verb O V =	–	–	–	1	–	1	1	–	–	–	–	–	–	–	1	2	–	3	1	10
C. ALL QUESTIONS =	3	3	–	10	19	47	14	10	3	8	–	2	2	–	2	5	10	18	11	168

[a] QW = question word; all figures are absolute

Table 28 *Kate's English declarative main clauses* [a]

TAPES:	1	2	3	4	5	6	7	8	9	10	11	12	13	14	15	16	17	18	19	TOTAL
A. Element in first position is the Subject																				
S finite verb (V) (O)=	9	65	1	–	18	1	15	11	17	11	18	9	10	23	28	14	9	–	–	259
B. Element in first position is a Y-element																				
Y S fin. verb (V) (O)=	–	9	–	–	6	–	5	12	8	2	9	3	9	14	10	6	22	–	–	115
C. Element in first position is an X-element triggering inversion																				
X fin. verb S (V) (O)=	–	3	–	–	–	–	1	1	–	1	6	2	–	–	1	–	–	–	–	14
D. Element in first position is a fronted W-element not triggering inversion																				
W S fin. verb (V) (O)=	–	4	1	–	4	–	3	1	2	–	1	–	–	–	3	1	1	–	–	21
E. English main clause declaratives: overview																				
S finite verb (V) (O)%	100	80.2	50.0	–	64.3	100	62.5	45.8	60.7	84.6	52.9	64.3	52.6	62.2	66.7	66.7	28.1	–	–	63.3
Y S fin. verb (V) (O)%	–	11.1	–	–	21.4	–	20.8	50.0	28.6	15.4	26.5	21.4	47.4	37.8	23.8	28.6	68.8	–	–	28.1
W S fin. verb (V) (O)%	–	4.9	50.0	–	14.3	–	12.5	4.2	7.1	–	2.9	–	–	–	7.1	4.8	3.1	–	–	5.1
X fin. verb S (V) (O)%	–	3.7	–	–	–	–	4.2	3.6	–	–	17.6	14.3	–	–	2.4	–	–	–	–	3.4
TOTAL EMC's NON-INT.=	9	81	2	–	28	1	24	24	28	13	34	14	19	37	42	21	32	–	–	409

[a] S = Subject; V = non-finite part(s) of VP; O = Object; fin. = finite; (V)(O) means V and O are optionally present; EMC's NON-INT. = English non-interrogative main clauses; for definitions of Y, X and W, please refer to section 8.2.2.1 in Chapter 8

Table 29 *Kate's English main clauses with a multi-component VP: word order patterns* [a]

TAPES:	1	2	3	4	5	6	7	8	9	10	11	12	13	14	15	16	17	18	19	TOTAL
A. Interrogatives																				
Group I =	–	2	–	–	3	–	2	2	1	1	5	2	2	11	16	5	7	–	–	59
Group II =	–	–	–	–	–	–	–	–	–	–	–	–	–	–	–	1	3	–	–	4
TOTAL A. =	–	2	–	–	3	–	2	2	1	1	5	2	2	11	16	6	10	–	–	63
B. Non-interrogatives																				
Group I =	8	21	–	–	4	–	2	6	4	5	13	5	10	9	11	6	17	–	–	121
Group II =	–	4	–	–	1	–	–	2	3	5	2	1	6	5	9	3	4	–	–	45
TOTAL B. =	8	25	–	–	5	–	2	8	7	10	15	6	16	14	20	9	21	–	–	166
C. All English main clauses with a 2-component VP																				
Group I %	100	85.2	–	–	87.5	–	100	80.0	62.5	54.5	90.0	87.5	66.7	80.0	75.0	73.3	77.4	–	–	78.6
Group II %	–	14.8	–	–	12.5	–	–	20.0	37.5	45.5	10.0	12.5	33.3	20.0	25.0	26.7	22.6	–	–	21.4
ALL E MC's WITH 2-VP=	8	27	–	–	8	–	4	10	8	11	20	8	18	25	36	15	31	–	–	229

[a] In Group I utterances no element intervenes in the Subject—finite verb—non-finite verb group; in Group II utterances there is another element within this group (usually immediately in front of the non-finite verb) (see section 8.2.2.2 in Chapter 8); E MC's WITH 2-VP = English main clauses with a multi-component VP

Table 30 *Kate's English interrogative main clauses*

TAPES:	1	2	3	4	5	6	7	8	9	10	11	12	13	14	15	16	17	18	19	TOTAL
A. Y/N-QUESTIONS																				
inversion =	–	2	–	–	1	–	–	1	1	–	7	–	–	9	11	5	4	–	–	41
rising intonation =	–	1	–	–	–	–	–	–	1	3	1	–	1	–	–	–	1	–	–	8
TOTAL ALL E Y/N-Q =	–	3	–	–	1	–	–	1	2	3	8	–	1	9	11	5	5	–	–	49
B. WH-QUESTIONS [a]																				
inversion =	–	3	–	–	3	–	3	1	1	1	1	3	2	8	7	4	7	–	–	44
no inversion =	–	–	–	–	–	–	–	–	1	–	1	1	–	–	1	1	–	–	–	3
lack of inversion =	–	–	–	–	–	–	–	–	–	–	–	–	–	–	–	1	–	–	–	2
TOTAL ALL E WH-Q =	–	3	–	–	3	–	3	1	1	1	2	4	2	8	8	6	7	–	–	49
C. ALL QUESTIONS =	–	3	–	–	4	–	3	2	3	4	10	4	3	17	19	11	12	–	–	98

[a] The row 'no inversion' includes non-inverted WH-questions with the Subject as question word; the row 'lack of inversion' refers to the inappropriate absence of inversion with a QW that is not in Subject position

Table 31 *The proportions of Kate's utterances with a Z vs. a U code* [a]

TAPES:	1	2	3	4	5	6	7	8	9	10	11	12	13	14	15	16	17	18	19	TOTAL
A. English																				
E Z-codes %	44.4	24.2	60.0	100	35.3	50.0	54.0	39.0	5.9	34.0	31.3	26.8	14.6	38.3	38.6	44.1	41.1	100	60.0	35.9
E U-codes %	55.6	75.8	40.0	-	64.7	50.0	46.0	61.0	94.1	66.0	68.8	73.2	85.4	61.7	61.4	55.9	58.9	-	40.0	64.1
E UTTERANCES =	18	128	10	2	85	2	63	59	34	47	80	41	41	115	171	93	95	3	10	1097
B. Dutch																				
D Z-codes %	75.5	55.9	41.2	38.4	66.7	61.4	76.6	59.2	50.0	48.5	63.2	65.8	60.4	85.7	75.0	76.1	50.4	42.1	54.6	56.6
D U-codes %	24.5	44.1	58.8	61.6	33.3	38.6	23.4	40.8	50.0	51.5	36.8	34.2	39.6	14.3	25.0	23.9	49.6	57.9	45.4	43.4
D UTTERANCES =	53	143	17	354	505	167	206	46	68	19	38	48	7	24	138	137	242	350	2703

[a] These codes refer to the Global codes Z on the one hand, and UA, UN, UY and UW on the other (see section 8.1.2 in chapter 8 for definitions); the figures here refer to all English and Dutch utterances, including those that were not fully transcribed

Table 32 *Kate's utterances with a U code* [a]

TAPES:	1	2	3	4	5	6	7	8	9	10	11	12	13	14	15	16	17	18	19	TOTAL
A. English																				
E affirmatives %	100	80.4	100	-	86.5	-	86.2	72.7	90.0	62.1	72.5	66.7	48.4	59.1	58.1	67.4	63.5	-	100	70.6
E negatives %	-	12.0	-	-	3.8	100	3.4	6.1	-	20.7	5.9	14.8	32.3	15.2	16.3	6.5	11.5	-	-	11.4
E Y/N-questions %	-	4.3	-	-	1.9	-	-	18.2	6.7	10.3	17.6	-	12.9	15.2	15.1	10.9	13.5	-	-	10.0
E WH-questions %	-	3.3	-	-	7.7	-	10.3	3.0	3.3	6.9	3.9	18.5	6.5	10.6	10.5	15.2	11.5	-	-	8.1
E UTTS. WITH U-CODE =	10	92	4	-	52	1	29	33	30	29	51	27	31	66	86	46	52	-	3	642
B. Dutch																				
D affirmatives %	41.7	73.3	100	75.3	36.4	64.7	45.7	77.2	69.6	57.1	85.7	61.5	83.3	-	60.0	75.9	68.9	64.2	77.6	68.8
D negatives %	33.3	21.7	-	19.7	20.5	9.6	14.3	10.1	13.0	17.1	14.3	23.1	-	-	-	6.9	11.5	20.9	13.8	15.2
D WH-questions %	25.0	5.0	-	4.5	36.4	22.5	28.6	3.8	8.7	20.0	-	15.4	5.6	-	40.0	13.8	3.3	9.0	6.6	11.6
D Y/N-questions %	-	-	-	.5	6.8	3.2	11.4	8.9	8.7	5.7	-	-	11.1	-	-	3.4	16.4	6.0	2.0	4.4
D UTTS. WITH U-CODE =	12	60	10	198	44	187	35	79	23	35	7	13	18	-	5	29	61	134	152	1102

[a] The figures here refer only to English and Dutch fully transcribed utterances

Table 33 *Kate's sentence types* [a]

TAPES:	1	2	3	4	5	6	7	8	9	10	11	12	13	14	15	16	17	18	19	TOTAL
A. English																				
simple sentences %	90.0	79.3	100	-	92.3	100	96.6	90.9	86.7	100	96.1	92.6	87.1	81.8	81.4	97.8	92.2	-	100	88.6
complex sentences %	10.0	14.1	-	-	5.8	-	-	6.1	3.3	-	-	3.7	6.5	1.5	4.7	2.2	5.9	-	-	5.0
compound sentences %	-	3.3	-	-	1.9	-	3.4	3.0	10.0	-	3.9	-	-	9.1	9.3	-	2.0	-	-	4.1
tag sentences %	-	3.3	-	-	-	-	-	-	-	-	-	3.7	6.5	7.6	4.7	-	-	-	-	2.3
TOTAL E UTTERANCES =	10	92	4	-	52	1	29	33	30	29	51	27	31	66	86	46	51	-	3	641
B. Dutch																				
simple sentences %	100	96.7	90.0	98.0	100	87.2	91.4	78.5	78.3	100	100	100	94.4	-	100	96.6	82.0	76.1	87.4	89.1
tag sentences %	-	3.3	10.0	.5	-	11.8	5.7	21.5	21.7	-	-	-	5.6	-	-	-	9.8	9.0	5.3	7.0
complex sentences %	-	-	-	-	-	1.1	-	-	-	-	-	-	-	-	-	-	1.6	11.2	3.3	2.1
compound sentences %	-	-	-	1.5	-	-	2.9	-	-	-	-	-	-	-	-	3.4	6.6	3.7	4.0	1.8
TOTAL D UTTERANCES =	12	60	10	198	44	187	35	79	23	35	7	13	18	-	5	29	61	134	151	1101

[a] All figures have as a basis fully transcribed utterances with a Global U-code only

Table 34 *How many constituents per clause?* [a]

TAPES:	1	2	3	4	5	6	7	8	9	10	11	12	13	14	15	16	17	18	19	TOTAL
A. English																				
clause constituents =	32	305	11	-	140	2	84	98	105	77	160	80	95	220	245	125	161	-	7	1947
clauses total =	11	112	4	-	56	1	31	36	34	29	53	29	35	78	102	48	57	-	3	719
CONSTITUENTS/CLAUSE :	2.9	2.7	2.8	-	2.5	2	2.7	2.7	3.1	2.7	3	2.6	2.7	2.8	2.4	2.6	2.8	-	2.3	2.7
B. Dutch																				
clause constituents =	35	161	20	553	116	523	91	217	59	90	20	35	46	-	14	61	182	390	415	3028
clauses total =	12	60	10	203	44	190	36	79	23	35	7	13	18	-	5	30	66	154	167	1152
CONSTITUENTS/CLAUSE :	2.9	2.7	2	2.7	2.6	2.8	2.5	2.7	2.6	2.6	2.9	2.7	2.6	-	2.8	2	2.8	2.5	2.5	2.6

[a] All figures have as a basis fully transcribed utterances with a Global U-code only

Table 35 *Clause constituents*

TAPES:	1		2		3		4		5		6		7		8		9		10		11		12		13		14		15		16		17		18		19		TOTAL	
A. English																																							
Subjects	%	31.3	35.4	18.2	–	–	–	–	25.7	50.0	33.3	29.6	31.4	24.7	29.4	26.3	29.5	30.0	31.0	26.4	30.4	–	28.6	30.2														
Direct Objects	%	21.9	8.2	18.2	–	–	32.1	–	23.8	28.6	24.8	18.2	14.4	22.5	25.3	13.6	14.3	18.4	21.1	–	28.6	18.3																
Monotransitive Verbs%	18.8	8.5	18.2	–	–	21.4	–	27.4	22.4	24.8	16.9	13.8	21.2	28.4	14.1	16.7	20.0	21.1	–	28.6	17.8																	
Intransitive Verbs	%	–	10.8	18.2	–	–	2.9	50.0	–	3.6	3.1	4.8	16.9	8.1	8.8	1.1	5.0	12.2	14.4	7.5	–	8.0																
Place Adverbials	%	9.4	8.9	18.2	–	–	1.4	–	1.2	2.0	3.8	15.6	7.5	10.0	6.3	5.0	6.9	8.8	5.0	–	–	6.5																
Subject Complements	%	3.1	9.5	–	–	–	1.4	–	4.8	1.0	1.0	–	7.5	3.7	2.1	11.4	6.5	8.8	3.7	14.3	5.3																		
Copular Verbs	%	3.1	9.2	–	–	–	1.4	–	4.8	1.0	1.0	–	7.5	3.7	2.1	9.5	4.9	–	3.7	–	4.8																		
Other Adverbials	%	–	3.9	–	–	–	–	–	–	1.9	3.9	–	5.0	1.3	–	3.2	3.7	2.4	3.1	–	2.6																		
Time Adverbials	%	–	2.0	–	–	–	1.4	–	1.2	1.0	4.8	1.3	1.3	2.5	–	1.4	1.2	7.2	1.9	–	2.0																		
Ditransitive Verbs	%	9.4	1.0	–	–	–	5.7	–	–	6.1	1.0	–	2.5	–	–	–	–	–	.6	–	1.4																		
Manner Adverbials	%	–	1.6	9.1	–	–	–	–	–	1.0	–	2.6	–	.6	–	1.1	2.7	–	2.4	.6	–	1.3																
Indirect Objects	%	3.1	1.0	–	–	–	6.4	–	–	4.1	1.0	–	2.5	–	–	1.1	–	–	.6	–	1.2																		
Complex Trans. Verbs%	–	–	–	–	–	–	–	–	–	–	–	–	–	–	1.4	–	–	–	–	.3																			
Object Complements	%	–	–	–	–	–	–	–	–	–	–	–	–	–	–	1.4	–	–	–	–	.3																		
PrepositionalObjects%	–	–	–	–	–	–	–	–	–	–	–	–	–	–	1.4	–	–	–	–	.2																			
CLAUSE CONSTITUENTS =	32	305	11	–	–	140	2	84	98	105	77	160	80	95	220	245	125	161	–	7	1947																		
B. Dutch																																							
Subjects	%	34.3	32.9	30.0	30.6	32.8	33.1	33.0	32.7	28.8	33.3	35.0	31.4	30.4	–	28.6	34.4	30.2	32.6	32.3	32.1																		
Intransitive Verbs	%	11.4	14.3	35.0	19.5	18.1	18.7	12.1	7.8	6.8	16.7	5.0	17.1	15.2	–	21.4	23.0	8.2	11.8	11.6	14.8																		
Monotransitive Verbs%	5.7	8.7	–	8.5	6.0	8.2	9.9	13.8	3.4	12.2	10.0	8.6	10.9	–	14.3	9.8	19.2	11.3	15.7	10.8																			
Direct Objects	%	5.7	8.1	5.0	7.6	4.3	6.9	9.9	7.8	5.1	14.4	10.0	8.6	6.5	–	14.3	6.6	21.4	12.1	16.9	10.3																		
Place Adverbials	%	5.7	11.2	25.0	8.9	8.6	12.6	7.7	7.4	8.5	10.0	10.0	20.0	2.2	–	14.3	3.3	7.1	7.9	8.4	9.2																		
Subject Complements	%	17.1	11.8	–	5.4	12.9	7.8	14.3	14.3	23.7	7.8	15.0	5.7	13.0	–	–	11.5	3.3	10.0	5.8	8.7																		
Copular Verbs	%	17.1	11.2	–	5.2	12.1	7.6	12.1	13.4	20.3	5.6	15.0	5.7	8.7	–	–	8.2	2.2	9.5	3.9	7.8																		
Time Adverbials	%	2.9	–	–	13.0	5.2	4.0	1.1	1.4	3.4	–	–	–	10.9	–	7.1	1.6	3.3	2.6	3.1	4.7																		
Manner Adverbials	%	–	1.9	5.0	.5	–	.4	–	.9	–	–	–	–	2.2	–	–	–	2.7	1.8	1.7	1.0																		
Other Adverbials	%	–	–	–	.7	–	.2	–	.5	–	–	–	–	–	–	–	1.6	1.1	.5	–	.4																		
Indirect Objects	%	–	–	–	–	–	.2	–	–	–	–	–	–	–	–	–	–	–	–	.5	.1																		
Ditransitive Verbs	%	–	–	–	–	–	.2	–	–	–	–	–	–	–	–	–	–	.5	–	.2	.1																		
CLAUSE CONSTITUENTS =	35	161	20	553	116	523	91	217	59	90	20	35	46	–	14	61	182	390	415	3028																			

Table 36 *Dutch and English spontaneous repairs*

TAPES:	1	2	3	4	5	6	7	8	9	10	11	12	13	14	15	16	17	18	19	TOTAL
A. Repairs as a proportion of the number of utterances per recording session																			
DUTCH =	3.8	.7	-	5.1	-	-	.8	1.2	-	-	2.9	-	-	-	-	12.5	-	10.9	12.4	7.1	3.8
ENGLISH =	-	4.7	-	-	-	-	-	-	3.4	2.9	-	-	2.4	4.9	5.2	6.4	3.2	8.4	-	10.0	3.7
B. Repairs per recording session as a proportion of the total number of repairs																			
DUTCH =	2.0	1.0	-	17.6	-	-	3.9	2.0	-	-	2.0	-	-	-	-	2.9	-	14.7	29.4	24.5	102
ENGLISH =	-	14.6	-	-	-	-	-	-	4.9	2.4	-	-	2.4	4.9	14.6	26.8	7.3	19.5	-	2.4	41

Index of names

Acunzo,M., 322
Albert,M., 337
Aldenhoff,J., 18, 28
Andersen,E., 311, 314, 315, 316, 318, 337
Anselmi,D., 322, 323
Antinucci,F., 53
Appel,R.,10
Ariza,F., 19, 28
Arlman-Rupp,A., 126, 150, 151, 235, 284
Arnberg, 9, 11, 34, 36, 58
Baetens Beardsmore,H., 96, 97, 103, 106, 340, 344
Bain,B., 10
Barrett,M., 31
Bates,E., 59, 280
Bellugi,U., 220, 266, 270, 272
Benedict,H., 31, 284
Bergman,C., 35, 36, 38, 48, 49, 90, 113
Berkele,G., 18, 32, 61, 62, 64, 138
Berman,R., 1, 18, 28
Berthoud-Papandropoulou,I., 336
Bever,T., 274
Bloom,L., 51, 213, 214, 226, 228
Bol, G., 143, 148, 151, 155, 282, 290, 291, 292, 293, 299, 301, 303, 304
Bowerman,M., 56, 113, 145, 343
Breston,A., 57
Bridges,A., 274
Brown,R., 14, 15, 51, 87, 88, 213, 219, 221, 224, 226, 228, 236, 271, 297, 304, 305
Bubenik,V., 12
Bybee,J., 161, 229
Cazden,C., 148, 229, 314
Chalkley,M, 226, 229
Champagne,R., 10
Chesterfield, 10
Chiat,S., 143, 144

Chomsky,N., 238
Chun,J., 10
Clark, A., 12
Clark,E., 9, 56, 57, 308, 311, 314, 315, 318, 320, 322, 325, 331, 333, 336, 337
Clark, H.,56, 57, 58
Clyne,M., 19, 28, 331
Clynes, D., 81
Comrie,B., 241
Crystal,D., 15, 84, 161, 162, 215, 241, 282, 290, 295, 299, 303, 304
Cummins,J., 10, 337
Davy,D., 161, 162, 215
De Geest,W., 118
de Haan,G., 82, 191, 192, 235, 241
De Houwer,A., 40
de Jong,E., 137, 138, 157
De Jonghe,H., 118
de Rooij J., 117, 120, 156, 168
De Schutter,G., 167, 238, 239, 241, 242, 243, 249, 253, 259
De Vooys,C., 107, 108, 176, 235
de Vriendt,S., 117, 118, 121, 235, 259
de Vriendt-de Man,M., 139, 207, 249, 254, 278
den Os, E., 149
Deuchar,M., 12
Deutsch,W., 122
Dodson,C., 97
Dore, J., 50
Doyle,A., 10
Ebeling,K., 314
Ellul,S., 11
Elwert,T., 2
Erreich,A., 272
Extra,G., 121, 142, 183, 186, 191, 199, 205, 206
Fantini,A., 90, 96
Flavell,J., 337
Fletcher,P., 60, 84, 144, 213, 215, 217, 218, 221, 222, 223, 224, 225, 227, 228, 229, 230, 233, 236, 241, 272, 273, 282, 290, 291, 295, 297, 299, 303, 304
Fokes,J., 336
Foppa,K., 320
Fox,B., 322
Fox,D., 226, 229
Franklin,M., 50

Index 387

French,A., 143
Fromkin,V., 113, 319
Furrow,D., 284
Galambos,S., 337
Gallagher,T., 322
Garman,M., 60, 84, 241, 282, 290, 295, 299, 303, 304
Gathercole,V., 228, 234
Geerts,G., 117, 120, 156, 168
Gerhardt,J., 213
Gerritsen,M., 241, 253
Gillis,S., 32, 142, 143, 149, 197
Gleitman,L., 60
Goldin-Meadow,S., 337
Greenbaum,S., 84, 85, 158, 164, 237, 238, 239, 261, 282, 299
Grieve,R., 337
Grosjean,F., 9, 34, 35, 50, 96, 113
Gruendel,J., 31
Haeseryn,W., 117, 120, 156, 168
Hafitz,J., 213, 226, 228
Hagen,A., 311, 318, 334, 337
Hakes,D., 333
Hakuta,K., 10
Halliday,M., 238
Hanlon,C., 297
Harder,R., 149
Harding,E., 9
Harrison,G., 11
Hasselmo,N., 339
Hassing,Y., 126, 150, 151, 235, 284
Hatch,E., 10
Hecht,B., 56
Hoefnagel-Höhle,M., 10, 149
Hoffman,C., 19, 28
Hofmans,M., 168
Hogan,T., 10
Hoppe,R., 336
Huang,J., 10
Hudson,R., 238
Huerta,A., 20, 28, 36, 104, 106, 112
Hurford,J., 180
Hyltenstam,K., 7
Ianco-Worrall,A., 10
Idiazabal,I., 11
ImedadzeN., 55, 64

Index

Ingram,D., 14, 271, 272
Iwamura,S., 314
Jansen,F., 241, 243
Januschek,F., 336
Jarovinskij,A., 10
Jekat,S., 15, 20, 32, 42, 61, 62, 64
Jisa,H., 11
Jobse,J., 126, 150, 151, 235, 284
Jogman,A., 149
Jonekeit,S., 9, 20, 26, 27, 36, 100, 111, 112, 113, 114
Joosten,J., 126, 150, 151, 235, 284
Kagan,J., 2
Kaltenbacher,E., 281
Karmiloff-Smith,A., 141, 306, 343
Käsermann,M., 320
Keeney,T., 213
Kempen,G., 311
Kess,J., 336
Kessler,G., 10
Kielhöfer,B., 9, 20, 26, 27, 36, 100, 111, 112, 113, 114
Kinsbourne,M., 274
Klein,R., 260
Klima,E., 266
Konefal,J., 336
Koster,J., 241
Kuczaj,S., 180, 219, 226, 229, 230
Kuiken,F., 143, 148, 151, 155, 282, 290, 292, 292, 293, 299, 301, 303, 304
Labov,W., 236
Lahey,M., 51
Langford,D., 320
Lanza,E., 11
Lappin,K., 12
Lattey,E., 113, 114
Laver,J., 113, 311, 318
Leech,G., 85, 158, 237, 238, 239, 261, 282, 299
Leemans,M., 247, 248, 251, 256, 259, 260
Lempert,H., 274
Leopold,W., 10, 14, 21, 29, 37, 38, 39, 46, 50, 63, 225, 233
Levelt,W., 311, 318
Liebman,E., 12, 35
Lifter,K., 213, 226, 228
Limber,J., 295
Lindholm,K,. 2, 3, 10, 35, 48, 49, 50, 53, 58, 106, 112

Lindsay,P., 333
Linnakylä,P., 10
Lipski,J., 104
Loffeld,M., 206
Lyons,J., 159
MacWhinney, B., 59, 280
Maratsos,M., 176, 180, 226, 229
Marshall,J., 336, 337
Matthews,P, 238, 305
McClure,E., 10, 90, 105, 106
McLaughlin,B., 2, 10, 35, 53
Meisel,J., 3, 7, 16, 21, 22, 32, 37, 44, 45, 50, 51, 54, 58, 59, 60, 61, 62, 63, 64, 188, 280, 281, 343
Métraux,R., 11
Meys,W., 301
Michaels,S., 314
Mikès,M., 12, 55, 64
Miller,J., 88
Miller,R., 50
Mills,A., 1, 44, 53, 116, 117, 143, 144, 343
Morton,J, 336, 337
Nagtegaal,D., 149
Nelson,K., 31, 284
Nooteboom,S., 114, 311, 318
Norman,D., 333
Nuckle,L., 12
Obler,L., 7, 337
Olmsted,D., 14
Padilla,A., 2, 3, 10, 12, 35, 48, 49, 106, 112
Palmer,F., 158, 161, 165, 210
Paprotté,W., 336
Parisi,D., 53
Park,T., 12
Peeters,A., 206
Pérez,R., 10
Peters,A., 60, 192
Pfaff,C., 10
Piette,A., 11
Poplack,S., 104, 105, 339
Porsché,D., 23, 28
Pratt,C., 337
Pye,C., 343
Quirk,R., 84, 85, 158, 164, 237, 238, 239, 240, 261, 263, 282, 299, 301

Index

Ramer, 50
Ramaekers,B., 247, 248, 251, 256, 259, 260
Redlinger,W., 10, 12
Reilly,P., 9
Rescorla,L., 31
Richards,B., 219
Rijpma,E., 118, 122
Rogers,S., 336
Rohde,W., 336
Romero,A., 10
Ronjat,J., 2, 23, 28, 32, 36, 40, 48, 49, 50, 51, 52
Rosansky,E., 13
Routh,D., 322
Saunders,G., 9, 23, 24, 25, 26, 27, 32, 34, 47, 60, 90, 101, 111, 112
Savasir,I., 213
Saywitz,K., 336
Schaerlaekens,A., 142, 143, 148, 149, 151, 171, 186, 191, 197, 199, 204, 205, 206, 208, 260, 261
Schuringa,F., 118, 122
Segalowitz,N., 10
Shatz,M., 314
Sinclair,A., 336
Slobin,D., 1, 55, 56, 58, 152, 161, 220, 229, 274, 325, 332, 336
Slockers,V., 149
Smith,C., 228
Smith, M., 11
Smith,N., 10, 14, 149
Smout,H., 73
Snow,C., 10, 126, 149, 150, 151, 235, 284
Sridhar,K., 104, 105
Sridhar S., 104, 105
Steele,S., 241, 263
Stockwell,R., 239, 259
Stoops,Y., 73
Svartvik,J., 85, 158, 237, 238, 239, 261, 282, 299
Swain,M., 25, 29, 30, 35, 50, 52, 63, 99, 101, 106, 111, 112
Tabors,P., 314
Taeschner,T., 2, 26, 30, 31, 32, 35, 39, 40, 41, 42, 43, 44, 45, 46, 47, 50, 52, 53, 54, 61, 62, 65, 101, 102, 111
Templin,M., 14
Theissen,S., 259

Tinbergen,D., 171, 183, 186, 191, 192, 194, 195, 196, 197, 199, 200, 201, 203, 204, 205, 206, 208, 260, 261
Tomasello,M., 322
Tracy,R., 192
Traugott,E., 241
Tsushima,W., 10
Tyack,D., 271, 272
Van de Craen,P., 73, 259
van den Toorn,M., 117, 120, 156, 168
van Driel,H., 206
van Driel-Karthaus,I., 206
Van Ginneken,J., 171, 172, 195, 196, 199, 200, 201, 203, 206, 208, 260, 261, 293
van Hauwermeiren,P., 167, 238, 239, 241, 242, 243, 249, 253, 259
van Ierland,M., 14, 259
van Peer,J. , 206
van Reydt,A., 149
van Wijk,C., 311
Verhulst-Schlichting,L., 142, 191, 194, 195, 205, 248, 249, 252, 254, 257, 260
Verlinden,A., 137
Vihman,M., 11, 35, 46, 108
Vila,I., 12
Vlahovic,P., 55, 64
Vogel,I,. 12, 149
Volterra,V., 26, 30, 31, 39, 40, 41, 42, 43, 44, 45, 46, 47, 54
Vorster,J., 126, 150, 151, 235, 284
Wagner-Gough,J., 12
Wanner,E., 60
Weist,R., 281
Wells,G., 7, 15, 83, 140, 143, 149, 152, 156, 218, 219, 220, 221, 225, 226, 230, 264, 266, 267, 270, 271, 273, 282, 283, 288, 289, 290, 291, 295, 297, 298, 302, 304, 305
Wentz,J., 10
Wesche,M., 25, 30, 63, 99, 101, 104, 106, 111, 112
Wijnen,F., 122, 138, 142
Wilkinson,L., 336
Willemyns,R., 72, 89, 156
Witkowska-Stadnik,K., 281
Wolfe,J., 213
Wong Fillmore,L., 10
Yau,S., 280
Zanón,J., 12